Library of
Davidson College

Janáček and Czech Music

Proceedings of The International Conference

(St. Louis, 1988)

Janáček and Czech Music
Proceedings of
The International Conference
(Saint Louis, 1988)

edited by
Michael Beckerman and Glen Bauer

STUDIES IN CZECH MUSIC No. 1

PENDRAGON PRESS
STUYVESANT, NY

Other Titles in the Series *STUDIES IN CZECH MUSIC*

No. 2 *The Opera Theater of Count Franz Anton von Sporck in Prague (1724–35)* by Daniel Freeman (1992) ISBN 0-945193-17-3

No. 3 *Janáček as Theorist* by Michael Beckerman (1994) ISBN 0-945193-03-3

Library of Congress Cataloging-in-Publication Data
International Conference on Janáček and Czech Music:
  (1988 : Saint Louis, Mo.)
    Janáček and Czech Music: Proceedings of the Internationa Conference (Saint Louis, 1988) / edited by Michael Beckerman and Glen Bauer. p. cm. -- (Studies in Czech music ; no. 1)
    Includes bibliographical references and index.
    ISBN 0-945193-36-x
    1. Janáček, Leoš, 1854-1928--Congresses. 2. Music--Czech Republic--Congresses. I. Beckerman, Michael Brim, 1951-   . II. Bauer, Glen. III. Title. IV. Series.
    ML410.J18I58
    780'.92--dc20   94-19222
                                                      CIP
                                                      MN

Copyright Pendragon Press 1995

Contents

Introduction MICHAEL BECKERMAN	ix
Part 1: Janáček and Czech Opera	1
Janáček's Recitatives JOHN TYRRELL	3
A New Hypothesis on the Theme of Janácek's "Russian" Operas JIŘÍ BAJER	21
Czech *verismo* in the 1890's JAN SMACZNY	33
"Pleasures and Woes": The Vixen's Wedding Celebration MICHAEL BECKERMAN	45
Part 2: Analytical Approaches to Janáček's Music	55
The "Old" and "New" Modality in Janáček's *The Diary of One Who Vanished* and Nursery Rhymes JAROSLAV VOLEK	57
Musical and Dramatic Organization in Janáček's *The Cunning Little Vixen* NORS JOSEPHSON	83
Janáček's First String Quartet: Motive and Structure of the First Movement ZDENEK SKOUMAL	93
Structure and Meaning in the First Movement of Janáček's *Concertino* FRED MAUS	107
Part 3: Czech Music Before Smetana	115
Antonio Vivaldi and the Sporck Theater in Prague DANIEL E. FREEMAN	117
Jan Dismas Zelenka's Setting of Psalm 150: "Chwalte Boha Silného" JAN STOCKIGT	141
18th Century Folk Music in the Czech Lands: Comments on the State of Research ZDEŇKA PILKOVÁ	155

CONTENTS

Cantor's Music, Local Repertories and Some Thoughts on the Need for a Bohemian Musical Topography   MARK GERMER   165

Vojtěch Jírovec and the Viennese String Quartet
ROGER HICKMAN   185

J. V. Voříšek and the Fantasy   KENNETH DELONG   191

Part 4: Editorial Approaches to Janáček   215

The Principles of the Janáček Critical Edition
JARMIL BURGHAUSER   217

Editorial Guidelines for the Compete Edition of Janáček's Works
BÄRENREITER AND SUPRAPHON, PUBLISHERS   221

The Performer as Co-Editor: Proposals for a New Complete Edition of Janáček's Works   PAUL WINGFIELD   243

Part 5: Janáček and the Contemporary World   253

Dvořák and Janáček: New Insights into an Old Friendship   ALAN HOUTCHENS   255

Romantic and Twentieth-Century Styles in the 1870's: Music for String Orchestra by Dvořák and Janáček   DAVID BEVERIDGE   263

The Program of *Balada Blanická*   HUGH MACDONALD   273

A Reappraisal of Janáček as Realist   MARILYN S. CLARK   283

Czechoslovak Presence at Schoenberg's *Verein*
JOHN H. YOELL   289

Henry Cowell, Leoš Janáček and Who were the Others?   EVA DRLÍKOVÁ   295

Leoš Janáček and His Influence of Slovak Music
MILAN ADAMČIAK   301

CONTENTS

Part 6: Janáček's "Danube" Symphony	309
Was Janáček Satisfied With His Symphony "The Danube"? ALENA NĚMCOVÁ	311
Janáček's "Danube": Some Notes on the Montage of the Symphony by the Composer and on its Reconstruction from an Autographic Draft MILOŠ ŠTĚDROŇ	321
Leoš Janáček's "Danube" Symphony—Original and Chlubna Versions JAKOB KNAUS	335
The Vocalise in "Danube" Symphony PETER SUSSKIND	341
Part 7: Janáček: Past, Present, and Future	345
The Reception of Leoš Janáček as seen through a Study of the Bibliography: A Preliminary Report JAROSLAV MRÁČEK	347
Leoš Janáček Today JIŘÍ VYSLOUŽIL	357
The Controversy between Reality and its Living in the Work of Leoš Janáček JAROSLAV JIRÁNEK	365
Janáček and the Dance of "Categories" JIŘÍ FUKAČ	
Index	389

To Alena Němcová

and

Vivian Abbott

INTRODUCTION

Leoš Janáček and Czech Music: Proceedings of the Conference "Janáček and Czech Music," May 24–29; Washington University in St. Louis

On May 4–9, 1988, the International Conference and Festival "Janáček and Czech Music" took place at Washington University in St. Louis. For many of us the event seemed to be a palpable chink in the casements of the cold war, since more than a dozen Czechs and Slovaks were able to participate in the event. Such a thing had scarcely seemed possible even two years before, and we were perhaps a little proud of ourselves for having achieved what appeared to be a breakthrough. Little did we know that less than two years later that chink would become a mighty crack and that The Wall would crumble, to be followed by the collapse of innumerable metaphorical walls which had been erected between the United States and Czechoslovakia.

If our rather limited diplomatic aims were soon superseded by far more dramatic developments, we still find ourselves in the midst of a much less monumental yet nonetheless formidable struggle to carve out an international field for the study of Czech and Slovak music. In this sense, the Janáček conference may be seen as part of an ongoing effort which, in this country, had begun with the "Smetana Centennial Conference" in San Diego, directed by Jaroslav Mráček, and which is continuing with conferences on Martinů and Dvořak.

It is hoped that the contents of this volume will reflect the diversity and vitality of this new field—indeed we see a rich array of scholarly styles and approaches. Although the majority of the articles deal with Janáček, we felt that it was quite important to have sessions devoted to Czech music before the "national" period. Within the specific area of Janáček studies, we tried to encourage diversity by arranging sessions on the operas, analysis, the Danube Symphony, and also on the relationship between Janáček and his contemporaries and the larger sphere of European culture. Finally we arranged two sessions dealing specifically with scholarly problems; one focussing on the future of Janáček research and the other on problems relating to the Critical Edition of the Works of Leoš Janáček, co-published by Bärenreiter and Supraphon.

Although we have tried to preserve the flavor of the original sessions as much as possible, we have moved several papers to categories where they seem more appropriate. Thus Nors Josephson's essay on the *Cunning Little Vixen* seemed more appropriate with the analytical papers, while Jan Smaczny's study of Czech verismo works fits in quite well with the collection of papers on Janáček's operas. We have not made undue efforts to standardize scholarly style, since often part of the individuality of a contribution lies in its method of documentation. Suffice it to say that we have only made such changes when it was necessary for the comprehension of some aspect of the work. Each series of papers is accompanied by a short introduction, outlining the basic questions in the area, and individual studies are preceded by some shorter comments which try to place both the study and its author in a slightly wider context.

The field of Czech and Slovak music owes a tremendous debt of gratitude to the International Board of Research and Exchanges (IREX), which has been responsible, more than any other organization, for making the conference and festival a success, and sustaining the field in its initial stages. At least seven participants in the event have, at one time or another, traveled to Eastern Europe on an IREX grant, and IREX helped substantially with the costs of the festival and this publication. On the other end, we must acknowledge the tremendous contribution of the Český hudební fund, who supported this effort in so many ways. Generous grants from both the U.S.I.A. and the N.E.H. also contrib uted to the success of the conference. We are also grateful to the administration of Washington University to Roger Hahn, and of course to the Music Department faculty and staff for their encouragement. I would especially like to thank my colleagues Jeffrey Kurtzman, Dolores Pesce, Roland Jordan, Craig Monson, Seth Carlin, Dan Presgrave, Mary Henderson, and Hugh Macdonald for their activities before, during, and after the conference and festival, and my students Ken Mitchell, Donna DiGrazia, Karen Trinkle, Cathy Irwin, Gary Zink and John Vitale for their gracious assistance.

Anyone who is familiar with the Janáček Conference and Festival knows that it could not have been possible without the efforts of Dr. Glen Bauer who is co-editor of this volume and assisted me throughout the preparation and execution of the project.

INTRODUCTION

The world has changed greatly since this project began, and we all look with the greatest hope to future projects. But this volume is testimony to all those who carried out their research under the old system, often under extremely difficult conditions, and managed to keep the flame of scholarship burning during hard times. I would like to dedicate this volume to two people who embodied this desire to bridge the gap between East and West, and who encouraged the study of Czech music in countless ways: Alena Němcová, head of the Music Information Center in Brno, and a contributor to this volume; and Vivian Abbott of IREX whose support and concern helped make it all possible.

Michael Beckerman

Part 1:

Janáček and Czech Opera

It is an understatement to say that there has been a boom in Czech opera, and that interest in the topic has never been greater. In the Fall of 1990 there were Janáček operas playing in both major New York houses, and in recent years there have been important productions in San Francisco, Chicago, Cincinnati, St. Louis and numerous other companies. The operas of Janáček have arguably attracted the most attention, indeed they are one of the real discoveries for American opera-goers in recent decades, and Janáček can clearly take his place with the greatest opera composers of our century.

    The papers presented here provide several perspectives on Janáček opera and those of some of his lesser known contemporaries. From specific consideration of Janáček's recitatives to a broader inquiry into Janáček's Russian sources, these essays aim to offer the latest thinking in this area.

Example 1. *Jenůfa* **(1908 vocal score, p. 201)**

Janáček's Concept of Recitative

John Tyrrell

The above-mentioned boom in Janáček opera has also been accompanied by a similar explosion of journalistic and scholarly work on Janáček and Czech music. More than any other scholar, it is John Tyrrell whose work has brought these fields into the mainstream of musicological discourse, and this on the highest possible plane. Through his work for New Grove, *his* Cambridge Opera Handbook *on Katya Kabanová and most recently* Czech Opera, *Tyrrell has offered panoramic, yet beautifully detailed views of Czech music from the 1850's to the 1930's.*

It stands to reason that a composer such as Janáček, who was virtually obsessed with human speech, would take some special approach to the composition of recitatives. In this study Tyrrell focuses on the problem of Janáček's recitative, particularly in the very early operas, in an attempt to chart the development of Janáček's mature vocal style.

In one of the best known passages in all of Janáček's operas, the Kostlenička brings Act 2 of *Jenůfa* to an end with the dramatic words "Jako by sem smrt načuhovala!"—as if death was peering in here. The figuration in the orchestra stops abruptly. Unaccompanied, the voice ascends to a high B-flat for the word "smrt" (death) and then leaps down almost two octaves to middle C for "načuhovala." And, at the highest point of the phrase ("smrt")—its longest note, there is the marking "recit." (Example 1-opposite)[1]

It is not clear what Janáček intended here. In practice today the pitches of "načuhovala" are often taken fairly freely, though such an interpretation is not supported by theoretical writings of the time. Janáček, for instance, was well acquainted with those of the singing teacher František Pivoda (1824–98), with whom he corresponded between 1879 and 1895.[2] In 1885 he printed Pivoda's article "Pěvectvo a

---

[1] Examples 1–3 are taken from the first, 1908, edition of the vocal score. More recitative indications crept into later editions. For instance the first "Quasi recit." on p. 87 of the current Czech vocal score appeared for the first time in the second (1917) ediiton; the second indication on that page was added editorially in the third edition.

Example 2. *Jenůfa* (1908 vocal score, p. 36)

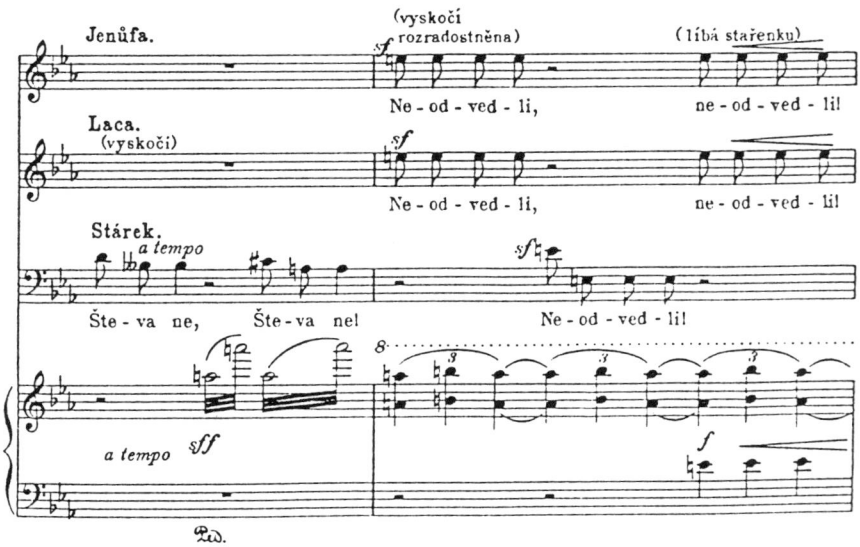

veřejnost" (Singing and the public) in his journal *Hudební listy*.[3] He used Pivoda's singing manual, *Nová nauka zpěvu* (1879), in his teaching and was responsible for its acceptance as a textbook at Czech teaching institutes.[4] The 1883 edition of the manual includes an account of recitative (pp. 230–6), most of which went word for word into Pivoda's later article in *Hudební listy* (on pp. 64–6, 74–6). Pivoda characterized recitative in the following way (my numbering):

1. Recitative is used in opera and in religious works in places "where the text expresses contemplation, reflection, explanations, prophecies etc.—in general where the content has predominantly to do with ideas."

2. Natural speech rhythms prevail; the length of notes is determined only by the length of the syllables.

3. Harmony is unimportant, chords having no function in recitative other than to fill in the gaps between sentences.

4. Dynamics are left entirely to the good sense of the singer; only the melody is set down by the composer.

5. As declamation, recitative avoids strict measuring of the note values according to the beat, recognizing as its only measure the natural rhythm of speech, generally expressed in 4/4 for easy comprehension.

6. There is no melody in the usual musical sense.

Though with this last point Pivoda declared that melody is unimportant in recitative, he does not suggest that pitches should actually be interfered with. Pivoda's point that dynamics are left entirely to the singer, can hardly apply to Example 1 in view of the accent markings on every syllable of "načuhovala" and the fortissimo marking at the beginning of the passage. The chief inference that might be made from Pivoda's observations on recitative in respect to Janáček's marking in Example 1, is that the words from "smrt" onwards need not to be sung in strict time.

This is not the only passage with a recitative marking in *Jenůfa*. The first comes in Act 1, when the mill Foreman, the Stárek, announces that Števa has not been called up by the army (Example 2, opposite). The words of this momentous announcement, a turning point in the act, need to be heard clearly by the audience. They are given here with great clarity since

---

[3]*Hudební listy*, ii (1885–86), 21–22, 29–30, 37, 45–6, 57–8, 64–6, 74–6.
[4]Helfert, ibid, 273.

Example 3. *Jenůfa* **(1908 vocal score, p. 77)**

they are delivered unaccompanied, on a monotone with minimal musical interest in rhythm and pitch. The marking "recit." implies (in view of the later "a tempo" marking) that the singer can take the passage in his own time: the single long-note notation allows him to set his own rhythms. After a dramatic pause, his final words "A Števa ne" (But not Števa) stand out in high relief by returning to strict time, to a given rhythm, and to new pitches. The Foreman is then joined by the orchestra and three more soloists. The musical purpose of the passage now becomes clear: it is a transition to an ensemble. Apart from their importance to the plot, these two bars have the clear structural function of leading into a set number, a familiar use of recitative.

Another passage from *Jenůfa*, in effect a bridge between two set numbers, provides an even clearer example of this sort of transitional recitative (Example 3, opposite). After the big concertato number for soloists and chorus in Act 1 ("Každý párek"), the sound of the xylophone is heard, pattering away to a repeated C-flat. Left alone with Števa, Jenůfa begins to reproach him for his drunken behavior. Her aria, marked "Allegro," is preceded by a short recitative sung over the repeated C-flats on the xylophone. In this example the rhythms and in particular the pitches to which these words are sung are more varied than in the other examples so far examined. The emphasized notes in the last bar are particularly interesting since the four pitches—B-flat, A-flat, E-flat, D-flat—provide the motivic basis for Jenůfa's following aria. Janáček cannot intend much in the way of rhythmic freedom here; there would be no point in his writing all these different note values. Nor could he intend the pitches not to be adhered to since the last group is so clearly related to what the orchestra plays next. And, with the initial dynamic mark (at the same time as the recitative marking), the decrescendo and crescendo markings and the careful accents, there is no question of dynamics being left "to the good sense of the singer." There is a link here with Example 1. The five Cs on "načuhovala" generate a five-note orchestral motif which is hammered out against changing chords, one of Janáček's most thrilling orchestral conclusions to an act. The only oddity is that the singer's notes which initiated the sequence are marked "recit." In other words, as in the recitative transition to Jenůfa's reproach aria, a vocal tag, marked "recitative," has generated an orchestral development. In these cases Janáček's use of the term seems to imply something different from its normal usage and from Pivoda's explanations.

This is one oddity about Janáček's use of the term "recitative" in *Jenůfa*. Another is that he used the word at all. It is not after all what one expects in an opera, written to a prose libretto by a committed realist at the beginning of the twentieth century. Here is Janáček writing a couple of years after *Jenůfa* was first performed.

> I wouldn't write operas if they had to have arias, recitatives, duets, ensembles etc. (*Moderní harmonická hudba*, 1907)[5]

The statement rings a little hollow for *Jenůfa* has all of these features, many in abundance. True, Janáček sought to diminish them when he prepared the work for publication—duets and in particular ensembles were reduced in length considerably, though not to their total exclusion, just as Janáček left in these puzzling recitative indications. Duets, ensembles and also recitative survive in even later operas. For instance in the Hussite excursion of *The Excursions of Mr. Brouček*, composed as late as 1917, there is one "free tempo" recitative, and one "quasi recitative" marking. There is no doubt, however, that with his statement quoted above Janáček wished to disparage the type of opera that employed recitative in a traditional way. That he retained this attitude to the end of his life can be inferred from a lecture on naturalism that he worked on in 1924, in which he wrote:

> Why should [man] be left out of naturalism in composition? Why must he be brought on with clumsy recitative? Why drugged with the over-sweet scent of songs?[6]

In other words Janáček saw both recitative and aria as inappropriate to the naturalistic concept he had of opera.

Jenůfa was not of course Janáček's first opera, and if we wish to understand the presence in it of what may appear to be isolated and puzzling phenomena, it is necessary to look at it in the context of his previous two operas, *Šárka* and *The Beginning of a Romance*. What becomes immediately clear from such an exercise is the much greater number of all the features that he dismissed in 1907: aria, duets and ensembles. As for recitative, there are twenty-three passages so marked in the first version of *Šárka*. *The Beginning of a Romance*, an un-

---

[5]Quoted in Bohumír Štědroň: "K Janáčkovým nápěvkům mluvy (zárodky jeho operního slohu)" [Janáček's speech melodies: the embryos of his operatic style], *Sborník pedagogické fakulty UK: Sborník k 60 narozeninám Josefa Plavce* (Prague, 1966), p. 255.

[6]Unpublished notes (p. 11) for a lecture on naturalism dated 5 February–4 March 1924: in Moravské muzeum, Hudební historické oddělení.

ashamedly set-number opera, has even more. There are marked recitative links between many of the individual numbers and in the final version, three substantial numbers are made up entirely of recitative. The opening number for Poluška includes six short recitative sections. Five are no more than an indication of "free tempo," ending with strict-tempo markings. The remaining one is more interesting and will be discussed later, after an examination of Janáček's use of recitative in his first opera, Šárka.

It is useful to distinguish three main versions of Šárka. The first was written in 1887 and was sent to Dvořák for his comments.[7] Janáček then revised the opera the next year, 1888. The new version was very different and was written out afresh, both by Janáček and by his copyist, Josef Štross, though only the copyist's score survives. Even this version today barely exists since thirty years later, from the summer of 1918 to early 1919, i.e. on the threshold of his final masterpieces, Janáček subjected the score to a radical revision, chiefly of the voice parts, thus creating the third version.[8] Or to put it another way, the third version is written over the second version in the same vocal score. There were further minor revisions before the opera was finally brought to first performance in 1925, but these need not concern us.

As a compendium of Janáček's changing views on recitative Šárka is a rich source of information. In the first version Janáček used the indication on twenty-three occasions. Twenty of these occur in the first two acts in fairly dramatic passages; a mere three occur in the tombeau-like Act 3. Within a year Janáček wrote another version of the opera to the same text in which the word "recitative" occurs only ten times. These are not always in the same places as in the first version, and the oscillation between the two provides a most useful tool for investigation. A few of these recitative markings survive right into the final version of the opera.

From the fact that between 1887 and 1888 Janáček eliminated more than half of the instances of marked recitative from his opera it can be argued that this was one result of Dvořák's advice. Dvořák himself used the word increasingly sparingly in his operas and by the 1890s

---

[7]Dvořák acknowledged receipt of the opera on 6 August 1887. Apart from a brief comment by Janáček in 1924 that Dvořák's assessment went "quite well" it is not known what Dvořák said about the opera.

[8]Examples 4–9 are taken from piano scores of the 1887 version (A 30.388) and of the 1888 version with Janáček's 1918 corrections (A 23.522), Moravské muzeum, Hudební historické oddělení.

Example 4a. *Šárka* (1887), Act 1, p. 19v.

hardly at all. In many cases recitative disappeared from *Šárka* when Janáček tightened it up, replacing the stop-go character of recitative-aria passages with a more declamatory vocal part over a more active orchestral background. In Example 4a from the first version of *Šárka*, an orchestra passage based on a short motif is briefly interrupted by unaccompanied recitative. The recitative itself has a limited pitch range. The rhythm, with triplets for the tri-syllabic word "vzhlédněte," is reasonably sensitive to Czech prosody, though it cannot resist a conclusive thump of Libuša when leading into the introduction to the next section—the chorus "Nás jímá strach," based on the earlier orchestral motif. It is clear why the term "recitative" disappeared from the revision (Example 4b). Although the voice part, in both 1888 and 1918, has something in common with the 1887 version, it is now heard over an active orchestral motif. This is a fairly common pattern in Janáček's elimination of recitative.

There are also examples where the term "recitative" was similarly omitted from the 1888 version but without substantial changes to the music. Example 5 is a type of recitative that Janáček frequently used. In the gaps between the vocal phrases the orchestra keeps up motivic activity; I shall call it "motivic recitative." In Janáček's 1888, and even his

Example 4b. *Šárka* (1887), Act 1, p. 29; (1918–19), Act 1, p. 55v.

followed by short orchestral interlude over which the words 'Nuž vzhlédněte' are repeated and at the end of which the remaining words 'Zde Libuša!' are given over a held accompaniment (in 1888 as 'recitative').

1918, revision the changes in voice part did not change the essential character of the passage. But although the passage stayed much the same, Janáček did not take over the term "recitative" into the 1888 version. Maybe this was just a slip, but it was one that was repeated on other occasions.

Janáček's reduction of recitative in 1888, whether by recomposition or by simply leaving out the indication, it too contradictory to suggest any general pattern of what was and what was not recitative in his view. Perhaps then it would be more helpful to look instead at those occasions where he *retained* the term "recitative" in his second version.

Example 5. *Šárka* (1887), Act 1, p. 16–16v.

The fact that despite his attempt to reduce recitative such instances remained, must surely mean that they are much more significant than those which Janáček omitted when he revised the score. But of the ten examples of recitative which can be found in the second version, only five are direct survivors from similar or identical passages in the first version, and none of these five are different in kind from those where Janáček omitted the term in his revision. In other words, all these may simply be considered as examples of Janáček's inconsistency, and it would be unwise to draw too many conclusions from them.

Rather more importance could perhaps be attached to those five examples of recitative which appear for the first time in the second version, swimming, so to speak, against the tide. Example 6 (next page) provides an instance of this. One can argue, furthermore, that it was no slip since the recitative in the second version was carefully worked out in advance. On the score of the first version one can see pencil traces where Janáček planned his revision, with the word "recit." included. The 1887 version placed the voice against a motivic accompaniment (Example 6a), hence no recitative. In the second version (Example 6b) this became the beginning of a new number: a typical "motivic recitative" with orchestral flourishes between the vocal phrases. In fact in his 1918 revision, with recitative still marked, Janáček even expanded the recitative since the next words, "Jsem Šárka, bojovnice Vlasty vítězné", set melodically in the second version a few bars later, were incorporated into the recitative.

In this example however, as in other similar ones, one can hardly point to any new element in the new recitative Janáček created in 1888. Like those in the first version, they are little more than examples of conventional uses of the term. They serve only to underline Janáček's somewhat limited and conservative acquaintance with opera at this stage of his life and there seems no point in spending any more time discussing them. Instead it may be more useful to draw attention to a few examples from *Šárka* which seem different and which may help to illuminate some aspects of his later style.

Example 7 (p. 15) is one of the oddest examples of a marked recitative that Janáček ever wrote. As the first example of recitative in *Šárka* it is also probably the first passage that he ever called "recitative." Whereas most recitatives attempt to diminish musical interest, this one is motivic. It is also longer than most other recitatives that he wrote— at least 16 bars up to the Meno Mosso based on the same motif (it is unclear how long the recitative indication is in force). And all the time the

Example 6a. *Šarka* (1887), Act 1, p. 22.

Example 6b. *Šarka* (1888), Act 1, p. 36; (1918–19), Act 1, p. 65.

Example 7. *Šárka* **(1887), Act 1, p. 6v.**

voice sings it is doubled in unison by the orchestra. It is hard to know what Janáček meant by this marking. Another composer might well have called it an aria.

It is not an isolated example. Later in the act (Example 8a, p.16) a steady quintuplet rhythm from the Allegro (10 bars, last one given) is interrupted by three recitative bars for Přemysl. When the orchestral motif resumes it turns into a chorus, and so the function of this recitative is again transitional—a short, seemingly freetempo solo before a strict-tempo chorus. But, as in the above example, Přemysl's recitative line is sung in unison with the orchestra. When this passage was revised (Example 8b, p. 16) the orchestral doubling—the chief argument against its being a recitative in the conventional sense—was removed. And, for good measure, so was the recitative indication!

One of the most interesting examples comes at the end of Act I of *Šárka* (Example 9, p. 17). In the 1887 version it begins as a "motivic recitative." Once again it is melodic, taking up a motif already given out by the orchestra, and which will form the main motif for the accompaniment to Ctirad's solo which concludes the act. In the light of the *Jenůfa* examples already discussed, this is familiar ground—a short vocal motif and related orchestral development which forms the basis for so much

Example 8a. *Šarka* (1887), Act 1, p. 8v–9.

Example 8b. *Šarka* (1887), Act 1, p. 10v–11.

Example 9. *Šárka* (1887), Act 1, p. 26v–27.

of Janáček's later operatic music. What is particularly intriguing is that Janáček designated such a passage recitative in the first place. A significant number of such "recitatives" in Janáček are unashamedly motivic and the motif frequently goes into the orchestra—or came from there in the first place. The example is in fact similar to Example 3 from *Jenůfa*, where notes of Jenůfa's recitative become the basis for the subsequent aria.

Poluška's opening aria in *The Beginning of a Romance* provides another similar example. As mentioned earlier, the five examples of marked recitative in this aria imply, from the tempo markings at their conclusion, that these passages are to be taken in free time. They are either unaccompanied or sung over held chords, but one, roughly halfway through the number, is quite different. It is a quotation of the familiar folksong "Žalo dívča," marked "Andante," and sung against a full accompaniment. It is not clear how far the recitative is to continue—possible to the end of the first verse (nine bars), before two bars for orchestra alone. The number continues with a series of variations, in voice and orchestra, on the folksong. This follows none of Pivoda's observations on recitative, but is instead similar to the unusual examples of recitative in *Šárka* and *Jenůfa*.

In a bird's-eye view of opera, given at an Organ School lecture in 1909, Janáček made a number of remarks about recitative:

> From secco recitative Gluck went over to "a tempo" recitative, i.e. by prescribing the beat it allowed the rhythm to develop and capture every verbal nuance. And this is the ideal of the latest modern opera. With "a tempo recitative" we stand on the threshold of the most recent opera.[9]

Note Janáček's term. In his account the harpsichord-accompanied "secco" recitative developed not into "accompagnato" recitative (or in Pivoda's description "obbligato recitative") but "a tempo" recitative. Of course the terms "secco" and "accompagnato" cease to retain their original meaning once a harpsichord is not involved, but it is interesting that Janáček seems to have thought of non-secco recitative as being in strict time, and that he saw a connection between recitative and the ideals of "the latest modern opera," He went on to state that recitative came "gradually ever closer to the model of the spoken word." Janáček saw a link between melodies from spoken words—his "speech melodies"— and the most developed type of recitative.

And this is borne out by an examination of recitative in Janáček's early operas. Together with a number of perfectly ordinary examples of recitative in *Šárka*, there are some that no-one else would have designated as such. They have much more in common with Janáček's familiar instrumental elaborations in his later works of themes given out by the voice. In this light it is hardly surprising that in the sketches for "rhapsody for orchestra," *Tarus Bulba*, Janáček originally conceived the three movements as three "recitative" sections.[10] (A trace of this origin survives in the opening tempo indication "Moderato, quasi recitativo"—Janáček added the "quasi" to the copyist's score, and when asked what it meant described it as "like a title").[11] Such a conception has nothing to do with Beethovenian or Lisztian orchestral recitative, which tends to be written for a single or unison orchestral

---

[9]Shorthand transcription of Janáček's lecture by Mirko Hanák as "Z přednášek Leoše Janáčka o sčasování a skladbú" [From Janáček's lectures on rhythm and composition], *Leoš Janáček: sborník statí a studií* (Prague, 1959), p. 169.

[10]Svatava Přibáňová: "K otázce vzniku Janáčkova Tarase Bulby" [On the question of the origin of Janáček's *Tarus Bulba*], *Časopis Moravského musea: vědy společenské*, xlix (1964), 225.

[11]See *Taras Bulba*, Souborné Kritické vydání děl Leoše Janáčka D7, ed. Jarmil Burghauser and Jan Hanuš (Prague, 1980), p. 161.

part, and which is merely an orchestral imitation of vocal gestures. The *Taras* "recitatives"[12] are all harmonized (if not at first, then soon after), in strict time, and above all motivic: they all initiate motivic processes, in much the same way that the more remarkable *Šárka* examples do, as well as Poluška's "recitative" folksong and most of the *Jenůfa examples*.

It could also be argued that many of the more conventional recitatives in *Šárka* and *The Beginning of a Romance* sound more like later Janáček than the set-numbers they separate. For one thing there is some attempt to take account of Czech prosody with triplets or quintuplets accommodating polysyllabic words. This makes an evident contrast to Janáček's practice in the more "melodic" portions of these works where lines of verse are fitted to regularly structured music, with inevitable verbal distortions. With recitative Janáček was confronted by the need to pay attention to the rhythms and, one might say, the melodies of words. It is possible to see in Janáček's use of recitative in *Šárka* the germs of his later concept of speech melody, and in his historical account of opera he seems to be saying as much.

There is one further link in the chain. The longest recitatives that Janáček wrote occur in *The Beginning of a Romance*. Three numbers, designated as "recitative," were originally to have been spoken dialogue.[13] In comparison with the spoken dialogue upgraded to recitatives in *The Bartered Bride* or *The Two Widows*, these recitatives went through an extra stage: from spoken dialogue in the first version, to spoken dialogue over instrumental music in the second (i.e. the melodrama), to recitative in the third. Since when he wrote these recitatives Janáček did not begin from scratch but incorporated into them the instrumental music of the melodramas,[14] Janáček was in effect adding a layer of words over a layer of existing music and calling the result "recitative."

Janáček travelled a long way from these early operas to *Jenůfa*, but in any consideration of his later vocal style, its relationship to the orchestra and in particular any evaluation of what he meant when stressing the importance of his "speech-melody" to opera, it is essential to look in more depth at the vocal style of his first operas. And in this Janáček's concept of recitative plays an important and vital part.

---

[12] See those printed in the collected edition pp. 125, 127, or the opening of the second movement, originally Rec. II."

[13] See Otakar Fiala: "Libreto k Janáčkovú opeře Počátek románu" [The libretto to Janáček's opera *The Beginning of a Romance*], *Časopis Moravského musea: vědy společenské*, xlix (1964), 211; the three numbers are 3b, 8b–9a–9b and 14b.

[14] See John Tyrrell: "The Musical Prehistory of Janáček's Počátek románu," *Časopis Moravského musea: vědy společenské*, lii (1967), 264–5.

A New Hypothesis on the Theme of Janáček's "Russian" Operas

Jiří Bajer

Jiří Bajer has been at the forefront of our recent exchanges with Czechoslovakia in his twin roles as a member of the Musicology Division of the Academy of Science and President of the Česká hudební společnost. He is a well-known scholar and administrator.

For many years, and for obvious reasons, certain parts of Janáček's context were all but ignored in Czechoslovakia. For example, the Czechoslovak government's ambivalent attitude towards Jews would have made a study of Max Brod's role a rather perilous undertaking. This is also true in terms of Janáček's relationship to Tomaáš Masaryk. In this paper, written more than two years before the "revolution," Bajer suggests that some of Janáček's philosophical and artistic goals must be seen in the context of contemporary events and ideas involving Masaryk and Russia.

Leoš Janáček would be very surprised if he learned that his two best pupils, the conductor Břetislav Bakala and the composer Osvald Chlubna, who should have been sympathetic to his artistic goals, changed the ending of his opera *From the House of the Dead* in an insensitive way. And he would definitely be disappointed that a full thirty years were to pass before his work had its premiere in the original version, including the original ending. This came about thanks to Jaroslav Vogel, through his reading of the opera *From the House of the Dead* at the National Theatre in Prague, where the new performance was presented as a real discovery on 10 May, 1958, in the year of the thirtieth anniversary of Janáček's death.

In his well-known monograph Jaroslav Vogel wrote convincingly about the opera and his motives for rehabilitating Janáček's ending.[1] It is not the intention of this paper to comment on Vogel's conclusions, but nevertheless one fact must be presented. Vogel writes that:

> Chlubna's nine-bar finale deviates too far from the musical style of the rest of the work, due to its somewhat superficial showiness.

[1] Jaroslav Vogel, *Leoš Janáček*, Prague, 1963, p. 361 (English translation).

I share this opinion and, moreover, I think that the modification is in conflict with the dramaturgical orientation of the opera, about which I shall speak later on.

The performance of Janáček's original version of the opera at the National Theatre in 1958 was well-received by qualified critics who understood the issues. One of the leading connoisseurs of Janáček's music, František Pala,[2] wrote, among other things, the following about Vogel's staging of the opera in the bimonthly *Divadelní noviny*:

> ... in Janáček's case the opera ends with a clamorous orchestral coda on a variant of the theme of the house of the dead, which is a protest. The eagle takes wing above the wide steppe, Goryanchikov departs, but the house of the dead continues to survive. This ending is written in the style of the work and its creator. No catharsis, because it would have a false ring! Let us merely recall the Nazi concentration camps! What could be more obvious? A protest or a hymnic catharsis? It is impossible to speak about a hymnic finale![3]

When seeking the inner motivations of Janáček's interest in Russian themes for his operas of the twenties, it is necessary to refer to Vogel's monograph once again. After Vogel analyzes the reasons for and against Chlubna's modification of the ending (and other dramaturgical modifications of the opera *From the House of the Dead*) he also expresses the following conclusion:

> In principle Janáček endeavoured to achieve a bright sound even in his most tragic works. Apart from the ending of the opera *From the House of the Dead*, *Kátya Kabanová* also represents an exception to this rule.

Where should we seek the explanation for these two conspicuous exceptions? Definitely not in chance circumstances! Neither existing literature on Janáček and his work nor my endeavors to answer this question has so far provided direct proofs in the form of, for example, Janáček's own words. On the other hand, indirect proofs and testimonies exist which permit at least a hypothetical formulation of certain arguments about the orientation of the contents and form of these two operas by Leoš Janáček.

---

[2]František Pala, 1887–1964. Music critic of prewar daily *České slovo*. He wrote mainly about J. B. Foerster, V. Novák and L. Janáček.

[3]*Divadelní noviny* (Theatrical Newspaper), Bimonthly of the Czechoslovak Union of Theatre Artists, No. 15 (1958).

It is well known that Janáček developed as an artist throughout his whole life and in what we might call a rising curve. He sought his own path until he was approximately fifty years of age, then in the next quarter of a century he found something at every step and churned out one work after another. This allows us to pose the question of whether a similar process of development, and particularly an acceleration of his life knowledge, also characterizes the sphere of his extra-artistic ideas. For this reason I have concentrated my interest on Janáček's so-called "Russophilism," because it was an important component of his personality. A considerable number of compositions from the last twenty-five years of Janáček's life originated from this impulse. Here, however, mention must be made of a special fact. In spite of the clear pioneering character and artistic vitality of his "Russian" works, into which the reality of the twenties penetrated in all possible ways, Janáček has practically always been presented as an enthusiastic Russophile of the late nineteenth century in the spirit of the enthusiastic tirades which he wrote in Vymazal's textbook of Russian in nine lessons at the time of his first journey to Russia.

The Russophilist climate of that time differed completely, however, from that of the twenties of the present century. National relations in the Bohemia of the nineties were extremely acute and tense. The Czech-German antagonism which existed in the Czech territory of the monarchy developed, in both economics and politics, into a permanent confrontation which gave rise to the opposed tendencies towards pan-Germanism on one hand, and to pan-Slavism on the other. At the same time Austria-Hungary developed ever more clearly as a power with a predominant Slavonic population which, at least in its more educated and cultured representatives, acquired strong self-confidence in relation to the internationally more active Russian empire. This growing self-confidence led to the idea that the historical moment of the Slavonic nations under Russian leadership had come. It was as though there existed no knowledge of the experience of more level-headed Czech travelers, who had previously become acquainted with Russian affairs and had been cured for all time of notions about pan-Slavistic utopias and about the leading position of tsarist orthodox Russia in the future of Slavonic nations.

Janáček's trusting idealism, which during his first journey to Russian made him write words such as: "At last the feeling of a Slav . . . rebirth! I shake off slavery . . . ," was later to be put to a hard test. From the time of Palacký and Havlíček the criticism of primitive Russophilism had progressed to the much finer and more differentiated forms elaborated by Tomáš G. Masaryk, which reflected the situation in the 1920s. Janáček encountered them on the pages of *Lidový noviny,* which played a large role which still has not been evaluated as part of the general development of his outlook.[4]

Most of the following deductions concerning Janáček's interpretation of Russian opera themes are based on a new perusal of seven volumes of *Lidový noviny* from the years 1920 to 1927, i.e. from the time of the completion of *Kátya Kabanová* to the composition, from the first sketches down to the last note, written by the composer's hand in the score of the *From the House of the Dead*. In the course of its over fifty year existence *Lidový noviny* was always a remarkable cultural and political paper which expressed the independent liberal opinions of a considerable part of the Czech intelligentsia. After the First World War it was particularly the younger creative generation, represented, for example, by the brothers Čapek, Kisch, Arne Novak and others, that contributed to this newspaper. The political viewpoint of *Lidový noviny* clearly inclined toward Masaryk's democracy, and the philosophical aspect toward his realism and humanity.

As is known, Janáček contributed to the newspaper from its very first volume, which appeared in 1893, up to the time of his death. In all he wrote 58 idiosyncratic feuilletons for it and from his readings in it gained impulses for a number of compositions. In other words, he helped to create *Lidový noviny* and it helped to create his political viewpoints. Here my study considers the question of the extent to which this newspaper influenced the deepening of Janáček's democratism and humanitarian thinking and the degree to which it helped to break down the residue of his trusting Russophilic idealism. I read the newspapers page by page—reports dealing with politics, the national economy and culture—and tried to see it through the eyes of Janáček himself, to determine how he would most likely have understood them. And in doing so I arrived at several probable conclusions.

For Janáček *Lidový noviny* can be said to have been a university of modern political thinking. He was even interested in reports from the economic sphere, a fact witnessed by a curious note from 23 September, 1921, in which, under Dr. Desiderius's drawing of Janáček there is printed a text alleged to have been written by Janáček himself:[5]

---

[4]Jan Racek and Leoš Firkušný, "Leoš Janáček and the People's Newspaper," see in *Leoš Janáček, Feuilletons from the People's Newpaper*, Brno, 1958. Editor's note: The *Lidový noviny* has been resurrected since the November Revolution.

[5]Hugo Boettinger, pseudonym Dr. Desiderius, 1880-1934. Well-known painter and master of the art of drawing. Often sketched Czech musicians, including Janáček.

From *Lidový noviny* I have already set Gellner's *Puppets* and *Song of the Unknown* and Těsnohlídek's *Cunning Little Vixen* to music; I still have to transcribe the air of the stock exchange house in music when the Czechoslovak crown drops by fifty points in Zurich.

Whether these words were really written by Janáček or not, their meaning is the same: to express through a joke a certain unknown characteristic of the composer—i.e. his interest in public events.

Exceptionally expressive reports and commentaries presented in the paper, for example, provided Janáček with a disquieting portrayal of Russian events. In the years 1920 and 1921 the first pages of the newspaper were dominated by reports from the civil war front and the testimonies of emigrants who flooded Czechoslovakia. *Lidový noviny* published, for example, several extracts from *My Notebook 1919–1920* by Dmitri Sergejevich Merezhkovsky[6] and, in serial form, Nazhivin's memoir novel *The Bolshevik Years of Trouble and Chaos*.[7] Here the "bábushka of the Russian revolution," Kateřina Breshko-Breshkovskaya,[8] also asked for the floor. She did not feel too safe in the new revolutionary Russia, because in the name of the revolution she wanted to "enlighten the whole nation and to make each person into a conscientious citizen" (30.1.1920).

It can be presumed that the official proclamation of representatives of the Czechoslovak government on its policy towards Soviet Russia had a substantial influence on Janáček's Russophile tendencies. For example, on 5 February 1920 *Lidový noviny* printed a speech made by the then Minister of Foreign Affairs, Eduard Beneš, on the international situation—a speech in which a considerable amount of space was devoted to questions connected with Czechoslovakia's relation to Russia. In it Janáček was able to read:

> ... [Beneš'] agreement in Slavonic and Russian matters with the opinions of the president ... the backwardness of the Slavonic world ... why did Russia collapse? Because it was a medieval country with no idea of what democracy means for the people.

---

[6] Dimitri Sergejevitsh Merezhkovsky, 1866–1941. Russian writer, left Russia in 1920.
[7] Ivan Fiororovitsh Nashivin, 1874–? Russian writer, translated very often into Czech.
[8] Kateřina Konstanty Breshko-Breshkovskaya, 1844–1934. One of the founders and leaders of the Russian political party named Eser (Social Revolutionaries). She supported the Temporary Government created in Russia after the March (February) Revolution. She left Russia in 1919.

The official government proclamations and semi-official deliberations on the theme of Russia appeared quite regularly and it would be a mistake to regard them as being of a biased anti-Russian nature. On the contrary, realism and an endeavor to understand the new conditions began to predominate in them. In the leading article published on 24 March, 1922, under the heading of "Our Russophilism" the writer admitted that "the Soviets will endure."

Of particularly conclusive importance was Masaryk's presence at the ceremonial opening of the Slavonic Institute in Paris in the autumn of 1923, on which occasion the president delivered a lecture on the need for Slavonic studies. In his speech he expressed the idea of building a barrier against pan-Germanism through the cooperation of the Slavonic nations, inspired by European culture. *Lidový noviny* devoted a whole page to this on 18 October, 1923, and it is almost certain that Janáček read it, because his admiration of Masaryk exceeded by far the degree of enthusiasm of the people as a whole for the person who deserved so much credit for bringing about national self-determination and state independence. Janáček arrived at a profound understanding of Masaryk's philosophy, ethics and social policy, strong proof of this being afforded, among other things, by his feuilleton headed "Engraved Words" published in *Lidový noviny* on 22 September, 1921. In it the composer described the impression he had gained from his meeting with Masaryk at Wilson Station in Prague on 16 September, 1921, and from his speech, from which he extracted several of Masaryk's ideas and recorded them in his characteristic way in notes:

> I am engraving several of the president's significant words in the notes of his own speech . . . : "we shall fulfill the tasks of the building-up of our state only through diligence and our broad political view."

—and at the very end of the feuilleton: "I do not like to speak about my feelings..."[9]

Janáček was able, of course, to gain a considerable amount of valuable knowledge about Masaryk's opinions in relation to tsarist, post-February and Soviet Russia from the first edition of Masaryk's work already published in 1925 under the title *A World Revolution*. However, I have no reports about this. On the other hand, a powerful effect was

---

[9]The feuilleton "Engraved Words" was first published in *Leoš Janáček, Feuilletons from the People's Newspaper*, Brno, 1938 (ed. Jan Racek and Leoš Firkušný). After that it appeared in Racek's publication *Triptychon*, Prague, 1948. It was omitted in the so-called "full edition" of Janáček's *Feuilletons from the People's Newspaper* (1958).

created by daily events such as Maxim Gorky's letter to Masaryk in which he sought help for the starving inhabitants of Soviet Russia, printed in *Lidový noviny* on 20 July, 1921, and Masaryk's almost immediate and positive reply of 5 August, 1921. There were quite a number of similar reports and many of them concerned factual recognition of the status quo in Russia and, simultaneously, the formulation of the democratic conception of the so-called eastern policy of the young Czechoslovakian state in which out-dated Slavonic and Rusophile opinions were substantially revised.

In this respect an important role was played by an article printed in *Lidový noviny* on 5 December, 1924, under the heading of "Minister Dr. Beneš on Our Relation to Russia." In it the reader could find the following:

> There are no arguments in the field of international affairs against diplomatic relations with Russia ... We reject the pre-war conception of the Slavonic policy not only because it was always shaped by the considerations of tsarist Russia, but also because it was always the domain of mostly reactionary elements.... The former formulations of the Slavonic policy must be different ... hazy ... Our present Slavonic policy must be different ... above all we do not want to confuse Slavonic policy with Russophilism ...

The article was most likely a modified version of Beneš's parliamentary speech dealing with Czechoslovakia's foreign policy, about which *Lidový noviny* published a report on 7 February, 1924, under the heading of "Czechoslovakia and Soviet Russia." And there, too, a quotation taken from Beneš's speech, "Without Russia European politics and European peace are impossible," appeared as a motto.

However, a complicated path runs between these readers' experiences, whose influence on Janáček cannot be proved directly on the basis of records, as it were, and his compositional work. And so it is more useful to place one next to the other so that possible connections automatically suggest themselves. For example, the *Glagolitic Mass* could document the years-long development of Janáček's Slavonic feeling. In his monograph Jaroslav Vogel wrote that the image of the *Glagolitic Mass* had lain dormant in Janáček's mind from the time of the Cyril and Methodious celebrations in Velehrad in which the young student Janáček participated. According to Jaroslav Vogel's notes, the composer returned to the idea of the mass at the end of 1921, but it was not until the latter half of 1926 that he finally completed the work. It is instructive that he expressed himself ex post facto on the *Glagolitic Mass* as follows:

> I wanted to portray here faith in the certainty of a nation, not on a religious foundation, but on a moral, strong one which takes God as a witness.

Let us compare this with an idea expressed by Masaryk in the book *Humanitarian Ideals*: "I want morality on a religious base, but a different religion to the one officially served up," says Masaryk in the conclusion entitled "About Important Things."[10]

The opera *From the House of the Dead* is a dramatic work, but its contents consist of humanity and morality "which take God as a witness." The choice of Dostoevsky's novel was in itself entirely unusual. After all, it was the *carmen horrendum* of the rule of Tsar Nikolai (as Herzen called it) and as such it was perhaps the first work in 19th century Russia to speak about the human dignity of prisoners often sentenced for petty reasons to long years of imprisonment in Siberian camps, where the worst conditions prevailed. However, if we consider Janáček's choice of Dostoevsky more profoundly in the light of all the impulses provided by the period of the first decades of the twentieth century, marked by dramatic events such as wars, revolution, starvation and the frustration of human destinies, it is not really so surprising. The composer could not, however, interpret the novel as the revival and squashing of slavery in the direct sense, but only as an Aristotelian catharsis, an emotional purification in a bath of dread and horror, which he actually achieved through the use of an exceptionally powerful style of expression.

The Aristotelian conception of the finale of the opera can be understood in terms of the then contemporary experience of events during which people were treated with anything but humanism. The press of the twenties carried alarming reports from all corners of the world—at a time when the civil war was still proceeding with great cruelty in Soviet Russia and starvation was setting in, Mussolini appeared on the political horizon, followed promptly by Hitler. The age of concentration camps had just arrived. Even in the serious *Lidový noviny*, reports and headlines appeared in the news items from Russia which shocked readers. As examples one can quote titles like: "Archbishop Tichon condemned to imprisonment!," "Sentence

---

[10]T. G. Masaryk, *Humanitarian Ideas*, Prague, 1930. First published in 1901, and thereafter in 1919, 1920, and 1927.

passed on Russian social revolutionaries!," "Death sentences for priests!," "Russian peasants oppose the government!" and others. Although Janáček did not react directly to such reports, their influence could have been reflected in his artistic endeavours through his efforts to find the most penetrating way of expressing the positive values of humanity—tolerance, moral greatness and, above all, an unshaken longing for freedom.

In the spirit of his individual poetics and social and humanitarian feelings, Janáček linked his last great compositions with his daily experiences. Expressive evidence of this is provided by one of his rarely quoted feuilletons which was printed, under the title "It is Getting Dark," by the rival daily called *Venkov* on 5 February, 1928.[11] Here the composer returned once again to the experiences which led along complicated paths to his concrete presentation of certain of his opera characters. In most cases Janáček presents specifically Czech reminiscences, including his own intimate interests, and not sources of inspiration of a general nature—in his Russian operas, for example, Russian or Slavonic ones. In Ostrovsky's *Storm*, for example, he initially perceived "a great deal of the emotionally touching, Slavonically soft." However, when he began to compose the text he identified Kátya with his mistress Kamila, about which he left several explicit pronouncements. However, in a letter to Max Brod dated 18 January, 1928, he wrote that his motives "are pinned to everything that is." I consider this short sentence to be an important key to the understanding of Janáček's creative ethics and poetics. On one hand Janáček distanced himself from academic composing, according to which so-called musical ideas are conjured up in the mind by means of freely improvising on a piano, while on the other hand he drew attention to more common, we might say more universally human motives in general and a typified artistic imagery in particular. And it is just about this that infallible proof is provided in the feuilleton published in *Venkov*,[11] where it is written:

> Musical composition is not as easy as simple reason would have it. Notes do not sit on the keyboard of the piano, they are not collected and poured on paper with ink. Madam! When I saw your tears in 1915 – a child in your arms, your husband away at war – your pain, suffering and despair filled me with a vision of *Kátya Kabanová*. Do not the nostalgia and sorrow you aroused in me lie in this melody?

---

[11]*Venkov* (Countryside), was the daily newspaper of the Republican Party of small farmers. It was published from 1906 until the Second World War.

There can be no doubt that this "Madam" was once again his beloved, Kamila Stosslova, but here raised to the level of a symbol of human suffering. In *The Makropoulos Case* Janáček was momentarily inspired to give a concrete portrayal to one of the characteristics of the image of Elena, something "that was here at the moment." In the feuilleton entitled "It is Getting Dark" the composer wrote about being under the deep spell of a strange woman:

> But on you, lady of Kounic Street, in a black fur coat looking as though moles themselves had shed it, I measured my three-hundred-year-old Elena Makropoulos! You were probably surprised that I, an unknown person, greeted you, unknown to me! You were suitable for Elena Makropoulos only due to your icy, beautiful face.

In both cases Janáček "inclined to the truth, to the coarse language of the elements,"[12] which must be interpreted on several levels of meaning.

Through Dostoevsky's novel *Notes From the House of the Dead* Janáček avowed the ethics of truth, "the coarse language of the elements" and the writer's art of finding "good human souls" even in the dreadful environment of a prison. He was exceptionally precise in his understanding of Dostoevsky, because what was captivating in the novel is also captivating in the opera, i.e. faith in Man, in his inborn positive characteristics. Janáček expressed his faith in the previously quoted letter addressed to Dr. Brod. Let us go further, however. Dostoevsky gained renown for his psychologically fine and precise characterization of his characters, for which Turgenyev had already expressed his recognition.[13] Masaryk, a connoisseur of Russian literature, appreciated the same thing about Dostoevsky. It is known that Masaryk based his arguments for his conception of democracy on faith in the individual, in his human values, his spiritual wealth and his immortal soul. The successful result of the transfer of Dostoevsky's model to an operatic form is not merely a mark of Janáček's dramaturgical skill! Connected with it is also the bold transposition of a general humanitarian idea from an environment which is remote as regards both time and place to the close world of the Czech idea of interpersonal relations. And, last but not

---

[12] From the feuilleton "To What I Confess," *Lidový noviny*, 13 February, 1927, and also a letter addressed to Max Brod, dated one day earlier.

[13] In a letter from Paris in 1861. See: *F. M. Dostoevsky and I. S. Turgenyev, Perepiska* (Correspondence), Academia Moscow, 1928.

least, at least a trace of the moral directives of Masaryk's form of democratism can be found here.

Speaking once again of Masaryk, whom the Moravian master, more or less of the same age, profoundly admired, I should like to draw attention to the noetic roots of Janáček's intention, proclaimed in the last years of his life, to pin his creative fantasy to "what is," i.e. to life's concreteness. In this respect, too, he stood close, even if mediatedly, to Masaryk's noetics and philosophy of realism, likewise called concretism. On more than one occasion Masaryk wrote that his concretism recognized individualities in nature, society and the whole world and that he tried to get to know these individualities. The opera *From the House of the Dead* portrays individual human destinies, thus also strengthening faith in a collective and its ability to achieve freedom. Here, however, faith in freedom is not mythologized. As Janáček's original ending shows, the myth of freedom was confronted here with a critical knowledge of reality, which was rougher than human longing. And thus it is true not only from the artistic, but also the noetic aspect. Every step from faith and myth to critical knowledge is valuable, especially if it is presented in such a suggestive way as in the opera *From the House of the Dead*. Janáček was not appreciated artistically for a long time in our country, but this has changed now. It is with regret that I must say that this does not yet apply to the understanding of Janáček's artistic and human integrity. In the eyes of some people Janáček is a strange mixture of genius and simplicity which must be explained and defended. I, on the contrary, have arrived at the conviction that in his mature years Janáček continued to develop both artistically and intellectually and that thanks to his talent, curiosity and thoughtfulness he arrived at a critical judgment with which he enriched and oriented his unfading imagination.

Czech Composers and Verismo

By Jan Smaczny

One of the dangers in a field like our own is the tendency to become insular, to evaluate material solely in terms of its Czech or Slovak quality, or lack of it. Another pitfall to be avoided is the glorification of an array of compositional demigods and Czech school "begats": Smetana begat Dvořák who begat Janáček, etc. Jan Smaczny, in his study of the interaction between Czech opera and verismo, provides a welcome tonic to both by looking outside the Czech Lands for influence, and focussing for a while on the little-known Richard Rozkošný. Smaczny is a versatile scholar who has published valuable studies on Dvořák, Janáček, and with Christopher Hogwood, on earlier music in the Czech Lands.

On January 4, 1891, Mascagni's *Cavalleria rusticana* was given its first performance in Prague, in a Czech translation by the indefatigable V. J. Novotný. It was an immediate and considerable success with twenty-eight performances being given in its first year followed by fifteen in 1892. After this, as Table 1 shows (page 43), Leoncavallo's *Pagliacci* had a comparable, if slightly less marked, success before numbers of performances fell to much more modest levels, though in both cases neither opera disappeared entirely from the repertoire. Whatever the fate of these operas as far as the audiences in the National Theatre in Prague were concerned, some Czech composers were sufficiently impressed to attempt what might be described as the sincerest form of flattery. It would be misleading to suggest that the Czechs established their own *verismo* school, but the response of a variety of composers, both young and old, was sufficient to ensure that the new realism became an important feature in the native repertoire.

The new interest in *verista* subject matter was by no means the prerogative of younger men. If Dvořák and Fibich stood aside from the tendency, two composers associated with the generation which provided some of the earliest operas for the Provisional Theatre, Bendl and Rozkošný made a significant contribution. Richard Rozkošný's Herzegovenian melodrama *Stoja*, premiered in the National Theatre on June 6, 1894, seems to have been the first concrete response to the novelty (see Table 2, page 43), and it was followed a little over a year later by Bendl's *Matka* or *Máti Míla*, given its first performance in the

National Theatre on June 25, 1895. Table 2 gives the operatic pairings enjoyed by *Stoja*: only once was it given a double bill with *Matka Míla*—evidently the authorities of the National Theatre did not feel that they had a Czech equivalent of the *Cavalleria rusticana-Pagliacci* axis on their hands.

Later manifestations of the new realism in Czech opera, such as Foerster's *Eva* (first performed in Prague in 1899) and, of course, *Její pastorkyňa* (first performed in Brno in 1904) understandably have claimed far greater interest than the pioneering efforts of Rozkošný and Bendl. But a full understanding of Janáček's achievement in *Její pastorkyňa* demands that some attention be paid to what has been hitherto an area of Czech operatic endeavor little examined by scholars.[1] Before looking a little more closely at Rozkošný's *Stoja*, the question of the broad influence of *verismo* in musical terms must be addressed.

Italian opera was a potent force in Czech musical theatre from as early as the 1860s. Smetana's debt to Verdi is clear on the occasion of his very first opera.[2] Later, Dvořák confirmed an enthusiasm for the same composer, something readily perceived in a number of his operas, when he spoke in warmly approving terns of Verdi to Charles Villiers Stanford.[3] As early as 1945 Alec Robertson[4] pointed out the near quotation of the first-act love duet from Verdi's *Otello* during Rinald's monologue at the beginning of the fourth act of Dvořák's *Armida*. It is, perhaps, a tribute to the strength of the Czech operatic tradition in the 1890s and early 1900s that the evidence for any palpable musical influence from *verismo* appears to be fragmentary. While Fibich avoided *verista* subject matter in his operas, he offers in *Šárka* (paradoxically given its highly national credentials) a clear sign that he had taken note of the fulsome lyricism of Puccini. The crucial moment in the love duet between Šárka and Ctirad in Act 2 of the opera is marked with this magnificent musical phrase:

---

[1] My article "Janáček and Czech Realism" touched briefly on the subject. See Jan Smaczny, "Janáček and Czech Realism," in *Jenůfa/Katya Kabanová*, ed. Nicholas John (London, 1985).

[2] See *Braniboři v Čechách*, vocal score (Prague, 1911, revised 1946), Act I, Scene 10, pp. 73–76 and Act 3, Scene 1, p. 181.

[3] C. V. Stanford, *Pages from an Unwritten Diary* (London, 1914) p. 112.

[4] A. Robertson, *Dvořák*, Master Musicians (London, 1945), p. 140.

Example No. 1

Notwithstanding a knowledge of and clear admiration for *Cavalleria rusticana*, Janáček's *Její pastorkyňa* shows little, if any evidence of its musical influence, although the uninhibited use of the shouted line "Hanno ammazzato compare Turiddu!" at the end of Mascagni's masterpiece might well have hovered in the background of Kostelnička's final sally in Act 2. A parallel with Puccini, however, makes itself felt at the end of Act 3 of *Její pastorkyňa* in the violin melody which appears over the pulsating accompaniment when Jenůfa and Laca are left alone. The theme (see Example No. 2), is strikingly similar to the melody of the duet, which is hammered out so blatantly at the end of *La Bohème* (see Example No. 3). If the means are entirely different, the musical outline is distinctly congruent.

Example No. 2

Example No. 3

Dvořák appears to have had no inclination towards attempting a *verismo* opera. Commenting on Dvořák's endeavour after *Armida*, Janáček made the following observation:[5]

> I believe *Armida* would have been his last opera in which a dense and impenetrable mist of chords pervaded the whole — his last opera in the old style. He was looking for a libretto which would break up the usual architectonic structure.

Sadly, Janáček's comment is also rather dense and impenetrable. It is possible that he was inferring a change in direction towards *verismo* by the older composer, but he could hardly be referring to Dvořák's last operatic project, *Horymír*, to a wretched libretto by Rudolf Stárek. The only thing that *Horymír* might, had it been completed, have had in common with an unchallengeably *veristad* opera, such as Jindřich Káan's Zola setting, *Germinal*, is that both have scenes set in a mine. However, we learn from the same reminiscence of Dvořák by Janáček, that the older composer was acquainted with *Madama Butterfly* and he possessed a score of Gustave Charpentier's *Louise*. Dvořák appears to have had a rather ambiguous relationship with the latter work. According to an account by the pianist Josef Faměra,[6] Dvořák was much absorbed with the score of *Louise* in early 1903. The musical language of the opera clearly presented Dvořák with a quandary since he spoke of it in the following terms:[7]

> "... this Charpentier is a curious musician. Everywhere he has false notes! For example, where he should have C he has C sharp, where A-flat he has A. Take this chord here, one can see it is wrong!" Suddenly, as if just remembering that I had been his pupil, he said, "So, how would you do it more satisfactorily?" Shyly, I gave my opinion. But Dvořák viewed me with disdain and pointing to the chord in question said, "No — this chord is fine!"

Faměra's account of Dvořák's worries concerning *Louise* is borne out by a scrutiny of the composer's score of the opera.[8] Dvořák made

---

[5] L. Janáček, "Za Antonínem Dvořákem" in *Dvořákův sborník, Hudební revue*, IV (October 1911, Nos. 8–9), p. 433.

[6] In O. Šourek, *Dvořák ve vzpomínkách a dopisech*, (Prague, 1938), p. 178.

[7] Ibid.

[8] I am very grateful to Jarmil Burghauser for allowing me to look at Dvořák's score of *Louise*. The text of the score is in German and was published by Hugel and Co.. On the first page Dvořák wrote "Koupil jsem od M.M. Urbánka 1903 v dubnu" (I bought it from Urbánka in April).

Example No. 4

a number of marginal comments at points where he found the harmony to be especially provocative. For instance, on page thirteen of the score Dvořák wrote: "These quints [consecutive parallel fifths] are very beautiful, but I cannot stand them!" A number of other consecutives are queried in the score and on page twenty he questions a progression involving diminished fifths (see Example No. 4). Dvořák's marginal comment asks "why not B and C sharp?" Despite his slightly prurient interest in this kind of exotic harmony, Dvořák was not above allowing similar progressions to invade his own work. Since Dvořák brought his score of *Louise* from Urbánek in April, 1903, shortly after the Prague premiere of the opera,[9] it cannot have been a direct influence on the prelude to Act 3 of *Armida*, one of the composer's most extraordinary harmonic passages, which was begun on October 8, 1902 (see Example No. 5). Here, a succession of consecutive fifths are concealed in a

Example No. 5.

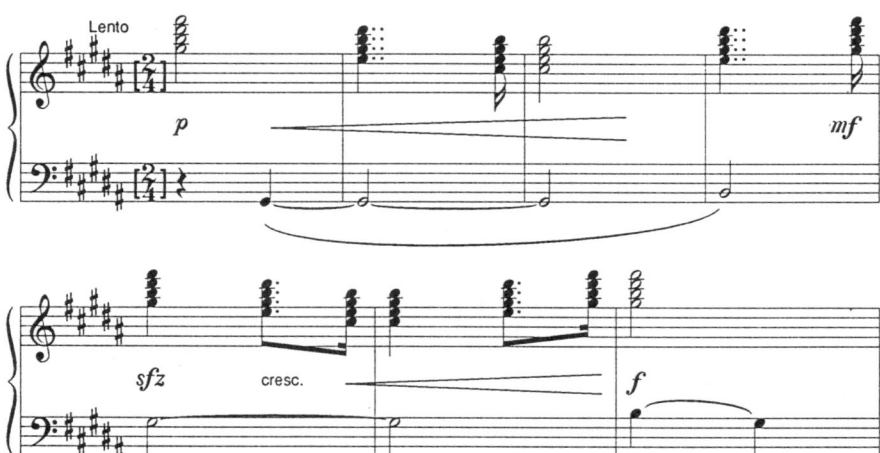

[9]February 13, 1903, in a translation by V. J. Novotný.

sequence of parallel sevenths bearing a family relation to the passage outlined in *Louise*. It is not beyond the bounds of possibility that Dvořák's fascination with the score of *Louise* may have resulted from the parallels to be found in the apparent harmonic excesses of Charpentier with his own developing style. Unfortunately the relatively sparse sketch material which survives from *Horymír* do not indicate a reinforcement of this direction.

To conclude this consideration of Czech composers and *verismo* a brief consideration of Rozkošný's *Stoja* is offered. The only readily available source for the work is a full score with a German text in the Klementinum in Prague. A further source concerning the opera, and one which may serve as evidence of a certain local popularity, is a pot-pourri of themes from the work published by Urbánek.[10] The fact that the pot-pourri focuses strongly on what appears to be the national element in the opera is a significant indication that Rozkošný has not abandoned his Czech credentials despite the location of the action in Herzegovina and the novelty of the subject matter. Example 6 is taken from the opening chorus of the opera after the overture and introduction; it is also the starting point of the pot-pourri issued by Urbánek. *Stoja* is Rozkošný's sixth opera and was composed some twenty-three years after his first, *Mikuláš*. Thus it is, perhaps, no surprise that a work

Example No. 6.

[10]Směs pro klavír na 2 ruce upravil skladatel, Urbánek, Prague.

Example No. 7.

which looks to new directions in atmosphere and subject matter still reflects the compositional characteristics of a style which was well-advanced in the opera *Svatojanské proudy*, premiered in the Provisional Theatre in 1871, and which had continued to mature over twenty-two years. In *Stoja* it is possible to observe a characteristic tendency towards easeful melody in compound time (see Example No. 7), something which amounts to a commonplace in *Svatojanské proudy*, and Rozkošný's methods of whipping up excitement remain an amplification of the techniques he adopted in earlier operas (see Examples 8 and 9, next page). In many senses *Stoja* is a work whose musical style would have come as no surprise to audiences familiar with Rozkošný's musical language and treatment of situation. It is the situations themselves which are so different from the content of such works as *Svatojanské proudy*, *Záviš z Falkenštejna*, *Popelka* and *Krakonoš*. Having pursued an operatic career which might be described as orthodox in terms of the repertoire of the Provisional and National Czech Theatres, Rozkošný was entering new territory. Where before the consideration of day-to-day life in a rural or occasionally urban context had been the province

Example No. 8.

Example No. 9.

of idealised comedy in opera, Rozkošný had taken a subject based on human passions in a mundane setting and given the Czechs their first taste of realism from a native composer. The libretto, by Otakar Kučera, is based on a short story by Joseph Conrad concerning the love, which has ultimately a tragic outcome, of Stoja, the wife of the remote and cruel Alexandr Pankarovič, for the sergeant Štěpán. The first review of the work in *Dalibor* by František Hejda[11] was quick to point out

---

[11]*Dalibor* (Roč, 1894), pp. 240–251.

Rozkošný's new departure with reference to earlier works. He also pointed out clear links with Mascagni's *Cavalleria rusticana*, suggesting that *Stoja* was, to an extent, riding on the popularity of the Italian work. Hejda also added the following:

> ... it would not be fair to emphasize the debt of *Stoja* to new trends in Italian opera ... Rozkošný, whatever the relationship of his new opera to "verismo", has remained conclusively independent, relying on rich melodic invention, ...

A final example (No. 10) may serve as additional proof of Rozkošný's ability in this area.

Example No. 10.

The individuality of musical style in *Stoja* is significant. If Rozkošný's compositional voice was a small one, Hejda's enthusiasm for his musical "independence" indicates the strength of belief in the Czech national style: a tradition which could absorb new trends in subject matter and atmosphere while still maintaining its integrity and quality of utterance. If *Stoja* is not a masterpiece of Czech *verismo* it serves as an indication of the vigour of a tradition which might yet produce masterpieces. Tracing the history of Czech national opera is a vexed and aggravating business even where only a single composer is concerned. Themes suggest themselves, from subject matter—for instance the historical-mythological trend and the country comedy—to musical genres such as ballet and aria; the folk-element is also a sturdy line of investigation and flourishes in the most unlikely places. But an overview of the tradition, which critics such as Hejda were quite clear existed, is much harder to achieve. It is possible, however, to assess, from time to time, like a hydrometer measuring specific gravity, the worth and intensity of the tradition. One method is by the response of Czech opera composers to new influences, and their encounter with *verismo* in the 1890s and 1900s provides us with such an opportunity. While Preissová's plays of 1889 and 1890 may have provided Foerster and Janáček with material which related more closely to the native soil, Rozkošný's *Stoja*, modest as it is, furnished persuasive evidence of a national style which is firmly established and ready to absorb and profit from new impulses, without losing its identity.

Cavalleria rusticana was premiered at the National Theatre in Prague on January 4, 1891 in a translation by V. J. Novotný entitled *Sedlák kavalír*. *Pagliacci* was premiered two years later on February 10, 1893, in a translation by V. J. Novotný entitled *Komedianti*. The two operas were paired in the same programme four times in 1893, and three times in 1896. Other operatic combinations comprised the following for *Cavalleria rusticana*: *L'Amico Fritz*, four times, and *V studni* once; for *Pagliacci*: *V studni*, three times, and *Stoja*, twice.

Pucinni's *Manon Lescaut* was premiered on April 24, 1894 in a translation by V. J. Novotný and played for six performances in the same year; it was not revived until the twentieth century. *La Boheme* was premiered on February 27, 1898 in a translation by V. J. Novotný entitled *Bohema* and given six performances in that year and none the following year.

Table 1

Performance record of *Cavalleria rusticana* and *Pagliacci* in the National Theatre in Prague in the 1890s.

	1891	1892	1893	1894	1895	1896	1897	1898	1899
Cavalleria rusticana	28	15	9	2	4	7	0	4	2
Pagliacci			19	5	5	7	3	1	3

Table 2

Operatic pairings with Rozkošný's *Stoja*. All performances were in the National Theatre in Prague.

1894

June 6 (premiere), Blodek: *V studni*

June 8, Leoncavallo: *Pagliacci*

June 11, —

June 13, —

June 25, Dvořák: *Tvrdé palice*

September 25, von Suppé: *Die schöne Galatea*

December 12, Leoncavallo: *Pagliacci*

1895

July 8, Bendl: *Matka Míla*

August 18, Bendl: *Česká svatba* (Ballet pantomime; given in the presence of the Emperor)

Pleasures and Woes: The Vixen's Wedding Celebration

Michael Beckerman

This study is part of the author's ongoing effort to articulate the power and variety of the musical pastoral. Focusing on the wordless wedding dance at the end of Act II in The Cunning Little Vixen, *he argues that Janáček's ability to convincingly combine opposing states is one of the keys to understanding his dramatic gift.*

At the conclusion of the second act of *Příhody lišky Bystroušky* the forest seems to erupt into a wild dance of joy as the animals celebrate the wedding of the vixen and the fox. Virtually all commentators have mentioned this scene as a conspicuously positive and affirmative moment in the opera. John Tyrrell refers to the act's "exhilarating close," [1] while Kurt Honolka speaks of the celebration as a "frölichen Hymnus."[2] Vogel writes of the "carefree rejoicing of the youngsters during the wedding round,"[3] Černohorská describes the scene as "vivacious wedding merriment,"[4] and Michael Ewans writes of "the total unity of the forest." Here is the opening of the dance:

Example 1.

---

[1] In the liner notes to the London Decca recording of the opera, conducted by Sir Charles Mackerras.
[2] Kurt Honolka, *Leoš Janáček* (Stuttgart: Besler Verlag, 1982), p. 217.
[3] Jaroslav Vogel, *Leoš Janáček* (Prague: Státní hudební vydavatelství, 1963).
[4] Milena Černohorská. Liner notes, Supraphon recording, conducted by Bohumil Gregor.

This passage occurs a total of four times in the course of the wedding scene. Yet the first two repetitions are followed by an interpolation which forms a marked contrast to it:

Example 2.

Eric Chisholm considers this "a happy waltz rhythm with block chord harmonies,"[5] but it is difficult to imagine how one could experience this example as a "happy waltz" of any kind. Thus it seems appropriate to ask what such music is doing in the middle of the Vixen's wedding, and what it signifies? In order to approach this question, however, we must go back to the first example and view it in the context of the opera itself, and also in the larger context of European musical symbols.

With its Lydian "folk" modality, simple phrase structure, syncopations, and melodic cells, all welded together by a drone, the opening passage corresponds to the traditional rustic dance, common throughout Europe for centuries, and especially resonant in the 19th century where it plays a central role in the development of "national music." It is also a vital part of the Czech tradition, as we know from the *Bartered Bride* and Dvořák's *Slavonic Dances*. Janáček's updated version has simply turned the peasants into small animals, a necessary transition, at any rate, since peasants don't usually dance in forests (since they would tend to trip and fall).

This particular type of rustic dance may itself be considered a subset of the pastoral mode, which from the middle of the 17th century on-

---

[5]Eric Chisholm, *The Operas of Leoš Janáček* (Oxford: Pergamon Press, 1971).

wards has a fairly straightforward set of musical conventions associated with it. On the level of presentation, pastorals tend to be displays, more concerned with demonstrating an abiding status quo than creating conflicts at a fundamental level. The key symbol involved in the depiction of the musical pastoral is the drone bass, which not only evokes the visual "outdoor" image of the bagpipes, but enforces harmonic stasis as well. Thus the pedal D-flat, which dominates the passage, is a bulwark against change, whether harmonic or affective.

I do not wish to imply that Janáček's pastoral is qualitatively neutral simply because it represents something eternal—i.e., the world of nature. Not all visions of nature need be the same. The passage is not only distinguished by its Lydian flavor and pulsing rhythm, but the accompaniment is rich in associations. Its parallel fourths (see Example 1—in brackets) suggest several important moments in the opera including the vixen's triumphant return to the forest,

Example 3.

and perhaps even the opening bars of the opera, with their undulating motive:

Example 4.

The relationship between the wedding scene and the work's opening is further reinforced by the reiteration of the pitches A-flat and F at the beginning, though in a D-flat Lydian rather than an A-flat minor context. Also significant is the 1-4-5 interval pattern in the accompaniment (circled in the second measure of Example 1), which is used frequently by Janáček as a specific symbol of the perfection of nature.

The resonance of the moment is even deeper, since the Lydian tune is an accelerated version of the introduction to the second act, where it is intoned by the offstage voices, the "hlas lesy" (voices of the forest). I believe that these wordless, off-stage voices have a potent symbolic significance, allowing the mysterious, incorporeal world of nature to seep onto the stage. They frame the second act, since they precede the wedding dance as well, and with their drone, offer us a musical image of the eternal world of the forest, something which "was in the beginning, is now, and forever shall be." Having the animal chorus sing the same melody in an accelerated, on-stage version creates the illusion of some undefinable natural spirit coming to life for an instant.

In trying to account for the section which follows (Example 2), Michael Ewans has written ". . . so all-embracing is the ecstasy of the celebration that even the music of Bystrouška's sobs is transformed into a joyous part of the energy discharged in this finale."[6] His comments may accurately describe the *effect* of the wedding scene, but certainly not the means used to achieve it, since the "music of Bystrouška's sobs" remains harsh in relation to the opening. The meter changes from duple to triple and the pedal vanishes. The harmonic stasis of the opening is replaced by harmonic flux, heightened by chromatic voice leading. There are no cadences, and the D-flat which dominates the opening is nowhere to be heard. There is also a fairly radical change of sonority, since the "voices of the forest," the sopranos and tenors who sing the first section, give way to the darker altos and basses in the second. Also, the use of percussion in the second section imparts a different quality to it.

In addition, the programmatic associations with this material recall the "worst" moments in the opera such as the Vixen's capture by the forester:

---

[6]Michael Ewans, *Janáček's Tragic Operas* (Bloomington: Indiana University Press, 1977), p. 158.

Example 5.

and more immediately, the moment preceding the wedding, when Bystrouška discovers that she is about to become an unwed mother:

Example 6.

We may also note links with the opera's opening measures, particularly with the distinctive cadence which appears numerous times in the first half of Act 1 (see Example 4).

Once again we are left with questions: Why does such dissonant material with unpleasant plot associations become part of the wedding celebration, and why isn't this mixture articulated by commentators on the opera? How do the two sections relate to each other? If we are calling the opening section a kind of pastoral, we might almost want to call the following section an "anti-pastoral," since it is composed of almost antithetical elements. Far from being unusual, however, the very identity of the pastoral, especially in 19th-century music, is bound up with such states of opposition, Indeed, it seems clear that what I have called the "anti-pastoral" is often an integral part of the pastoral mode itself. We may thus consider that the storms in the *Four Seasons* or Beethoven's "Pastoral" Symphony, or the unison "development" section of the "Dance of the Buffoons" from Mendelssohn's *A Midsummer Night's Dream*, far from being unusual occurrences in the pastoral mode, are essential to its impression. As stated earlier, pastorals tend to be static tableaux illustrating unchanging states. Composers and playwrights do not, however, *display* stasis on stage, but rather create *illusions* of conditions such as stasis. One way composers have found to "depict" stasis in music is to juxtapose it, however, briefly, with an opposing illusion, that of flux. In this sense, we may compare the second section of the Vixen's wedding with Zerlina's chromatic swoon, which occurs within the context of Don Giovanni's pastoral seduction.

If I have not misrepresented the views of the numerous critics who have "read" the final moment of the second act as an expression of joy, then it might appear that Janáček has created an illusion of immense rejoicing by juxtaposing his updated version of the traditional rustic wedding with its antithesis.

But this may be too simple, and does not account for the fact that the secondary material goes almost unremembered. Actually, the reasons for the ease with which we balance the diverse material of the opening sections may possibly be found in the third section of the dance:

Example 7.

This passage can be said to reconcile some of the basic conflicts between the opening sections. The tension between D-flat and A-flat minor is resolved in the opening two bars, with both pitches appearing in the alto part as well as in the bass line. There is no pedal, but rather a shifting between D-flat and C-flat, somewhat less stable than in the beginning, but still a shaping force in the passage. The phrase structure, though once again less regular than the opening, transforms the triple meter into something less intrusive, something more like the waltz Chisholm alluded to. The harmonic profile of this section lies midway between the first two sections, featuring two shorter sections with pedals on D-flat and A. Programmatically too, this third section has mixed elements. The parallel sixths in the alto part recall the first entrance of the Vixen in the first act, rather a neutral moment in the opera,

Example 8.

while the motive in the first four measures is an augmentation of the passage accompanying the Vixen's return to the forest:

Example 9.

Also, in terms of texture, the third section neatly combines all the voices instead of keeping them separate. Finally, we may note, in successively rising intensity, the presence of Janáček's 1-4-5 pattern at the end of each phrase.

Yet one cannot easily see Janáček calmly plotting such a series of musical illusions apart from their relationship to real life in general, and specifically to the plot of the *Cunning Little Vixen*. We may keep in mind how important the juxtaposition of opposites is in the opera itself and quote Janáček's famous line from a letter to Max Brod: "Spring in the forest—but also old age." [7] In the same letter Janáček wrote of a shooting during a wedding in a small village, where the culprit, after some time in jail, was welcomed back to his village with open arms:

> For me it confirmed that ordinary people do not consider evil a lasting stigma. It happened and is no more ... so bad and good follow one another again.

Janáček, as we know from other writings, was predisposed to think in terms whereby opposing tendencies are presented and somehow, reconciled. It is possible, though, that the direct cause of Janáček's choice in this scene might have been his reading of Těsnohlídek's description of the Vixen's wedding in his novel:

> The wedding itself was magnificent, so magnificent that we cannot even describe it—and besides, at least half of the reading public, on their way through this vale of tears, has experienced the pleasures and woes that go with a wedding.... The banquet was wonderful. A mixed choir of blackbirds, thrushes, finches, and robins gave a vocal concert.[8]

What a strange way to describe a wedding, in terms of "pleasures and woes," yet the narrator remembers the proceedings as magnificent despite the contrary elements which comprise it. It is certainly probable that this scene in the novel had a great resonance in Janáček—he certainly seems to have remembered the mixed choir of birds—and it is even possible that the *wordless* aspect of the scene derives from the phrase "we cannot even describe it." It seems likely that Janáček, too, tried to combine pleasures and woes, but in such measure, and in such a context, that we remember the magnificence precisely because it has come about through the controlled contrast of elements. In this case, a primary element "pleasure," the Lydian dance, calls attention to itself, while the second section, "woes," seems to direct the focus *away* from itself, modifying and intensifying our experience with the outer frame.

[7] In a letter to Max Brod, March 11, 1923.
[8] From the English version of the novel, published as *The Cunning Little Vixen*, translated by Robert Jones, Tatiana Firkušný, and Maritza Morgan (New York: Farrar, Straus & Giroux, 1985).

While accomplishing this Janáček has, despite his reputation as a somewhat primitive, white-hot scribbler, artfully recalled almost all of the opera's primary material in this minute and a half of music.

Actually, the structure of the wedding dance is a microcosm of the overall structure of the second act, which is a kind of large ABA with the "hlas lesy" on either end. Just as the outer sections of the wedding round "conceal" the inner conflict, so too do the pastoral moments of the second act condition the way in which we hear its two disruptive elements—the Vixen's retelling of her escape from the forester, and the sexual conflict between the Vixen and the Fox, which is ultimately resolved only by the wedding.

One can even expand this model to account for the effect of the opera as a whole, and wonder that an opera which contains so much violence, death, pain, and deep sadness could possibly be thought of as a genuinely happy and positive work; but the juxtaposition of opposing forces is Janáček's greatest strength as a dramatist. What other figure could possibly have immediately preceded one of the most potent moments in all opera, the culminating catharsis of the forester, with a talking, stuttering baby frog?

Part 2.

Janáček, Theory, and Analysis

The last decade has seen an explosion in the field of Music Theory, with a proliferation of journals, conferences, organizations, and approaches. The present collection of papers was meant to address two separate but related needs. First, it was a response to Jiří Vysloužil who, in Volume 1 of the *Leoš Janáček Society Newsletter* lamented the difficulty of integrating musical analysis into the large monograph on Janáček presently in progress, saying that "the state and level of musical analysis fail to cope with the great demands of the project. Neither have adequate analytical methods been so far developed which would encompass Janáček's musical and literary output . . . " We certainly hope that the papers in this section may suggest new directions in the field.

Second, by offering a collection of papers on a composer like Janáček we are trying to counteract a tendency towards a rather narrow repertoire in musical theoretical discourse, where a relative handful of composers receive perhaps a disproportionate amount of scrutiny.

It is our hope that the following studies, from a variety of perspectives, will provide a dynamic starting point for additional theoretical work dealing with the music of Janáček and other Czech composers.

The "Old" and "New" Modality in Janáček's *The Diary of One Who Vanished* and "Nursery Rhymes"

Jaroslav Volek

Jaroslav Volek died a little more than six months after the Janáček Conference took place. He was one of the finest and most fertile minds in the field. Volek studied composition with Šín, Hába, and Řídký, and later studied aesthetics and philosophy, coming under the influence of Mukařovsky and Utitz. He served as a Professor on the Arts Faculty at Charles University, and was also Chairman of the Musicological Section of the Czechoslovak Composers Union. He dealt with broad theoretical questions and difficult analytical problems with equal intensity, lucidity, and grace. In his study on The Diary of One Who Vanished *he argues, among other things, that in its own way, modality is as striking a departure from tonality as is atonality. Further, in a close reading of the work he shows how extraordinarily effective structures can be created through the interaction of modality, tonality, and chromaticism.*

I.

Before I actually go into the subject matter of my paper I have to give some explanation of the terminology and methodology: I can hardly assume that the greater part of the audience here is familiar with my former studies on modality concerning both the system in general and modal features in the works of Janáček, Bartòk and other composers in particular.

1. Contemporary ("modern") modality—or rather the renaissance, revival and development of the principles of "historic" (medieval) or folklore modality in the "artistic" ("art") music of our century—may be seen as the foundation of the progressive trend in those structures of the musical syntax which are based primarily on the *pitch* of tones (melody, chords, harmony, polyphony, etc.). This trend has managed to avoid both rigid conventional ties with traditional major-minor dualism as well as their total destruction and nivelization. Contemporary modality does not lead to atonality, but nevertheless produces tensions and stimulating im-

pulses in proximity to the *limits* of tonality. To put it in general terms: movement in the neighborhood of any "limit," without overstepping it except in a few occasional cases, is a potent source of meaningful innovations, a kind of "vibration" of the very basis of musical diction (its "dictionary" included) which stirs up hitherto unexploited forms of tension: all this constitutes fertile ground for Janáček's rhapsodic nature and inexhaustible vitality. In this respect his modal invention in no way lags behind his analogous experiments in the tectonic (form), sonic (instrumentation), and metrorhythmic realms, and so on.

2. In my paper I use the semantic antonyms: *syntagma* and *paradigm* (paradigm*a* in the original Greek version). A syntagma is a concrete form or structure, actually sounding either in our "real" or "inner" hearing, a concrete composed or improvised music. A paradigm is derived ("sedimented") from a certain number of syntagmata and has the character of a disposition, of a possibility to be used in creating other "new" syntagmata. It is something given to the composer beforehand, a kind of "alphabet," "dictionary," or repertoire, and settled in his experience, memory, skill, etc. The existence of a paradigm conditions—within certain bounds, given by various taxons like style, region, historical epoch, number of instruments, etc.—the choice of tones (plus various grades of preference among them), the choice of intervals or other relationships between tones, and the choice of chords and their stable connections (e.g. cadences), etc. These are paradigms (paradigmata) with regard to pitch and, as may be seen, they can be specifically melodic, chordal, harmonic (relation "chord : chord") or "global," i.e. concerned with all these components (for example when we speak broadly of the diatonic, chromatic, modality, or dodecaphony and similar subjects). There are various ways of demonstrating paradigms: in the form of a scale or even of the whole keyboard, in the form of "models" for the building of chords or for their joining together, but also in the form of verbally expressed rules, prohibitions and recommendations. For stylistic reasons we shall often substitute the word "paradigm" with the—in this case highly synonymous—words "infrastructure" (the syntagma then being "only": structure), "background," or "pattern."

3. The term *inflection*, especially "diatonic inflection," denotes a phenomenon which occurs very often in the folk music of Eastern and Southern Moravia (the Moravian-Slovak borderland) as well as in that of Hungary, South Poland, and the Balkan countries, but also of Turkey, Spain, and that of oriental folklore as a whole. An inflection involves the lowering or raising of the originally "established" tone, usually by

semitones, exceptionally by whole-tone shifts, within a limited area of a musical syntagma (e.g. immediately in the motif, theme or its repetition, transposition, variation, etc.) in the development of the melody, provided that key or tonal center does not change. Such a shift takes place at some, potentially in any, degree of the scale. The newly "included" tone necessarily changes the actual mode (given by a fixed consecution of the intervals), but only for a moment. This change is either merely transitory or one in which the initial constitution of the modal "background" is not "forgotten." Thus the resulting effect of these micro changes is the appearance of *two* (exceptionally: three) more or less equivalent "representations" of a single degree in the scale. In other words: two or three alternatives stand here "paradigmatically" beside each other. So the assumption for musical comprehension of the inflection is the idea or conception of the gradual basis[1] of such a type of melodic paradigm, which is displayed or shown in the form of an ascending or descending scale (or respective part of the scale). This basis is determined by degrees, not by the concrete single tones of the "written" scale: the degree is to be identified with a small group of alternating tone pitches, not with one tone. In this sense our "feeling" of the degree surely has the character of a "metro-structural" orientation (for instance we "know," hearing either the major or minor third, that we "find ourselves" at the III. degree of the scale): the scale—as a paradigm—works as the "background" for the melodic syntagma, but the structure of the degrees lies "behind" its tones as a "background of background."

The relationship of tones in inflection differ fundamentally from the relations between diatonic and chromatic tones, which are products of major-minor dualism and functional harmony whereas the inflection is essentially a modal phenomenon. Chromatic tones have a secondary, derived character (the melodic "envelopes" of diatonic tones, additionally constructed semitone relations in altered chords); they constitute a complementary filling out of the primary diatonic plan. In an actual syntagma chromatic tones are syntactically bound to diatonic tones—at least until their frequency and growing independence reach the phase of total chromatization and of destruction of the whole major-minor pitch hierarchy, which leads to atonality.

If there is an initial mode in any of the diatonic scales (either of the so-called "pure" diatonics—heptatonic consecutions on the white

---

[1] Editor's note: *gradualini baze* = gradual basis. It seems that Volek is here referring to something which shifts by degrees.

keys—or in the "modified" diatonics, in which the semitone distances are placed more closely than in the "pure" diatonics), then we may speak of *diatonic* inflection, which directly infers that both tones of a inflection are diatonic, which is clearly shown by the way they are treated in the given context. Inflection may also be simultaneous, which leads to sharp dissonances when both inflection-tones are heard (for instance in different voices or in the vocal part in the instrumental accompaniment) simultaneously. Inflection is a very ancient phenomenon, as in the medieval opposition: "B-rotundum: B quadratum." It also exists in the ordinary major scale (at the VIth degree, therefore we can use in the key either the major or the minor subdominant) as well as in the ordinary minor scales (again in the VIth degree, but also at the VIIth one, see the so-called "melodic minor scale"). Another sample of inflections can be found in the so-called "blue notes" in negro spirituals and in Jazz (and in all jazz-influenced music): these are inflections at the IIIrd and VIIth degree, sometimes even exposed simultaneously. In this category of inflections may also be included the "sudden" (but only momentary) alternations of major and minor keys (of the same tonal center) within a small area, so favored in the romantic epoch of music and especially by Dvořák.

However, European musical notation does not enable an easy differentiation between the notes of a *diatonic* inflection and chromatic tones. For this reason both phenomena in question, in principle so widely different, were not distinguished enough in music theory. Moreover, composers who consciously used modal inflections spoke of them in a rather conflicting manner, using the word "chromatic" in terms such as: "modal chromatic," "chromatic diatonics" and the like: and in all these terms the word "chromatic" functions in a misleading manner.

4. Janáček's manner of notation in *The Diary of One Who Vanished* (further referred to as DV) does not contribute to the discovery of his modal paradigms. Janáček, in theory an advocate of tempered tones, indulged in superfluous enharmonic carelessness in practice. An incredible number of completely "unnecessary" enharmonic spellings renders an ex post facto analysis difficult, by disguising a continuation in the mode as a fictive change, or, on the contrary, by hiding a real change with equally confusing spellings (mainly where there is an opportunity of applying Janáček's favored signs "b" and "b-flat"). It is no wonder that editors attempt to replace this often very superficial complication with a new transcription. Nevertheless the very possibility of using inflections and modal modulations in order to expose all the 12 tones of the tempered scale in a brief area creates an objective problem for graphic notation

designed only for heptatonic scales. It is important not to succumb to the optical suggestion of the notes at first sight but to try through patient hearing to clarify for oneself the "true" modal-tonal determination and classification of each tone, chord and interval.

5. The question of modal and tonal changes. The modal-tonal stability found in folklore structures of modality—where generally one mode prevails, or at most there is an oscillation between two centers of modality (bi-centrism)— are not to be expected in the works of a composer as educated as Janáček. This lack of stability is also due to the fact that chamber music (DV being one example) as well as other species and categories in the zone of "art" music, are deeply dependent on key changes and modulation in their tectonics . In DV, as a cycle consisting of 22 numbers, each short section could of course be tonally unified "inside," while ostensibly differing "outside," i.e. in the relations between one number and another. However, the opposite is inclined to be true. Janáček has endowed (from this point of view) most of the sections with "inner" motion, reacting thus in his specific way to the poetic text, which usually exposes some remarkable change or turn (in the attitude of persons, in the mood, situation, or conflict) with the help of very nice metaphors in each strophe. This corresponds to the fundamental context of the entire cycle, describing various stages of the "vain" struggle of a "well-bred" young man from the country village with the erotic challenge embodied by the "strange," unknown Gypsy girl.

The inner semantic and dramatic motion even within short numbers of DV results in the notable fact that 50% of the numbers end in a different key (with another tonal center) from the one they begin with. Among these changes only two cases work as a preparation of the "attaca" toward the following number. Janáček thus breaks the almost "inviolable" rule in the formal construction of short musical pieces (respected otherwise in his own piano compositions). In the "long" vocal compositions or in symphonic poems such a difference would draw no special attention. It is possible to think that Janáček considered the numbers of the cycle as dramatically and epically similar creations, only composed in very condensed form, somehow "en miniature." It is perhaps important to add that yet another of Janáček's vocal compositions, "Nursery rhymes," involves an even greater proportion of such an abandoning of the initial key (14:2). Perhaps the humorous and caricature-like characters of the text and of the original illustrations by the painter Josef Lada which inspired "Nursery rhymes" provided an impetus for changing keys similar to the semantic gesture of the "story" in DV. Nevertheless the increasing density of this feature can suggest a more general motivation, independent of the concrete contents of both compositions. In his last mature works Janáček seems to have followed his inborn inclination to express himself in very rhapsodic idioms, thus loosening his ties to the tradition even in this—earlier untouched—principle (the balance of keys). Henceforth he also attacks the borderline of tonality in an indirect sense: he does not try to fix the inner coherence of numbers by framing them with parts written in identical keys.

The change of keys within relatively short numbers makes a determination of the modes more difficult because their centers (which must be identified in order to name the mode) are often not sustained for a sufficiently long time or with enough "power" (not enough structural affinities) to stabilize their positions as centers. Therefore we do not object to describing some examples of the modal context in DV as *ambivalent*, as balancing or oscillating between two centers. On the other hand, by careful and repeated listening to the music we have found that in most cases it is possible to find the one "true" center, even if it is a bit "hidden" in the more complicated context, and especially if we will not be misled by the above-mentioned "enharmonic" notation. The uncertainty or ambiguity of the modes is further supported by the reduced texture of the sound, sometimes also by the preference of what we call "fourth-second intervalics" in the melodic shapes (vocal line, ostinato patterns, piano, etc.) and in the chords as well. In the conclusion of number 13 there even appears a touch of bitonality (piano: m.d. in G major, m.s. in B-flat minor).

The "whirlpool" of keys within the numbers is surprisingly compensated by Janáček's tendency towards the excessive use of certain tonal centers, dominating in particular numbers. The work involves a peculiar hierarchy at the top of which stand two key centers: the central position is occupied by the tone A-flat (A-flat major, A-flat minor), which appears at the beginning of 10 numbers and at the end of 11 (one half of the total); the next position is occupied by D-flat (5 starts, 3 endings). Together these two forms of centralization occupy two thirds of all the key determinations. Moreover, Janáček's well-known sense for contrast gives way to this hierarchy when two numbers "in A-flat" follow immediately one after the other (9–10, 20–21), though the expression of the pieces is different. There is an analogical connection between 18 and 19 (written "in D-flat") where the connection is strengthened by the motivic similarity of the tunes. The same motivic connection happens again between the A-flat minor numbers, 17 and 21.

After these introductory remarks we can pass over to the proper topic of our paper.

II.

Janáček's composition *The Diary of One Who Vanished* for tenor, alto, three female voices and piano is thoroughly imbued with modality. Among 22 numbers there are 16 (70%) which are built on a different basis than common major-minor dualism. Beside these five other numbers can be labelled as "major" or "minor" in the ordinary sense with inflections which, owing to their clear influence on the melodic context, bring to the music an "echo" of modality (see for instance 20, 21). The alternation of M3 and m3, i.e. the inflection at the IIIrd degree, works much the same way in the flowing stream of music. Moreover, the inflections are used in undoubtedly modal structured sections. In sum: we find them in at least 14 numbers (ca. 64%). nine numbers show both forms of modality, the initial or constant modal basis and the variable changes (inflections) within. By the way: in our statistical analysis, the original aeolian mode (6, 12) is not counted as a modal phenomenon, even though its occurrence in the major-minor system is rare (compared with the so-called melodic or harmonic minor). On the other hand it is necessary to acknowledge the full modal background in such numbers or areas where the intervalics are identical with the ascending direction of the melodic minor scale but used on the contrary in the descending motion (that concerns the upper tetrachord of the scale, see for instance the beginning of 2).

The modal "climate" is indicated—and sometimes directly evoked—by the concrete syntagmatic selection or preference of the consecutive intervals either in the vocal line or in the accompaniment. We focus mainly on the "large" or "skipping" intervals which are not the mechanical projection of a concurrent chord. Secondly we think of the very frequent, and for the DV (and Janáček generally) typical, fourth-second intervalics used in the structuring of the melody or of the chords and ostinato patterns (figurations). We have found in DV two major forms of this system: 1. a "narrow" one, in which the extension (ambit) of the P4 is filled in by M2 and m3 (counting it in tempered semitones, we get two consecutions: 2+3=5 and 3+2=5). Here the relation between the step of M2 and the whole ambit of P4 (perfect fourth) is significant :

Figures 1, 2.

2. the "broad" form: in which the ambit of the P5 is filled in by the intervals M2 and P4 (2+5=7 and 5+2=7):

Figures 3, 4, 5, 6.

Both forms can be combined:

Figures 7, 8

Figures 9, 10

All these examples avoid semitones (they are anhemitonic), but the "fourth-second" intervalics can also produce hemitonic structure (with semitones, with tritones, etc.). The sound of such contexts is more "sharp," e.g.:

Figures 11, 12, 13, 14.

and evokes the impression of the *modal* (not tonal) transposition.

The modal integrity of the descending motifs is interesting:

Figures 15, 16.

Figure 15, from the end of number 11, reveals—in the ambit of P5—partial shapes A flat-G flat-E double flat and G flat-E double flat-D flat, both of which involve outstanding hemitonic sharpening, produced by the lowering inflection of the VIth degree in G flat major. In spite of the fact that the accompaniment here—various non-modal harmonies changing in rather quick modulation—does *not* have a modal character, the motifs are able to preserve their modal "status."

The contribution of fourth-second intervalics to the modal sound of the music is possible to affirm safely in 13 numbers of DV (in more than 50%, namely in 1, 3, 4, 9, 10, 11, 14-17, 19, 21, 22); in 15, 17, 21 and 22 such intervalic consecutions have *thematic* importance.

Another factor supporting the modal structuring is the use of the so-called "mediants"—shifts of the basic tone in a chord or ostinato pattern to the distance either of M3 or m3 (in whatever direction). Such progressions are also found in the major-minor system (especially in the early and mature stage of its chromatization), but Janáček also exploits them for transitions from one mode to another, and sometimes uses the opportunity to change the tonal center.

The modal elements, and particularly the inflections in DV often lead to structures that seem to be a part of the *whole* tone scale. But it is for the most part a different whole tone organization from that which is commonly found, for instance in the music of Claude Debussy. This difference will be explained later.

As regards the diminished or augmented intervals, it depends on the context: for example intervals being generated by the chromatic process remove us from the modal diction. On the other hand, if they are produced by the structure of the chosen mode or by some inflection within the mode, then the modal character of the syntagma (melody, chord, etc.) is considerably accentuated.

A special "chapter" of modal expression involves rhythmically pregnant ostinato patterns (figurations), sometimes acquiring the quality of little "mini-motifs" though having largely a coloristic function. Among them we find chromatic shapes (ascending or descending chains of semitones), but also structures on the borderline of modality, e.g. in intervalic steps 1-1-2 or 1-2-1 (16) or in the steps like G flat-F flat-G, and A flat-G-B flat (piano in 9), reminding us of the "cells" of Olivier Messian's technique. In other ostinato patterns, Janáček uses whole tone effects to support the modal climate of the music through a very simple but clever method: within the framework of the "normal" minor melodic scale he isolates its inner whole-tone part (from IIIrd to the VIIth degree of the scale).

Figure 17.

Finally we should mention several pentatonic shapes in DV. These shapes may also be understood as the manifestations of a modal "deviation" from the rules and routine of the major-minor convention, though such shapes are realized mostly in the framework of its intervalic selection (19; 9 bars 17–23).

Figure 18.

III.

The modes used as the paradigmatic backgrounds of musical syntagmas in DV are to be viewed neither in the narrow frame of traditional historic terminology nor in the locally limited ethnographical aspects. Using the terms of Glareanus' complete system of medieval modes, we do it deliberately for the purpose of comprehensible designation of all the modal phenomena and of quickly hinting their particular features. Every modal structure or mode can be, of course, expressed exactly in intervalic consecutions (the first tone being taken mostly for the tonal or modal center). The appearance of such a sequence of ciphers (for instance :1221222; 1=semitone, 2=the whole tone) does not reveal to us—at first glance—the "point" of difference between the mode and common major-minor dualism, the degree at which the decisive, characteristic, modal "deviation" lies. So the term "phrygian mode" must be used to describe "Janáček's phrygianism," but not without realizing, of course, that it certainly has something to do with similar patterns in Moravian folklore, but only very little with the phrygian mode of the Middle Ages. Nevertheless the term "phrygian" succeeds in drawing our attention to the "sensitive" point of the scale (IInd degree). Analogically the word "lydian" implies the distance of an augmented fourth between the I and IVth degrees, etc. In many cases there may appear more than one deviation of this sort; then it becomes necessary to choose "combined" names like "phrygian-lydian" or names of other origins (for instance "Naturskala" in German) if they are either already known and used, or comprehensible from the musicological point of view.

As a composition lasting between 20–25 minutes and including 22 numbers, DV is extraordinarily variegated in terms of the use of relatively fixed modal scales and patterns, to say nothing of a lot of actual inflections. The exact number of different modal paradigms is not easy to state since some of them are not fully developed (see for instance the first two bars of 16) and others move on the boundaries between modality and the chromatics of the major-minor system. Nonetheless it is possible to identify 16–18 modal "models" or paradigms. This number is very great indeed, evoking the impression of an extraordinary creative invention on the part of the composer, comparable to, or even exceeding the variety of the modes in the folklore collections, which contain two or three thousand folk tunes from the regions where the modal heritage is still living and thoroughly investigated.

The *Dorian* mode occurs at the end of 5 (A-flat minor with F), in the first bars of 10, and for a moment we hear it also at the end of 19 (tone C in relation to the center E-flat). In the same number, bars 18–23 are also dorian in spite of the "masking" notation (using #): the initial D-flat major with modal hints of the fourth-second intervalics and of the pentatonic omission of the IVth and VIth degrees comes after a short modulation back into the D-flat major in mm. 12–17, but now two sudden inflections F-E-flat and C-C flat (enharmonically noted) change it into the dorian D-flat (which is confirmed also by the tone B-flat in m. 21).

The *Lydian* mode (in its genuine form, not in its combination with the minor third, see more about this later) is found in relatively few places: it seems that its "euphoric" tension does not suit the emotional "climate" of DV. We can record only passing moments of its "color" in 2 (mm. 21–24, inflection D-D-sharp by the dominant tending toward A major). On the other hand the progression in m. 9–13 of 8, looking "optically" like a clear lydism is actually a graphic illusion: the tune does not abandon the initial key of A-flat major, but emphasizes its subdominant zone.

The *Phrygian* mode is evident in the initial motif of 13 (the intermezzo of the piano) and in all its transpositions:

Figure 19.

Another phrygian element comes into being through inflection at the II degree in A-flat major of 7 (mm. 5–7). In spite of the notation "as if" in A major, this passage is a subdominant harmony in A-flat minor (phrygian second B-double flat-D flat-E-flat).

The *Mixolydian* mode appears in 2 (mm. 20–21 on the center E) and, similarly, in 19 (mm. 8–9, center E-sharp, in the piano interlude). Further, passages in number 1—bars 9–12 (after the transposition of the same motif), bars 13–17 and, finally, the climax of this entire gradation in b. 18–19—can only be considered as a sequence of mixolydian shapes (on C-sharp, F-sharp, A), for the other possible explication (changing dominant harmonies) fails, as supposed dominant harmonies do not resolve to their tonics.

The introduction of 15 is an impressive modal moment. In spite of the fact that the piano accentuates the tone A-flat (with the trill), the vocal melody can only be understood in D-flat (with the inflection at the IIIrd degree). This motif is twice followed by two bars of a piano interlude which develops it as if in A-flat minor: so we hear in them the important tone C-flat. Nevertheless, the repeated return of the melody in D-flat prevents us from realizing a change of keys here. Therefore, the interlude is better described as minor dominant in D-flat. This means that the mixolydian seventh C-flat penetrates into the pitch selection of the piece (there occurs *no* C—ionic seventh—in the whole area).

Abandoning "pure" diatonics we find ourselves first of all in the realm of "modified" diatonics (scheme: 121222 with all the rotations). The combination of the aeolian lower pentachord with the major (ionic) tetrachord (the shared pivot-tone of both the shapes lying on the Vth degree) is striking, and identical with the ascending melodic minor scale. The modal "point" here is that such a selection of pitches also appears (and frequently) in a descending direction where it works as a modal "deviation." This is the way number 2 begins (in A-flat minor):

Figure 20.

And in number 11 the alto sings:

Figure 21.

It is interesting that both these expositions of the "minor-major" scale are transformed into special forms of phrygian structure by the ensuing inflection.

More important and more essential for Janáček's style is a group of modal infrastructures which has a character of partly quite new, partly already known, combinations of the primary modal background. These infrastructures involve Janáček's favorite among all the modes, the so-called "Lydian minor" scale (*das lydische moll*). In the lower pentachord we find the m3, and in the ascending step of the augmented second a lydian (augmented) fourth, the interval of a tritone from the basic tone of the mode. This "Lydian minor" pattern is well-known from other Janáček works, beginning with the opera *Jenůfa*. The variety of upper tetrachords we find adjoined to this shape now, however, is somewhat surprising. The minor third, in spite of the presence of the lydian fourth, dictates that the global character of the mode belongs into the group of "minor" scales. We are accustomed to say: phrygian, aeolian, dorian minor (moll) and mixolydian, ionic and lydian major (dur). So it is logical to expect that the continuation of the combined mode will be—in its upper part—also a minor (aeolian) one. But such a context appears only in 15 (mm. 14–18)

Figure 22.

and similarly in 16 (mm. 6–9) on the same tones "in D-flat":

Figure 23.

In other cases the mode looks different. There is a very clear presence of the dorian sixth (M6), exposed long enough at the beginning of 11 (B-flat beside the fourth G in D-flat minor) to be taken into consideration.

Figure 24.

One should also note a striking figurative portion of the piano part in 17 (b. 13), again "in D-flat." The dorian sixth appears as far as in the next bar, where the lydian fourth is already present—by a nice example of the inflection-technique—alternating with the "normal" G-flat.

The most complicated and original lydian minor mode appears immediately at the beginning of 1—like a sign of the modal saturation of the whole work. Over the lydian minor piano passage (with the center on E) hovers the vocal melody in which the tones C-sharp and D-sharp, ergo the components of the major (or ionic) scale, prevail:

Figure 25.

A combination of *phrygian* and *dorian* elements can also be found in DV. In the alto solo of 11 (mm. 45–52), the first bars sound like a combination of the lower pentachord of minor and the upper tetrachord of descending major. Yet in the subsequent four bars appear inflections on the VIIth and II degrees (the central tone of the mode being D-flat, i.e. inflections lead to the notes C-flat and E-double flat = phrygian second). But the situation on the VIth degree does not change, and the dorian sixth, absent in the original phrygian mode, remains in evidence here:

Figure 26.

The same combination is found for a few measures in 19 (4 bars before the end: E-flat minor with the dorian sixth is modally confronted with the phrygian note F-flat).

The mixolydian mode is complicated several times as well, mainly by the occurrence of the lydian fourth (this combination is known under the German name "Naturskala"), e.g.:

Figure 27.

(the lydian fourth is "masked" by the enharmonic use of the note C). This context changes more and more into a whole tone structure in the following bars (21–24), losing even its tonal orientation. Similar selections can be found also at other places, always with the strong touch of whole-tone consecutions.

An extraordinary paradigm is represented by the mode that like a magic "fluid" (the text expressed here involves the charming evening mood in nature: "along the lake side the air is soft with glowworms") veils the whole introduction of 3 (with the center on F-sharp):

Figure 28.

In the lower pentachord we find the intervals 1312, something like a "phrygian major" with the step of the augmented second between degrees II and III; the upper tetrachord has the character of the aeolian mode. This combination produces a mode which is known from Spanish folklore: if another augmented second appears in the upper tetrachord (between degrees VI and VII) the whole pattern changes into the so-called "major Gipsy scale" (different from the current Gipsy scale in minor). Janáček used this "Spanish" scale in *Jenůfa* and before him

Dvořák used it in his *Requiem* ("Quid sum miser"). In the DV its actual sound is made more peculiar by the fact that the vocal motif begins twice with the tone E, that is with the m7 (at the VII degree). Such a start reminds one of a certain antiquity in folklore (and not only in the Moravian one): in this way the strong position of the VII degree (and of the triads rooted in it) is manifested in modal music, because it is able to substitute for the dominant in relation to the tonal center.

12 bars of quasi-recitative in the part of the Gypsy girl (alto) in 10, beginning in b. 50, involve "rules" of a very interesting infrastructure, possibly used here for the first time. First of all: the tone G in the bass line of the chord which briefly appears in the song four times is indeed the tonal center of the mode, though at first sight—optically—this chord looks like the dominant harmony from C minor (with bass tone G). Nevertheless upon this center is developed the paradigmatic consecution (G-A-flat-B-C sharp-D-E-flat-F-G), in which very heterogeneous modal elements are blended: phrygian second, minor third, lydian fourth, aeolian sixth and seventh, some of them showing truly opposite tendencies and affinities. We can see in the queer structure of this mode Janáček's successful attempt to express in a lapidary abridgement certain semantic contradictions induced into the content of the DV by the text and by the increasing moral conflict of the story.

Another appearance of phrygian elements in the major scale involves the combination of the lower phrygian pentachord with the upper tetrachord of the ionic mode. In 2 Janáček begins with the A-flat minor-modally "colored" by the M6 and M7 in the descending motion. Then (mm. 8) a phrygian inflection at the IInd degree forms the phrygian A-flat minor: this paradigm is supported by the chord: B-double flat-D-flat-F-flat, "masked" in the notation as the A major triad, but in fact a "clear" subdominant harmony from A-flat minor. The new selection still has to be related to the (now latent) center A-flat, which leads to the modal pattern 1222221 (A-flat-B-double flat-C flat-D-flat-E-flat-F-G) in which the "surviving" major sixth and seventh from the beginning of the piece, together with the phrygian lower part of the structure, produces a massive whole-tone block. Moreover, the whole tone character of this area is strengthened by the fact that the latent center A-flat is overridden by the step: B-double flat-G (written as A-G), i.e. by the step of a diminished third:

Figure 29.

The whole-tone consecution is further emphasized not only by sforzatos in the tenor and in the piano chords, but also by the consequent parallelism of chords, which is a generally-known feature of whole-tone verticality in the music of Debussy and others. The center A-flat, though overridden in the melody, does not lose its "power" of orientation. We are therefore confronted with a unique form of whole-tone structuring, one different from the *hexa*tonic form used in the exotic cultures or in musical impressionism, where either no tonal centrality exists or the tonal center is identified with one of the tones in the whole-tone chain. In Janáček there is no whole-tone-hexatonic as such, no six-tone pattern; but we are confronted with a *hepta*tonic structure offering the possibility that the central tone can be set quasi "outside" of the actual context. This is surely a new and remarkable phenomenon in the development of modality. The same structure is repeated in following bars of 2, yet based on another center (D-flat), and again it is accomplished with the help of a phrygian lowering of the IInd degree (tone: E-double flat). The transfer of the motif (and of accompanying chords) into the other (the second and last possible one) whole-tone "scale" (about the semitone lower or higher) is affirmed again by the striking sforzato of the piano:

Figure 30.

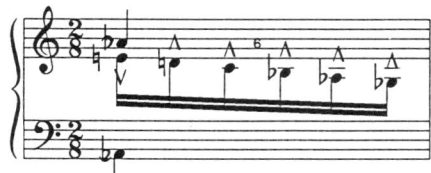

This new form of whole-tone structuring is not limited to 2. The evidence of its influence reappears in the Poco piu mosso section of 19 (once again on the tonal center D-flat):

Figure 31.

In the most articulated and the longest number, 10, in which the alto sings her "Gypsy prayer" (from the dramatic point of view the decisive moment of the "story"), Janáček introduces another peculiar mode, a mode with the diminished fifth (the interval between the tonal center A-flat and the Vth degree E-double flat being a tritone). The same interval occurs in the so-called "locrian" (inaccurately named hypophrygian) mode (1222122) from the Glareanus system; but there is no augmented second between the I and IInd scale degrees in the locrian mode. Janáček's paradigm could perhaps be called the "diminished aeolian scale" apart from the inflection at the IInd degree stirred up by the short modulation toward the new center D-flat (m. 7) where the motif is repeated:

Figure 32.

The same background is also evident in the Meno mosso section of 15, if the center is considered A-flat, though orientation around D-flat is also possible (ambivalence):

Figure 33.

A mirrored opposition to this intervalic "deviation" with the diminished fifth are those shapes with the *augmented* fifth. Janáček tends to such a "morphology" in 16 (in the set of chords, m. 1), and perhaps also in 10 (the cadence of the "prayer"); in both cases with a strong accent of the whole-tone structuring. However, the chief manifestation of this form of modality comes in 17 with its undoubtedly original, not to say peculiar infrastructure (m. 15, etc.). The scheme of this mode can be understood as 2132121: G-A-B-flat-C-sharp-D-sharp-E-F-sharp-G. The "lydian minor" (see above) is combined here with the "superlydian" progression to the "raised" Vth degree and with the conclusion of the scale in the major mode.

Figure 34.

This selection of the tones and intervals is so queer that one could offer another explanation, taking the tone c-sharp (noted so only in the vocal line) as D-flat (that means instead of an augmented fourth the interval is considered a diminished fifth). By this approach the IVth degree will disappear from the selection, and D-sharp, as representative of the Vth degree will change into the m6. However, the question of what to do with two "pretenders" on the VIIth degree (E=F-flat and F-sharp) remains? In any event, a certain ambivalence in this pattern is not excluded. The same infrastructure is emphasized by the "ff" of the piano in the section "Vivo" (mm. 30–31).

Apart from the "content" of single and syntagmatic structures there is something particularly meaningful in this paradigm: the contradictions between the lowering and raising of the degrees in addition to the loosening of the stability of the mode by abandoning the firm position of the P5 at the Vth degree, indicate a sort of "expansion" or "depression," that is a deformation. This all reflects very well the fierce desire, affection and haste of the hero (tenor), "Now I hurry often at the evening to the wood . . . ," and—at the same time— the definitive breaking away from his moral obstructions, expressed previously with feelings of sadness (in 16).

One also encounters model meanings of augmented intervals in 13 and 22. This time it is the augmented second between the Ist and IInd degrees which counts. In 13 (m. 8, 10) the tone A (upon the center G-flat) can be felt as a chromatic note (leading to the M3 B-flat), but in the whole context of this piano passage there is something (for instance the descending skip from the same pitch, now written as B-double flat to the tone D-flat) which indicates the possibility of modal conception, too. We can also claim that the shape E-F-sharp-G in 22—sung as it is literally prescribed "in the greatest exaltation" at the conclusion of the whole cycle—has a modal character. Here it seems that the tone F-sharp (in F-flat major) is indeed the expression or a sort of symbol of the new life the hero is beginning, and of the two alternative theoretical explanations, the modal explanation is better than the chromatic one.

IV.

The modern, contemporary and "artificial" modality (though arisen spontaneously from the roots of folklore) is in no case the type of paradigm (or: paradigmatic system) which leads to an antagonistic "fight" against other paradigms, or to the suppression and "tabuization" of them in the name of the "progress" and paradigmatic intolerance, which was typical for the final stages of the destruction of the major-minor dualism. Janáček was able to exploit different paradigmatic backgrounds in a relatively small area —as I have taken the opportunity to show in another of my studies about modality—without the slightest loss of the uniqueness and integrity of his personal style. Moreover, he was able to use the juxtaposition of distinctly articulated syntagmatic units, each of them being influenced by another background, to suggest tectonic effects and to express very different semantic, psychological and dramatic levels or situations. Thus modal diction differs positively from paradigms of other types, in principle contradictory to it, for instance a very clear and "persuasive" major (dur) or, on the other hand, the almost hypertrophic chromatization leading to the loss of tonality.

Nevertheless, the DV is full of modal progressions which make its "language" exciting through their mobile variability which supports the expressiveness (not to say "expressionism") of the composition and are able to produce the proper tension for the "story" (sometimes even to create the effect of "purposeful," semantically justified "deformation"). One might say that the DV reaches its artistic goal only because tonality is not excluded. A "big" paradigmatic confrontation arises here as if in the second "plan": we project the actual syntagmata to the background of the modal paradigms, but we feel these paradigms—as a whole—still as "bold" and inspiring deviations from ordinary major-minor systematics which more or less serves as the "meta-background." In this way the fundamental semantic gesture of the cycle is served, something like the basic "wave" of its message and emotionality. Janáček, however, makes such a confrontation more effective by incorporating a certain plasticity through his use of the above-mentioned changing paradigms. There are places in the DV where the thread of its "love story" is suspended, interrupting the course of action and events. These include both moments of temporary relaxation (where pleasure and delight come in turn) and moments where the basic conflict is sublimated, as if to create a Platonic "beholding of the essence" of the matter (even if it as fatal one, see 6). In such cases Janáček uses (mostly in a slow tempo) a very "clear" and "eloquent" major with fully expressed harmonic functions, with a more compact sound. Now, something like a little miracle unfolds from this: that which elsewhere sounds conventional, here brings refreshing and emotionally rich music (thanks to Janáček's invention and to his courage to move for a while in the opposite direction—back to the non-modal means) partly due to the particular texture and sound, but mostly because the score includes the indication "dolce." And so already in 1 the excited and "nervous" modal uneasiness (in the story caused by the first attack at the sight of Zefka by the boy) is compensated with tonal harmonies of the "Adagio" section (in A-flat major with the minor subdominant D-flat).

There is another "island" in the "ocean" of Janáček's modality (and in much of the chromatics as well), again involving the complete harmonic cadence: it is a passage in the Meno mosso section of 6 (D-flat major, the text: "Who there waits for me now . . . "). The third and most beautiful "extempore" of this kind comes in 10 (19 bars of Adagio sung by three female voices, an erotic challenge "stopping the time"—the words: "The blouse from her breasts she lowered a little . . . "). It is written in a placid A-flat major with a rich exposition of all the harmonic functions. To this group belongs also the short, rather epic, area calming down the foreground excitement in 11 (the text: "A few twigs she broke off"), and the 6 bars of Meno moss in 17 ("A few leaves I'll draw aside"). The simple A-flat major, apart from concurrent inflections at the VIth degree, is used in the sole gay, humorous number (20) of the whole work. Finally, such a characterization at least partially refers to the conclusion of DV in 22 (E-flat major), especially in the piano interlude.

On the other hand, Janáček does not avoid chromatics. Often it is only a slight contact with the modality (various ambiguities), mainly in the ostinato patterns. The chromatics work frequently as a connective element in the modulations or modal changes as well; and so no special meaning is to be "read" from this use of them. A special aspect of chromatic function involves the increasing of tonal uncertainty, which brings an end to modal vacillations: chromatics also play a role in transitions to the whole-tone segments or in their development (final bars of 16). Intervals like the tritone, diminished third, augmented fifth, etc. (even if their origin is of a modal source) also help to intensify the chromatic sound of the context in question, but this is merely another example of the already-mentioned ambivalences.

Several times, however, the chromatics also acquire a certain semantic importance and "meaning," e.g. in 5 (the text: "It's hard for me to plow, I slept little") with the passing chromatic parallel sixth and similarly the chromatic descending shifts in the penultimate section of 13 (this number is often called "Intermezzo erotico"). In this connection it is also possible to mention 8 (the symptomatic words in the text being "dark eyes", "witch eyes", and in addition the reluctant confession of the tenor). Some chromatic details can also be found in 1, 3, and 6. Trying to estimate the total share of chromatics in the structure of DV, we are inclined to speak of 10–15% of the entire context. This is enough to conclude that this paradigmatic background—in purposeful "cooperation" with the modal structures and with the "persuasive" major parts—also has its own important function in the DV.

The conclusion of our analysis can be a short one. The DV is a "treasure island" and, at the same time, a "textbook" of modern "artificial" modality, a document demonstrating the immense possibilities of modal principles for the innovation of musical language, and reflecting their new stage of development in contrast to the situation in the 19th century. These newly opened horizons also represent a good possibility for resisting the entropic, destructive tendencies which can end in the substitution of extrasensual factors for the necessary sensual contact between our hearing and the sounding music.

But if we consider the unity of the very good, very condensed and poetic text (its author being unknown), and Janáček's music as its sublimation, and further, when we realize the masterly acquired coherence of the relatively small areas endowed with different meanings, contents and expressions (in the average in the extension of 4–6 bars), then we can see the import of the modality in such a type of "unitas multiplex" principle in yet another light. Janáček's basic approach to his task involves the montage of discrete units, a general method which may not be familiar in music, but is known in the technology and tectonics of the cinema. The DV is a composition which already in the 1920s may be said to have "struck" the structural homology (or at least its possibilities) in the relation between two different kinds of art, or between two different systems of artistic communication: one of them being very ancient and the other just born. This statement has very little to do with the qualities of so-called "film music"—which is a component of the motion picture, adding to the visual basis of it—because unlike Janáček's work, such music generally follows the "ordinary" ways of its evolution, and the sudden pauses, determined by the decisive organization of the film sequences, are so often felt as a sort of "violence" against the musical accompaniment of the film. Back to Janáček's music: if we are right with the just mentioned tectonic parallel, then we must admit that this approximation could be realized only in such a mixture of paradigms which is used in DV: under the hegemony of the "open" modality a symbiosis of it and other two types of infrastructure (chromatics, major-minor diatonics) standing historically and ethnographically next to the modality. In *The Diary of One Who Vanished*, Janáček succeeded in establishing quite a new model of musical "narrativity".

Musical and Dramatic Organization in Janáček's *The Cunning Little Vixen*[1]

Nors S. Josephson

Perhaps the only basis on which music should be evaluated is in terms of the response of enlightened listeners upon repeated hearings. But there has grown up in the last decades another way of postulating artistic quality: by demonstrating through a detailed consideration of a musical score that a work is composed of tightly drawn, coherent, and highly logical permutations of basic materials. We have always had evidence concerning the effectiveness of Janáček's work in performance—there is hardly another 20th century composer who has been so successful. In this paper Nors Josephson, a gifted analyst and author of numerous studies on Janáček, argues that Janáček's Cunning Little Vixen *reveals the same care for the details of motivic permutation and organization which we have come to expect in the works of the most doctrinaire dodecaphonic composers.*

Like most of Janáček's operatic masterpieces, *The Cunning Little Vixen* is based on a recurring intervallic matrix that is heralded at the very outset of act I: scene i, **12:1**,[2] one that appears to symbolize the "eternal feminine" element (namely, the Vixen and her human counterpart, Terynka) and the regenerative life cycle embodied in nature. This intervallic formation may be reduced to pronounced parallel fourths (a-flat'-e-flat'-g-flat'-d-flat', henceforth labelled motive *x*), in addition to a superimposed chromatic voice-leading (a-flat'-g'-g-flat'- over accompanying c-flat'-b flat, g-a-flat, or motive *y*) that forecasts analogous intervallic cells in Janáček's contemporary works from the 1920's, *The Makropulos Case* and *Youth*.[3] *X*'s two sequential fourths are frequently combined to form a freely pentatonic aggregate with connecting second

---

[1] In the following discussion, bold numbers refer to rehearsal numbers of the Universal Edition vocal score (no. 7564, Vienna, 1924); thus **6:5** signifies 5 measures *after* no. 6, while **5:6** indicates 5 measures *before* no. 6.

[2] See my previous article, "Conflicting Polarities and Their Resolution in the Music of Leoš Janáček," *Časopis Moravského Musea: Acta Musei Moraviae* 65 (1980), 141–48, in particular 141–42.

[3] See "Conflicting Polarities," 142.

intervals (such as d-flat'-e-flat'-g-flat'-a-flat'), notably in the Vixen-dominated scenes I:ii (12:1, 8:9, 11:2 and 18:7 [fifths]), II:i (**1-7**), II:iii (**25, 26** and **6:31**) and II:iv (**46, 48:4, 60** and **71**). Of the latter, the erotic metamorphoses in II:iii, **26** and especially **6:31**—when the schoolmaster gazes rapturously at the mysterious sunflower—are again recalled by the poacher Harashta and the forest ranger in **III:i, 8:5** and III:iii, **9:48-48:7**, respectively, when they in turn recount their romantic experiences with Terynka. The ranger's amorous recollections are gradually transformed into a pantheistic vision of the forest's regeneration (III:iii, **51:3**–11), one based on essentially the same sequential fourths (a-flat-D-flat, C-flat-F-flat) that underlay his reminiscences of Terynka at **48:7**. (Significantly, even the ensuing semitonal modulations to [implied] D-flat, D, E-flat and E [**52:2-53:4**] recall those of 2:**49**–5:**51**.) Analogous pentatonically-inspired fourth aggregates dominate the close to act III:iii, **55-58**:28, which depicts the ranger's encounters with the Vixen's child and the frog, and also completes the regenerative life cycle by returning to the main characters and dramatic framework of act I:i (see Ex. 1 for x's above-mentioned transformations). Indeed, the little Vixen's dance theme at 5:**56** (which restates its initial appearance in III:i at **15**) is but a melodic variant of its mother's semitonal y motive from I:i (compare 12:**1**, **11**:16 and **13**).[4]

Example 1. X's Metamorphoses

[4]Similar evocative echoes of y occur during the nature voices in II:iii, **45**:2 (a flat"-g"-e flat").

ORGANIZATION IN THE CUNNING LITTLE VIXEN

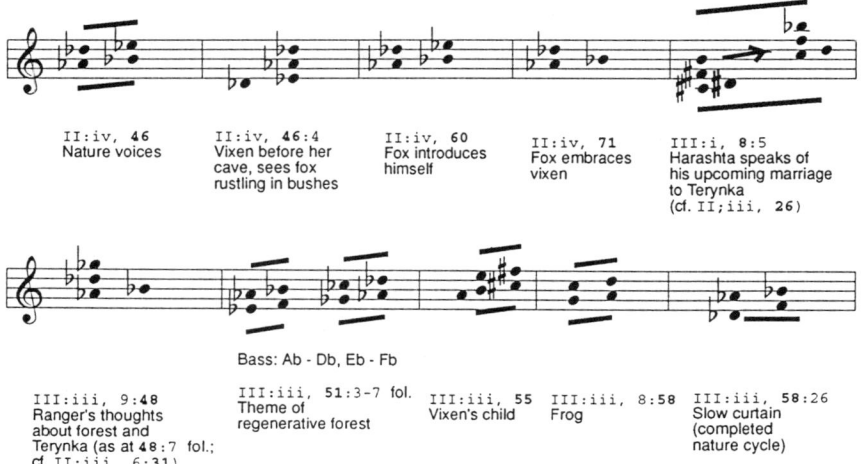

This impressive intervallic cohesion is also supported by the overall harmonic organization, in that x's initial pitches from act I:i—a-flat, G-flat, E-flat and D-flat—also determine the principal tonal centers and their linking modulations in all three acts:

Example 2: Principal Tonal Centers in The Cunning Little Vixen

Act:Scene	Rehearsal No(s.)	Main Tonal Centers			Basic Tonal Movement in Each Scene
		Ab ab	Gb Eb eb	Db db/c#	
I :i	12:1, 4, 18:5	x			ab-eb/Eb-Db-Ab/ab
	3		x		
	8:9		x		
	9		x		
	4:13	x			
I :ii	12:1, 15	x			ab-Gb-Db-Eb
	11:13, 10:14		x⁵		
	18:7			x	
	6:22, 26:4-16		x		
II :i	1			x	Db-Ab-Gb
	7:14	x			
	8:24		x⁵		
II :ii	9, 11, 23:9		x	x	Gb-Db-Ab
	13:6	x			
	24	x			
II :iii	6:31, 40:8			x	
	34:4		x		
	4:41	x			
II :iv	2:45, 62:2, 69:5			x	Ab-db/Db
	2:46, 46:4, 64,			x	
	68, 75, 82				x
	59, 65:4, 68:5				x
III :i	12:1-7:6, 11:8		x		db/c#-Eb-Db-ab-Gb-Eb
	1:8, 2:8, 31, 33:7			x	
	22, 31:4	x			
	27:4		x		
	29		x		
III :ii	34:1, 44		x		Gb-Eb-ab-Gb-Db
	34:4	x			
	38, 38:3			x	
	46:4		x		
III :iii	5:48	x			Gb-Ab-Db
	48:7, 51:3			x	
	2:55, 58:12				

⁵These Gb instrumental interludes both tonicize Gb's upper major mediant, Bb, as at I:ii, **13**:5, **3**:14, **6**:15 and II:i, **8**:38.

Moreover, Janáček is careful to set up a consistent pitch hierarchy between these interrelated tonalities. Since D-flat represents the central tonic of the entire opera, it is often employed for emphatic dramatic resolutions. Some prominent examples include the Vixen's women's liberation sentiments in I:ii, **18**:7, her narrated escape into the forest in II:iv, **59** (here in d-flat minor), in addition to the numerous (D-flat) erotic declarations in act II, as in II:iii, **34**:4 (schoolmaster's love for Terynka), II:iv, **75** (fox's love for the Vixen) and II:iv, **83** (marriage dance of the forest animals). Much the same is true of the Vixen's moving love music in act III:i at **22**:5, as the married couple discusses future children; this expressive theme recurs at the Vixen's death and again at the end of the entire opera (III:iii, **58**:12, here at the original D-flat pitch level) to symbolize the continuity of love and regenerative life.

In surveying the overall tonal structure of *The Cunning Little Vixen*, one observes a consistent tendency for the weaker, more atmospheric and elegiac a-flat *minor* of acts I and III:i–ii to gradually resolve to the stronger a-flat *major*, or the dominant of the eventual tonic D-flat, as in acts II and III:iii. The latter consolidation process is supported by an increasing stress on D-flat's subdominant G-flat, which is often associated with the people's scenes (especially II:ii and III:ii) and the forest ranger in particular; significantly, the latter character eventually effects a dramatic resolution between the animal and human spheres in act III:iii. The final member of the initial *x* motive, E-flat, is often accorded a coloristic supertonic (or dramatically entertaining) function, as during the ballet numbers in I:i, the Vixen's high-spirited escape at the end of I:ii and notably in III:i–ii, as in III:i, **31**, where the Vixen mocks Harashta by quoting the chicken's music from I:ii, **17**.

The pitch hierarchy just outlined—with a-flat and G-flat resolving to the more conclusive supertonic E-flat and tonic E-flat—is also supported by Janáček's conspicuous juxtaposition of the two whole-tone scales on C and C-sharp/D-flat (here labelled wh-t I and wh-t II, respectively).[6] Since wh-t I features both a-flat and G-flat, while wh-t II includes the more affirmative, stable E-flat and D-flat (which terminate all three acts), wh-t I is more frequently encountered at the outset, wh-t II at the close of the three acts, as emerges from the following table:

---

[6]One is reminded of Janáček's similar juxtaposition of wh-t I and wh-t II in his contemporary compositions *Youth* (1924), *Concertino* (1925) and *Sinfonietta*: ii (1926); see my article, "Formale Strukturen in der Musik Leoš Janáček's," *Časopis Moravského Musea: Acta Musei Moraviae 59* (1974), 103–118, especially 110–14.

Example 3: Usage of Wh-T I and Wh-t II in The Cunning Little Vixen

No. of Instance	Act:Scene	Rehearsal No(s).	Wh T I	Wh-T II	Dramatic action or Theme
1.	I : i	6:6-8:9	x		Forest ranger enters out of breath
2.	I : i	12:9-9:17		x	Gnat's ballet (E♭-D♭-B keys)
3.	I : i	11:16, 14-15:2		x	Ranger captures Vixen
4.	I : ii	2:1-2:9		x	Orchestral introduction depicting courtyard of ranger's house
5.	I : ii	5-5:22	x		Dachshund yearns for love
6.	I : ii	6:9-1:7	x		Starlings' gossip about sexual escapades
7.	I : ii	12:10-13:4, 13:11		x	Vixen (in shape of gypsy girl, Terynka) weeps while sleeping
8.	I : ii	16-18:4		x	Chickens obey rooster (B-E♭-G-C#-A-E♭-C# keys)
9.	II : i	22:1-1	x		Orchestral introduction
10.	II : i/ii	8:8-22	x		Orchestral transformation music (including tavern noises of II: ii)
11.	II : ii	9:12-1:11, 12-1:13	x		Terynka's seductive influence on minister, schoolmaster and ranger (Fatalistic, descending variant of x)
12.	II : ii	14:2-14	x		Ranger's bad experience with Vixen (compare no. 6 above)
13.	II : ii	B16:5-17:1	x		Minister warns of woman's sinful love
14.	II : ii	19-20:3	x		Minister escapes angry crowd (compare no. 10 above)
15.	II : iii	3:28-28:15	x		Schoolmaster slips in forest
16.	II : iii	11:38-40:7	x		Minister recalls seductive Terynka (variant of no. 11, with empathetic dotted rhythms at 40)
17.	II : iv	50:9-14, 2:55-55:7, 56-56:7, 58:3-5		x	Vixen criticizes her human upbringing and describes her confrontations with ranger
18.	II : iv	3:61-1:64	x		Vixen's free life style ("ideal modern woman")
19.	II : iv	74-1:75	x		Fox loves Vixen's soul, not her body
20.	II : iv	2:78-79:6	x		Owl's gossip about Vixen and fox
21.	II : iv	81-1:82	x		Fox and Vixen approach woodpecker to get married

22.	III :i	**4:6-6:8, 9-10, 4:12-1:**x 15			Harashta's depraved character and his intention to marry Terynka (cf. no. 11 and especially dotted rhythms of no. 16, together with Vixen's dance rhythms from II:iv, **69**: and **74** in III:ii, 7:7)
23.	III :i	**16-17:**7, **8-1:**18	x		Vixen warns children of ranger's trap
24.	III :i	**17:**8-15, **18-1:**20		x	Vixen and her children criticize ranger's stupidity in setting trap
25.	III :i	**21:**7-17	x		Vixen warns of anticipated gossip about future children
26.	III :i	**23:**8-11	x		Foxes hear Harashta's boisterous approach
27.	III :i	**24:**7-14, 9:27-27:3		x	Harashta chases, tries to shoot Vixen
28.	III :ii	**3:**39-39:5	x		Ranger describes empty fox den (variant of no. 23)
29.	III :ii	**3:**47-47:**18**		x	Ranger returns to woods
30.	III :iii	**8:**58-58:**12**		x	Little frog causes ranger to sink back into his dream

Of the two whole-tone patterns, wh-t I tends to be utilized for neutral scene depictions (as in nos. 4 and 9), physical movement on stage (nos. 1, 14, 15, and 21), noise in general (nos. 10 and 26), pernicious gossip about unorthodox life styles (cf. the inter-related nos. 6, 12, 18, 19, 20) and Terynka's causing of moral depravity (nos. 11, 13, 16 and 22). On the contrary, wh-t II tends to effect dramatic resolutions (as does its tonic member Db), notably as the Vixen tries to liberate herself from her human bondage (nos. 7 and 17) or criticizes the ranger's renewed attempt in Act III to trap her (no. 24). (In this connection it is noteworthy that wh-t II is also employed for the two instances in the opera when the Vixen is actually victimized by mankind [nos. 3 and 27].) Moreover, the other animals in captivity (as the dachshund's yearning for true love in no. 5, or the chickens in no. 8) are accorded a clear supporting function for the Vixen's strivings for freedom, since they, too, outline wh-t II formations, as did the gnat's ballet in no. 2. Once the Vixen has perished in Act III:i, the other forest animals and the ranger assume her wh-t II mantle in nos. 29 and 30 and thus again effect a dramatic resolution between the human and animal spheres.

Since the wh-t II instances are less numerous (and less obvious) than those of wh-t I, Janáček is careful to buttress the cumulative resolving impact of wh-t II by tonicizing its modal fifth (a) and sixth (B) scale degrees at key dramatic moments, most of which directly involve either the liberated Vixen or her children. In Act I (when the Vixen is often depicted in captivity) these modal inflections tend to be limited to occasional upper appoggiaturas of a-flat (compare the a-harmony in I:i, **1**:6) or the upper minor mediant of the Vixen's frequent a-flat minor triads (usually spelled as B's enharmonic equivalent, C-flat). In Act II, however, A and B major are often tonicized as independent key areas and are characteristically associated with the liberated vixen, as in x's poetic metamorphoses in II:ii, **2:8-3** (B major), II:iii, **41** (again in B major) and especially II:iii, **43**:2 (apotheosis in A major, as the Vixen successfully escapes her pursuers). An analogous dramatic event, namely the Vixen's realization that the fox truly love her (cf. II:iv, **73**) again provokes an impassioned B major outburst that has been subtly prepared by introductory wh-t II patterns in **72**:6–11, and which is further confirmed by related E-flat harmonies in **73**:3 and finally another key member of wh-t II, the D-flat major downbeat at **75**. The same harmonic cycle—B-D-flat-D-flat—is reiterated in **76**:7–**77**:12 as the foxes descend to their love-making in the vixen's cave. Moreover, sublimated wh-t II patterns are also outlined during the ensuing wedding chorus **87–3:88** (compare stress on C-flat and A). Furthermore, a similar modal stress on D-flat: bV, bVI and bVII (or the fourth, fifth and sixth degrees of wh-t II) is clearly evident in the introduction to Act III, whose ostinato bass accentuates D-flat, G, B, and A. These pitch areas recur in climactic fashion during III:iii, notably at 7–**3:49** (B), **51**:7–12 (C-flat), **55** (A), **57** (repeated B) and the final apotheosis of the Vixen's love theme, (originally stated in III:i, **22**:5–6 and **32**:4–5 [depicting the Vixen's death]) at **58**:20–28, with its prominent melodic line, b'-a'-g-sharp'/c-flat'-b double flat'-a-flat'.

In conclusion, Janáček's musical organization of his opera *The Cunning Little Vixen* clearly supports the principal dramatic issues and relationship outlined in the libretto. Just as the two embodiments of the "eternal feminine" complex—the Vixen and Terynka—are musically interrelated through various subtle permutations of motives x and y, much the same holds true for the principal male characters in Terynka's life, who tend to be associated with erotic metamorphoses of x. As the drama progresses, the latter x variants tend to assume fatalistically descending, dotted rhythmic patterns set to wh-t I pitches.

Since the regenerative natural cycles become more prominent in Acts II and III, the ultimate tonic D-flat and its crucial major dominant

A-flat are increasingly balanced by a growing stress on D-flat's dominant, G-flat, which often leads to circle-of-fifths *musical* cycles. Simultaneously, D-flat is further confirmed by subtle linear gravitations[7] during the redemptive wh-t II patterns (stressing D-flat's supertonic E-flat and modal flatted seventh B), that are particularly evident towards the end of all three acts. While such an intense correlation between musical idiom and dramatic structure is not unique to the early twentieth century (one encounters a similar relationship in Berg's contemporary opera *Wozzeck*, a work Janáček deeply admired), *The Cunning Little Vixen* nonetheless remains a particularly striking example of extremely cohesive musico-dramatic unity, in which extensive intervallic permutations ultimately govern the entire opera's tonal, linear, and consequently dramatic framework.

---

[7]Similar linear tendencies are observable in the final, third acts of Janáček's remaining two operas, *The Makropulos Case* and *From the House of the Dead*; see "Conflicting Polarities," 142–43 and 146–47.

Janáček's First String Quartet: Motive and Structure of the First Movement

Zdenek Skoumal

Despite the fact that the Schenker industry has been a growing concern for several decades this is, to my knowledge, the first published article anywhere which tries to apply general Schenkerian principles to the work of Janáček. At the very least, Skoumal, who has recently received his Ph.D. dissertation at C.U.N.Y., demonstrates that a careful analysis reflects the very same "unity" in Janáček's work that we find in composers who are more conventional subjects of the Schenkerian art, such as Beethoven, Brahms, or Mozart.

It is well known that Janáček's music is constructed from short motivic ideas which fit together in a mosaic-like fashion. The motives are relatively easy to detect; the repetitions of short phrases and frequent ostinati focus our attention on this very feature. However, it is substantially more difficult to see how the motives are organized in coherent larger structures. That which can be accomplished relatively easily in a traditional musical language through harmonic prolongations and melodic expansions becomes a problem in a 20th-century style that is turning away from conventional harmony and counterpoint. Though Janáček's music always remains tonal—it makes a clear distinction between consonance and dissonance, it mostly uses diatonic scales (major, minor, modal), it treats the triad as the primary harmonic unit, it displays unambiguous tonal centers (focusing on a specific pitch and a related triad)—and yet in his later works the harmonic and melodic structures are frequently dissimilar to those found in traditionally tonal compositions. Is there a palpable system which gives the music order and unity, or must we be content with simply explaining his structures as "intuitive" creations? The following analysis of the first movement of Janáček's *First String Quartet* addresses this problem. I focus on individual motives and explore their roles as organizational elements both at the musical surface and at deeper structural levels.[1]

---

[1]My analysis clearly owes much to analytical ideas developed by Arnold Schoenberg and Heinrich Schenker. Although I do not propose to amalgamate their widely differing theories, I have found several concepts useful in the analysis of Janáček's music. (cont.)

In the analysis I use the terms "cell," "cell complex," and "motive." By cell I understand an unordered collection of two or three pitch classes which acquires special significance in the course of a piece. The pitch-class content of the primary form of the cell may be altered through chromatic alteration, transposition or inversion. Transposition and inversion are self-explanatory; chromatic alteration involves a semitone shift of one of the cell members on the condition that at least one of the constituent intervals remains unaltered. This operation is justified on two grounds. First, Janáček's music is tonal. In tonal music the interval content of motives is commonly altered to suit the underlying harmony (consider, for example, tonal answers of fugues). Second, Janáček himself acknowledged that the motives are flexible entities: "I know very well that the melodic material in my work changes according to the circumstances under which it is used."[2] Jaroslav Vogel adds: "melodic intervals are diminished or augmented (especially when, at a moment of crisis, the theme "bends" under the pressure of dissonant harmony)."[3] In Janáček's music a cell is a relatively elastic structural element where the relationship of the primary form and the variants is obvious and logical.

A cell complex is a collection of three or more pitch classes from which two or more cells are derived. A motive is a cell that is stated linearly—its members are ordered. It also tends to be associated with a specific rhythm.

Schoenberg's *Grundgestalt* helps one to understand the structural implications of motives, while Schenker's concepts of prolongation and structural levels allow us to discuss motives at more remote levels of structure.

The analysis uses a graphing technique derived from that of Schenker, one which shows the relative structural importance of notes. The following list presents notes in order of increasing importance:

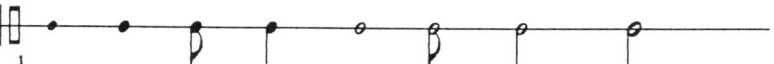

Beams join notes that form important motives or connections. For clarity, octave placements of pitches may be altered and pitches nay be enharmonically respelled. Square brackets show my additions.

[2]Leoš Janáček, *Letters and Reminiscences*, ed. Bohumír Štědroň, trans. Geraldine Thomsen (Prague: Artia, 1955), p. 143.

[3]Jaroslav Vogel, *Leoš Janáček: A Biography*, revised and edited by Karel Janovicky (New York: W. W. Norton & Company, 1981), p. 16fn.

Form

The present form of the work dates from 1923, although there is strong evidence to suggest that this movement was largely composed by 1908 or 1909.[4] These dates place it squarely in Janáček's middle period, a period characterized by juxtaposition of traditionally tonal compositional practices and novel ideas. The overall layout of the movement clearly follows tradition: it is a sonata form. As is common in Janáček's sonata forms the Development is relatively brief—more like an interjection between the Exposition and the Recapitulation—but otherwise the movement follows the traditional formal pattern faithfully; both in terms of thematic arrangement and tonal structure.[5] The following chart shows the formal divisions.

Exposition	First Subject	mm. 1–45
	Second Subject, Part 1	46–56
	Second Subject, Part 2	57–71
"Development"		72–85
Recapitulation	First Subject	86–132
	Second Subject, Part 1	133–148
	Second Subject, Part 2	149–161
Codetta		162–164

The movement is non-traditional in that the form does not grow out of the standard tonal syntax; there are no balanced, symmetrical phrases, and few goal-oriented harmonic progressions. The sonata form is more of a mold into which Janáček's motivic musical language fits.

---

[4] See Paul Wingfield, "Janáček's "Lost" Kreutzer Sonata," *Journal of the Royal Music Association* 112/2 (October 1987), pp. 229–256.

[5] For more on Janáček's sonata form see Miroslava Kanková, "Sonátová forma v díle Leoše Janáčka" [Sonata Form in the Works Of Leoš Janáček], *Opus Musicum* 14/5 (1982), 135–140, and Vaclav Felix, "Příspevek k poznání specifických rysů Janáčkova sonátového slohu (Analyza jeho Sonáty pro housle a klavír)" [A contribution to the recognition of specific characteristics of Janáček's sonata style (Analysis of his Violin Sonata)], *Živá hudba* 7 (1980), pp. 127–44.

Motivic Material

The generating idea for the entire movement is the following cell complex:

Example 1.

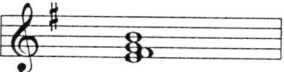

It represents all pitches heard in measure 1, and it also appears as a chord on the downbeat of measure 3. From this complex we can derive four three-note cells.

Example 2.

Cells X and Y play a critical role in the structure of this movement. Cell Z becomes important in the second movement, while the triad as a cell is structurally secondary—it appears on the musical surface as a natural consequence of the tonal nature of Janáček's music.

Example 3 shows chromatic alterations of X and Y along with their inversions, as well as some motives they generate. While many more motives are possible, those below are particularly important in this movement. Note the whole tone nature of Y^3. Though whole-tone elements are secondary in this movement, those that do appear can be said to originate in this motivic variant. I shall draw attention to them when appropriate.

Example 3.

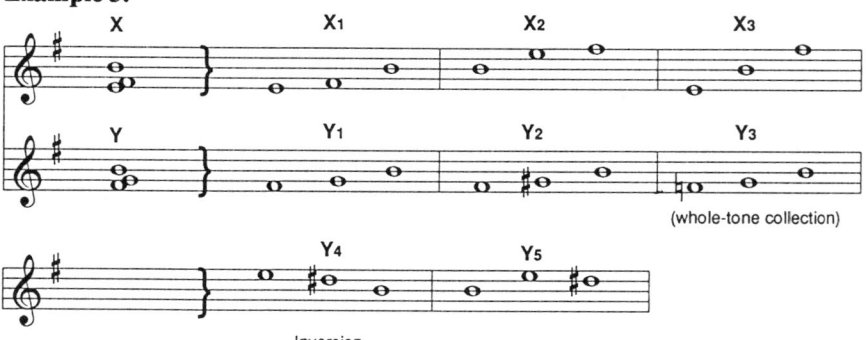

Exposition: First Subject

The opening two measures present cell Y harmonically (violin II, viola), while motives X^1 and Y^2 form the melody (violin I). Measures 3–11 sustain cell Y and feature an energetic cello melody constructed from motives X^1, X^3, Y^1, Y^2, and Y^3 (some in retrograde; Example 4).

Example 4.

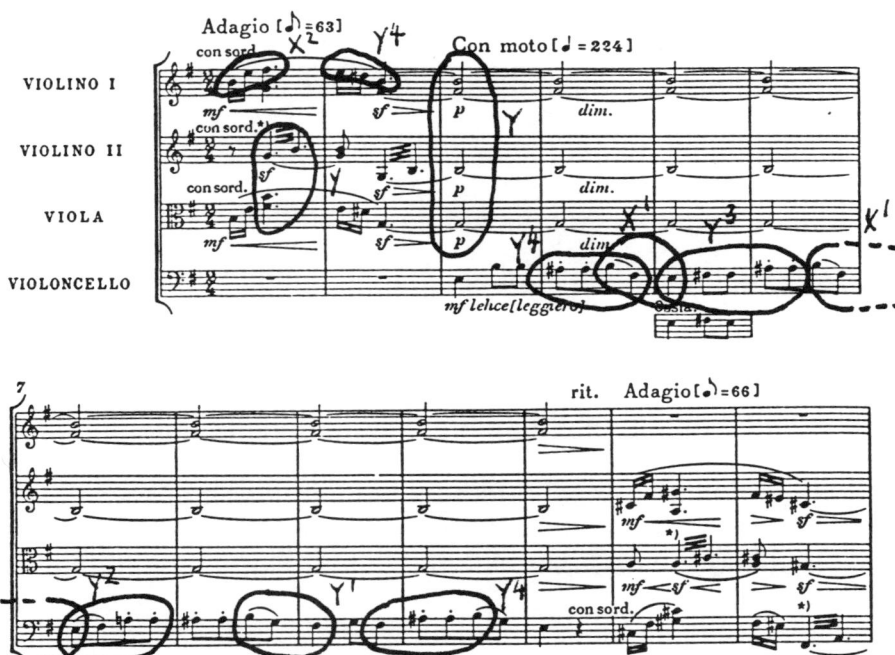

This entire phrase is repeated in F-sharp minor (measures 12–22), and B minor (measures 23–33). Measure 34 marks the end of this part of the first subject by the return of the E minor harmony and a retrograde statement of X^2, *now heard in the lowest voice* (measure 1 presented this motive in the highest voice). The transpositional path of the three phrases outlines motive X^1 (Example 5).

Example 5.

Measures 34–45 act as a transition to the second subject; their bass motion outlines motive Y^5 (permuted, see Example 6).

Example 6.

Thus the structure of the first subject arises from an expansion of motives X^1 and Y^5, and in this way reflects the pitch structure of the opening melody (Example 7).

Example 7.

Exposition: Second Subject

The second subject is in two parts: part 1—measures 46–56, and part 2—measures 57–71. Intervalically, the melody of part 1 is closely related to the cello melody in measures 3–11. This relationship becomes obvious in the Recapitulation, where the second subject returns in the tonic key (Example 8).

Example 8.

The ostinato of part 2 is motive X^1 and its retrograde, transposed up a fifth to the dominant. The viola's melodic figure in measure 59 is assembled from the same familiar motives. Even in a construct this small the motives emerge at different structural levels, most important being the level that takes into account the harmonic context of the passage. The motive of that level is Y^2 (Example 9).

Example 9.

The overall harmonic motion of the second subject mirrors the harmonic motion of measures 1–33. Cell Y is once again an important harmonic unit and it again moves along the outline of motive X^1 (as we saw in Example 5). Despite the new harmonic context it does so at the original pitch level. This section however differs from measures 1–33 in two important ways: 1) since it is in the dominant key, certain harmonic alterations are inevitable, and 2) the motion of Y is somewhat disguised by the interjection of a more traditional harmonic progression. It is here that we see most clearly the aforementioned juxtaposition of old and new techniques.

The first harmonic alteration is a change from Y^1 to Y^2—akin to a change from minor to major (Example 10; for easy reference I label the three transpositional levels of Y^3 [1], [2], [3]).

Example 10.

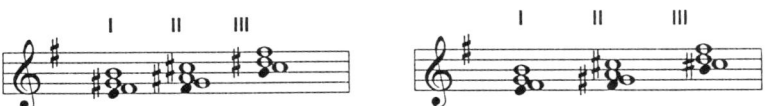

The second alteration is a replacement of notes which belonged to motive X^1 by notes suitable for the B major context (Example 11).

Example 11.

The motion of Y is disguised in that harmony [2] in measures 50–51 is immediately followed by a descent and a return of [1] in measure 54. This is to prepare the traditional 6/4–5/3 resolution of measures 55–56.

Example 12.

The implications of that cadential activity are compelling. The status of the 6/4 harmony in measures 46–49 is questionable; it could be interpreted as either a tonic or a dominant. It is preceded in measure

45 by its own dominant to suggest that it functions as a tonic, but that dominant is surprisingly brief and hence the tonic is unconvincing. Only the harmonic motion of measures 55–56 forces us in retrospect to hear the entire section (measures 46–56) as a prolongation of the dominant. Harmony [2] is thus only a neighbor to a prolonged [1], not on par with [1] and [3] as it was in measures 1–33. Yet when it arrives in measure 50, the parallel with measure 12 is unmistakable. An absolute parallel to measures 1–33 would not prolong the dominant and bring back [1] in measure 54; it would retain [2] until the end of measure 56. Janáček apparently felt the need to better establish the dominant key area and hence reverted to a conventional harmonic process in measures 52–56.

The arrival of part 2 of the second subject in measure 57 features only motive X^2; as we saw earlier Y^2 (harmony [3]) is embedded in the viola's melodic figure in measure 59. The figure appears three times (varied the third time) and then the entire harmonic motion is reversed: harmony [2] returns in measures 62–64 (cf. violoncello part here and in measures 50–51), and harmony [1] returns in measures 65–67 (cf. violin I here and viola in measures 46–49).[6]

The bass motion of the second subject likewise displays a strong motivic influence. As we just saw, F-sharp is the most important bass note in the second subject, part 1. In the same way part 2 (measures 57–71) stressed the bass note B. Taking into account the opening tonic of the movement we once again see an expansion of the X^1 motive, this time at an even deeper structural level (see Example 13).[7]

---

[6] The structure of the second subject utilizes an often-cited characteristic of Janáček's musical language: the frequent appearance of triads with an added second or sixth. The added notes do not significantly change the basic quality or function of the chord (as a flat seventh would, for example), but they do provide another note that will be in common in certain harmonic changes. If a tonic chord contains an added second, three of the four notes will remain when the harmony changes to the dominant with an added sixth. Note that the chord with the added second (the tonic) is the cell complex here, and the chord with the added sixth (the dominant) is cell Y and its inversion.

[7] This type of structural design—the appearance of a motive in different structural levels—is sometimes described as "motivic nesting," see Charles Burkhart, "Schenker's 'Motivic Parallelisms'," Journal of Music Theory 22/2 (Fall 1978), pp. 145–175.

Example 13.

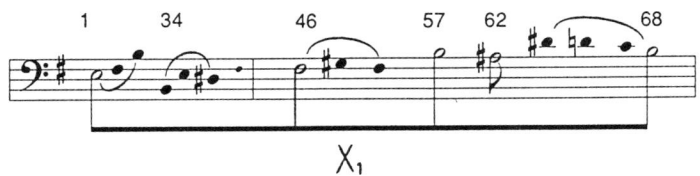

Development

As mentioned earlier, this section is relatively brief; it mostly restates the melodic material of the second subject, part 1. Harmonically, it retraces the structure of measures 36–45. Just as the second subject followed the harmonic motion of measures 1–33, the Development continues that process for measures 34–45, the remainder of the first subject (Example 14).

Example 14.

First subject

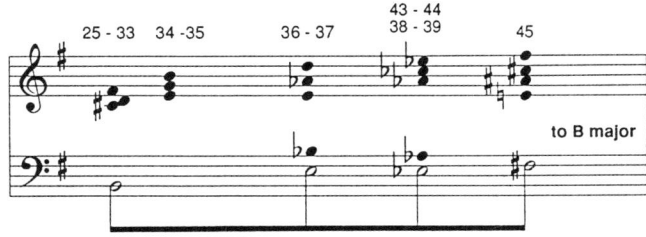

Second subject/Development

Measures 72–77 parallel measures 34–37; note that the whole-tone nature of measures 75 and 77 is related to the whole-tone structure of measures 36–37. The A-flat major 6/4 harmony of measure 78 parallels the A-flat minor 6/4 of measures 38–39 and 43–44, and the dominant of E minor (measures 82–85) parallels the dominant of B major (measure

45). The dominant of measures 82–85 is in a 6/4 inversion, thereby providing the same bass note (F-sharp) as did the dominant in measure 45. Thus the harmonic structure of the first subject returns as the structure of the second subject and the Development.

The bass motion of the Development is simple, but as such it connects with the bass of the Exposition to imitate the opening cello melody (Example 15).

Example 15.

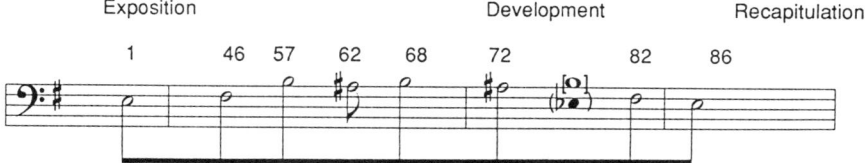

Recapitulation and Codetta

These sections are rather straight-forward; I shall simply point out three noteworthy features. Measures 86–87 are a repetition of measures 1–2, with the addition of a melodic fragment in the viola (measure 86) and cello (measure 87). The two fragments begin as literal statements of motives Y^1 and X^2.

The first subject structure in the Recapitulation does not outline any of the motive; instead, the E minor tonic is prolonged by a descending whole-tone scale. This is the fullest realization of the whole-tone potential inherent in motive Y^3 (Example 16).

Example 16.

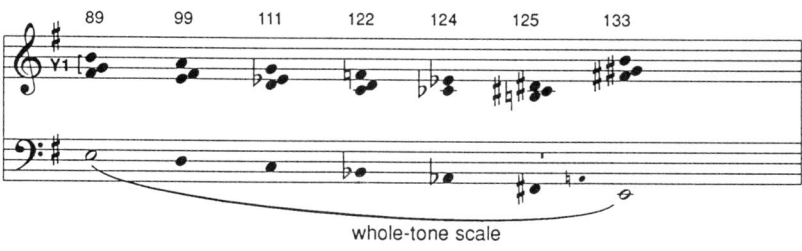

The second subject now appears in the tonic major. The statements of motive Y^2 contain the identical pitches in the tonic as they did in the dominant (cf. measures 46–51, viola and violoncello, and measures 133–140, violin II and viola).[8]

As a summary of the preceding analysis, Example 17 shows graphically the structural features of the entire movement. Here I have restored some of the original octave placements in order to make the correspondence with the score clearer. I have also made an effort to allign similar events within the four systems to show the structural parallels among the various sections of the movement (this is why several blank areas appear, for example, between measures 33 and 34).

How did Janáček organize a composition? Certainly, in this work there is the sonata form, but as we saw the movement contains none of the dynamic elements which give the sonata form its vitality. The governing structural principles here include expansions of basic motives over large spans of music, motivic nesting on several levels, and the use of similar harmonic designs for disparate sections of the movement. They give the music profound order and unity; Janáček's unique rhythmic sense gives it life and vigor. Perhaps the most magical feature of the movement is the seemingly natural marriage of novel structural techniques and traditional form. It is a testimony to Janáček's genius that the offspring of that union is an esteemed work of art.

Example 17. Janáček: String Quartet No. 1/I

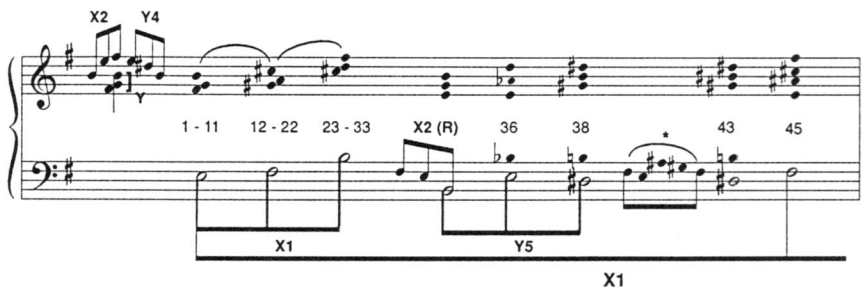

---

[8]This is possible because of the unique property of the added-note chords mentioned in footnote 5.

JANÁČEK'S FIRST STRING QUARTET

– Second Subject

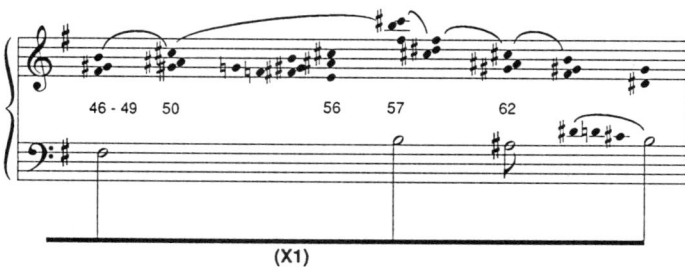

"Development"

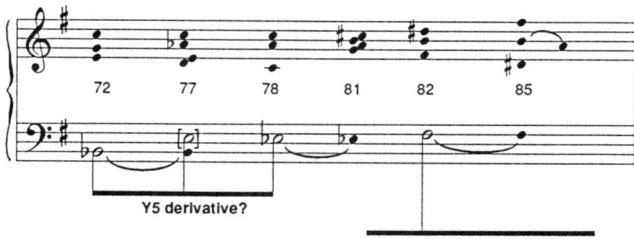

Recapitulation – First Subject

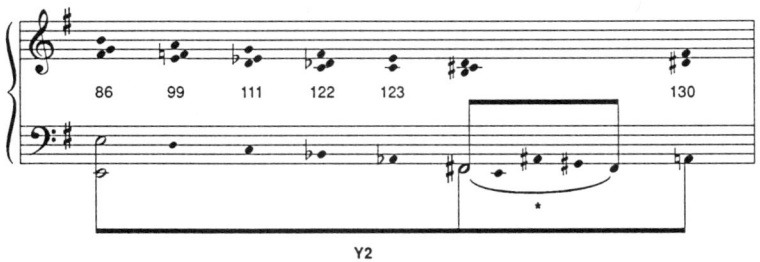

– Second Subject

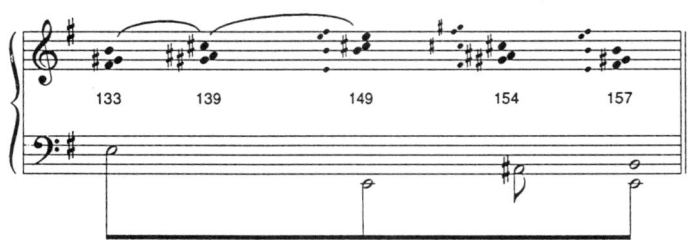

Structure and Meaning in the First Movement of Janáček's *Concertino*

Fred Everett Maus

Fred Maus is not, by trade, a Janáček scholar. Yet after I heard one of his lectures which dealt in part with the issue of "animism"—the belief that all objects have a natural life or soul—I asked him to have a look at some of Janáček's writings. It seemed to me that Janáček was an animist's animist. The result of this is the following study which searchingly, and with no little elegance, combines a close reading of the score with bold speculations about metaphor and musical drama.

I.

I am not here as a Janáček specialist, but as a music theorist with an interest in aesthetic issues. Several months ago Michael Beckerman suggested that some of Janáček aesthetic ideas might intrigue me. And he was right: certain aspects of Janáček musical thought, as expressed in some of his essays and in his compositions, have turned out to be very pertinent to my own preoccupations.

Today I want to explore a part of this territory by speculating on musical structure and musical meaning with reference to a particular composition, the first movement of Janáček's *Concertino* for piano and chamber ensemble. In view of my limited knowledge of Janáček's work, not to mention the complexity of the general aesthetic issues, the following remarks must be understood as conjectural. It is a privilege to be able to present them to such a knowledgeable audience.

II.

Jaroslav Vogel's discussion of the *Concertino* in his biography of Janáček raises several important issues, and his treatment will provide a good starting point for my remarks. Vogel begins by noting that the piano concerto medium could easily have led to "academic" results, but that Janáček approach is fresh and original. He links the work to Janáček's love of nature, and quotes the composer's own brief description of the piece, which consists in part of anecdotes about animals. Vogel also sketches a formal description of the piece. I shall begin with this last matter, returning to the others later.

Vogel observes that the first movement of the the *Concertino* "hints at sonata form." He identifies an introduction, up to No. 1 in the score; at that point the "allegro proper" begins. The material marked "Meno mosso," he suggests, "could be called the second subject." After the development section, in which Vogel identifies a "waltz-like motif," the recapitulation occurs; Vogel notes that the material returns in reverse order, "with the introductory bars returning at the end."

It is easy to wonder what "sonata form" might be in music as remote from the classical style as the *Concertino*. Vogel's discussion suggests that he conceives of sonata form primarily in terms of thematic repetition and contrast. But his wording is cautious, and no doubt this reflects his awareness that classical sonata form is not merely thematic in nature; at the least, one would have to describe an appropriate coordination between large-scale harmony and thematic patterning in order to regard the piece as an instance of sonata form, and the claim would be stronger if the large-scale harmonic relations could be shown to be dramatized in some way. Vogel's tentative sonata-form analysis cannot be augmented along these lines. But this is the result of an easily-corrected error in Vogel's proposed analysis. Though the movement does not rely on major and minor scales, a listener can easily identify tonic pitches and tonic triads for a number of different local keys; in particular, the opening measures establish a g minor triad as tonic; at 1, e-flat minor appears, and this key remains in effect until 2. In light of these key relations, one can regard mm. 1–9 as the first subject in a sonata-form pattern; the next passage would constitute a transition, and the second group would arrive at 1. In other words, harmonic structure argues against Vogel's sonata-form suggestion, in which the g minor material serves as an introduction, but in favor of a sonata form structure in which, as in many of Haydn's pieces, repetition of the opening material marks the arrival at the secondary key.

In fact, Vogel is right to invoke sonata form, even if the particulars of his analysis are wrong. The organization of this movement has much in common with classical sonata form, and where it diverges, a comparison with sonata procedures is helpful in characterizing Janáček's piece. Closer examination of the beginning and end of the movement—its "exposition" and recapitulation," perhaps—will substantiate the point.

In classical sonata form, the first and second groups are in closely related keys; an important criterion of closeness is the retention of pitch material in the move from one key to the other. Normally, g minor and e-flat minor would not seem to be particularly close. But there is no reason, given the material of this piece, to compare the keys by comparing their conventional minor scales; comparison can more relevantly be based upon the actual pitches of the opening piano melody, heard as establishing a referential collection of pitch-classes. Among the various transpositions of this pitch-class collection, most will preserve two common pitch-classes between the original and its transposition, while the other transpositions leave only one common pitch-class. So the structural possibilities of tonal music, where key relations can be differentiated subtly in terms of pitch-class retention, do not arise from this opening pitch material. In moving to a tonic of e-flat, Janáček preserves as many common tones as possible, but other transpositions would have done the same.

The precise effect of the move from g to e-flat depends, of course, on *which* common tones are retained, and on how they are used in the actual thematic material. The opening theme places strong emphasis on the half-step ascents that move to the third and fifth of the triad; Janáček's choice of a transposition level that retains a and b-flat associated the pitches of the two statements through this prominent feature.

However, Janáček's transposition cannot have been motivated primarily by a desire to maximize continuity, for there is another transposition that would have sounded much more directly pertinent to the opening. By moving the theme to b-flat, Janáček could have retained b-flat and c-sharp (or d-flat) as common tones. These pitches are emphasized in the opening melody by repetition and rhythmic treatment. The local tonic pitch would have been a member of the g minor tonic triad, as in normal tonal practice. The substitution of d-flat for d as a stable tonic triad pitch would sound like a direct response to the first horn figure, which answers the piano d with c-sharp. For these reasons a move to b-flat would be more straightforward and purposeful than Janáček's move to e-flat; the point of this hypothetical alternative, of course, is to clarify by contrast the somewhat discontinuous effect of the actual succession in the piece.

The e-flat melody drives forcefully toward the a and b-flat, making a goal of pitches that were originally internal to a strong ascent. Treatment of these pitches as a goal emphasizes the shared pitch classes, stressing the point of contact with the opening. The transitional passage preceding the arrival at e-flat, in the long measure before 1, also directs attention to the role of a and b-flat as common tones. The horn, by playing its motive in successive whole-tone transpositions, creates a chromatic ascent formed from its upper notes. That ascent begins with c-sharp-d, and continues until it reaches a-b-flat. In other words, the horn part links the two half steps that appear in the opening; the piano, so to speak, recognizes the point of intersection and seizes the opportunity to reintroduce the theme.

A classical sonata form piece moves from its initial tonic to a closely related secondary key. In the new key, the sound is richly complex because, while much pitch material is retained, the common material functions very differently within the new key. At the same time, the pitches tend to retain a strong implication of their original function, so that the music of the second group typically has an ambivalent quality that somewhat destabilizes the local tonic. In comparison, the beginning of the second group in the Janáček movement retains very little pitch material from the first subject, and the sense of subtle, passive reinterpretation of pitch material is missing. But the beautiful new melody that appears before 2 introduces precisely the kind of complexity that I have described. It presents, in its high notes, a d-c-b-flat descent, followed by b-flat-a-flat-g. Obviously these pitches refer back to the opening, outlining a g minor triad even while the accompanying harmony establishes an e-flat tonic. Having reached e-flat through a rather tenuous link, Janáček expands the pitch material of the new key in a way that brings it closer to the starting point.

So far, the sonata form model, generalized somewhat beyond the pitch materials of classical tonality, serves fairly well. But is has taken us only two thirds of the way through the passage that should presumably constitute the exposition. The remaining section, from 2 to the repetition, returns to the transition and most of the second group, but with the harmony consistently revised so that at every point the pitch relations are more irregular; no single tonic emerges. The lyrical melody that closes the section begins as though it will restore an e-flat tonic—

e-flat major, as at the very end of the earlier statement of this material. But a-flat emerges as the local tonic; the a-flat minor triad appears as one of Janáček's characteristic consonant six-four chords. The six-four creates a vivid sense of the a-flat triad as, specifically, a substitute for the b e-flat triad that would sustain the previously established tonic. When the bass moves to a-flat, the harmony drifts to an unprecedented g major, immediately giving way to g-flat or f-sharp major. In short, the passage uses, but drifts away from, the major triads corresponding to the two minor tonic triads established earlier.

The long line that emerges from the melody is, in a way, more straightforward in its relation to the larger context than are the shifting harmonies. The melody descends from high g down to b-flat (notated a-sharp), once again referring to the g minor triad; the reference remains clear despite the internal complexities—the emphasis on e-flat, the play between d and d-flat, b and b-flat. The g-f-e-flat and d-c-b spans unfold parts of the e-flat and g triads; the last span, d-flat-c-flat-b-flat, can be heard as essentially concerned to correct the b to b-flat, restoring an element of g minor.

This passage, concerned with g and e-flat as tonics but affirming neither, does not follow the sonata-form model; more precisely, it does not fit the pattern of a normal sonata exposition. In loosening the grip of the secondary key, referring back to the overall tonic, moving through slightly distorted versions of earlier music in a somewhat exploratory way, the passage takes on many traits of the beginning of a development section.

The last ten measures of the movement are essentially a repetition of the first nine measures, with the addition of a final chord, chords at the beginnings of phrases, and altered dynamics. The second group, however, does not return in g minor; rather, just before 5, the melody from the second group returns, with g and then e-flat in the bass. Though the bass notes refer to the tonics of the opening sections, the harmony presents consonant six-four chords, implying local tonics of c and a-flat. As before, the effect is that g and e-flat triads are specifically evaded. The passage does not resolve the large-scale harmonic tension in the manner of a classical recapitulation; rather, the passage serves as a point of recall, gesturing toward resolution without actually providing it.

III.

I would like to turn now from formal issues to questions of interpretation, drawing on Janáček's writings. Janáček often approaches musical issues through descriptions of nature, especially sounds in nature, and some of this material will be helpful in deepening an understanding of the *Concertino*.

Janáček's involvement with natural sounds goes beyond purely sensuous interest in intriguing aural phenomena; he regards birdsong, for instance, not as mere patterned sound but as expression. The sounds of human speech or, equally, of birdsong, he writes,

> are a recognizable password with which one can easily become the guest of someone else's soul. The little soul of a bird, the human soul of a man, it's all the same. They intrude violently for they are outcries of a soul! (80)[1]

Janáček's view affects his detailed descriptions of birdsong; in writing about the many brief melodies in a thrush's song, he states that

> the thrush's character is superficial. He has plenty of witty ideas, but he tears them up by their roots. By the second song, it appears as if he has already forgotten the first one. It seems to me as if he has no complicated reactions. (84)

Similarly, in describing the single note produced by the flight of a bee, Janáček writes that

> the sustained tone, constant and unvarying, suggests to us an eager search, a sharp mind, and a consciousness full of impressions lived through and remembered. (48)

In such passages Janáček speculates on the psychology of relatively simple animals. But he also animates inanimate nature, as in this passage:

> the water hurries away, and in its hurry stumbles over every little stone. It chatters and shouts and grumbles: "out of my way... out of my way!" it cries. (68)

For Janáček, a sound is a revelation of the inner world of the person or animal that makes the sound; or, as in the case of the water, it is an in-

---

[1] This and all the other citations on this page are taken from *Leoš Janáček: Leaves From His Life,* edited and translated by Vilem and Margaret Tausky, New York: Taplinger Publishing Company, 1982.

vitation to *imagine* such an inner world. The importance of these views lies in Janáček's effort, in his compositions, to specify sounds that would evoke such responses from his listeners. Just as Janáček, hearing rushing water, personifies the water as hurrying, grumbling, and so on, so his music invites such vivid imaginative perception.

In commenting on the first movement of the *Concertino*, Janáček tells of trapping a hedgehog, preventing it from returning to its lair.

> He was cross but he toiled in vain. He could not make it out. Neither could the horn in my first movement. All it could manage was this grumpy motif[2]

—and Janáček quotes the first three-note horn figure from the *Concertino*. Clearly Janáček is not proposing a *program*, involving a story about a hedgehog, for this movement. Rather, he proposes an analogy: the behavior of the horn in the first movement is *like* the behavior of the trapped hedgehog. In other words, a listener can understand the horn part dramatically, as the behavior of a character in a story, and the result may be a pattern of behavior like that of the trapped hedgehog. It is revealing, in light of the passages I quoted earlier, that the hedgehog analogy does not deal with sounds, but more generally with the *behavior* of the trapped animal. The sounds in a musical composition need not be imagined as sounds made by a physically embodied dramatic character, but can be imagined more abstractly as expressive behavior. Thus, the first movement of the *Concertino* can be understood as presenting a story about the interaction of two characters; the piano part presents the behavior of one character, the horn part the behavior of the other. In thinking about the interaction of these characters it is best, I would suggest, not to press Janáček's hedgehog analogy too far; rather, the drama should be understood, as much as possible, in musical terms, as a drama of musical characters. And the dramatic construal will be more convincing if it manages to incorporate analytical detail. By narrating the events at the beginning of the movement I can illustrate the dramatic quality of the music.

Though Janáček's own description focuses on the hedgehog as a model for the horn part, both the piano and the horn are established at the beginning as restricted in their behavior. Indeed, the piano simply repeats the same melody three times. But the melody is coherent and self-sufficient, while the horn figures sound as though they are inac-

---

[2] Jaroslav Vogel, *Leoš Janáček*, New York: W. W. Norton, 1981, p. 305.

curately derived from the piano part. Having misquoted the piano three times, the horn part pauses and then, on the basis of the materials with which it is already involved, attempts to put together a long, continuous span. To do so, it returns to the three-note figure from which it first took its cue. Reproducing the piano's pitch material more accurately, the horn creates an utterly rudimentary succession, substituting a uniform chromatic ascent within the harmony of a whole-tone scale for the minor key of the opening. The horn seems to be preparing for a third set of transpositions when the piano interrupts, insisting on a tonal center and on its original material. As I suggested before, the piano's intervention is precipitated by recognition of one of its original half-step ascents; the relatively discontinuous sound of this transposition makes sense dramatically, since the transposed version is the piano's desperate attempt to recover control of the piece rather than the goal of a purposeful progression. After a brief, noisy conflict between the piano's trilled e-flat and b-flat, affirming the new key, and the horn figure, the piano rises rapidly in two passages that can be heard as ridiculing the horn—mimicking its three-note figures but demonstrating speed, agility, and range that put the horn to shame. With the horn temporarily silenced, the piano now works to establish greater continuity between its two key areas by creating significant intersection of the pitch material between the new key and g minor. This momentary equilibrium is interrupted by the horn which has, rather irrelevantly, developed a new way of proceeding with its motive, no longer confining itself to whole-tone-related transpositions. The piano responds with disorientation, losing the stability that it achieved briefly.

The first movement of the *Concertino* creates, in its horn part, a dramatic character of animal-like simplicity and intensity, and displays its tense interaction with a somewhat more flexible character. Such vivid drama and closeness to nature are fundamental to Janáček's unique achievement. To appreciate these qualities, one must go beyond the range of conventional musical analysis, following the animistic tendencies of Janáček's own writings about music.

Part 3:

Czech Music Before Smetana

A good deal of the attention paid to Czech music, especially in English-speaking countries, has been directed towards the period from 1860 onwards, and focussed primarily on four major figures, Smetana, Dvořák, Janáček, and Martinů. This has sometimes had the unfortunate effect of overshadowing the fascinating work which has been done on earlier historical periods. It is for this reason that we followed the tradition established by Jaroslav Mráček and convened a special session at the conference to explore ideas and deal with issues raised by Czech music before Smetana.

    The papers in this section cover the period from the Baroque to the early 19th century, and address a wide array of topics. In many of these, the issue of] "Czechness" plays absolutely no part, which is entirely appropriate, since most of the work in our field has nothing whatsoever to do with articulating the Czech quality of a specific composer, work, or context. The quality of these papers and the significance of the material they deal with are testimony to the fact that the exploration of Czech music before Smetana is one of the most fertile and exciting areas in historical musicology.

Antonio Vivaldi and the Sporck Theater in Prague

Daniel E. Freeman

Undoubtedly one of the most significant musical events to occur in Prague during the late eighteenth century was the foundation in 1724 of a public opera theater in one of the palaces of Count Franz Anton von Sporck. Under the directorship of the impresario Antonio Denzio, the Sporck theater flourished for about a decade as a colony of the Venetian operatic world, and it engendered productions of Italian opera elsewhere in central European cities during the 1720's and 1730's. Many talented Italian singers and composers were attracted to Prague, and the Sporck theater probably provided the composers Gluck and Stamitz, both of whom spent much of their youths in Prague, with their first exposure to opera. The greatest interest of the Sporck theater lies, however, in the intriguing connections it maintained with the composer Antonio Vivaldi, perhaps culminating in a personal visit during the early 1730's. What Vivaldi's collaboration with the Prague opera company produced will be sampled later during this presentation. But to understand how and why this collaboration came about, it will be convenient to begin with an overview of the origin, significance, and operation of the Sporck theater drawn from documents I gathered in the State Central Archive in Prague.

I have said that the Sporck theater was a Venetian colony; it imported nearly all of its personnel and repertory from that city. Not a single work performed in the theater was composed by a native Bohemian, and when the Italian librettos were translated for the local audiences, the language was German, not Czech. The reasons for this are of course to be found in the political conditions during the so-called *doba temna*, when Bohemia was dominated by a largely German Catholic nobility imposed on Bohemia by the Hapsburg monarchy after the Thirty Years' War. Count Sporck was a member of this new nobility, and, under the circumstances, it is easy to understand why he and his entire class had little to do with native Bohemian culture, preferring to find sources of prestige in emulation of the taste and patronage of the imperial court in Vienna. In the realm of theater and music that meant, of course, Italian opera. Sporck's opera productions did not, however, come directly from Vienna, nor from nearby Dresden or any other German center, but directly from Venice. The reasons for that are found in more particular circumstances.

Prague had seen very few Italian operas before Count Sporck opened his theater; since 1627 there had been only a handful per generation.[1] The fashion caught on, however, during the celebrations in Prague surrounding the coronation of Emperor Charles VI as King of Bohemia in 1723, the highlight of which was a performance of Johann Joseph Fux's *La costanza e fortezza*. Among the famous and obscure musicians who gathered in Prague for this event was evidently a Venetian impresario by the name of Antonio Maria Peruzzi, who, sensing an opportunity, petitioned the Bohemian *Statthalterei*, the highest civil authority in Bohemia, for permission to produce Italian opera on March 16, 1724.[2] Peruzzi, however, had no singers, so he contacted his father in Venice, who engaged Antonio Denzio, tenor, impresario, and friend Antonio Vivaldi, to form a company in May of 1724.[3]

It was Antonio Peruzzi who first turned for assistance to Count Sporck, one of the wealthiest and most prominent of the new nobility in Prague.[4] Sporck actually put up no money in Peruzzi's venture and had no financial stake in the company, but he did refurbish the comedy theater in his palace to make it suitable for operatic performances, in return for which he took credit for being the company's patron. His motivations were social rather than artistic, as he frankly confessed in his correspondence. The

---

[1] An overview of operatic performances in Prague before the foundation of the Sporck theater can be found in Oscar Teuber, *Geschichte des Prager Theaters* I (Prague:1883), pp. 32–60; Renate Brockpäler, *Handbuch zur Geschichte der Barockoper in Deutschland* (Emsdetten: 1964), pp. 313–23; Jaroslav Hach, "Operní divadlo v šlechtický rezidencích a na městkých scénách," *Dějiny českého divadla* I (Prague: 1968), pp. 248–262; and Daniel Freeman, *The Opera Theater of Count Franz Anton von Sporck in Prague (1724–35),"* Stuyvesant, NY: Pendragon Press, 1992, pp. 17–22.

[2] The original petition is preserved in Prague, Státní Ústřední Archiv, manuscript series SČM (=Staré České Místodržitelství), shelf no. 1724/VIII/d/39.

[3] A copy of the original contract between Peruzzi and Denzio, which describes an operatic venture that was to include performances in Dresden and Leipzig as well as Prague, is preserved in SČM 1724/XI/d/7. A transcription may be found in Freeman, "The Opera Theater," pp. 281–84.

[4] A copy of a contract between Peruzzi and Count Sporck, signed June 4, 1724, is preserved in SČM 1724/XI/d/7. A transcription may be found in Freeman, "The Opera Theater," pp. 285–86. At first, Peruzzi was engaged to provide an opera company for performances on the Sporck estate of Kuks only. In the autumn of 1724, however, Count Sporck allowed Peruzzi's company to perform in one of his Prague palaces for its own profit. Although previous literature on the Sporck theater holds that Count Sporck "invited" Antonio Denzio and his company to Bohemia, the contract between Peruzzi and Denzio demonstrates that it was Peruzzi who was responsible for bringing Denzio to Bohemia.

original purpose for engaging the opera company that Peruzzi promised to send from Italy, in fact, was merely to impress the wife of one of the leading courtiers at the Imperial court in Vienna.[5] Eventually, Count Sporck was able to derive a considerable amount of prestige from the early success of the opera company, but rarely even bothered to attend its performances after the death of his wife in 1726.

Thus, in spite of the free use of Sporck's theater, the Peruzzi-Denzio opera company was essentially a free enterprise operation in which box-office receipts were expected to pay the expenses. They never did, of course, and the following ten-year history of the venture is thoroughly documented in the records of the Bohemian *Statthalterei* and its magistrates, before whom an endless series of suits and petitions were filed by singers, instrumentalists, designers, suppliers, and impresario, usually in attempts to recover contracted payments. Although Denzio very soon wrested control of the company from Peruzzi because of financial default,[6] Denzio himself ended his Prague opera career in debtor's prison. The story is not new. It is told all over Europe, wherever impresarios attempted to make Italian opera a commercial success.

In all, Denzio produced fifty-seven operas for the Sporck theater between 1724 and 1735, normally two in the autumn, two during Carnival, and two in the spring of each year. For repertory, Denzio drew heavily on works in which he had appeared in northern Italy before coming to Prague in 1724, works for which his relative Pietro Denzio had served as impresario, and on other older operas originally produced in northern Italian centers ten, fifteen, or even twenty years earlier.[7] Apparently the scores for such old operas were inexpensive to obtain and the Prague audiences, isolated from operatic trends in Italy, would likely no have realized how stylistically old-fashioned most of the works presented in the Sporck theater were. Composer like Giovanni Porta, Tomaso Albinoni Francesco Gasparini, and Antonio Vivaldi dominated, while fashionable Neapolitans such as Vinci, Porpora, or Hasse were represented almost not at all. A large number of the Denzio productions were pastiches of arias, often by several different composers, assembled into operas based on librettos that Antonio Denzio concocted

---

[5]This is confirmed in a letter of Count Sporck to Count Johann Wilhelm von Thürheim dated August 16, 1724. Copies are preserved among the Sporck copybooks in Prague, Státní Ústřední Archiv, manuscript series A, inventory nos. 485 and 486.

[6]The bitter dispute between the two impresarios that resulted in Peruzzi's ouster from the operation of the Sporck theater is detailed in the large number of documents contained in SCM 1724/XI/d/7.

[7]A complete evaluation of the origins of the Sporck theater repertory is provided in Freeman, "The Opera Theater," pp. 101–46.

or adapted from earlier Venetian versions, or on torsos of complete operas with many arias replaced. As we shall see, Antonio Vivaldi's operas seemed to have been one of the most favored sources for these substitute arias. These conditions were in general the result of the slender finances of the Denzio company, which did not permit the commission of large numbers of new works of the ability to purchase scores representative of the latest operatic styles.

Considering the difficult finances, it seems remarkable that Antonio Denzio could have assembled such an illustrious and experienced group of performers for eleven seasons of opera in Prague.[8] They included Anna Maria Giusti, Maria Catterina Negri, Antonio Maria Laurenti, Anna Cosimi, and Giovanni Dreyer, along with some less well-known singers for minor roles. But whether famous or obscure, the singers Denzio engaged for Prague, year after year, had, for the most part, been associated with one another in Italy through an extensive network of collaboration in earlier productions, quite frequently in productions for which Antonio Vivaldi had been either composer or impresario, sometimes both. Vivaldi's assistance in helping to procure these singers is the first area in which his connections with the Sporck theater is firmly documented. A report of Antonio Denzio dated February 20, 1725, whose rediscovery and contents I announced in a paper delivered at the international musicological conference of the 1986 Prague Spring Festival, states that Vivaldi was responsible for negotiating the engagement of several female singers for the Sporck theater during its second season of 1725–1726.[9] One may well be surprised to see a composer such as Antonio Vivaldi engaging in this sort of traffic in singers, but in fact, Vivaldi was at this time in the middle of one of his most active periods as an impresario producing a large number of works at the Teatro Sant'Angelo in Venice. Since Denzio had appeared as a singer in several of Vivaldi's operatic productions of the 1710's as did his wife Elisabetta,[10] it would not be surprising that Vivaldi might have been willing to perform this type of service for Antonio Denzio.

---

[8]Biographical information concerning the singers who appeared in the Sporck theater can be found in Ibid, pp. 117–212, and Maria Skalick, "Die Sänger der italienischen Oper in Prag 1724–1734 (Materialen aus den Libretti des Graf F.A. Sporckschen Operntheaters)," *De musica disputationes Pragensis* II (Prague: 1974), pp. 147–69.

[9]The original, preserved in SČM 1725/II/d/24 is transcribed in Freeman, "The Opera Theater," 289–91. A copy is also preserved in Prague, Státní Ústřední Archiv, manuscript series A, inventory no. 486, pp. 702–4.

[10]See Anna Laura Bellina, Bruno Brizi, and Maria Grazia Pensa, *I libretti vivaldiani* (Florence: 1982), nos. 12.a, 32.1, 37, 38.1 and 52.

The connection between Denzio and Vivaldi revealed in this document may thus go far toward offering an explanation as to how Denzio was able to attract such excellent singers for the Sporck theater during the remainder of the 1720's without ever having to travel back to Italy. There is, in fact, considerable circumstantial evidence to suggest not only that Vivaldi continued to send singers to Prague, but also that Sporck theater singers were sent back to Italy for Vivaldi's use.

In the case of the singer Lorenzo Moretti, for example, who sang in Prague from autumn of 1724 until spring of 1726,[11] it is very interesting to note that he was engaged at the Teatro Sant'Angelo in Venice in the autumn of 1726 immediately after his departure from Prague.[12] Vivaldi was the impresario of the Teatro Sant'Angelo during the 1726–1727 season, and two of his operas, *Dorilla in Tempe* and *Farnace*, were performed there at this time.[13] The singer Angela Capoano, who appeared in the Venetian productions of *Dorilla in Tempe* and *Farnace*,[14] was engaged in the Sporck theater immediately after her appearances in the Teatro Sant'Angelo. A connection with Vivaldi is especially likely since two of the arias in her Sporck theater roles were taken from *Dorilla in Tempe* and *Farnace*. It is possible that Capoano was traded by Vivaldi for the singer Maria Catterina Negri, who appeared in three operas of Antonio Vivaldi in the Teatro Sant'Angelo in Venice immediately after her departure from Prague at the end of the 1726–27 season.[15] Vivaldi was the impresario in this theater during the 1727–28 season as well.[16] Other notable singers in the Sporck theater during the late 1720's, such as Antonio Maria Laurenti, Francesco Braganti, Antonio Gaspari, and Margherita Gualandi, also appeared in Vivaldi's operas at one time or another, and Vivaldi's assistance may have been used to attract these singers to Prague also, even though they did not appear in the Teatro Sant'Angelo just before their arrivals in Prague.

---

[11]Skalick, "Die Sänger," and Freeman, "The Opera Theater," pp. 295–359, list all roles of Sporck theater singers.
[12]See Taddeao Wiel, *I teatri musicali veneziani del settecento* (Venice: 1897; rpt. Leipzig: 1979), nos. 250, 252 and 255; and Bellina, *I libretti vivaldiani*, nos. 16.1 and 18.1.
[13]See Reinhard Strohm, "Vivaldi's Career as an Opera Producer," *Essays on Handel and Italian Opera* (Cambridge: 1985), pp. 131 and 154–55.
[14]See Bellina, *I libretti vivaldiani*, nos. 16.1 and 18.1.
[15]Ibid, nos. 18.2, 36.1 and 40.
[16]See Strohm, "Vivaldi's Career as an Opera Producer," pp. 131–2 and 154–55.

One suspects rather strongly that the decline in the calibre of Sporck theater singers beginning in 1729 may have been prompted at least in part by the loss of Antonio Vivaldi as an agent. After the spring of 1728, Vivaldi temporarily ceased his activities as an impresario and would not have been available to help engage singers for the 1729–30 season in Prague, the first in which a noticeable decline in the artistic stature of Sporck theater singers is apparent. From this time until the dissolution of the Denzio company in 1735, the Sporck theater generally had to rely on singers who were already active in the central European region.[17]

Vivaldi's purely musical connections with the Sporck theater can be divided into two areas: performances of complete operas attributed to him in the Sporck theater librettos and the presence of aria texts in many other Sporck theater librettos apparently borrowed from miscellaneous Vivaldi operas. The complete operas attributed to Vivaldi are listed in Table One and are six in number: *La tirannia castigata* (1727), *Farnace* and *Argippo* (1730), *Alvilda regina de' Goti* (1731) and *Doriclea* and *Dorilla in Tempe* (1732). Of these six, earlier Italian performances are known for only three, *Farnace*, *Dorilla in Tempe*, and *Doriclea*. *Farnace* and *Dorilla in Tempe* were both performed in the Teatro Sant'Angelo in Venice during the 1726–27 operatic season, whereas *Doriclea* is a version, with new title, of the opera *La constanza trionfante* (1716), an opera in which both Antonio and Elisabetta Denzio appeared in the original Venetian production.

The alterations seen in the Sporck theater productions of these three Vivaldi operas appear to have been a function of the isolation of the Sporck theater from the Italian operatic world, its principal source of singers and repertory. In particular, this isolation meant that it was impossible for the impresario to engage singers on a temporary basis if a certain voice type were required for a specific opera. The singers engaged for a season could not be substituted, and opera frequently had to be altered to fit the requirements of the Denzio company.

The biggest problem that Denzio faced was a chronic shortage of male sopranos. He could often get around the problem through the expedient of transvestite roles, but if their were not enough women available, castrato roles had to be eliminated or transformed into tenor roles. In the Sporck theater production of *Farnace*, for example, the castrato role of Gilade was transformed into a tenor role by the substitution of all of the arias and the addition of new recitative. In *Doriclea*, the castrato role of Olderico was

---

[17]This phenomenon is documented in Freeman, "The Opera Theater," pp. 295–359.

eliminated entirely, and because his character was so intimately bound up with that of his lover Eumena, her role had to be jettisoned as well. The elimination of their arias necessitated the addition of several new scenes, which served to expand the role of the title character Doriclea and her conflict with the evil character Artabano. The Sporck theater was very fortunate in having at its disposal an impresario like Antonio Denzio, who was a gifted librettist in his own right. It would appear that about a dozen of the Sporck theater librettos were expressly written for Prague by Antonio Denzio,[18] and his talents were naturally very valuable when operatic plots needed to be altered to suit the capabilities of the Sporck theater company.

Denzio's abilities as a librettist and arranger of operatic pastiches is also evident in the three other Vivaldi productions, the most remarkable achievement undoubtedly the Sporck theater production of *La tirannia castigata* in 1726. It is well known that early eighteenth-century impresarios would assemble new operatic productions by gathering miscellaneous arias, often by many different composers, and fitting them into dramatic contexts different from those in which the arias originally appeared. *La tirannia castigata*, however, is a type of operatic pastiche almost without precedent in the early eighteenth century, in which the arias of just one work, Antonio Vivaldi's *La costanza trionfante* (1716) were rearranged and altered textually by Antonio Denzio to fit a completely different libretto with entirely different characters. In all, only five of the arias and choruses in *La costanza trionfante* were left unused.

The Sporck theater production of Vivaldi's *Alvilda regina de' Goti*, on the other hand, is a more conventional operatic pastiche in which the arias and choruses were drawn from several operas, specifically Antonio Vivaldi's *L'inganno triofante in amore* (1725), *Dorilla in Tempe* (1726) and *Rosilena ed Oronta* (1728). In the case of *Argippo*, however, only four of its arias have readily apparent models in earlier works of Vivaldi, and since Vivaldi is not known to have set the text earlier, there has been speculation that it was arranged specifically for the Sporck theater with Vivaldi present for the performance.[19]

---

[18]Denzio's authorship of the following four dramas is documented in librettos or *Statthaalterei* documents: *La caduta di Baiazetto* (spring, 1728), *La pravit castogata* (Lent, 1730), *Santa Maria Egizziaca* (Lent, 1734) and *Praga nascente da Libussa e Primislao*. Other dramas likely to have been written by Denzio include *La fortunata sventura* (spring, 1725), *La reit fortunata* (spring, 1726), *Amore trionfante* (carnival, 1729), *Sansone* (Lent, 1729), *Gli amori delusi* (carnival, 1730), *Gli amori amari* (carnival, 1732), *La bilance infallibile* (Lent?, 1733 and *Ermelinda* (carnival, 1734).

[19]Strohm, "Vivaldi's Career as an Opera Producer," pp. 132 and 156.

In addition to the complete operas performed in the Sporck theater, there can be little question that a great number of individual Vivaldi arias found their way into Sporck theater operas attributed anonymously or attributed to others, the vast majority of which have been completely unsuspected by Vivaldi scholars. Only two of these arias are attributed to Vivaldi in the Sporck theater librettos, both in the margins of the libretto for the second Sporck theater production, *L'innocenza qiustificata* (1725). Vivaldi scholars have long suspected also that the first Sporck theater production, *Orlando furioso* (1724), contains at least some arias of Vivaldi despite the unequivocal attribution of the music in the libretto to Antonio Bioni, a minor Venetian composer who was attached to the Denzio company during its first season.[20]

But aside from these two instances of aria borrowings known to Vivaldi scholarship, it would appear from an analysis of the Sporck theater librettos that Antonio Denzio frequently attempted to fill out his productions with Vivaldi arias, often altering the texts slightly, or even quite substantially, to make them suitable for the new dramatic contexts into which they were inserted. These borrowings are listed in Tables Two and Three. Since no music survives from any Sporck theater production, and little music survives even from the original Vivaldi productions, it is not possible to confirm positively whether or not the same music was used, but the patterns of borrowing that can be observed in the Sporck theater repertory strongly speak against the possibility that the presence of these texts in the Sporck librettos is coincidental. The text borrowings appear to have been drawn repeatedly from only a small repertory of Vivaldi operas and do not have the character of a random sampling. The operas favored in the 1720's were *Arsilda regina di Ponto* (1716), *Armida al campo d'Egitto* (1718) and *Candace* (1720). In about the year 1730, there appears to have been a fresh transmission of Vivaldi's music, and the operas *L'inganno trionfante in amore* (1725), *La fede tradita e vendicata* (1726), *Siroe re di Persia* (1727) and *Rosilena ed Oronta* (1728) became favorite sources of arias in the Sporck theater. Undoubtedly, Antonio Denzio had either complete scores available to him on which he could draw freely, or else aria collections that included arias from the Vivaldi operas mentioned. The arias listed in Table

---

[20]See Bellina, *I libretti vivaldiani*, no. 38.4; Eric Cross, *The Late Operas of Antonio Vivaldi 1727–1738* I (Ann Arbor: 1980), pp. 242–3; Brockpäler, *Handbuch*, p. 317; and Reinhard Strohm, *Italienischen Opernarien des frühen Settecento*, Analecta Musicologica 16/II (Cologne: 1976), p. 257. The issue of the presence of Vivaldi's music in this production is thoroughly discussed in Freeman, "The Opera Theater," pp. 178–86. See also "*Orlando Furioso* in the Bohemian Lands: Was Vivaldi's Music Really Used?" *Informazioni e studi vivaldiani* 14 (1993): 51–73.

Three, which are even more likely to represent the use of Vivaldi's music, appear to have been transmitted by individual singers directly from previous roles in Vivaldi's operas.

All of these practices of assembling new operas out of old arias with new words fitted to existing music naturally raises questions about the dramatic integrity of the resulting pastiches and about current standards and conceptions of text-music relationship. A thorough treatment of this question, even within the context of the Sporck theater, would entail the analysis of dozens of librettos, clearly not a task for this presentation. However, a representative example is illuminating.

Given below is the text of "Armata di furore," an aria sung in Vivaldi's *Armida al campo d'Egitto* in 1718 and then partially retexted in order to fit into the Sporck theater production of *Il confronto dell'amor coniugale* of 1727.[21] In the original context, the title character Armida vents her fury at her false lover Emireno, who has just rejected her, and whom she wishes, at this point, to die in battle:

> Armata di furore
> D'un finto amore in campo
> Co' vezzi, co' prieghi
> Io vo, che si pieghi
> Quell'alma superba.
> Che un simulato ardore
> All'ira avvampo,
> Il vanto del suo pianto
> Ancora serba.

In the Prague opera, the character Cesonia, wife of the deranged emperor Caligula, expresses her anger at the news that her husband would like to repudiate her, just as he had his first wife. Cesonia's anger, however, is directed at her rival Messalina, and the text of Vivaldi's aria was altered accordingly:

> Armata di furore
> Sarò crudel Megera:
> Nè pianti, nè prieghi
> Faran, che si pieghi
> Quest'alma sdegnata.
> Il mio sprezzato amore
> Farà vendetta fiera
> Della rivale altera
> Ed ostinata.

---

[21]The source of the music for this example is Turin Biblioteca Nazionale Universitaria, manuscript Fo 38.

One reason why this or any aria in the appropriate style could be transferred from one to another opera is that the text expresses a generalized passion that might arise in many typical *opera seria* situations. The infrequent reference to a specific situation could be changed without altering the syllable count in each line or the rhyme scheme. If the general passion implied by the second text is essentially the same as the first, then the new text should correspond with the affections of the original music pretty well. In this case, the music, given as Example One, suggests fury, an active, expansive emotion occasioned by pain, according to the early eighteenth-century theories of affections; it is characterized by rapid tempo, active rhythm, many wide intervals, loud dynamics, octave doubling, energetic, syllabic delivery of text, but minor key, and episodes of dissonant harmony and mild chromaticism.

The connections between music and text here are more subtle than the expression of a general affect, however, and the new text conforms to the music with surprising precision. In both texts, lines 1 and 2 contain the first thesis: a metaphor involving battle, which is reflected in the recurring opening motive suggestive, perhaps, of a field-trumpet signal. Lines 3 and 4 in both texts, however, contain an antithesis of this, referring to charms, or tears, and entreaties—passions adequately reflected in the music that sets these lines, in measures 13–16, with much lighter texture, absence of the basses, softer dynamics (as marked in measures 3–6 of the opening ritornello), conjunct rather than disjunct melodic motion, ana a chromatically descending tetrachord in the viola line. Notice that even the anaphora of the first text, with two phrases of three syllables each ("co' vezzi, co' prieghi"), is reflected in the alternation of two complementary motives in the music (measures 13–16), and the substitute text likewise preserves this musical-rhetorical relationship with the parallel line ("n pianti, n prieghi"). Then the synthesis that follows the antithesis, "Quell'alma superba," line 5 in the first text, is set to music that combines the melodic leaps of the first phrase, the thesis, with the syncopated figure of the antithesis. In this case, the substitute text parallels the original, replacing the key word "superba" with a comparable word, "sdegnata." The parallels are continued in the "B" section of the da capo aria also.

1	Armata di furore	1	Armata di furore
2	D'un finto amore in campo	2	Sarò crudel Megera;
3	Co' vezzi, co' prieghi	3	Nè pianti, nè prieghi
4	Io vò, che si pieghi	4	Faran, che si pieghi
5	Quell'alma superba.	5	Quest'alma sdegnata.
6	D'un simulato ardore	6	Il mio sprezzato amore
7	Al sdegno d'onde avvampo,	7	Farà vendetta fiera
8	Il vanto del suo pianto	8	Della rivale altera
9	Ancora serba.	9	Ed ostinata.

1	Armed with fury	1	Armed with fury
2	at a false love within the camp,	2	I will be a cruel Megera:
3	with charms, with entreaties,	3	neither tears nor entreaties
4	I want to wound	4	will suffice when
5	that haughty soul.	5	this angry soul is wounded.
6	Feigned ardor,	6	My rejected love
7	which ignites my wrath,	7	will have its proud revenge
8	in the guise of his tears	8	on the haughty
9	is nonetheless contained.	9	and stubborn rival.

In the end, it seems, perhaps, a matter of little significance whether Antonio Denzio fit new texts to Vivaldi's music, or whether Vivaldi did it himself according to Denzio's specifications. They certainly collaborated very closely, sharing the roles of impresario, contractor of singers, arranger of operas, and provider of materials. In the course of the collaboration, Vivaldi may have even traveled to Prague.[22]

The circumstantial evidence that has been raised to suggest a visit rests most importantly on a request of Vivaldi's father in September of 1729 to be released from his duties at the Cathedral of St. Mark's in Venice in order to accompany his son to Germany, a geographical expression that could well have included Bohemia at that time. Other whereabouts for Vivaldi are unknown during much of the years 1730

---

[22]See Michael Talbot, *Vivaldi* (London: 1978), pp. 78–9 for an excellent brief discussion of this possibility.

and 1731, and it is known that Vivaldi preferred to be present for performances of his operas. Five of the six Vivaldi operas presented in the Sporck theater were produced during the period in which he was most likely to have visited Prague.

There is also another very intriguing piece of evidence for this hypothesis. Three instrumental compositions in Turin bear a dedication to "his Excellency Count Wirtbij." There seems little doubt but that this must refer to Count Johann Joseph von Vrtby, who, as Supreme Burgrave in Prague, was the principal member of the Bohemian *Statthalterei* from 1712 until his death in 1734. Unfortunately, the small number of surviving documents associated with the Vrtby household yield no information on Vivaldi's relationship with the count,[23] and neither of the chief sources of our information concerning the operation of the Sporck theater—the Sporck correspondence and the records of the Bohemian *Statthalterei*—offer any confirmation of a personal visit. Thus, the possibility of a personal visit is still an open question.

Vivaldi's extensive musical connections nonetheless illuminate activities associated with Vivaldi's career as an impresario never before suspected. Particularly intriguing is the service Vivaldi provided Denzio in procuring singers who were not involved with Vivaldi's own operatic productions. The documentation of this practice leaves open the possibility that he may have provided this service commonly to other impresarios. The use of unattributed Vivaldi arias in Sporck theater librettos certainly invites speculation that a vast body of Vivaldi's arias were disseminated in the early eighteenth century operatic productions without attribution to the composer that still remain undetected. Close scrutiny of repertories from other operatic centers may well yield similar widespread borrowing. There is no reason to believe that the Sporck theater was exceptional in this regard. The new information presented here concerning Vivaldi's connections with the Sporck theater thus demonstrates that the study of even an isolated outpost of the Venetian operatic world such as such as Prague can provide many interesting insights into the operations of Italian operatic production in the early eighteenth century, It is surely no wonder that the Sporck theater is a source of such great fascination to scholars of Vivaldi's music.

---

[23]These documents are described in Jiří Tywoniak, *Vrtbovský* rodinný archiv (Prague: 1963), pp. 1–3.

TABLE ONE
Sporck Theater Operas Attributed to Vivaldi

la terannia castigata (carnival, 1726)

Farnace (spring, 1730)

Argippo (autumn, 1730)

Alvilda regina de' Goti (spring, 1731)

Doriclea (carnival, 1732)*Dorilla in Tempe* (spring, 1732)

+ two arias in the pastiche *Linnocanza giustificata* (carnival, 1725)

TABLE TWO
Possible Borrowings of Vivaldi Arias in Sporck Theater Productions Not Attributed to Vivaldi

From *Ottone in villa* (Vincenza, 1713):

"Frema pur, si lagna Roma" (parodied in the anonymous *Arrenione* of 1726)

From *Orlando finto pazzo* (Venice, 1714):

"Sentire che nel sen" (parodied in Matteo Luchini's *Amore trionfante* of 1729)

From *Nerone fatto Cesare* (Venice, 1715):

"Comincia à naufragar" (parodied in Francesco Feo's *L'amor tirannico* of 1727)

From *Nerone fatto cesare* (Brescia, 1716):

"Questa sorte a quel ch'io sento" (used in the anonymous *Il tradimento tradito* of 1732)

From *La costanza trionfante* (Venice, 1716):

"Un baccio un vezzo, un riso" (parodied in Antonio Bioni's *Armida abbandonata*)"Viva l'amor, viva la pace" (Coro) (parodied in Antonio Costantini's *Impermestra* of 1731)

From *Arsilda regina de Ponto* (Venice, 1716):

"Fingi d'aver un cor" (used in the anonymous *Tullo Ostilio* of 1727)

"Dove sei bel volto amato" (parodied in the anonymous *Il confronto dell'amor coniugale* of 1727)

"Se un cor soffrir saprà" (used in the anonymous *Tullo Ostilio* of 1727)

"Ancor la tortorella" (parodied in the anonymous *Il più fedel fra vassali* of 1733)

"Son come farfalletta" (used in the anonymous *Tullo Ostilio* of 1727)"Di Carridi li vortici ondosi" (used in the anonymous *Achille in Sciro* of 1727)

From *L'incoronazione di Dario* (Venice, 1717):
> "Fermo scoglio in mezzo al mare" (parodied in the anonymous *Il confronto dell' amor coniugale* of 1727)

From *Il vinto trionfante del vincitore* (Venice, 1717):
> "Son frà l'onde e son frà i venti" (parodied in the anonymous *Il tradimento traditor di se stesso* of 1727)

From *Armida al campo d'Egitto* (Venice, 1718):
> "Sento brillarmi in sen" (used in Giuseppe Boniventi's *Venceslao* of 1726)
>
> "Armata di furore" (parodied in the anonymous *Il confronto dell'amor coniugale* of 1727)

From *Candace* (Mantua, 1720):
> "Si bel volto che v'adoro" (used in the anonymous *Tullo Ostilio* of 1727) "Voglio sperar" (parodied in Francesco Gasparini's *La fede tradita e vendicata* of 1727)

From *Giustino* (Rome, 1724):
> "La cervetta timidetta" (parodied in Matteo Luchini's *Amore trionfante* of 1729 and the anonymous *Praga nascente da Libussa e Primislao* of 1734)

From *Artabano re de' Parti* (Mantua, 1725):
> "Sì che ti renderai" (parodied in Francesco Feo's *L'amor tirannico* of 1727)

From *L'inganno trionfante in amore* (Venice, 1725):
> "Al balenar del brando" (used in the anonymous *La verità nell'inganno* of 1730)
>
> "Tra le catene ancor" (parodied in Tomaso Albinoni's *Merope* of 1731)
>
> "Se ingrata nube" (used in the anonymous *Sidonio* of 1732)

From *La fede tradita e vendicata* (Venice, 1726):
> "Cor di figlia, e cor d'amante" (used in Antonio Costantini's *Impermestra* of 1731)
>
> "Quando amore fa preda d'un core" (parodied in the anonymous *Il tradimento tradito* of 1732)

From *Cunegonda* (Venice, 1726):
> "Se avvien ch'io mora" (parodied in Tomaso Albinoni's *Didone* of 1731)

From *Dorilla in Tempe* (Venice, 1726):
> "Al mio amore il tuo responda" (parodied in the anonymous *Aristeo* of 1729)

From *Siroe re di Persia* (Venice, 1727):
> "Se tu mi vuoi felice" (parodied in the anonymous *Penelope la casta* of 1730)
> "Se al ciglio lusinghiero" (parodied in the anonymous *Penelope la casta* of 1730)
> "Vedeste mai sul prato" (parodied in the anonymous *Penelope la casta* of 1730)
> "Frà sdegno ed amore" (parodied in Giovanni Porta's *La costanza combattuta in amore* of 1728 and the anonymous *Penelope la casta* of 1730) "Torrente cresciuto" (parodied in the anonymous *Penelope la casta* of 1730)

From *Orlando* (Venice, 1727):
> "Benche nasconda" (parodied in Antonio Costantini's *Impermestra* of 1731) "Qual candido fiore" (parodied in Carlo Francesco Pollarolo's *Publio Cornelio Scipione* of 1729)

From *Rosilena ed Oronta* (Venice, 1728):
> "Furibonda a me dinante" (used in the anonymous *La pravità castigata* of 1730) "O placa il tuo furor" (parodied in the anonymous *Il più fedel fra vassali* of 1732) "Leggo in quel torvo aspetto" (parodied in the anonymous *Penelope la casta* of 1730)

TABLE THREE
Arias Sung by Sporck Theater Singers in Earlier Vivaldi Operas

For Angela Capoano:
> "Giace languente" (performed in Vivaldi's *Dorilla in Tempe* of 1726 and Francesco Gasparini's *La fede tradita e vendicata* in the Sporck theater in 1727) "Langue misero quel valore" (performed in Vivaldi's *Farnace* of 1727 and the anonymous *Il tradimento traditor di se stesso* in the Sporck theater in 1727)

For Margherita Gualandi:
> "Non deesi prestar fede" (performed in Vivaldi's *Ottone in villa* of 1729 and the anonymous *Praga nascente da Libussa e Primislao* of 1734)

For Maria Monza:
> "Se ricerco un faggio, o un fiore" (performed in Vivaldi's *Ottone in villa* of 1729 and the anonymous *Praga nascente da Libussa e Primislao* of 1734)

For Lorenzo Moretti:
> "Darà della sua fede" (original attributed to Vivaldi in the Sporck theater production of the pastiche *L'innocenza giustificata* in 1725; repeated in the anonymous *Nel perdono la vendetta* of 1735)

Example: Complete score of "Armata di furore" with two texts

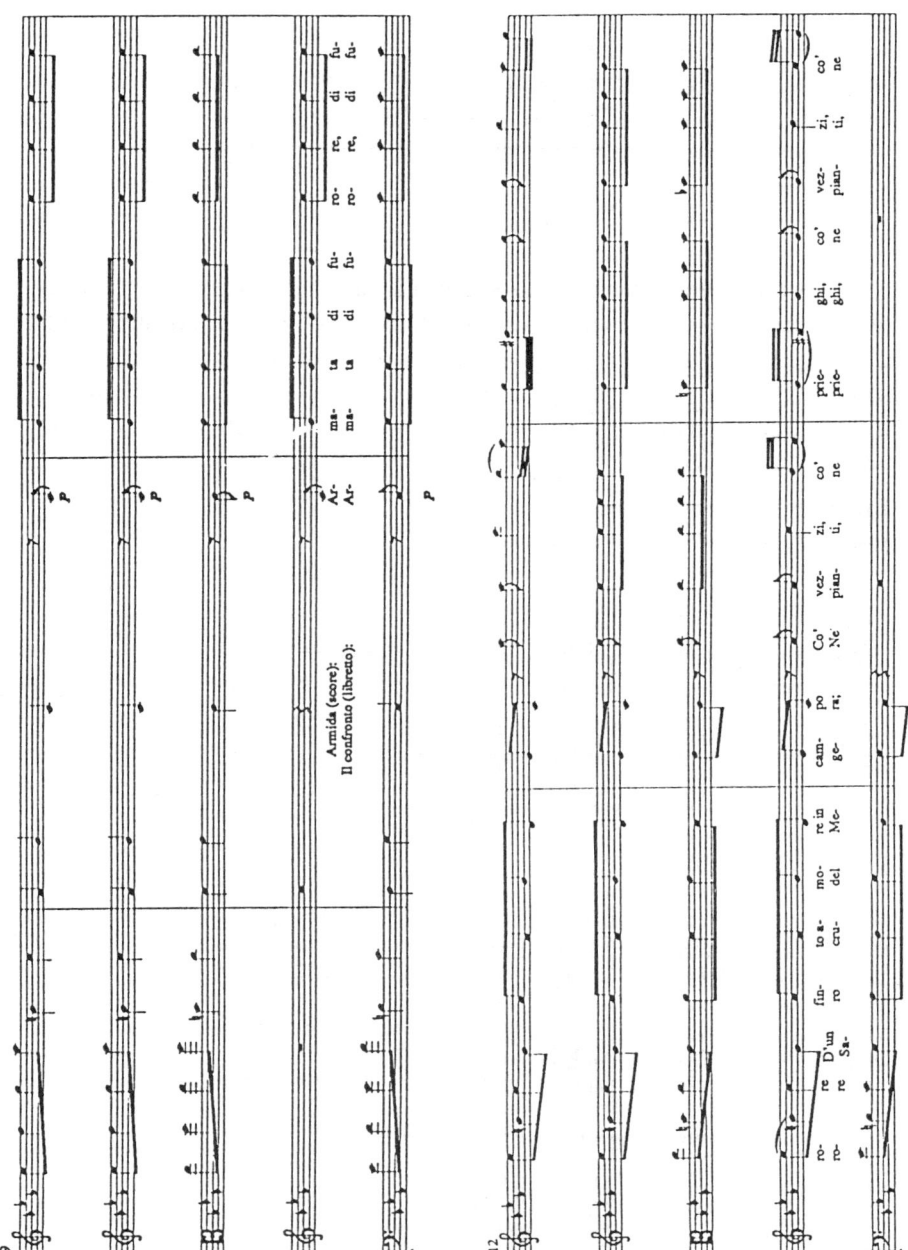

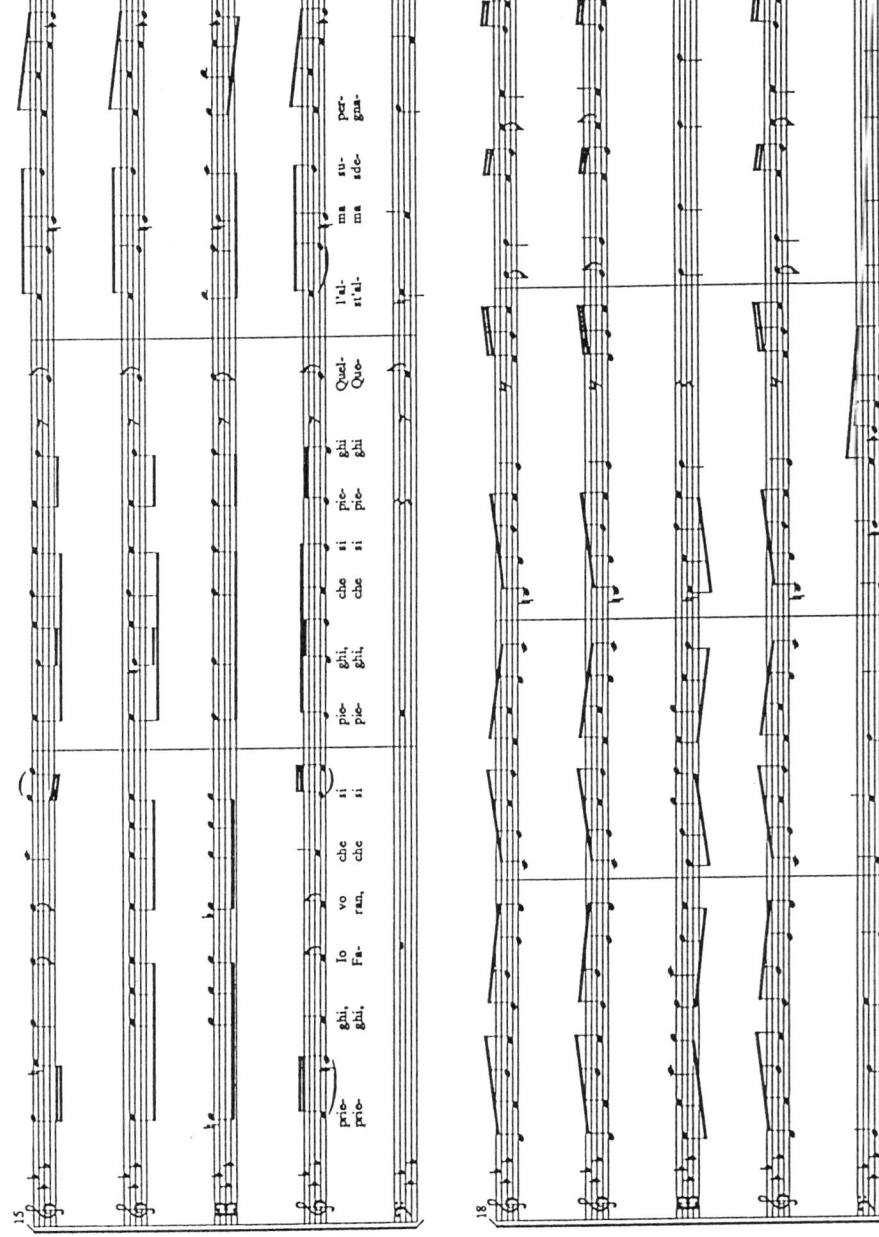

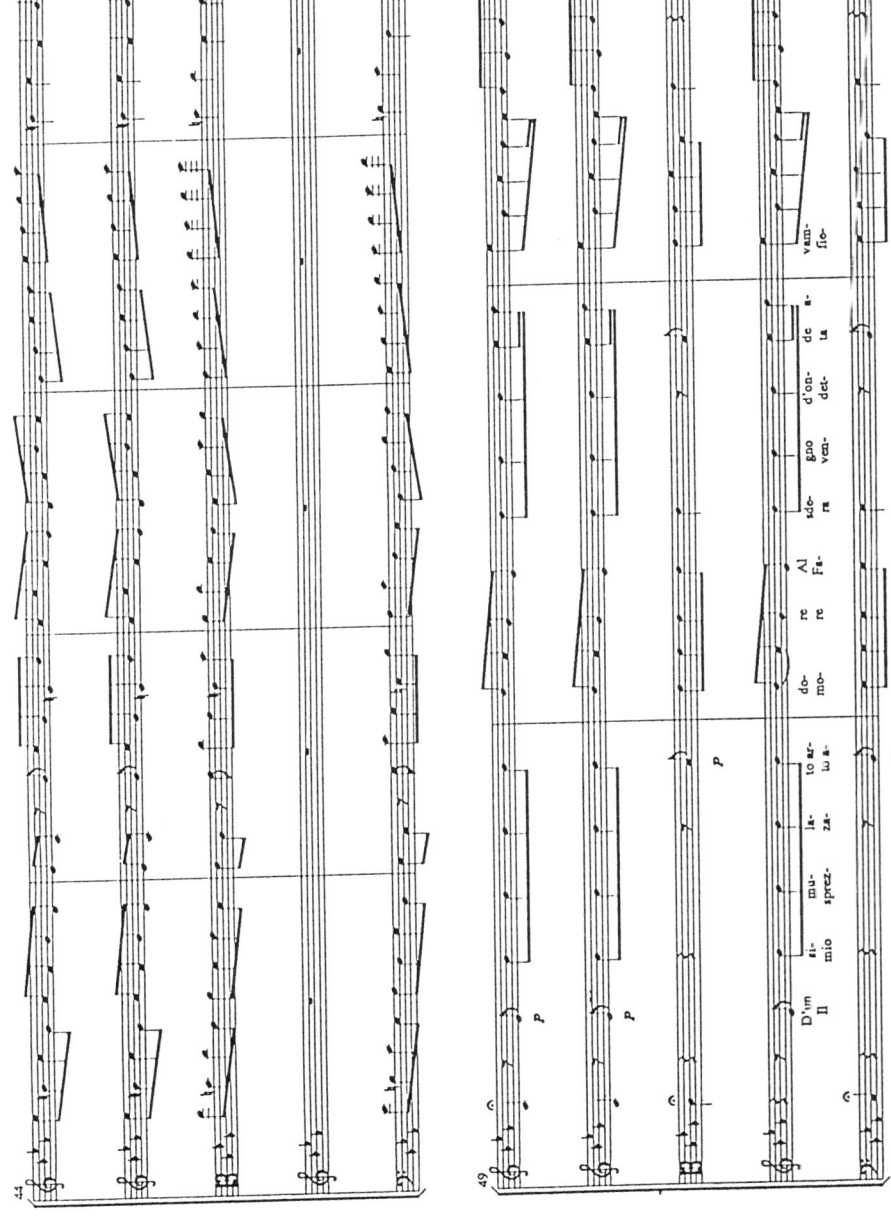

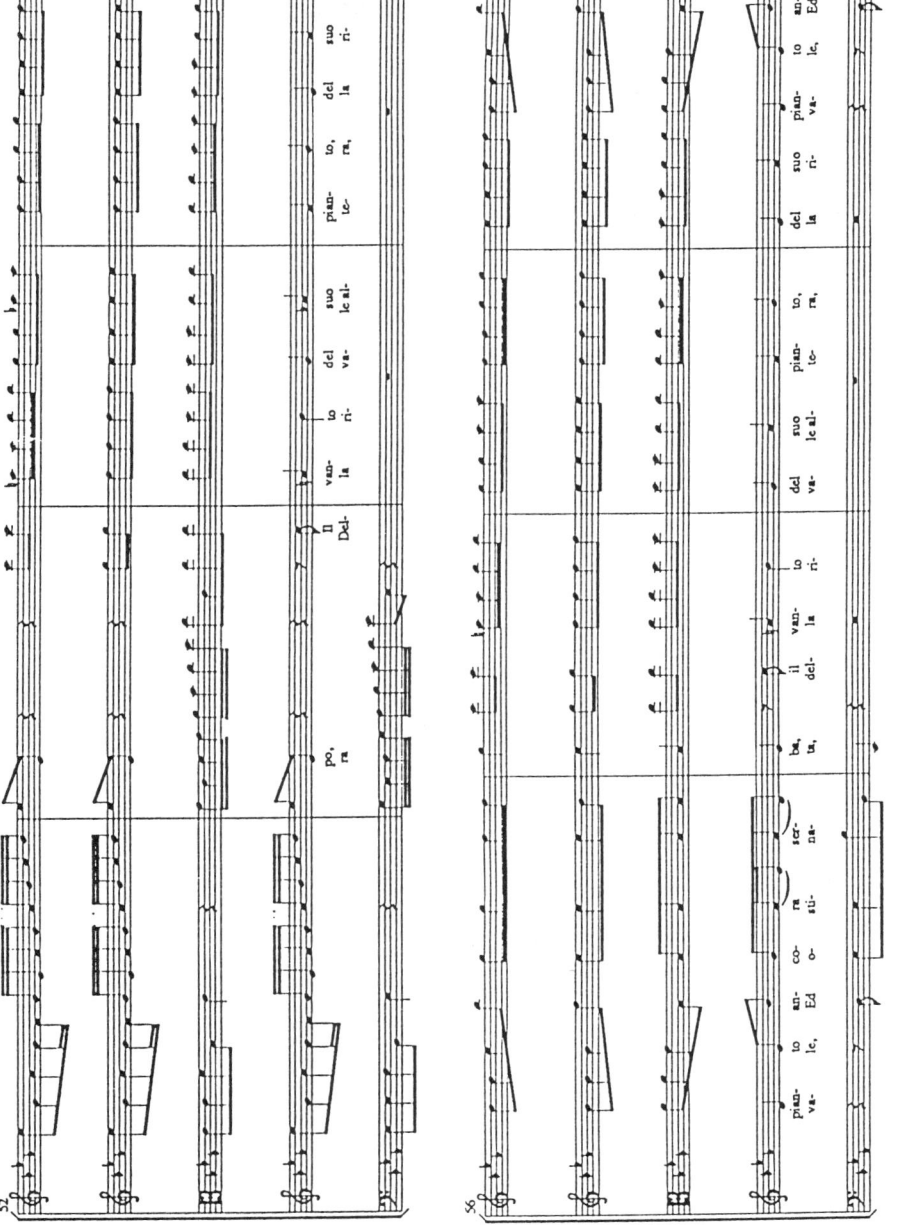

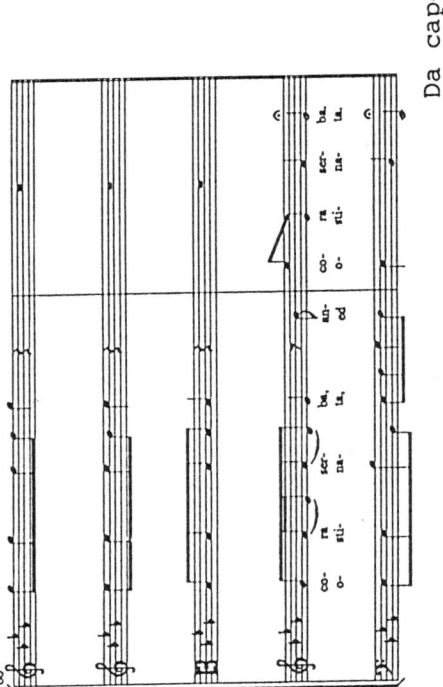

Da capo

Jan Dismas Zelenka's Setting of Psalm 150: Chvalte Boha Silného

Janice Stockigt

Introduction

Among the lists of liturgical compositions of Jan Dismas Zelenka (1679–1745) one work is unique. It is a setting of what appears to be the Kralická Bible version of Psalm 150. Not only is this work remarkable in the context of Zelenka's output, since all his religious works are usually setting of Latin texts (with the exception of the three Italian oratorios), but in the context of the repertoire of the Catholic Court Church in Dresden where most of Zelenka's works were deposited, it appears to be an oddity.

In the output of any composer unexplained works invariably give rise to speculation. This work is no exception. In the context of Zelenka's life and work, clarified only in recent years, the specific religious and political positions of his patrons would appear to exclude the need for a setting of this translation of this psalm. The present study approaches the work primarily from the context into which Zelenka placed this composition, his *Inventarium*. Viewed from this point, it is possible to form an hypothesis concerning the date of the work and to speculate as to Zelenka's reason for placing this Protestant composition into the repertoire of the Dresden Catholic Court Church.

Zelenka in Dresden

Zelenka's presence in Dresden is first recorded in 1711, not as a composer but as a player of the violone. He arrived there soon after the establishment of the Catholic Court Church (1708), a necessity due to the conversion of the Elector of Saxony, August II (*der Starke*) to Catholicism. This move that enabled him to become the successful candidate for the crown of neighboring Poland (1697). The influx of Polish Catholic nobility to Dresden, the many Italians and French present at the Court and the royal position of Friedrich August I, as he became upon his coronation, demanded such an establishment. The Court theatre was transformed into a Royal Chapel and a set of regulations drawn up.[1] On Maundy Thursday, April 5th, 1708, the church was inaugurated. Although most of the *Kapellknaben* associated with this church had been recruited in Bohemia,[2] and instruments, including a "Grosse Bassgeige" had been purchased for use in musical services of this church, it does not appear that Zelenka's position in Dresden was formally associated with the Catholic Court Church until at least ca. 1731.[3] For almost twenty years he was listed and paid as a player of the violone in the Court Orchestra.

It is certain that from ca. 1716 until 1719 Zelenka was in Vienna as a student of Fux. During part of that period the Electoral Prince of Saxony, also a convert to Catholicism, was in Vienna forging links between the Imperial House of Austria and the Court of Dresden. In 1719 he married Maria Josepha, daughter of Joseph I of Austria. As Electoral Princess and later, as Electress of Saxony and Queen of Poland, Maria Josepha's piety and musical tastes were to have a powerful influence on the music of Dresden Catholic Court Church. In the same year, 1719. Zelenka returned to Dresden taking with him a collection of music that was later to enrich the repertoire of the Court Church. It should be noted that parts of this collection became important to Zelenka in later years as a source of compositional inspiration through reworkings and revisions.[4]

In 1716 Johann David Heinichen had been engaged in Venice as *Kapellmeister* to the Dresden Court. Until his death, part of Heinichen's

---

[1] "Reglements du Roi pour l'Eglise et Chapelle Royale, ouverte aux Catholiques" 1708. These regulations are discussed by Wolfgang Horn, *Die Dresdner Hofkirchenmusik 1720–1745* (Stuttgart: Carus Verlag, 1987) Chapter 2, Parts 2 and 3 and by Moritz Fürstenau, *Zur Geschichte der Musik und des Theaters am Hofe* ... Dresden: 1862. Facs, reprint Leipzig: Peters, 1971) Part II, p. 35. Fürstenau cites the regulations as "Reglements et Ordonnances du Roy pour l'Englise publique et Chappelle royale 1708."

[2] The Institute of Kapellknaben is discussed in both sources given above. Horn, Chapter 2, Part 3 and Fürstenau, Chapter 3. This recruitment of the *Kapellknaben* from Bohemia was necessary because of the lack of Saxon Catholic boys.

[3] I am indebted to Daniel Freeman for drawing my attention to a letter written by Zelenka in ca. 1729 in which Zelenka signed himself as "Giovanni Disma/Zelenka. Compositore/di S: M: Re di Polonia." See Daniel Freeman: "The Opera Theater of Count Franz Anton von Spork in Prague (1724–35)" (Ph.D. diss. University of Illinois, 1987).

[4] *Collectaneorum Musicum Libri Quatuor*. SLB Mus. 1-B–98. A collection of Music by Morales, Frescobaldi, Poglietti, Palestrina, Battiferi, Froberger, Fux, Ragazzi, Bernabei and Zelenka. Jarmil Smolka has pointed out that at least two vocal works attributed to Zelenka are complete or partial reworkings based upon ricercari from Frescobaldi's *Fiori Musicali*. See notes accompanying the recording Jan Dismas Zelenka, *Litaniae Omnium Sanctorum* etc. Cond. Vaclav Neumann and Lubomír Mátl. Soloists, Czech Philharmonic Chorus and Orchestra. Supraphon 1112 4251–53 ZA.

duties involved the musical requirements of the Catholic Court Church. In this he was assisted by Zelenka who, between 1720 and 1730 composed a large part of his entire output, especially between 1725 and 1729, the year of Heinichen's death.[5] Together, Heinichen and Zelenka, through composition and acquisition, established a multi-faceted repertoire to serve the church.

On January 17th, 1726, Zelenka began to catalogue his collection of liturgical music, possibly in expectation of official recognition in the form of an appointment, His *Inventarium*[6] is of inestimable value, not only as a basis for the cataloging of his works and establishment of a chronology, but also in demonstrating the transmission of Catholic liturgical works between Italy, Austria, Bohemia and Saxony. Further, the *Inventarium* provides evidence of Zelenka's significant contribution to the entire repertoire of the Catholic Court Church, verified by later catalogues. In 1731 he was listed in the *Hof- und Staats- Calender* as "Contra-Basso & Compositeur," in 1733 as "Compositeur" and from 1735 as "Kirchen-Composit." In the meantime, Johann Adolf Hasse had been appointed as *Kapellmeister* to the Dresden Court.

The Motet Listings of the *Inventarium*

Under the rubric *Mottetti* in the *Inventarium*, sixteen works are listed. They are given below as they appear on pages 61 and 62. The ZWV (Z) number assigned by Reich,[7] together with the Dresden source and approximate datings are added.[8]

---

[5]Almost all surviving works of Zelenka are held at the music department of the Sächsische Landesbibliothek, Dresden, under the signature Mus. 2358.

[6]*Inventarium rerum Musicarum variorum Authorum Ecclesiae Serventium* . . . SLB Bibl.-Arch. III Hb 787ᵈ. See Jaroslav Buzga "Zelenkas Musikinvertar aus der Katholischen Schlosskapelle in Dresden," *Fontes Artis Musicae* (31–4 October-December 1984), pp. 198–206. It should be noted here that an important study by Wolfgang Horn and Thomas Kohlhase is due to be published late 1988: Zelenka-Dokumentation. *Jan Dismas Zelenkas Kirchenmusikalisches Repertoire an der Dresdner Hofkirche Quellen und Materialien zu Zelenkas Leben und Werk* (Weisbaden: Breitkopf and Härtel).

[7]Wolfgang Reich, *Jan Dismas Zelenka Thematisch-systematisches Verzeichnis der musikalischen Werke (ZWV)*. Heft 6. Studien und Materialien zür Musikgeschichte Dresdens. (Dresden: Sächsische Landesbibliothek und Hochschule für Musik "Carl Maria von Weber," 1985). [8]From Reich and Horn.

Table 1

[Key]	[Number]	[Title and Scoring]	Author	Identification
C	1	Proh quos criminis etc. Tenor Solo W:2 Flaut 2, Travers 2, Viola e Basso Cont: NB De Nativitate D:	Z	Z 172 / SLB Mus. 2358-E-34 / 1723/ca.1729
C	2	O quam Suavis de V: Sacramen Ten: Sol: W2 obo 2 ad lib Viol e Bass. Con:	Ariosti	SLB Mus. 2156-E-1 / Zelenka's copy 1722-28
E#	3	O magnú, de Nativitate D. Alto solo W:2, Viola e Basso	Zelen:	Z 171 / SLB Mus. 2358-E-501 / 1723/ca.1728
D	4	Perfice etc. De tempore a 4 W:2 Viola e Basso Con:	Caldara	Missing in Dresden
g	5	Resonate de Martyre à 9 W:2 Viola e Basso Cont:	Mancini	SLB Mus. 2203-E-1
g	6	de Temp: Basso Solo, W:2 Oboe 2 Corni di Cacia 2 Viola et Basso Conti:	Zel:	Z 165 / Missing in Dresden
g	8	Pange lingua à 4 : pro Stationibus Theophorica Stromenti ad libitu	Z	Z 159 / SLB Mus. 2358-E-23 / Missing in Dresden
[c]	7	[deleted] Haec dies à 4 W:2 Viola e B : Conti	[Zelenka]	Z 169? / SLB Mus. 2358-E-21? / ca.1730
a#	9	Gaude Plaude [Gaude Laetare?] Tenor Solo de SS: Trinitate W:2 Oboe 2 ad lib Viol. e Basso Con:	Z	Z 168 / SLB Mus. 2358-E-35 / 17.5.1731
C	10	Guadia mille a 6 CC:2 AA2 Ten: ba: W.2 Viole e Basso	Z	Listed by Reich as a missing or unidentified work
?	11	Quid Statis de B:V:Maria. Basso W.2 Oboe 2 Viola, Trom (?) 2 Tym e Basso cont.	Z	Listed by Reich as a missing or unidentified work

[Key]	[Number]	[Title and Scoring]	Author	Identification
C	12	Mottetto Barbara dira effera! a contralto Solo Wiolini 2 Oboe 2 Viola, Fagotto e Basso Continuo	Z	Z 164 / SLB Mus. 2358-E-36 / ca.1733
D#	13	Huc pastores Alto W.2 Oboe 2 Flauti 2 Viola	Handel	SLB Mus. 2410-D-66a
[G]	14	In turbato Mare irato Sopran Wli 2 Obo 2 Viola e Bass Contin.	Vivaldi	SLB Mus. 2389-E-2
[F]	15	Sum in medio tempestatú Sop W.2, Oboe 2, Viola e Basso Conti:	Vivaldi	SLB Mus. 2389-E-1
?	16	Angeli cementes Sop: Solo.	Hasse	Unclear

In a thematic catalogue of music of the Dresden Court church drawn up in 1765,[9] thought by Reich to be the result of a stock check made at the end of the Seven Year War, five motets of the nine composed and listed by Zelenka in his *Inventarium* are given in the listing of Zelenka's works under the title *Motetti*. They are all solo motets.

Table 2

[Section]	[Location]	[Author / Title / Instrumentation / Incipit (not given here)]	[Score]	[Parts]
13	5	No. 1 Gaude Laetare a Sopr. Solo con Stromenti	-	-
13	6	No. 2 Pro Nativitate Dni O magnum mysterium a Contr. S. con Strom. e Flauti	-	-
13	7	No. 3 Pro Resurrect Dni Barbara diva a Contr. S. con Strom. d Fagti obo e Corni	-	-
13	8	No. 4 Pro quos criminis a Tenore Solo Wni Vla obo e 4 Flauti	-	-
13	9	No. 5 Chwale Boha Sylneno a Basso Solo co Wni oboè et Corni	-	-

---

[9]*Catalogo [thematico] della Musica di Chiesa [catholica in Dresda] composta Da diversi Autori secondo l:Alfabetto* 1765. Now in the Deutschen Staatsbibliothek, Mus. ms. theor. Kat. 186. Many errors are to be found in this catalogue.

In another thematic catalogue (ca.1775)[10] the same set of motets is given. A set of parts to accompany the score of number 5 is not indicated in this later catalogue. The musical incipit given for number 5 is identical in both catalogues, with the absence of articulation marks in that of 1775.

Example. (1765)

In 1861–2 Moritz Fürstenau, in a footnote to the list of Zelenka's vocal compositions, stated that one of the five motets was in the Bohemian language. The instrumentation given by Fürstenau matches that of the catalogues.

> Eine dieser Motetten ist in böhmischer sprache componirt "Chwale Boha sylneho" für eine Bass stimme mit 2 Violinen, Viola, 2 Oboen, 2 Waldhörner und Bass.[11]

The autograph of this motet no longer exists in Dresden. But a copy of the score of a motet *Chvalte Boha silného* is to be found in the National Museum, Prague.[12] No direct evidence exists to link this example with Zelenka's motet *de Temp[ore]*. We are entirely dependent upon secondary sources and the strong circumstantial evidence they provide concerning the scoring. In the article on Zelenka in *New Grove*, Camillo Schoenbaum has incorrectly listed *Chwalte Boha sylného* as also

---

[9]*Catalogo [thematico] della Musica di Chiesa [catholica in Dresda] composta Da diversi Autori secondo l:Alfabetto* 1765. Now in the Deutschen Staatsbibliothek, Mus. ms. theor. Kat. 186. Many errors are to be found in this catalogue.

[10]*Catalog della Musica de Chiesa, composta da diversi Autori Secondo l'Alfabetto. Armaro IIIza., principiando dalla Littera S sino Z con l'aggiunta degl'Autori senza Nome*. The approximate date of this catalogue is given by Reich in the introduction to *Thematisch-systematisches Verzeichnis*, pp. 8–10. This publication is accompanied by a facsimile of the listings of Zelenka's works from this catalogue.

[11]Fürstenau II, p. 78.

[12]The following items are kept in the Narodni Museum, Prague under the siglum XXIV F I:
    1) Score entitled "Chvalte Boha Silného". . . Zelenka
    2) Piano arrangement of the work
    3) parts
The score is undated. The year "1895" is marked at the end of the piano arrangement.
I am indebted to the staff of this library for making a copy of the score availabkle to me in 1984. I acknowledge with gratitude the information on the further sources, provided by Dr. Jana Fojtíková, Chief of the Music Archive there.

existing in England as a setting of *O Sing unto the Lord*.[13] A recording of the motet *Chvalte Boha silného* has recently been released.[14]

Before proceeding to discussion of the Prague copy of Zelenka's setting of Psalm 150, it is necessary to return to the list of *Mottetti* in the *Inventarium* because in that context, it is possible to form an hypothesis concerning the approximate date of this composition and to speculate upon its inclusion in the repertoire of the Catholic Court Church of Dresden. This hypothesis rests upon the belief that Zelenka entered the *Mottetti* in chronological order of composition or acquisition.

From the appearance of the entries, numbers 1 to 11 seem to have been made at the same time followed by the single entry of number 12. (Here it should be noted that in the *Inventarium* Zelenka initially listed the first two works under the rubric *Cantate*, p. 25. The entries were then deleted and placed as numbers 1 and 2 under the rubric *Mottetti*. Thus, it is likely that all the Motets were entered some time after 1726). Numbers 13, 14 and 15 were later additions. All entries are in the hand of Zelenka with the exception of number 16. Although Reich dates the first entry, *Proh quos criminis* ca. 1729, the autograph score was certainly copied by Zelenka before mid–1726.[15] According to Horn, the copy of number 2 was made by Zelenka between 1722 and 1728.[16] The score of number 3, *O magnum mysterium* (not autograph) has been dated by Reich as ca.1728. (It is possible that this working is the second of two.)

---

[13]Ms Tenbury 603. Bodleian Library, Oxford. Peter Ward Jones, music librarian from that library, has communicated that this *Anthem* (no. 3 - Zelenka), in the hand of a "Taylor," is one of many mid–19th-century English adaptations found in a series of Tenbury volumes. This adaptation is for treble solo, four-part choir and organ. The music does not correspond with any incipits for Zelenka's works to be found in the catalogues. Perhaps the adaptation was made by Edward Taylor (1784–1863) who, in 1830, translated and adapted Spohr's "Last Judgement," which led to "an intimacy with Spohr, at whose request he subsequently translated and adapted the oratorios, "Crucifixion . . . ," 1836 and "Fall of Babylon . . . ," 1842, from *A Dictionary of Music and Musicians*, ed. Sir George Grove. In 4 vols. (London: Macmillan, 1889). Other adaptations made by Taylor are: Mozart's *Requiem*, Graun's *Tod Jesu*, Schneider's *Sündfluth*, Spohr's *Vater Unser* and Haydn's *Jahreszeiten*.

[14]Included in the recording cited above, Note 4.

[15]At least two changes in Zelenka's handwriting provide a firm basis for the determination of broad guidelines for dating. They are: the usual manner of writing the bass clef ⨏: changed ca.1728–1729 to ⨏ ᛐ: ; observed by H. Unverricht in *Zur Datierung der Bläsersonaten von J.D. Zelenka* (Musikforschung XV, 1962) and the present writer's observation on Zelenka's adoption of a stroke to raise the figure 4, , ca. 1726 (early). In the autograph score of *Pro quos criminis* both ⨏: and #4 are to be seen, thus placing the writing of this autograph before March/April 1726.

[16]Horn, p. 160.

If number 4 is indeed the motet *Perfice (gressus meos)* by Caldara, as is suggested by Horn, it must have been composed in or before 1729, when it was performed on the sixth Sunday after Pentecost in Vienna.[17] No date is yet available to this writer for number 5, the Mancini motet. The autograph scores of number 6, *de Temp[ore]* and number 8, *Pange lingua* are lost. There is no absolute means of identifying which of Zelenka's two settings of *Haec dies*, number 7, is meant here.[18] Slight evidence exists that the later setting of ca. 1730 is intended in the list *Mottetti*: On page 1 of the autograph of Z 169 appears #8, which corresponds to the eighth position of the listing of *Haec dies* despite the reversal of numbers 7 and 8 in the *Inventarium*. The only dated autograph in the list is number 9, *Gaude Plaude*, or *Gaude Laetare*, which was completed on May 17th 1731. Numbers 10 and 11 are lost or unidentified works (Reich). *Barbara dira effera* number 12, is dated by Reich as ca. 1733. Number 13 has been identified by Horn as a reworking by Zelenka of the aria *Son confusa pastorella* from Handel's opera *Poro*, first performed in London in 1731.[19] Horn suggests that perhaps the transmission of this work to Dresden was via the Dresden Court composer Ristori, who composed two arias used as interpolations in the 1736 London revival of that opera. The two autograph motets of Vivaldi are undated,[20] and the Hasse (?) work, number 16, was not entered by Zelenka. Thus, a case could be made for the supposition that these motets in the *Inventarium* have been entered in chronological order of composition and/or acquisition. If this conjecture is accepted, the date of the untitled sixth entry *de Temp* would be between the time of the copying of *O magnum mysterium*, i.e. at the latest ca.1728 (*de Nativitate D.*) and May 1731.

A significant feature of the list of motets in Zelenka's *Inventarium* is the reworking not only of his own compositions but also those of other com-

---

[17] Friedrich W. Riedel, *Kirchenmusik am Hofe Karls VI (1711–1740)* (München- Salzburg: Katzbichler, 1977), p. 265. Dr. Brian Pritchard (University of Canterbury, New Zealand) has communicated the information that this motet/offertorium may very well date from 1718–1720 when Caldara wrote most of his offertoria. Only a few date from the 1720's.

[18] Two settings by Zelenka of *Haec dies*, Z 169 (C Major, ca. 1730) and Z 170 (F Major, ca. 1726) exist in autograph score in Dresden. Zelenka listed these works variously under the rubrics; Offertoria (F Major, therefore Z 170), Hymni (F Major, therefore Z 170) and Mottetti (Z 169?).

[19] Horn, p. 136.

[20] According to Horn these motets of Vivaldi were probably transmitted to Dresden through Pisendel, director of the Dresden Court Orchestra and former pupil of Vivaldi.

posers. These reworkings range from minor amendments to complete overhaul of text and orchestration. Four of the surviving works listed are known to have been amended and Horn suspects that two others might have been similarly treated. In 1723 Zelenka composed *Sub olea pacis* (A 175), also known as *Melodrama de Sancto Venceslao*, a secular latin-comedy commissioned by the Jesuit Clementinum College of Prague as its contribution to the festivities surrounding the coronation of Austrian Charles VI as King of Bohemia. This work represents a major achievement involving considerable effort by Zelenka. But since it was a "one-off" composition it became, not unreasonably, a rich source to be tapped by him for the musical requirements of the recently established Catholic Court Church in Dresden. At least three single items of the *Inventarium* come from *Sub olia pacis*. They are the two motets *Proh quos criminis*, a parody of a recitative and aria from act 2 of the Melodrama; *O magnum mysterium*, the aria of which is a parody of an aria from act 3 of the Melodrama (and also listed under the rubric *Arie* as *Dormi parve, dormi Deus*); and a further work, listed under the rubric *Offertoria* in the *Inventarium* as *Angelus Domini Descendit* (Z 161). *Mottetto a 4* is written on page 1 of the autograph, dated 28 Marzo 1725.

Amendments known to have been made by Zelenka to works of other composers listed under *Mottetti* are to the composition of Mancini *Resonate vos lyrae sonorae* and to *Huc pastores* by Handel. Of the textual alterations to the Mancini motet, Horn writes "This . . . was performed in Dresden in honor of St Inatius Loyola as indicated by a textual alteration in the first recitative. "In aeterna gloria/fortis Laurentii resonet victoria," the original text, has been replaced. The amendment reads "In aeterna gloria/divi Ignatii resonet victoria."[21] To the music of Handel's aria *Son confusa pastorella (Poro)*, Zelenka has added a latin text appropriate to Christmas. "All aspects [of the operatic pastorale milieu] have been translated into the liturgical."[22] Two other works from the list of motets are considered by Horn to be possible parodies: they are *O quam Suavis* of Ariosti and *Angeli cementes* of Hasse (?) with the possibility that the latter work is not by Hasse but yet another parody based upon an aria *Angelicae merites adeste frequentes* from *Sub olea pacis*.[23]

---

[21]Horn, p. 176.
[22]Horn, p. 136.
[23]The title *Angeli cementes* is thought by Horn to be a corruption of *Angelicae mentes*. No work of Hasse even distantly relates to this title. Horn, p. 138.

Chvalte Boha silného

Chvalte Boha silného is a G major setting of Psalm 150 for solo bass voice, violins 1 and 2, viola, oboes 1 and 2, horns 1 and 2 (in G) and organ continuo. The work is in three sections. In the first (Allegro un poco), verses 1 and 2 are set for solo voice, strings, oboes and continuo. In the second section (Vivace), verses 3, 4 and 5 are set with the addition of horns. The third section is a slightly altered and shortened reprises of the opening, but with horns added, with the setting of verse 6 and a concluding alleluja. Although the text in the Prague copy matches exactly that of the Kralická Bible it is now not possible to ascertain whether any alterations were made during his copying of the original. In the eighteenth and nineteenth century references to this work, the title is given as *Chwale Boha Sylneho* (1765, ca.1775) or *Chwale Boha sylneho* (1861–2). The missing letter to from the Chwalte is an error, unlikely to have been made by the Bohemian Zelenka. The w of Chvalte and y of silného are spellings usual until the early nineteenth century.[24] The missing letter "t" from Chwalte suggests that the compilers of the catalogues of 1765 and ca. 1775 and Fürnsteau worked from a version not made by Zelenka.

With the exception of the scoring for horns, used by Zelenka in many instrumental and few liturgical compositions (usually with trumpets), the basic four-part scoring of violins 1 and 2, viola and basso continuo together with ad. lib. oboes is that which seems to have developed in Dresden between the late 1720's and early 1730's. Oboes, with the dual roles of ripienists and soloists, were an important feature of the Dresden Court Orchestra as they are also in this work. A principal feature of this motet is the marvelous writing for the two horns, especially in the second movement. Although the bass lines of Zelenka's autograph scores usually specify only keyboard (organ or cembalo), surviving sets of parts suggest that 'cello and tiorba were used as part of the continuo with the re-enforcement of *violone* and *fagott* during ritornelli sections. With the exception of the occasional use of the terms *Tutti* and *Solo*, the frequent indications seen in Zelenka's scores from the late 1720's of *Tutti, Rip*[ieni], *Solo/Soli* are not to be found in the Prague copy. Dynamic markings are present, usually of "p" when the instruments accompany the singer and "f" in the ritornello sections. Because of the text of Psalm 150, all the specified instruments have important solo roles to play.

---

[24]This has been pointed out by Dr. George Marvan, Professor of Slavic Languages, Monash University, Melbourne.

When considering the almost classical instrumental scoring (4 part strings, 2 oboes, 2 horns) one is reminded of the passage from Charles Burney:

> The Bohemians are remarkably expert in the use of wind instruments, in general; but M. Seger...says, the instrument upon which their performers are most excellent, on the Saxon side of the Kingdom, is the hautbois; and on that of Moravia, the tube or clarion."[25]

The text of the Prague copy is precisely based on that of the *Kralická Bible*:

1.	[Halelujah]	1.	Praise ye the Lord.
	Chvalte Boha silného pro svatost jeho.		Praise God in his sanctuary.
	chvalte jej pro rozšíření síly jeho.		praise him in the firmament of his power.
2.	Chvalte jej ze všelijaké moci jeho,	2.	Praise him for his mighty acts:
	chvalte jej podlé veliké důstojnosti jeho.		praise him according to his excellent greatness.
3.	Chvalte jej zvukem trouby, chvalte jej na loutnu a citaru	3.	Praise him with the sound of the trumpet: praise him with the psaltery and harp
4.	Chvalte jej na buben a píštalu, chvalte jej na husle a varhany	4.	Praise him with the timbrel and dance: praise him with stringed instruments and organs
5.	Chvalte jej na cymbály hlasité chvalte jej na cymbály zvučné	5.	Praise him upon the loud cymbals: praise him upon the high sounding cymbals
6.	Všeliký duch chval Hospodina	6.	Let everything that hath breath praise the Lord.
	Halelujah.		Praise ye the Lord.

Kralická Bible (last edition, 1613)   *King James' Version*

Some discrepancies between the spellings of the Prague copy and the text given above occur, e.g. zvuke, citharu, housle, cimbly.

---

[25] Charles Burney, *The Present State of Music in Germany, the Netherlands and the United Provinces*, ed. Percy A. Scholes as *Dr. Burney's Musical Tours in Europe* (London: Oxford Univ. Press, 1959), p. 135.

The first bar of this motet is a very familiar one. The motif of a descending octave leap followed by a semiquaver rest and a scale passage to the rhythm ($\frac{4}{4}$ ♩ 𝄾 ♫ ... / $\frac{4}{4}$ ♩ 𝄾 ♫) is to be found in many of Zelenka's works. The motif is almost a personal signature and its affect that of a call for attention. The style of the first section is relatively uncomplicated. The harmonic movements and modulations to closely related keys are direct and predictable. Nevertheless the impression of the movement is one of noble simplicity appropriate to the text of verses 1 and 2. But the setting of the following three verses is so literal that an unexpected quality of humor is exposed. The solo bass singer, in the role of cantor, calls for praise with the *trouby* and pairs of horns respond; with *loutnu a citharu* and violins with pizzicato viola bass answer; with *buben a píšťalu* and a pair of oboes accompanied by a rustic, percussive tonic-dominant bass reply; with *husle a varhany* and all strings with *Pleno Organo* react in unison; with *cimbály hlasité* and *cimbály zvučné* and staccato violins retort. This rich and riotous antiphonal play between singer and instruments is drawn to order with the announcement by the solo singer of verse 6 and the opening theme returns. The final section concludes with the setting of *Alleluia*. Throughout the motet the considerations of the text always determine the music.

Speculations

The questions raised by the setting of *Chvalte Boha silného* are; what was the purpose of this composition which used the Protestant vernacular text and why does it appear in the repertoire of the Dresden Catholic Court Church? Were the commissioner of the motet known we would be helped in answering the questions and these answers might shed some light on the rather scant knowledge of Zelenka's position in Dresden during the period of this composition, ca. late 1728 to May 1731. The strongest speculation arises from the suggestion of Jarmil Smolka[26] that the motet was composed for a community of religious emigrants from the Czech lands living in conditions of religious tolerance in the Saxon-Polish kingdom. The combination of the psalm text from the Kralická Bible, instrumentation and forthright nature of the setting would support this suggestion. In Dresden in 1670 a church of Bohemian Lutherans was formed under the Bohemian pastor Martinius. He had obtained an order from the Court that Bohemians taking refuge in that city should unite with the Lutheran church or quit the

---

[26]In notes to accompany the recording, see Note 4.

country, which many chose to do.[27] It is apparent from the accounts of Protestant migrations from the Czech lands that these people found great joy in hearing sermons preached in their own language. This factor, together with the desire to maintain special liturgical features, led to the disinclination of many of these spiritual descendants of the United Brethren to formally unite with Lutheran communities, a move that would have given them a degree of protection. It seems that in several communities disputes arose over this matter, including the settlement of Herrnhut. Of all the settlements formed by migrations during the first half of the eighteenth century, this is the one most likely to have commissioned Zelenka to make the setting of *Chvalte Boha silného*. Herrnhut, dating from 1722, developed under the patronage and protection of Count Zinzendorf.[28] This Lutheran nobleman held the office of king's councillor at the Court of August II from 1721 to 1727. His family connections with Protestant nobility, his ecumenical outlook (in 1727 he sponsored a combination hymnal and prayer book for Catholic), his organizational abilities and above all, his extraordinary tolerance enabled Herrnhut to develop into a powerful independent movement capable of retaining its own identity without merging with the Lutheran Church. Important events occurred during the probable date of the Motet setting of Zelenka which might have warranted the commission of a special composition. They are:

1727: A set of rules regulating the legal and spiritual life of Herrnhut were drawn up and confirmed (July 4th).

1728: These statutes were rewritten, calling for loyalty of Lutheran forms of creed and worship but with specific provision for the retention of certain customs of the Bohemian Brethren (November 11th).

1729: The final legal conclusion of the document of 1728 (August 8th).

1731: The community met and determined by lot not to unite with the Lutheran community (January 17th).

If Zinzendorf did commission this work for Herrnhut from Zelenka, the community would have retained the original score. This

---

[27] A. Bost, *History of the Bohemian and Moravian Brethren*, trans. and abridged. Third edition (London: The Religious Tract Society, 1848), p. 120.
[28] See A. Lewis *Zinzendorf, the Ecumenical Pioneer* (Philadelphia: SCM Press, 1962) and J.R. Weinlick, *Count Zinzendorf* (Nashville: Abingdon, 1956).

would explain the supposition that a copy was in the archives of the Dresden Court Church.

Conclusion

But we are still left with the problem of why the work was placed by Zelenka into the repertoire of the Catholic Court Church of Dresden. The Kralická Bible was banned in Bohemia and thus it is highly unlikely that it would have been used as the basis for any composition performed in that church which, from its inception, had close ties with Bohemia. The Jesuits in Dresden, including the first director of the Catholic Court Church, Father Moritz Vota SJ, belonged to the Bohemian provincial order.[29] Therefore, on the basis of our knowledge of Zelenka's reworkings, it is suggested that he included this work in the *Inventarium* with the intention of altering the text. This would explain the lack of title and the empty space preceding the remark *de Temp* of the sixth motet entry. Two possibilities occur. Perhaps Zelenka planned to substitute a liturgically acceptable version of the psalm text, for example, either that of the Svatováclavská (Wenceslaus) Bible (1677–1715)[30] or that of a catholic latin version. Or perhaps *Chwalte Boha silného* was listed simply in order to have a spare musical work, which could be adapted in an emergency using any text appropriate to a particular occasion within the temporal cycle.[31] It is still hoped that further researches will uncover the exact origins of this unexpected work by the Bohemian Zelenka.

---

[29]Horn, p. 38.

[30]Listed in the National Union Catalog Pre–1956 Imprints. This bible was a translation from the Vulgate made by three Jesuits, Jirú Konstane, Matej Václav Steyer and Jan Barner and published in Prague between 1677–1715.

[31]In Vienna, "de Tempore" signified motets without a specific liturgical/seasonal purpose. See Riedel, p. 159.

Eighteenth Century Folk Music in the Czech Lands: Comments on the State of Research

Zdeňka Pilková

The relationship between folk music and art music is one of the great bugaboos in our field. Indeed, one might argue that the popularity of Czech music outside Czechoslovakia (and also, sometimes, within it) results from the perception of its "folkness." Even those of us who should know better are sometimes seduced by an illusion which equates the folk quotient of a work with its value: the more folklike, the more Czech; the more Czech the better.

Zdeňka Pilková has been an active scholar in this area for decades. She has written extensive studies on early Czech music, Mozart, and Haydn, and in this essay she cautions us against making facile generalizations about folk music by pointing out the vagueness of a range of terms associated with the very word "folk." She also warns us of the dangers of asserting that this or that composer employs "Czech themes" before we fully understand our methods of coming to such a conclusion and the preconceptions we bring to the endeavor.

If there is a link between Janáček and the eighteenth century, it may be found in the realm of folk music. That is why, as a specialist in the music of the eighteenth century, I have chosen this topic for my study.

The music of the lower social classes has been a part of musical development from the earliest beginnings to the present day. Since folk music is for the most part orally transmitted, written notations have been preserved for later periods only at random. However, a variety of documents and objects relating to a folk culture give more information about it. In Czechoslovakia folk music has been more or less systematically recorded since 1819. A number of collections were already in existence before Janáček began his own collecting activity, and at present the files of ethnographic institutes in Prague and Brno contain written records of more than thirty thousand folk songs. As we go further into the past, however, direct sources decrease in number. For the eighteenth century there are only a few incidental records in the Czech Lands, and in addition several little hand-written song books which were written down by some musicians for their own use, especially for providing dance music.[1] It is evident that this orally transmitted folk music and composed art music interacted on numerous levels and involved a wide variety of contacts. In doing research on art music the music historian meets with a number of questions which require a more detailed knowledge of the spontaneously created music of the time. However, there are usually no direct sources, and the indirect ones produce only hypotheses.

My reflections were inspired by such difficulties in the course of research involving Czech art music of the eighteenth century. Here I would like to inquire into the state of research on the musical folklore of our country, and into the current terminology employed in musicology when such problems are approached. My reflections are based on the music folklore materials of Bohemia and the western regions of Moravia, which form a certain, though rather differentiated cultural historical whole. Materials relating to the eastern regions of Moravia and Slovakia are thoroughly different in structure and belong to quite another cultural historical sphere.

There is a very clearly defined boundary between these two spheres of folk music in our country. It divides Moravia into two parts from south to north. Musical ethnographers have been able to determine this boundary precisely, nearly village by village. The eastern style, with which Janáček was associated, is asymmetrical, with modal elements and vocal "recitative" style in the melody. The western type, about which I will speak, is more symmetrically organized, though not in terms of phrase length: periods of five, six and seven measures are very typical. This type we might call more "instrumental."

We all use terms such as "folk song," "folk dance," "folk music." I will use them too, since they do facilitate communication. But these terms are very inaccurate and ambiguous, as I will try to prove.

---

[1] These oldest small collections are discussed in more detail in the book/edition by Jaroslav Markl, *Nejstarší sbírky českých lidových písní* (The Oldest Collections of Czech Folk Songs), (Prague: 1987).

Comment No. 1: On the term "folk"

The reason for the inaccuracy of terms like "folk song" and "folk dance" lies in the very term "folk." The question, however, is very complicated and would provide more than enough material for an enormous interdisciplinary symposium. The way this term has been handed down in Czech musical historiography until recently is very significant: the implications of the term have their roots in a rather idealized conception of the peasantry and of its role in society, which originated in the period of the Enlightenment. It was then taken over during the Revivalist period and by Romanticism, which were initially represented most importantly by F. L. Čelakovský in the Czech Lands).[2] At earlier stages the expression "folk" denoted large sections of rural population without any further specification. In fact, however, this term comprised heterogeneous groups with wide social differences. For this reason, historians are now using much more precise terms (e.g. "rural subservient sections," "unprivileged rural and urban sections," "the section of urban craftsmen and retail dealers," etc.)

This seemingly theoretical speculation has practical consequences in relation to the musical activity and repertory of the eighteenth century. Among statements frequently used in journalism, as well as in musicological literature, we find, for example, "the people in the church sang religious folk songs." To whom does the word "people" actually refer? We know that in certain rural districts, where there was the residence of estate management, but without a special manor church (e.g. at Dolní Lukavice, where Joseph Haydn was engaged for some time), both the peasantry, the employees from the castle, and nobility of the manor gathered for worship in the same church on Sundays and feast days. They all sang, for example, the same repertory of Marian songs. Can this gathering be called the "folk"? Did they sing religious "folk" songs? As for the latter, this term is now beginning to be replaced by more factually accurate terms, for it is clear that these songs belong to the realm of composed music, even though many are anonymous, and large sections of the population appropriated them from printed hymn books for their own purposes. This is why hymnologists now prefer to use the term "strophic song of religious content."

---

[2]František Ladislav Čelakovský, *Slovanské národní písně* (Slavic National Songs), 3 vols., (Prague: 1822–27).

Yet another question concerns the village schoolmaster—who usually represented a sort of personal link between music in the manor-house, where he used to help with music or teaching children, music in the choir, where he was often engaged as *regenschori*, and music in the pub, where he used to play with other musicians for dances. Was this schoolmaster the representative of "the folk"? And can the music he produced with his band on Sundays be regarded as "folk music"? In this case, musicology could draw inspiration from the terminology and results of an allied field, ethnomusicology. Scholars in this field draw a subtle distinction between "authentic" or "rustic" village bands and more advanced schoolmasters' bands.[3] Although the latter type of band did not use such traditional folk instruments as bagpipes and cymbals, they were the real embodiment of rural musicality in the second half of the eighteenth century. Both of these examples, and a host of others that could be drawn, make the commonly used term "folk" fairly inexact and vague from the point of view of the music itself.

Comment No. 2: On the terms "folk song" and "folk music"

Naturally there is extensive specialized literature concerning this theme, and individual authors have different interpretations of the term "folk music." The broadest conception in foreign literature was recently supported by Herman Strobach,[4] who uses the phrase to describe the entire vocal repertory of large sections of the population, from Gregorian chant to the music produced by amateur ensembles in the present. In current Czech musicological practice and, above all, in musical journalism, the term "folk music" denotes the musical creativity of subservient sections of rural population before the period of industrialization, but not as a whole. This term covers only a certain part of their musical activity, namely secular folk songs employing Czech texts and instrumental music.

When considered in terms of later compilations, our earliest collections of folk songs, originating under the influence of the Enlightenment, reflected the state of folk music in a relatively objective manner. They include small song books of the eighteenth century, the collection of Jan Jeník

---

[3]Ludvík Kunz, "Historical Accounts of the Horn in the Folk Instrumental Music of the 18th and 19th Centuries in the Czech Lands," in *Das Waldhorn in der Geschichte und Gegenwart der tschechischen Musik* (Prague: 1983), pp. 128–137; Jaroslav Markl, "Mundstückinstrumente in der Musikfolklore Böhmens," Ibid, pp. 105–122.

[4]Herman Strobach, *Deutsches Volkslied in Geschichte und Gegenwart* (Berlin: 1980).

of Bratřice,[5] and especially the so-called "Gubernatorial Collecting," which was organized by Austrian authorities and started in 1819. Many collectors, primarily teachers and priests, took part in it. B. D. Weber then compiled a part of this material into the *Kolovraty Manuscript* (1823). Another part of the Gubernatorial Collecting was edited by J. Rittersberg as *Česke narodní písně* (Czech National Songs, 1824).[6] These collections have recorded not only folk songs, but also ballads and various kinds of very unsophisticated tunes. We also find that the texts were written down, almost entirely without moralistic censorship. Later collectors (from Čelakovský on) skewed the selection process so that the finished product would fit with their romantic conceptions of "the people" and conform to their own aesthetic tastes. This resulted in considerable intervention in the choice of songs, texts, and even resulted in modifications of musical structure in collections with printed tunes. By now, ethnographers have worked out methods (on the basis of musical and textual analysis) which enable us to distinguish different types of songs in the wider repertory as they were originally written down: authentic folk songs, semi-authentic folk songs, and songs which had been accepted as folk songs from various sources. The results of this research are of great importance for musicologists involved in eighteenth-century art music.

Comment No. 3: On the problem of so-called "urban folklore"

Today it is clear that folk music was not only the music of rural communities, but that there was also urban folklore, which must be differentiated in another manner. While so-called "rural folklore" varied primarily according to the individual regions (the songs and dances of one region, formed sometimes by only a cluster of several small localities, had characteristic features different from those of other regions), urban folklore reflected the qualities of social groups corresponding to the varied stratification of the urban population. The ranks of craftsmen, for example, had their own repertory, as did groups such as students, soldiers, etc.

These spheres of the music repertory were not, of course, strictly separated, and were no doubt rather interwoven, as for example in the pub. In addition, urban folklore was influenced by music that people heard at church, at various ceremonies, and at military marches through

---

[5]Jaroslav Markl, "Rozmarné písničky (Humorous Songs) Jana Jeníka z Bratřic" (Prague: 1959). (a critical edition of this collection)

[6]Complete critical editions of the Kolovraty Manuscript, Rittersberg's publication and other smaller collections are contained in Markl, *Nejstarší sbírky*.

the town; and by ballad songs and contemporary "hits" from operas and singspiels, which often arrived in smaller towns in the form of religious compositions.[7]

As a matter of fact, the musical folklore of the rural population was also influenced by religious music, ballads and other phenomena, which may have included the repertory created and brought home by students of various schools and convents. Thus this music of "spontaneous creativity" was influenced in numerous ways, which does not, however, make it less valuable. The process through which various kinds of music were adapted in the sphere of rural and urban folklore was, as ethnographers emphasize nowadays, a creative process in itself, and therefore the thesis about so-called "decayed" music is not only old-fashioned but entirely false as well.

The problem of identifying the musical repertory of the rural and urban populations is also complicated by certain historical events, primarily the Josephinian reforms of the 1780s, which caused a population drift: the sections of rural population of lower social standing moved to the towns, especially to those in which the fast-growing textile industries provided opportunities to make a living. In addition to other tunes, these country folk certainly sang tunes they had brought from their native region and adapted them to their new surroundings. Unfortunately, very little is known about this interesting process in which the original songs changed under the influence of urban folklore, and vice-versa.[8] In any case, the complexity of all these phenomena and processes makes it rather tenuous for the music historian to estimate what might have been taken over into art music. Therefore, we must be very careful about our judgments.

---

[7] Ballad songs ("kramářské písně") may be described as follows: a man (or a pair of men) came to the marketplace with a large sheet of paper containing pictures referring to a "terrible story" (e.g. an assassination, but there were also songs about the lives of saints, and about newly imported fruits, etc.). He sang the song and simultaneously showed the story in pictures. Afterwards, people could buy the text of this song on a small print (of one or two sheets). As for the melody, at the bottom of the page there was usually a remark such as "it ought to be sung like..." followed by a text incipit from a well-known folk song. Ballad songs were a kind of contemporary newspaper.

[8] Markl, *Nejstarší sbírky*, p. 170.

Comment No. 4: On the term "Czech folk music" and the traditional point of view

While this term is still commonly used by musicologists, ethnographers prefer the terms "folk music of Bohemia " and "folk music of Moravia." All these problems with terminology have historical roots, which date back to the Revivalist period and derive from the specific position under the control of the Hapsburg monarchy in which the Czech Lands found themselves after 1620. Until recently Czech scholars were concerned only with songs to Czech texts, although a population of both Czech and German nationalities shared one territory. German songs were of great interest only to German authors, who often took a nationalist-chauvinist position between the two World Wars, and sometimes even later.[9] But the results of the Gubernatorial Collecting started in 1819 had already proved that the repertory of the population of the Czech Lands contained songs with both Czech and German (sometimes even bilingual) texts. It is evident that both types of songs were performed not only in the places where both nationalities were intermixed (as in some towns and border areas), but even where they lived separately to some extent (as in areas where one village was Czech and another German). With the exception of a single study,[10] no Czech musicologist has thus far undertaken a deeper inquiry into the German folk songs of the Czech Lands.

Comment No. 5: On the so-called "specificity" of Czech folk music

This rather complicated issue is closely connected with problems which belong to the field of music historiography. In the eighteenth century, the Czech Lands were not a closed union; the ethnic boundaries coincided with neither the boundaries of the individual countries of the Hapsburg monarchy nor the state frontier. Folk music spread to the Czech Lands through various kinds of mechanisms (through the migration of students, soldiers, village fiddlers, etc.) not only from the neighboring lands, but often even from very distant countries. We know that folklore phenomena (fairy tales, folk stories, etc.) often moved great

---

[9]E. g. Karl Michael Komma, *Das bömische Musikantentum* (Kassel: 1960).
[10]Jaroslav Markl, "Deutsche Volkslieder in Böhmen, gesammelt im Jahre 1819," *Beiträge zur Musikwissenschaft 1* (1959), pp. 23–27.

distances throughout Europe. The same is true of folk music, a particularly suitable means of social entertainment. Under these circumstances the question of the specific identity of Bohemian and Moravian folk music is extremely complicated. Numerous tunes circulated throughout the whole of Central Europe, or at least through the Austrian Lands (e.g. the lullaby "Hushaby, my angel"). In studies published by foreign authors, Czech music historians often happen to find a tune which might be described as a "typical Neopolitan song," for example, but which is known to them as a Czech folk song. At the same time, apart from such similarities there were also clear differences, and Czech musical folklore does have some characteristic features, which has been proven by ethnographers in a number of studies. However, the problems have not yet been elaborated upon as a whole. A musicologist, trying to distinguish certain specifically Czech melodic or rhythmic idioms from Italianate elements in either religious or secular composed music from the Czech Lands during the eighteenth century, is confronted with a by and large unsolvable task at this time.

Comment No. 6: On the chronologically different layers of the folk repertory

In the eighteenth century repertory of the rural and urban populations, the most varied chronological layers were concurrently in existence; from the residues of Gregorian chant to the latest songs of the period, which originated under the influence of ballad songs of secular as well as religious content. Musical and textual analysis can distinguish these layers to some extent, but only approximately. A more exact location in time has been, with a few exceptional cases, very difficult to determine so far, although it would be of great interest for a music historian in specific cases. Hymnologists are faced with this problem most frequently, but even those who are involved in the study of eighteenth-century art (composed) music often need a more accurate knowledge of the probable time a particular song or group of songs originated. There are many tunes which recall the melodic and metro-rhythmical models of the music of early classicism. The problem of so-called "Mozartisms" in folk music of the Czech Lands is discussed most often. It would be important to know if specific melodies, which are so irresistibly reminiscent of certain melodies by Mozart, appeared as a result of the popularity of his works, or whether they had occurred in the musical repertory of the people even before, and had been, together with other melodies of a similar structure, a reason for the positive reception of Mozart's works in Bohemia.

From the previous comments it is clear that the stage of research into spontaneous musical creativity in the Czech Lands does not by any means enable us to answer many questions that are posed by historical musicology in connection with the relationship of this kind of music to art (composed) music. It is necessary to wait until the extensive files of records of folk songs and instrumental music, which have been collected for decades, have been explored in a more detailed and systematic manner. Until that time, all statements which appear in both Czech and foreign literature claiming, for example, that "in František Benda's (or J. V. Stamic's, etc.) works we can find a marked reflection of Czech folk dance, the typical Czech musicality of the rural people..." must be considered as mere observations of an accidental melodic or metro-rhythmic coincidence, which can be thoroughly misleading and, in any case, are not based on profound analysis. To create the conditions for such analysis represents one of the unfulfilled tasks of musicology and musical ethnography in our country.

Cantor's Music, Local Repertories, and Some Thoughts on the Need for a Bohemian Musical Topography

Mark Germer

Mark Germer's richly detailed work on the pastorella and pastoral mass in Austria, Bohemia, and Poland has always drawn our attention to the overlapping of borders: geographical, social, economic, cultural, and religious. In his study presented here he raises profound questions about subjects which range from current debates about the notion of the canon, to the very sources of Czech "musicality" in the 18th century.

In the years immediately ahead, as "audience interaction" claims more space in critical discussions,[1] we can brace ourselves to be reminded often of a rather mundane truth: the question "what shall we make of the music of the past?" (that is, what interest does it hold for us now) is very different from the question "what music did people of the past choose to know?" Perhaps the first sound some of us are likely to hear, upon settling in at a hitherto unfamiliar archive, is the sound of our own voices muttering about the preponderance of musical sources and documents which really do not interest us—sources which almost seem to distract us, as if obscuring our view of the rare materials we have come to study. More than once a mildly exasperated colleague has asked me rhetorically, did I have any idea of the number of Auber sources in Paris alone; or did I have any conception of the number of times the works of Volkmann appear in 19th century concert programs. Such moments, of course, are moments of reckoning with a musicological commonplace: that the grafting and pruning which goes into evaluating the legacy of the past has little if anything to do with patterns of production and consumption in a given era—indeed, an observation so fundamental that we may be surprised when literary historians seem only now to

---

[1] Variants on the study of reception now include spillover from "reader-response" theory and from investigations into how audiences come to confer on works of art a "canonical" status. Compare two very different approaches that have appeared recently in *19th-Century Music*: Beckerman 1986–87 and Kallberg 1987–88.

be pondering its meaning.² It might be said that here, with the nurturing of a canon of revered works, is the juncture where those who are involved with the grafting and pruning part company from those who chart the history of ideas or study music-making as an aspect of human behavior. But I think it would be better to say that here is the juncture where they come together; for the two approaches coincide in their recognition that what was heard in, say, the 19th century bears little relation to what we now think of as 19th century music.

The difficulties are compounded the farther back in time we go, as the modern delineation of a canon requires more and more scholarly artifice, and as what we are left with is mainly a record of what was heard, and an ever vaguer sense of what hearing it meant to the majority of an intended audience. Yet in the 18th century, from which vast repertories of music remain wholly unknown to us,³ a great deal can be said to hang on this duality in our approach to the music of the past. A reluctance to grapple with music which has never acquired a "canonic" significance has led to something rather worse, I think, than our mere inability to capture the experience of music by people of the past who held it to be significant. Such a reluctance can also steer us away from historical interpretations of wide cultural relevance.⁴ I am not the first to point out, for instance, that during the period in Czech history so notable for its tide of awakening national consciousness—the decades surrounding 1800—the vast majority of musical works brought to performance (and subsequently preserved in archives) belonged to the milieu of the church.⁵ Naturally this has much to do with the conservative nature of established institutions, even those undergoing paroxysms of reform, and with the nature of musicians who conservatively cling to them. Nevertheless the sources convey a picture of musical life in Catholic Central Europe that is at the very least religiously motivated, if not fundamentally religious in character. It would not be too much of

---

[2] Surprised but not ungrateful: my opening remarks are inspired by Darnton 1986–87. The loose dichotomy between historical and aesthetic considerations has its best explication in Carl Dahlhaus' *Grundlagen*, English translation 1983, chapter 7, esp. 95–101; also the circumstances in which the distinction is artificial, chapter 10 *passim*.

[3] A recent assessment by Helmut Hucke (1982, 191: "Die italienische Kirchenmusik des 17.\18. Jahrhunderts stellt bis heute eine *terra incognita* dar . . .") may be extended to include all of Catholic Central Europe, save perhaps the great Hofkapelle; yet even here, as Bruce MacIntyre has shown (1986), much depends on sufficient acquaintance with local traditions.

[4] There is at least one striking exception to this rule of reluctance that can be taken as a model: Kauper 1979, esp. chapter 2 on the interplay of local traditions in the music of urban churches.

[5] Hůlek 1983.

an exaggeration to say that 18th century music in South-German and West-Slavic areas *is* first and foremost church music.

This fact does not sufficiently reverberate in the musical historiography of the period, despite a long tradition, stemming in part from Burney, of attributing the phenomenal outpouring of music in the Czech lands to the rigorous teaching of music in the parish schools. Bohemia does appear to be an extreme case. There can be no doubt that the primary schools in the villages, along with the order gymnasia of the larger towns, facilitated an intense cultivation of music and helped to transform the Bohemian churches they served, to borrow a description from Oscar Kokoschka, into veritable "palaces of the poor."[6] Nor was the role of the sacristy factotums called *kantoři* in any sense negligible—though the popularly celebrated notion of the village cantors as protonationalists is a myth, borne of the spirit of creating canons. Still the interpretation accepts too much at face value, and does not begin to penetrate to the social and cultural premises which might explain either the vastness or the exceptional competence of the extant repertory. A recent discussion by Flotzinger, which emphasizes the frankly workaday conditions for music making in rural Austrian churches in the same period,[7] seems to cast the Bohemian evidence in even starker relief. Burney himself remained ambivalent, at once voicing admiration for the Czech cantors and the scope of their teaching and finding the initial results "rude and coarse." On the other hand, to a person accustomed to judging the "state" of a nation's music by the quality of its church service,[8] the limited modern acquaintance with the most prevalent manifestations of 18th- century Bohemian musical practice would no doubt seem a bit puzzling.

I propose nothing so ambitious as to knit together all the loose ends I have exposed, but in drawing out some of those threads even further, I hope to suggest a way for relating the legendary production and consumption of church music throughout Bohemia to its broader cultural context. To a degree, perhaps, it is an attempt to provoke interest in a body of music primarily for what it reveals about the people who

---

[6]Kokoschka 1942; Cf Mandrou 1960, 902: "... l'èglise baroque sort d'une socièté rurale, oú le pauvre a trouvè les richesses que la vie quotidienne lui refusait." The view represented by Kokoschka understands the artistic impulses of the Catholic baroque in Central Europe as a humanizing influence; without scratching the surface of a vehement debate in Czech historiography, I should emphasize that this view has its detractors: see, roughly from the time of Kokoschka's remark, Čapek 1940, notably at 23.

[7]Flotzinger 1985, 147, 150–52.

[8]Burney 1775, I:227; II:1–25 *passim*.

cultivated it. But it is also an attempt to comment on the seeming paradox of such an intense practice of "mainstream" or "supranational" music in rural areas, far away from the influence of urban centers. We might distinguish three problems: 1. whether the flood of musical creativity in the Czech lands admits of explanations which run deeper than that derived from Burney; 2. whether evidence of such explanations can be discerned in the music itself; and 3. whether the cultural phenomena we describe are of more than strictly local relevance.

The role played by the parish schools in this matrix ought not be undervalued, but the tendency has been rather to lean in the opposite direction; and the argument that schools and cantors thrived in the main to supply the nobility with musicians may be judiciously discarded. In general, accounts of the history of primary education should make us wary of too exalted claims for the efficacy of the lower schools during the entire age of recatholicization. In fact, there seems to be consensus that the broad-based achievements of Czech pedagogy before 1620 were never again reached after Catholic consolidation.[9] Both the orders and the secular church edifice approached this locally-valued heritage slowly and tentatively, more or less leaving it to fend for itself. Some rural schools evidently succeeded in perpetuating a basic curriculum according to the talents (or the existence) of a schoolmaster, while others coped less happily with the parlous conditions of country life.[10] Only at the end of the 17th century did Catholic interest in the state of the schools accelerate,[11] and then only for pragmatic reasons: schools attached to every parish could serve as a guard against heretical infiltration, and schoolmasters could be charged with assisting the priest in drilling children in the catechism. Official attention to the condition of the schoolhouse and to the proper maintenance of its master arose from the need for ideological monitoring. In Austria generally, as James Melton has discovered, "What appears in Catholic visitation reports as a school sometimes signified little beyond oral catechistic instruction by the church sacristan."[12] Indeed it is instructive to recall that, during the antiheretical campaigns of Charles VI, such watchfulness over the lower schools took the form of state intervention. In 1732, the Emperor him-

---

[9]Palacký 1970. Some sectarian schools were reorganized by Catholic parish clergy, but a shortage of confessionally reliable teachers guaranteed that a great many would never reopen.

[10]The tentative generalizations here are distilled from: Hanzal 1972, Hejnic 1974, Paleček 1971, Bartůšek 1978.

[11]Ryneš 1965; Ostrowski 1971.

[12]Melton 1988, 8.

self issued a directive that teachers were obliged to instill the fear of God in their pupils; and the following year his commission on religion proposed that schoolmasters who cooperated in surveillance with but meager enthusiasm should themselves be placed under surveillance.[13] It is a characteristic feature of the age (as in this decree handed down from above) that duties of cantors are stipulated in contracts and ordinances only insofar as the *spiritual* supervision required in their execution is prescribed. Pedagogy is alluded to only in the sense of benevolent inculcation; the cantor is expected to supervise the music for mass in much the same matter-of-fact way he would supervise the cleaning of the church; and the daily pursuit of education may be regarded as preparation for the weekly regimen of devotions and mass. The Jesuit—and later Piarist—gymnasia, of course, picked up the educational slack (if only for the select few), while parishes no longer required of schoolmasters a mastery of Latin, let alone the subjects traditionally imparted through its study.[14] By the onset of the 18th century, a practical facility in music had effectively replaced that in Latin as the governing criterion to be weighed in engaging a schoolmaster; cantors' contracts seem transparent on that. Only wealthier communities were capable of supporting more than this single sacristy factotum.

This much, in outline, is the familiar backdrop: village churches, whether administering to populations on soil owned by demesne lords, monastic houses, or incorporated towns, uniformly pursued musical programs in conjunction with the lower schools, whose cultural significance otherwise diminished. That received wisdom remains an impression. We know far too little about the inner workings of parish life during the Counter Reformation,[15] and we have every reason to believe that regional distinctions in practice would have been sharply drawn.[16] Moreover, even in light of the Catholic emphasis that it does trace, the outline sidesteps the fundamental question: what was the impetus and aspiration underlying the exceptional Bohemian investment in music?

---

[13]Engelbrecht 1982–86, III: 95.

[14]Ibid. II: 174–84.

[15]Part of the problem lies in the nature of historiographical literature on education in general; thus Rab Houston in a wide-ranging review article (1983, 279): "The study of education and literacy has become less anecdotal and parochial but the lack of a proper context prevents us from understanding its place in social development. Education is dealt with too much in its own terms." Similarly there is much to be done before all the local arrangements (e.g. patronat law and the laws of incorporation) by which parishes operated can begin to be appreciated.

It is often remarked that the Czech lands constituted by far the richest of Habsburg dominions. But that has, rightly, been considered a misleading statement unless accompanied by the recognition that the Habsburg treasury's appetite for Bohemian riches was nothing less than voracious. Well over half the monarchy's entire tax burden fell to Bohemia, Moravia, and Silesia, with scarcely any practical return from Vienna in the way of economic integration of those lands.[17] Locally, of course, the state-empowered feudal system provided a cushion for the privileged orders of society, enabling landowners to survive economically adverse periods: the Bohemian peasant churchgoers we have been considering fared markedly worse than their counterparts elsewhere in the *Erblande*. Child labor and the sale of serfs persisted to the 1780's, in a land where only one percent of the peasant population was classified as "free," and where 246 different kinds of labor service to the seigneur were specified in Moravia alone.[18] The nobility in some cases seem not to have grasped the level of penury and disease on their own estates, except perhaps when marauding bands of homeless, futilely proscribed by the authorities, began to pose a serious threat.[19] As late as 1771, an imperial commission on Bohemia described extreme destitution among the peasants in communities across the land.[20] As Arcadius Kahan has written, the entrenched feudalism of East-Central Europe proved effective in its ability "to shift the impact of declining incomes onto the serfs and to keep the majority of them at a subsistence level . . . In the process of preserving the institution of serfdom intact," Kahan adds, "not only did the serf owners become brutalized, but the whole body politic became dehumanized and permeated by elements of lawlessness."[21] If in this regard the dates 1680 and 1775 come too easily to mind as a convenient frame of reference, it is because the peasant uprisings of those years are so powerfully symbolic of what for the vast majority of Bohemia's population was not an era of economic initiative

---

[16]The French historian Marie Ducreux (1986) is preparing a study on the organization of Bohemian parishes. Kučera 1975 is the only source I have found suggesting the importance of regional religious distinctions. A number of questions bearing on local musical practice are potentially relevant here, such as the degree of tolerance of sectarian traditions, the negative or positive relations between sacristans and parishioners, even the number of schoolmasters recruited from neighboring as opposed to distant locales.

[17]Klíma 1955, 186–98.

[18]Blum 1978, 31; 42; 50; 58.

[19]Weingarten 1720, 266–68, 343–46.

[20]Stark 1937, 417.

[21]Kahan 1973, 99.

and reward, but rather one of severe subjection, impoverishment, and decline. Lawlessness, incidentally, in Counter Reformation Europe could be discerned in terms other than those of open revolt; and the condition of poverty left a great many of this society's underclass vulnerable to even more sinister accusations—a point that will presently prove interesting to raise again with regard to music of the cantors.

That a relationship would emerge between widespread material distress and the intense cultivation of music has been postulated by diverse writers[22]—sociologists of art as well as historians of economic trends. The idea can be construed as a corollary of the theory that baroque aesthetic impulses emanated from the 17th century atmosphere of crisis that permeated Catholic Europe.[23] Periods of exceptionally vital humanistic activity, according to this reading of events, tend to follow closely upon times of economic stagnation and instability, while a preoccupation with music in particular bespeaks the absence of any reconciliation between a culture's ideals and its reality. I claim no priority in invoking here the image of music as retreat from an unsavory reality, having borrowed it from a neglected gem of musicology by David Burrows.[24] But I do think the point can be bolstered by investigating repertories beyond Burrows' exclusively secular focus, namely repertories of Counter Reformation provenance intended for and propagated by a fairly wide cross-section of the population. For, notwithstanding its instances of extravagance and ostentation, the Catholic baroque encompasses patterns other than the predilections of elitist patronage. Indeed, one of its more intriguing aspects is the space allotted to indigenous vernacular forms. The artistic and musical expression of Counter Reform echoes through every level of society, its learned and esoteric programs aimed, utterly without irony, at eliciting a universal and mass response.[25] And it is in the realm of devotional art where the essential conflicts of baroque concern (conflicts like that between life's ideals and its reality) are worked out at their most basic level, mirrored, so to speak, in the strategies of aroque spirituality. Worked out,[26] internalized, but not explained. For it is here too where the interplay between elite and popular modes of discourse embodies a kind of rhetorical accommoda-

---

[22]Lalo 1921, chapter 4; Koenigsberger 1960.
[23]Mandrou 1960.
[24]Burrows 1971; a Bohemian parallel to the economic stagnation described by Burrows is suggested for the mid–18th century in some of the data presented by Lom 1971.
[25]Cf e.g. Spaemann 1984.
[26]That is, assimilated through repetition, imagery, allegorical presentations.

tion between the extremes of privileged and nonprivileged society—or in Kenneth Burke's nice formulation, a "rhetoric of courtship between contrasted social classes."[27] To extract an explanation of worldly conflict from the devotional repertories of Counter Reform would be to deny their very nature, their role in affirming the world; as alien to the baroque turn of mind "as it would be to argue that relations of traditional authority are the result of rational arrangements between superiors and inferiors."[28]

By way of pursuing that line of reasoning let us not obscure the main point, that the abundant creativity and undeniable grandeur of the Austro-Bohemian baroque rested on a fragile socioeconomic base;[29] and that this condition may be discerned in the musical proclivities of the age. Now there is no imperative to extrapolate from this a general principle: writers who explore the interrelations of economics and exceptional cultural activity tend to disclaim any crude implication of cause and effect.[30] But when the repertories themselves make direct allusion to troubled circumstances, we may recognize some measure of contemporaneous "agreement" with the modern characterization of baroque as the product of instability and decline, of discontent and accommodation. That is the case, for instance, in a number of 18th-century pastorellas—that is, in examples of a paraliturgical genre marked by its verisimilitude—wherein villagers wonder aloud about what they can afford to offer the son of God, the usual solution being such symbols of wealth as food or livestock; peasants portrayed in these works occasionally even resign themselves to their poverty and to the realization that the have nothing material to give.[31] That realization, too, supplies the standard rationale for shepherd music-making as it is depicted in Christmas iconography and verse (their offering consists of song and dance). Yet the symbolism of the shepherds is tricky. In regions of intense recatholicization, shepherds barely clung to the margins of society. They were typically counted among the misfits and outcasts of a society grown callous toward vagabonds and beggars. Their separateness left them susceptible to the most heinous charge a villager could bring against his neighbor in Counter-Reformation Europe: that of necromancy and cavorting

---

[27]Burke 1950, 124.
[28]Bloch 1974, 71.
[29]Evans 1979, 442–44; the opposing view, as expressed for instance by Polišenský (1967, 121) lacks the sophistication of Evans' analysis.
[30]Lopez 1952.
[31]Prague Muzeum české hudby XV.F.342; VI.A.109; Brno, Ústav dějin hudby A.6357.

with the devil. The witch trials involving shepherds in Bohemia[32] reveal this is no trivial imputation to the sorts of individuals featured in pastorellas, and we may take the willingness of villagers to bring testimony against them as evidence of the tensions in communal society to which we have already alluded. In a way, the pastorella is a record of the rural population in the middle of the conflict that characterizes baroque devotional artistic expression.[33] As Geoffrey Chew observed twenty years ago,[34] the folk instruments either invoked or actually utilized in pastorellas were the very *Bettlerinstrumente* associated with vagrants and other disreputable types. Moreover, the impetus toward accommodation that, I suggest, lies behind the flourishing of the genre would also help to explain the toleration at Christmastide of a kind of "institutionalized" begging, by the very actors entrusted with the annunciation of Divine Birth to the village on Christmas Eve.[35] An exceedingly popular church music form with both rural and urban branches of development,[36] pastorellas have been cherished as cantors' music par excellence, a comment on their musical inventiveness, on the number of works that survive, and on their central position in the oeuvres of schoolmasters and other church composers of Central Europe. Their dominant theme is the annunciation to the shepherds, that is, the approach to earthly mortals by the heralds of heaven's authority. Altogether the repertory constitutes an extraordinary appropriation of the pastoral convention ubiquitous in elite culture as—in the words of one critic which seem particularly apt here—"a form of the religious idea, a means of pitting the ideal creatively against the real."[37] That *pastoral* functions as a kind of code of balance and

---

[32] Antl 1900; Schulz 1903; Kočí 1973, 153–54 with a late example (1756) from Jistebnice on the Lobkovic estate. Cf the case described by Ilwof (1897, 247–48) wherein the loss of animals to wolves is blamed on a herdsman's pact with the devil—this as late as 1771. Though the number of witch trials declined in Bohemia and Moravia after 1700, popular belief in contracts with the devil persisted, to judge from a government order of 1758 expressly denying such things; in fact punishments for devil possession remained in the lawbooks until Joseph II struck them fully two decades later (Gottschall 1979, 97).

[33] Cf Struth 1949, 87: "Beim Volk besteht die Tendenz zur Sinnenhaftigkeit, die keiner abstrakten Denkhilfen bedarf, bei der Kirche die zur Vergeistigung. Die Geistigkeit des Volkes ist natürlich und frisch, während die Kirche ihre Lehre in ein wohl durchdachtes und geordnetes System fasst. Daraus ergibt sich eine Spannung, die das Volk zu einer Auseinandersetzung zwingt. Die Hirtenlieder zeigen das Volk in dieser Auseinandersetzung."

[34] Chew 1968, 184–85. Legal decrees and even penal codes often grouped outlaws and itinerant players of the bagpipe, hurdy-gurdy, dulcimer, etc: Krickeberg 1983, 102.

[35] Schroubek 1974, 460: "Hier ist das ursprüngliche Heischerecht für bestimmte Berechtigte—Schullehrer, Chorsänger, Nachtwächter, den Ortshirten—in der Tat zu jener Bettelei geworden...."

[36] Berkovec 1987, 55–67.

[37] Haffenden 1987, 32, quoting an anonymous source.

civility in relationships between unequals; that it "embraces the commotion of social opposition within the calm of its form"[38] did not escape the propagators of Austro-Bohemian Catholicism in their quest for social consensus, just as it does not today escape the anthropologists concerned with problems of cultural hegemony, nor students of 20th-century political propaganda.[39]

Pastorellas are church music in the conventional sense, despite their vernacular texts and musical styles. Not only were they copied, performed, and disseminated in the same manner as other church music, but also the musical and textual means by which they established seasonal relevance often parallels that of liturgical genres.[40] Yet at the same time pastorellas came to life within a larger framework than that of the mass and its accompanying forms, borrowing heavily from indigenous traditions of popular religious devotion. Indeed part of their attraction lies in the fact that they belong to that peculiarly baroque explosion of popular creativity called, for want of any better designation, "semifolkish" (pololidový, halbvolkstümlich).[41] The most telling consequence of this promiscuous parentage, I would like to suggest, is the striking tendency for pastorellas to share melodic phrases, rhythmic motives, opening formulas, and even structural plans—in short, characteristics typically associated with orally transmitted repertories. In addition, the degree to which pastorellas circulated anonymously or surfaced recast by different cantors seems to overstep the boundary where misattribution suffices as the only logical explanation (see example).[42]

---

[38]Ibid., 6: "Society thus requires the pastoral hero at once to embody and to purge it of its own dissenting impulses. Both insider and outsider, he is the necessary and welcome token sacrifice, and thus paradoxically the very model of a 'unifying social force.'"

[39]Rosaldo 1986, 97; Featherstone 1986, 161. There was also an eighteenth-century resonance to this political aspect, though its frame of reference was courtly pastoral; in certain economic theories of the age John Marino (1986, 131–32) sees "pastoral ideology as a mentality that imposed its imaginary version of the countryside on rural socioeconomic reality."

[40]Chew 1968, 176.

[41]Palas 1964, 53–63; Beneš 1968–69, 61–62. This is to say that pastorellas developed neither in isolation from "civilization" on the one hand, nor beneath a veneer of church protection on the other. By invoking these terms I wish to point to the resilience and recuperative power which baroque Catholicism discovered in popular culture. Here I differ from those who see musical life in the country as a distinct area of inquiry; rather, I believe the whole notion of a separate folk culture—*Volksbarock*, *selský* barok, etc.—must be called into question.

[42]The manuscripts in the example are as follows: Český Krumlov, Okresní archív 2851\596 (Matěj Novák, prov. Prachatice); Prague, Museum české hudby, VI.B.41 Jiří Linek, prov. Bakov); Sandomierz, Seminarium Duchowni, A.VIII.1 (Anon., prov. unknown); Prague, Mčh [uncat] (Anon., prov. Ženzný Brod).

Not to put too fine a point on it, pastorellas possess something of the appearance of collective property, each piece a "reworking" of the collective tradition, with little emphasis placed on the individuality of the work or on the proprietorship of the author.[43]

It is this aspect of the genre, its schizophrenic dissemination as both church music and collective cultural property, that underscores the popular origins of Bohemia's musical ascendancy in the late 17th and 18th centuries. Though here is not the place to elaborate that idea fully, I should like to take it as a peg on which to hang a few concluding remarks. The reworking of favorite pastorellas in a given parish suggests the evolution of what might be described as canons of essentially local significance. It is too convenient to dismiss the acts of rescoring, retexting, truncating, and supplementing as merely pragmatic adjustments without seeing them also, however small the scale, as tacitly critical acts as well. Indeed the reason one early extant work, by the cantor Kadeřávek, can be rescued today from its incomplete source is that a later cantor based one of his own pastorellas on it[44] (that in itself constituting a rescue of sorts, revealing the values of a different generation). The point, of course, is not that older pieces were salvaged on a large scale; yet the rural circulation of church music in a vernacular idiom, with or without attribution to one cantor or another, signifies a genuine contemporaneous interest in regional traditions that extends back well before the "historicizing" nineteenth century—indeed it is a good *baroque* problem that musicologists are recognizing all too belatedly. A considerable challenge lies ahead, it seems to me, in distinguishing such local canons one from the other insofar as the evidence of these and other "overlapping" sources can be read, allowing for lin-

---

[43]Finnegan 1973, 133. I offer this interpretation as an alternative to that in Chew 1968, where it is suggested (177–79) that composers of pastorellas "avoided" complexity and originality, being inherently conservative and resistant to change. It seems to me that the phenomena I describe can be placed in a positive, rather than a negative light, perhaps in the manner that ethnomusicologists describe certain music repertories as supplying a general but vital coherence; William Belzner (1981, 731), working from a premise that he derives from classic studies by McCallester and Merriam, finds that music can embody "elements of continuity within a culture, even as that culture undergoes dramatic transformation."

[44]Berkovec 1987, 46–47. There is much in Berkovec to emend the notion that pastorellas and other church music genres seldom circulated from place to place in rural areas. As early as the 1750s, works by Dubrovice cantor Paus and the Citoliby cantor Kopřiva were copied by Linek, cantor at Bakov, to take just one other example. Also, to say in the present context that pastorellas of both the rustic and more refined variety reached audiences at both ends of the social spectrum is not to downplay the distance between privileged and unprivileged classes, but rather is to underscore it (cf note 41 above).

guistic, religious, and other regional peculiarities, such that they may one day offer a place to begin in positing a musical topography. I see no reason why this problem should be considered merely an ethnographic one. The task should be approached on the same scale that the Swedes have recently announced for a similar period, including cooperation across internal and national borders; though in contrast to that project, the source material for Bohemia must be counted among the richest of Europe, and surely one of the most intriguing by virtue of its complicated Counter-Reformation history. On the encouraging side, however, the historical criteria for a topography encompassing the "semifolkish" devotional repertories of Central Europe have already been outlined by Leopold Nowak.[45] It is time we take up his challenge.

Finally there is an important difference between the reworking of compositions which in any event typically incorporate recognizable, seasonally-relevant motifs, and another kind of reworking that readily comes to mind with regard to Bohemian choir lofts toward the end of the eighteenth century—the kind of reworking involved in molding pastorellas and other church music out of, say, operatic set pieces. It is a phenomenon whose implications are at the same time obvious and difficult to assess. Examples range from pastorellas adapted from *Don Giovanni* and *Zauberflöte* (as in a German contrafactum of "Là ci darem," or a Czech version of Papageno's aria) and from Peter Winter's *Das unterbrochene Opferfest* (set to a Czech text in the former Jesuit church at Březnice to entire masses made up of numbers from *Così fan tutte* and from Wenzel Mueller's *Der Zauberzitter*.[46] In imagining the theatricality of services bedecked by this music, we need not question the sincerity of choirmasters who borrowed from the operatic stage any more than we should fail to respect the sincerity of choirmasters whose inspiration was equally profane but far from the limelight. In any case such adaptations continued long into the nineteenth century, apparent-

---

[45] Andersson 1986; Nowak 1970. By far the most important work in this regard being undertaken in Czechoslovakia is that by Jan Trojan; see especially his survey of cantors in Moravia (1984).

[46] Aria pastorella [arranged from *Don Giovanni*]: Prague, Muzeum české hudby, III.D.159, prov. unknown; Pastorella pro Tribus Regibus [*Zauberflöte*]: Miličín, kostelní archiv, without shelfmark (see Berkovec 1987, 132-33, and in the plates following 272, plate 17, reproducing the title page); Pastorella del opera Sacrifficio Interrotto: Hudební oddělení, Universitní-Státní knihovna, sbírka Březnice, 416 (see Pešková 1983, 212-13); Missa Solemnis . . . del Kozafantin [a kind of anagram for Così fan tutte?]: Fibiger collection, Bakov (see Tomandlová 1958, 48); Zauberzitte Messe: prov. Paseky nad Jizerou, Památník zapadlých vlastenců.

ly unimpeded by reformist attacks. Most important, that the practice can be readily documented in country parishes[47] where the operas themselves were never heard attests to a vital musical culture deriving its momentum from previous generations of local church musicians. The village cantors who in this way acclaimed and ratified the universal appeal of cosmopolitan musical culture can thus be seen extending a secularized baroque world view into the early nineteenth century, shedding light on the interaction between genres of local and translocal significance—and thus joining in the delineation of the international repertory's canons.

References

Andersson, AV Gregor. "Projektrapport: Stadsmusikantväsendet i Sverige under 1600-och 1700-talet," *Svensk Tidskrift för Musikforskning* 68 (1986): 101–106.

Antl, Theodor. "Čarodějní pastýři na Třeboňsku roku 1663," *Český lid* 9 (1900): 293–99.

Bartůšek, Vàclav. "Vývoy školství na Podblanicku ve druhé polovině 17. století v první třetině 18. století," *Sborník vlastivědnýc h práci z Podblanicka* 19 (1978): 185–212.

Beckerman, Michael. "In search of Czechness in music," *19th-Century Music* 10 (1986–87): 61–73.

Belzner, William. "Music, modernization, and westernization among the Macuma Shuar," *Cultural transformantions and ethnicity in modern Ecuador*, ed. Norman Whitten (Urbana 1981): 731–48.

Beneš, Bohuslav. "Die ästhetische Auffaussung der Wirklichkeit in der mitteleuropäischen halbvolkstümlichen Literatur," *Ethnologia Eruopaea* 2–3 (1968–69); 59–64.

Berkovec, Jiří. *České pastorely*. Praha 1987.

---

[47] In metropolitan centers professional musicians provided an obvious point of contact between theatrical and ecclesiastical institutions; thus the graduals with Latin texts based on excerpts from Mozart's *Thamos* and on the finale from *Clemenza di Tito* (now in the Loretto collection of the Lobkovic family archives), along with pastorellas drawn from operas by Cimarosa and Piccini, all came from the hand of Josef Strobach (1731–94), first violinist at the Italian Opera in Prague and choirmaster at several Prague churches (see Pulkert 1973, I:215, 235, 124). It is perhaps harder to see the connections in the case, for instance, of an "Aria de Beata Virgine" based on Leporello's register aria, copied for the village church at Rychnov nad Kněžnou (Muzeum české hudby, XIII.A.76; two pages of the manuscript are reproduced in Volek\Pešková 1987, 113; cf also the following plates at 114–15).

Bloch, Maurice. "Symbols, song, dance, and features of articulation: is religion an extreme form of traditional authority?" *Archives européennes de Sociologie* 15 (1974): 55–81.

Blum, Jerome. *The end of the old order in rural Europe.* Princeton 1978.

Burke, Kenneth. *A rhetoric of motives.* New York 1950.

Burney, Charles. *The present state of music in Germany, The Netherlands, and United Provinces,* 2d ed. 2 vols. London 1775.

Burrows, David. "Music and the 'nausea delle cose cotidiane'," *The Musical Quarterly* 57 (1971): 230–40.

Čapek, Jan. *Z kulturních dějin českých* XVII. a XVIII. století, Knihovna pokroka 166. Praha 1940.

Chew, Geoffrey. *The Christmas pastorella in Austria, Bohemia, and Moravia,* dissertation, University of Manchester, 1968; revised version to be published in *Kirchenmusikalisches Jahrbuch* (1989).

Dahlhaus, Carl. *Foundations of music history;* trans. J.B. Robinson. Cambridge 1983.

Darnton, Robert. "Literary history and the library," *The Princeton University Library Chronicle* 48 (1986–87): 145–51. Ducreux, Marie-Elizabeth. personal communication, 2 January 1986. Engelbrecht, Helmut. *Geschichte des österreichischen Bildungswesens.* 4 vols. Wien 1982–86. Evans, Robert. *The making of the Habsburg monarchy 1550–1700: an interpretation.* Oxford 1979. Featherstone, Simon. "The nation as pastoral in British literature of the Second World War," *Journal of European Studies* 16 (1986): 155–68.

Finnegan, Ruth. "Literacy versus non-literacy: the great divide?" *Modes of thought: essays on thinking in western and non-western societies,* ed. Robin Horton and Ruth Finnegan (London 1973): 112–44.

Flotzinger, Rudolf. "Über den Bildungseffekt und die 'andere' Konservität katholischer Kirchenmusik," *Geistliche Musik: Studien zu ihre Geschichte und Funktion im 18. und 19. Jahrhundert,* ed. Constantin Floros et al.; Hamburger Jahrbuch für Musikwissenschaft 8 (Laaber 1985): 143–55.

Gottschall, Klaus. *Dokumente sum Wandel im religiösen Leben Wiens während des Josephinismus,* Veröffentlichungen des Instituts für Volkskunde der Universität Wien 7. Wien 1979.

Haffenden, John. "Introduction" to William Empson, *Argufying: essays on literature and culture* (London 1987): 1–63.

Hanzal, Josef. "Nižší školy v Čechách v 17. a 18. století," *Muzejní a vlastivědná práce* 10\80 (1972): 152–70.

Hejnic, Josef. "Jihočeský školství v 15. –18. století," *Jihočeský sborník historický* 43 (1974): 54–60.

Houston, Rab. "Literacy and society in the west, 1500–1850," *Social History* 8 (1983): 269–93.

Hucke, Helmut. "Vivaldi und die vokale Kirchenmusik des Settecento," *Antonio Vivaldi: teatro musicale, cultura, e società*, ed. Lorenzo Bianconi and Giovanni Morelli; Studi di Musica Veneta, Quaderni Vivaldiani 2 (Firenze 1982): 191–206.

Hůlek, Julius. "Poznámky k otázce kořenů hudby českého národního obrození," *Město v české kultuře* 19. století, ed. Milena Freimanová (Praha 1983): 329–36.

Ilwof, Fanz. "Hexenwesen und Aberglauben in Steiermark: ehedem und jetzt," *Zeitschrift des Vereins für Volkskunde* 7 (1897): 184–96, 244–54.

Kahan, Arcadius. "Notes on serfdom in Western and Eastern Europe," *Journal of Economic History* 33 (1973): 86–99.

Kallberg, Jeffrey. "The rhetoric of genre: Chopin's Nocturne in G minor," *19th-Century Music* 11 (1987–88): 238–61.

Kauper, Russel. *The sacred works of Augustin Holler (1744- 1814): little known aspects of religious music in eighteenth-century Munich*, dissertation, University of Southern California, 1979.

Klíma, Josef. *Manufakturní období v Čechách*. Praha 1955.

Kočí, Josef. *Čarodějnické procesy: z dějin inkvizice a čarodějnických procesů v českých zemích v 16.–18. století*. Praha 1973.

Koenigsberger, Helmut. "Decadence or shift? changes in the civilization of Italy and Europe in the sexteenth and seventeenth centuries," *Transactions of the Royal Historical Society*, fifth series, 10 (1960): 1–18.

Kokoschka, Oscar. "An approach to the baroque art of Czechoslovakia," *Burlington Magazine* (November 1942): 263–68.

Krickeberg, Dieter. "On the social status of the Spielmann in 17th- and 18th-century Germany," *The social status of the professional musician from the Middle Ages to the 19th century*, ed. Walter Salmen, trans. Herbert Kaufmann and Barbara Reisner (New York 1983): 95–122.

Kučera, Jan. "Příspěvek k problémům lidového náboženství v 17. a 19. století," *Sborník historický* 23 (1975): 5–33.

Lalo, Charles. *L'art et la vie sociale*. Paris 1921.

Lom, František. "Die Arbeitsproduktivität in der Geschichte der tschechoslowakischen Landwirtschaft," *Zeitschrift für Agrargeschichte und Agrarsoziologie* 19 (1971): 1–25.

Lopez, Robert. "Hard times and investment in culture," *The Renaissance: a symposium* (New York 1952): 19–33.

MacIntyre, Bruce. *The Viennese concerted mass of the early classic period*, Studies in musicology 89. Ann Arbor 1986.

Mandrou, Robert. "Le baroque européen: mentalité pathétique et révolution sociale," *Annales* 15 (1960): 898–914.

Marino, John. "The state and the shepherds in pre-Enlightenment Naples," *Journal of Modern History* 58 (1986): 125–42.

Melton, James. *Absolutism and the eighteenth-century origins of compulsory schooling in Prussia and Austria*. Cambridge 1988.

Nowak, Leopold. "Studien zur einer Musiktopographie Niederösterreichs," *Österreichische Musikzeitschrift* 25 (1970): 84–95.

Ostrowski, Wincenty. *Wiejskie szkolnictwo parafialne na Śląsku w drugiej polowie XVII wieku*, Prace Wrolawskiego Towarzystwa Naukowego A/145. Wrocław 1971.

Palacký, František. "Obyvatelstvo českých měst a školní vzdělání v 16. a na vačátku 17. století," *Ceskoslovenský časopis histrický* 18 (1970): 34568.

Palas, Karel. *K problematice krajové pololidové literatury 18. století*, Spisy University J.E. Purkyně 97. Praha 1964.

Paleček, Jaroslav. "Školství kraji Vltavském v 17. století," *Sedlčanský sborník* (Sedlčany 1971): 61–86.

Pešková, Jitřenka. *Collectio ecclesiae březnicensis: catalogus collectionis operum artis musicae*, Artis musicae antiquioris catalogorum series 3. Praha 1983.

Polišenský, Josef. "Gesellschaft und Kultur des barocken Böhmens," *Österreichische Osthefte* 9 (1967): 112–29.

Pulkert, Oldřich. *Domus lauretana pragensis: catalogus collectionis operum artis musicae*, Artis musicae antiquioris catalogorum series 1\1–2. Praha 1973.

Rosaldo, Renato. "From the door of his tent: the fieldworker and the inquisitor," *Writing culture: the poetics and politics of ethnography*, ed. James Clifford and George Marcus (Berkeley 1986): 77–97.

Ryneš, Václav. "Farářské relace z let 1676/7, 1700/1," *Acta regionalia* 1 (1965): 106–12.

Schroubek, Georg. "Volksfrömmigkeit und Brauch," *Bohemia sacra: das Christentum in Böhmen 973- 1973*, ed. Ferdinand Seibt (Düsseldorf 1974): 455–64.

Schulz, Václav. "Pastucha čaroděj roku 1690 na Křivokláte2," *Český lid* 12 (1903): 110–11.

Spaemann, Cordelia. "Wallfahrtslieder," *Wallfahrt kennt keine Grenzen*, ed. Lenz Kriss-Rettenbeck and Gerda Möhler (München 1984): 181–92.

Stark, Werner. "Niedergang und Ende das landwirtschaftlichen Großbetriebs in den böhmischen Ländern," *Jahrbücher für Nationalökonomie und Statistik* 144 (1937): 416–49.

Struth, Sigrid. *Das weihnachtliche Hirtenlied*, dissertation, Johannes-Gutenberg-Universität, 1949.

Tomandlová, Eva. "Horčičkův seznam hudebnin z pozůstalosti bakovského učitele Augustina Fibigera," *Miscellanea musicologica* 5 (1958): 7–131.

Trojan, Jan. "Kantoři na Moravě a jejich hudební aktivita v 18. a 19. století," *Sborník prací filozofické fakulty Brněnské univerzity*, řada H, 19–20 (1984): 113–18.

Volek, Tomislav and Jitřenka Pešková. *Mozartův Don Giovanni: výstava k 200. výročí světové premiéry v Praze 1787–1987*. Praha 1987.

Weingarten, Johann von. *Codex Ferdinandeo-Leopoldino-Josephino-Carolinus: pro haereditario Regno Bohemiae, ac incorporatis aliis provinciis*. Prag 1720.

THE JANÁČEK CONFERENCE, 1988

Music Examples, Vocal Incipits

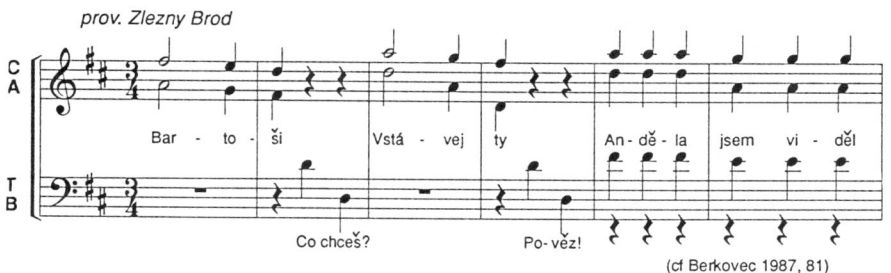
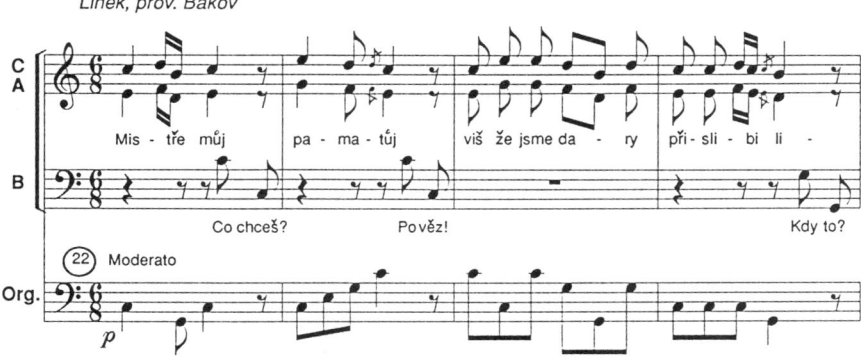

Vojtěch Jírovec and the Viennese String Quartet

Roger Hickman

Though we have hopefully distanced ourselves from the perspective which insists that Classical Music is something which was done by Mozart, Haydn, and sometimes Beethoven, there are still many significant aspects of the style which have not been adequately addressed. One of these concerns the development of the string quartet, and the role played by Bohemian-born composers in this process. Roger Hickman is a musicologist and a conductor who has been studying the music of some of these Bohemian composers for over a decade. His essay here focuses on the stylistic development of the quartets of Jírovec (Gyrowetz).

This year marks the tenth anniversary of my research into Bohemian composers of string quartets. Never did I imagine that there would be such a wealth of material to sustain this endeavor for a decade. Yet, in concentrating on Vienna alone, I have found an array of outstanding Bohemian musicians whose works had a significant impact on the shape of the 18th- and 19th-century quartet.

Among the composers that I have encountered are Florian Leopold Gassman, Emperor Joseph's favorite composer, whose brilliant career was cut short in 1774 by a riding accident; Vanhal, a popular composer whose fluid, melodic style comes closer to that of Mozart than any other composer except for J.C. Bach; Leopold Koželuh, who was hailed by Gerber to be Europe's favorite composer in 1792; František Kramář, who was to become Vienna's most prolific quartet composer; and Pavel Vranický, an important conductor and composer in Vienna who was greatly admired by Fétis. Yet, based on the qualities of their works, the composers that I have been most impressed with are two Bohemians who do not receive as much publicity as the others—Paul Vranický's younger brother Antonín and the fascinating figure Vojtěch Jírovec. While I would like to extol the virtues of both of these worthy figures, in interest of time, I must restrict my remarks to a brief overview of the quartets of the latter.

Jírovec was born in České Budějovice in 1763, and later studied music in Prague and Brno. Fétis reports that Jírovec spoke Latin, Bohemian, German, Italian, French and English. He was also well-versed in the sciences and jurisprudence and was later employed in diplomatic affairs. Jírovec was an extremely prolific composer, and although the number of his compositions declined considerably during the 1820s, we can view him as the longest surviving member of the "Viennese Classical School."

In 1785, he went to Vienna and shortly thereafter began a European tour of Italy, France, London, and Germany. His first set of string quartets were composed during a visit to Rome in 1786–87. According to his autobiography, these quartets were "received with such great applause in the world, that they were stolen by Imbault in Paris, published in 1788, and, in a very short time, seven new editions appeared."[1] The success of this initial endeavor led to the publication of twelve more quartets in the following year. As one might expect, the style of these early quartets does not reflect the traditions of Vienna, but shows the strong influence of Paris. They contain two or three movements, they are tuneful, and they exhibit a simple and light character, features that are the essence of the *quatuor concertant* as conceived by Boccherini and Pleyel.

But the light and delicate nature of these early works was quickly abandoned. With his fourth set of quartets, published in 1793, a new theatrical flair began to assert itself. My first two examples, taken from the opening movement of the string quartet in D, Op. 25, No. 1, will illustrate this abrupt change. (See Examples 1 and 2, opposite.)

Perhaps the most obvious element of the new style is the virtuoso treatment of all four quartet members. But, even more significant are the orchestral features—abrupt contrasts of mood, bold unisons, repetitious rhythm—and the theatrical gestures, such as the dramatic silence before the second theme. It is works like this that led Heinrich Koch to write in 1802: "it is today a difficult task to distinguish between the theater and chamber styles or to specify a precise difference in character between them."[2]

You may have noticed in the second example that the second key area was not in the expected dominant (A major), but in the lower mediant (F major). To my knowledge, this is the earliest instance of a

---

[1] *Lebensläufe deutscher Musiker von ihnen selbst erzählt*, Vol. III.IV: *Adalbert Gyrowetz*, ed. by Alfred Einstein (Leipzig, 1915): "... welche in der Folge so grossen Beifall in der Welt erhielten, in Paris bei Imbeault gestochen und in sehr kurzer Zeit durch sieben Auflagen erneuert und gekrönt wurden."

[2] Heinrich Koch, *Musikalisches Lexicon* (Frankfurt on Main, 1802), pp. 821–822: "daher ist es heut zu Tage auch eine schere Aufgabe, zwischen dem Theater- und Kammerstyle eine Grenzlinie zu ziehen, oder von beyden eine bestimmten Unterscheidungs Charakter anzugeben."

Example 1. Gyrowetz, Opus 25 No. 1, I, mm. 267–2

Example 2. Gyrowetz, Opus 25 No. 1, I, mm. 36–48

Example 2. cont.

substitute dominant. And unlike the early substitute dominants of Beethoven, the new key area does not heighten formal tensions, but serves to relax tensions, as in the manner of the Romantic sonata form.

These two new elements—the theatric orchestral qualities and the loosening of formal tensions—continue to appear in the published quartets of Jírovec through the end of the 1790s. Let us look at two additonal examples, both taken from Opus 29, published in 1799 (Examples 3 and 4, opposite). In the first, the chordal confirmation of the dominant key (D major) in the exposition is undercut by a B-minor chord. Following some chromatic shifting, the second theme begins in E flat, in mid-phrase an augmented-sixth chord corrects the harmony, and we move back to the dominant.

In the second excerpt from Opus 29, (Example 4) we again find a substitute dominant. The second key area in the E flat movement is set in C major, the major submediant. Again note the theatrical elements: multiple-stopped chords, rhythmic repetition, abrupt contrasts. In particular note the theatrical cliche of closing and lingering on the single dominant pitch before resolving into the new key area. Once the new area has arrived, all tensions are unravelled with the flowing conjunct second theme.

After Opus 29, only six more quartets by Jírovec were published, all in the early 19th century. With these works, two additional changes can be observed: an increase in the proportional size of the development section and an ever freer harmonic treatment. The development section of Opus 44, no. 2, for example, contains 73 measures, only 12 less than the exposition. The proportional size of the development is larger than any in Beethoven's Opus 18 quartets. In addition, listen to the extent of the chromatic shifting.

Example 3. Gyrowetz, Opus 29 No. 2, I, mm. 40–55

Example 4. Gyrowetz, Opus 29 No. 1, I, mm. 47–60

Example 4, cont.

The string quartets of Jírovec undergo as much change during the late 18th century as those of any other quartet composer. His earliest works reflect the popular, tuneful style of the Parisian *quatour concertant*. During the 1790s, virtuoso displays and orchestral features created a new theatrical conception of the genre. In the early 19th century, the quartets of Jírovec also begin to exhibit a freer harmonic idiom and proportionally-large development sections.

Now a number of these features can also be found in the works of Haydn and Beethoven, but what distinguishes the quartets of Jírovec from those of the two classical masters are the broad flowing melodies and the loosening of Classical sonata principles. In these respects, we must link Jírovec with the early Romantic movement of the 1790s. His quartets point toward the style of the next generation of quartet composers—of Kramář, Hansel, Romberg, and Schubert. As noted by Charles Rosen, the Romantic movement derived not merely from Haydn, Mozart and Beethoven, but even more importantly from many lesser-known composer,[3] among the names of whom, the Bohemian Vojtěch Jírovec cannot be omitted.

---

[3]Charles Rosen, *The Classical Style* (New York, 1972), p. 384.

J. V. Voříšek and the Fantasy

Kenneth DeLong

We often consider unity of style and design to be one of the hallmarks of the Classical style, yet scholars like Hugh Macdonald have pointed out that sometimes disunity seems to be one of the artistic goals of a particular work. This is nowhere more so than in the late 18th and early 19th century genre known as the Fantasy. Here, disruption and disconnectedness may be stressed over continuity and flow. This phenomenon has been noted in the work of such figures as C.P.E. Bach, Mozart, and Beethoven, but in this study Kenneth DeLong, an expert on early 19th century piano music, sheds new light on the relationship between Voříšek and the elusive Fantasy.

During the early nineteenth century, an improvisation, based either upon a known theme or sui generis, was frequently included in public concerts given by touring pianists.[1] These improvisations, usually placed last in the program, were much admired by audiences and marveled at fully as much as the quality of the playing in the set pieces. The pianist and composer Johann Hummel (1778–1837), for example, was as highly regarded for his improvisations as for his brilliant pianism and was held to be the principal heir of Mozart and Beethoven in this respect.[2] And Ignaz Moscheles (1794–1870), Hummel's principal pianistic rival during the 1820s, was a near equal in this respect.[3]

The usual term given to such improvisations, and also to written-out compositions in an improvisational style, was "fantasy," a word which even

---

[1] The concert programs cited in Mary Sue Morrow, "Concert Life in Vienna 1780–1810," (Ph.D. diss., Indiana University, 1984), pp. 292–418, demonstrate the practice of including improvisations in instrumental concerts during the the period, a practice which became more pronounced with the rise of solo concerts (usually with accompanying singers and instrumentalists) during the next generation. See also Alice Hanson, *Musical Life in Biedermeier Vienna* (Cambridge, 1985), pp. 82–126.

[2] Joel Sachs, *Kapellmeister Hummel in England and France*, Detroit Monographs in Musicology, No. 6 (Detroit, 1977), pp. 17–65; and Henry Pleasants, trans. and ed., *The Musical Journeys of Louis Spohr* (Oklahoma, 1961), pp. 109–10. Any weaknesses in the area of improvisation tended to be noticed quickly by contemporaries and to bring opprobrium upon the pianist. See for example V. J. Tomášek's caustic comments upon Daniel Steibelt's improvisations in Adrienne Simpson and Sandra Horsfall, "A Czech Composer views his Contemporaries," *Musical Times* 115 (1974), pp. 287–88.

[3] Carolyn Gresham, "Ignaz Moscheles: An Illustrious Musician in the Nineteenth Century" (Ph.D. Diss., University of Rochester, 1980), pp. 12–18.

by the early nineteenth century already had acquired a long, often confusing, terminological history.[4] Broadly speaking, it referred to the act of public improvisation, but it also was used to describe compositions in which a certain freedom in the relationship between thematic ideas was present, and in which the "flight of the imagination" formed a central compositional impetus-features which often resulted in a "loose" musical structure. By the middle of the eighteenth century, the keyboard fantasy was firmly established as a distinct and separate genre, and although it was ostensibly concerned with freedom of expression, it was in reality bound by well-defined conventions regarding its musical content and style.[5] Rooted in a long-standing tradition of keyboard improvisation, the fantasy was also the form in which eighteenth-century ideas regarding the nature of musical genius and imagination were most clearly expressed, ideas that continued to hold sway into the early years of the nineteenth century.

These ideas regarding the fantasy, both with respect to its style of performance and to its expressive content, are discussed in the writings of several prominent baroque and classical theorists, including Johann Mattheson, C. P. E. Bach, and Daniel Gottlieb Türk, all of whom treat the fantasy primarily in terms of its manner of performance and intended effect upon an audience. Mattheson indicates that fantasies should be performed

> ... without a theme or subject, now agile, now hesitant, now one voice, now many voices; occasionally, for a short while, in tempo, occasionally without measure, however, not without a suitable intention, namely to precipitate and establish astonishment.[6]

C. P. E. Bach, the most prominent mid-century fantasy composer, devotes considerable space to the Free Fantasia in his *Essay on the True Art of Playing Keyboard Instruments* (1753), stressing the need for boldness in modulation, variety in pianistic figuration, and skill in the handling of chromaticism, especially in descending bass lines.[7] Through his many works in this form and through his widely read book, C.P.E. Bach

---

[4] The characteristics of the fantasy during the late-2eighteenth and early-nineteenth century are fully elucidated in Peter Schleuning, *The Fantasia*, trans A. C. Howie (Cologne, 1971); and Jesse Parker, "The Clavier Fantasy from Mozart to Liszt: A Study in Style and Content," (Ph.D Diss., Stanford University, 1974).

[5] The final chapter of C. P. E Bach's *Essay on the True Art of Playing Keyboard Instruments*, trans. and ed. by William J. Mitchell (New York, 1949), pp. 430–445, gives a useful summary of mid eighteenth-century conventions surrounding the keyboard fantasy.

[6] Johann Mattheson, *Der vollkommenne Capellmeister* (Hamburg, 1737), I, Ch. 10, para. 93.

[7] C. P. E. Bach, *Essay*, pp. 430–445.

became the natural point of reference for later writings about the fantasy and compositions in the fantasy manner.[8]

Toward the end of the century theorists were still discussing the fantasy in terms of actual performance, but now distinctions were drawn between different types of fantasies—distinctions that also applied to written-down fantasies. Türk, writing in 1789, states that

> the fantasy, in the main, is improvisatory, although there are cases where the fantasy, like other compositions, is written down prior to performance. A fantasy is called free when it does not rely on a rhythm, ... when it freely modulates, and when it thoroughly gives way to capriciousness without following a definite plan. Those fantasies which do follow a definite plan, and where more homogeneity is observed, are called bound.[9]

From examining the writings of these and other theorists and from studying the fantasies composed during the period, it is possible to draw some general conclusions regarding late eighteenth-century views of how the musical mind is supposed to work when functioning in an improvisatory context, and, consequently, what sort of piece a fantasy is supposed to be, whether freely improvised or written down. In brief, a fantasy should contain several attractive and spontaneously generated ideas, but they need not be worked out thoroughly or extensively. It may employ a wide variety of textures, figurations, and musical topics—all freely juxtaposed. Consequently, there can be many changes in tempo, since the flow of ideas will often be varied and irregular. Occasional passages in the "strict" or "learned" style may well be included since they show a mastery of hallowed compositional techniques. The direct power of the musical imagination should also inspire passages that will amaze and delight the listener with their harmonic boldness and ingenuity, often the result of remote modulations and chromaticism. To effect a direct, empathetic contact with the audience, a fantasy may sometimes assume a declamatory manner and may take on the gestures of recitative; a fantasy may also contain passages of technical virtuosity. Finally, the whole should have a unity that is not necessarily evident immediately but is, however, the result of a gifted musical mind working in a concentrated span of time.

The best-known written-down examples that exemplify the conventions just mentioned are the fantasies of C. P. E. Bach and the Fantasies in

---

[8]A. Peter Brown, *Joseph Haydn's Keyboard Music: Source and Style* (Bloomington, 1986), pp. 219–29, stresses the importance of C. P. E. Bach's *Essay* with respect to Haydn's keyboard music.

[9]Daniel Gottlieb Türk, *Klavierschule* (Leipzig, 1789), p. 395.

C and D minor of Mozart. The Mozart fantasies, with their extended harmonic range, multiplicity of thematic ideas, declamatory stance, and sectional structure are, perhaps, the most convincing expression of the fantasy style as it was understood in the late eighteenth century. With the advent of the virtuoso composer-pianists of the early nineteenth century, the fantasy entered upon a new era. The eighteenth-century type of fantasy was gradually altered to incorporate the newer melodic styles and notions about musical structure, and the "free" fantasy as described by Mattheson and practiced by C. P. E. Bach was largely dropped. Fantasies became larger, and as the range and variety of musical ideas expanded, composers increasingly felt the necessity to unify their sprawling and occasionally disjointed works through some overall organizing principle. Accordingly, the fantasy began to borrow techniques from already existing stricter forms, especially sonata, rondo, and variation forms. Many early nineteenth-century fantasies are, in fact, formal hybrids, having structures which are governed by key relationships or thematic interconnections, as in Schubert's familiar *Wanderer Fantasy* or Beethoven's two sonatas Op. 27, which are subtitled "quasi una fantasia."[10]

This newer approach to the fantasy was noticed and described by Heinrich Koch as early as 1802:

> The musician, in the case of the Free Fantasy, seizes any pleasing thoughts that come to him and welds them together without any apparent inner relationship, so that his improvisation will have the value of a truly creative ability. So must the written-down Fantasy have the appearance of a free inspiration, to differentiate the Fantasy from compositions with fixed forms. Many pieces in the fantasy style select the exterior contours of the definite form-type, as in the case of the Sonata Quasi Fantasia which possesses the outline of the sonata.[11]

Since from its inception the fantasy was the medium for individual expression, it was only natural that during the early nineteenth century the fantasy became one of the primary vehicles through which composers began to express their burgeoning romantic instincts. By adding fantasy elements to their squared-out post-classic structures, composers produced fantasies which have the surface of romanticism, but still cling to the characteristic melodic idioms, rhythms, and pianistic figurations

---

[10]Beethoven's relationship to the fantasy style is treated in Malcolm Bilson, "The Emergence of the Fantasy-Style in the Beethoven Piano Sonatas of the Early and Middle Periods," (Ph.D Diss., University of Illinois, 1968).

[11]Heinrich Christoph Koch, "Fantasie," *Musicalisches Lexicon* (1802; rpt. Hildesheim, 1964), pp. 296–97. (Translation mine)

of a classical heritage—compositions which occupy a twilight zone between a retrospective orientation toward the formal patterns of sonata and fugue and the later developments that stress free variation, thematic transformation, and bravura display.

The Czech-born composer and pianist Jan Vaclav Voříšek (1791–1825) was with Beethoven, Ignaz Moscheles, and Johann Hummel one of the best-known improvisors in Vienna, especially during his early years in the city when he was most active as a pianist (1813–23). His principal biographer, Aloys Fuchs, who was able to observe him at first hand, compared Voříšek to both Hummel and Moscheles as being among the finest ex tempore players of his time and describes him as a fluent improvisor on both the organ and piano, equally at home in either a strict or free style. His outstanding ability in this area was evident also in his work as a continuo player, and he was, apparently, one of few musicians in early nineteenth-century Vienna who could fluently realize a figured bass at sight.[12] Voříšek's talent for ex tempore playing was, apparently, initially evident in his organ playing, something that Fuchs stresses in his description of the composer's boyhood musical experiences:

> On the excursions to neighboring towns, the organ of the visited place was his main object. He practiced and fantasized often entire afternoons on the organ behind various closed church doors, and here one heard and saw him sunk into deep inspiration, into which the piano was never capable of moving him.[13]

Fuchs also describes the typical performance context of Voříšek's improvisations during his Vienna years and compares him favorably to his famous contemporary Moscheles:

> Voříšek had no rival at the time except Moscheles, and these two competed with each other in the honorable art [of playing the piano] for the glory of the victory. Yet both were completely different in their playing, and could in this way be very well juxtaposed. Very often it happened that both played one evening for the very same society, and if Moscheles surpassed Voříšek through his neat and extremely brilliant playing, it was, however, agreed upon that the latter excelled the former in extemporaneous fantasizing; for in this genre, where the individual genius ex-

---

[12]Herfrid Kier, *Raphael Georg Kiesewetter: Wegbereiter des musikalischen Historismus* (Regensburg, 1968), pp. 57–82; and idem, "Kiesewetters historische Hauskonzerte," *Kirchenmusikalisches Jahrbuch*, 52 (1968), 95–119.

[13]Aloys Fuchs, "Biographische Notizen über Johann Hugo Worzischek," *Monatsbericht der Gesellschaft der Musikfreunde* (Vienna, 1829), p. 151. (Translation mine)

[14]Fuchs, "Notizen," p. 153. (Translation mine)

presses itself most unmistakably, Voříšek was surpassed only by his model, Hummel.[14]

Fuchs goes on to describe in some detail the ways in which Voříšek actually improvised. In so doing, he provides evidence of the concurrent existence of the older eighteenth-century tradition of fantasy playing, with its basis in the learned style, and newer, more virtuoso styles based upon characteristic variations:[15]

> His fantasies could be placed into two classes, the division being based upon whether the musical material for the fantasy was his own or drawn from existing melodies. In the first case were fantasies of this type: one thread taken from the extent or self-chosen theme, spun forward into a highly regular whole, without brilliant figurations, usually in four voices, and not rarely contrapuntal throughout, and in the severe style. In this he avoided, however, through harmonically surprising moves and truly ingenious modulations, and a few hints at virtuosity, all the things that would weary the listener.... In the second case, namely where to do the preceding would have been unsuitable, he chose for himself an especially popular, lightly arranged theme, which, after he had done brilliant variations, soon exchanged for another in exactly the same style, and always combined the two in the most interesting manner, and so constructed them into a single, tactful, and well-fitting potpourri.[16]

Although he wrote only one work that is explicitly improvisatory in style, much of Voříšek's output derives to a considerable degree from his ability to improvise and from his mastery of the conventions surrounding improvisation as they were understood during the early Romantic period. Voříšek's one published fantasy, like those of his contemporaries, represents the writing-down of what was probably an improvisation that was reworked for publication. Because of its size and its relationship to his improvisational style, the Fantasy in C major, Op. 12, is one of Voříšek's most important works, revealing most clearly the working of his musical mind.[17] The Fantasy in C major is Voříšek's first attempt at writing a large solo piano work different in character and form from the rhapsodies and impromptus with which he had been occupied during his first years in Vienna. As with

---

[15]Voříšek apparently owned a copy of C. P. E. Bach's *Essay*, now located in the Czech National Library (Music Division). I would like to thank Dr. Zdeňka Pilková for bringing this fact to my attention.

[16]Fuchs, "Notizen," pp. 153–54. (Translation mine)

[17]It is available in two modern editions: *J. V. Voříšek*, Ausgewählte Klavierwerke, ed. Dana Zahn (Munich, 1971); and Jan Sykora, ed., *Česti klasiková*, Vol II, Musica Antiqua Bohemica 20 (Prague, 1954).

many of Vořišek's pieces, the exact date of composition is unknown, although the date of publication was about 1822.[18] A portion of the Fantasy, the concluding allegro con brio, does exist in manuscript, however, and is dated 1817.[19] It seems probable that the first section of the two-part fantasy was composed after this date and was combined with the previously composed allegro to form a more substantial, large-scale work. In its final published form, the Fantasy consists of two parts: a florid andante in C major, and a related allegro con brio in C minor.

The first section of the Fantasy is highly varied thematically and reveals Vořišek's mastery over those features previously mentioned that comprise the fantasy style. It is an example of the type of improvised fantasy described by Fuchs as characterizing Vořišek's manner of improvising. The Fantasy opens with a long-held C (See Example 1), a dramatic call to attention suggesting importance and authority. It announces the principal melodic idea, a simple one, that is merely a C major chord inflected by chromatic neighbor tones. These seemingly innocent chromatic touches eventually prove to be a central element of the fundamental, germinal motive for the entire Fantasy. Initially, this two-measure idea is directly answered (mm. 4–5) and extended to lead toward the cadence in measure eight. Outwardly simple, these opening eight measures are remarkable for the way in which every facet of the music contributes toward one basic gesture: the growth from a single note into an entire phrase. Structurally the phrase is a single harmonic unit, in which tension gradually accumulates until its release in measure eight. This building of tension is accomplished by the extending of a simple I IV V I progression over a tonic pedal, by the gradual increase in dynamic level, and by the hemiola rhythm which drives the phrase toward its conclusion. Instead of being followed by a counterstatement or developed in some other manner, the idea is immediately abandoned and followed by three measures of "marking time" (m. 8–10) before another idea, completely different in character, emerges. A cadence is approached in measure sixteen only to be avoided and is ultimately reached in measure twenty-one. These twenty-one measures, the opening tonic-defining section of what eventually becomes a sonata-based harmonic structure, contain a number of apparently unrelated ideas or fragments of ideas—all freely juxtaposed-that establish the characteristic stance of an improvised fantasy.

---

[18]J. V. Vořišek, *Ausgewhälte Klavierwerke*, ed. Dana Zahn (Munich, 1971), Preface.
[19]The autograph is located in the Deutsche Staatsbibliothek in East Berlin.

Example 1. *Fantasy in C major*, Op. 12, Movement I, mm. 1–22,

Following a transition to the dominant that contains still more rapid changes in style and figuration, a smoothly phrased "second theme" is presented. (see Example 2) Although on the surface this theme appears to be new, it is actually a transformation of the opening chromatically decorated motive: the single initial note (the tonic in the first instance, here the dominant) is now elaborated by arpeggiation to present a new melodic shape, but the chromatic neighbor tones characteristic of the germinal motive are retained. Thus transformed, the second theme is presented as an

Example 2. *Fantasy in C major,* Op. 12, Movement I, mm. 36–50.

antecedent-consequent melody, much in the manner of an operatic cantilena. With its rapid and strongly accented appoggiaturas, simple harmonic background, and decorative melodic style, this theme is typical of the florid, operatically influenced melodies popular during the nineteenth century, a melodic style characteristic not only of Hummel and Moscheles, but also of Weber and other pianist/composers of the period.

The extension of the dominant key-area takes the form of a large contrapuntal section that eventually builds to a climax and a cadence. This contrapuntal passage strikes a serious, "learned" note that contrasts sharply with the popular, "modern" style presented immediately before. The passage is also a fine example of typical "faked counterpoint" in a fantasy context: presented as two upper parts supported by a walking bass, the passage strives to demonstrate the composer's (or improvisor's) prowess at handling the most severe style of all-chromatic counterpoint. By preserving the in-

Example 3. *Fantasy in C major,* **Op. 12, Movement I, mm. 51–68.**

tegrity of the walking bass (the most immediately striking element of Baroque style), the music diverts attention momentarily from the two upper parts, which in reality prove to be little more than harmonic filler with a few suspensions. (See Example 3, mm. 50–54) Following a rapid move through the circle of fifths (mm. 55–57), the passage grandly emerges from its contrapuntal rigors to make a forceful, free-style cadence in the subdominant, only to have the cadence thrust aside by a whimsical, pianissimo Neapolitan-sixth chord that leads to an even more striking show of contrapuntal chromaticism (mm. 60–63). On the surface this is impressive indeed. But for Voříšek, fluent with the idioms of Baroque harmony and fluent in the art of continuo playing, the passage represents no great originality and consists

Example 4. *Fantasy in C major*, **Op. 12, Movement I, mm. 86–99.**

largely of stringing together a number of Baroque-style contrapuntal cliches. In a fantasy context, however, the intended serious note has been struck.

Example 5. *Fantasy in C major,* **Op. 12, Movement I, mm. 117–24.**

The development section is concerned with two phases of action: (1) an intensified treatment of the contrapuntal passage just discussed; and (2) the gradual evolving of the sixteenth notes into a triplet figure that gathers intensity to reach a climax on a fortissimo Neapolitan-sixth chord, the point of greatest intensity in the section. (See Example 4) Structurally this second phase is handled with considerable skill. A Baroque-style texture (mm. 86–87) is transformed into a free-style, broken chord texture (mm. 88) that is eventually organized into a four-member modulating sequence that descends by thirds, tonicizing the keys of E-flat, C, A-flat, and F (mm. 89–95). Because each member of the sequence consists of four quarter-note units in a triple meter context, the measure rhythm is constantly irregular, adding considerably to the accumulation of tension. Following a harmonic pause in F minor (mm. 95–96), the music drops a final third to D-flat, which is treated as the Neapolitan-sixth chord of the tonic, C major. The entire passage is tautly constructed and demonstrates Voříšek's ability to create passages of striking harmonic intensity.

The recapitulation is compressed and the order of the two thematic ideas is reversed. When the opening, germinal theme is presented a final time just before the end, it is given in full dress, with rolled, fortissimo block chords (Example 5). A standard feature of the early Romantic fantasy style, it is nevertheless used here to good effect, providing both a sense of thematic unification and also an effective summing up of what has gone before.

Like the first part of the Fantasy, the second section forms an independent sonata-form unit. The central melodic idea with its characteristic chromatic semitone inflection is recast in bravura style to

Example 6. *Fantasy in C major,* **Op. 12, Movement II, mm. 1–16.**

provide a sharp contrast to the essentially lyric and rhapsodic manner of the opening movement. Together with the thematic transformation of the opening idea, a further unifying feature is provided by the presence of the triplet rhythm that both concludes the opening section and opens the final section. This triplet rhythm persists throughout the entire final movement, giving it the quality of an impassioned *moto perpetuo*—a typical finale style for the period and also readily found in the music of Hummel and Weber. (See Example 6)

As with certain of his piano rhapsodies and impromptus, Voříšek appears to have had a specific model in mind for the composition of the movement. In this instance the model is likely to have been Hummel's Fantasy in E-flat major, Op. 18, one of Hummel's best-known works and published only a few years before in 1811.[20] Hummel's Fantasy, like Voříšek's, is a multi-sectioned work, and it is the concluding section of the Fantasy that apparently provided the inspiration for the final movement of the Voříšek Fantasy. (See Example 7) As can be readily seen from Example 7, Voříšek adopts Hummel's textures, basic affect, and pianistic figurations. In fact, the final movement of Voříšek's Fantasy is a virtual paraphrase of the Hummel model.[21] Where Hummel is prolix and discursive, however, Voříšek is concentrated and structurally taut. And although it lacks some of the technical brilliance of the Hummel work, Voříšek's Fantasy is stronger in musical substance and avoids unnecessary longeurs.

Example 7a. Hummel, *Fantasy, mm. 1-3.*

Voříšek, *Fantasy,* **mm. 1-3.**

---

[20]Dieter Zimmerschied, *Thematisches Verzeichnis Johann Nepomuk Hummel* (Hofheim, 1971), p. 22. It is worth noting in this regard that Voříšek was a student of Hummel from about 1813 to 1816, played his music in public, and took over Hummel's class of piano student when he left for Stuttgart in 1816.

[21]The issue of "modeling" in early nineteenth-century music is discussed in Charles Rosen, "Influence: Plagiarism and Inspiration," *Nineteenth-Century Music* 4 (1980), pp. 87-100; with specific reference to Voříšek, this matter is treated in my dissertation "The Solo Piano Music of J. V. Voříšek" (Ph.D. Diss., Stanford University, 1982), pp. 74-111 and 122-140.

Example 7b. Hummel, *Fantasy*, mm. 18–20.

Voříšek, *Fantasy*, mm. 7–9.

Example 7c. Hummel, *Fantasy*, mm. 31–34.

Voříšek, *Fantasy*, mm. 48–50.

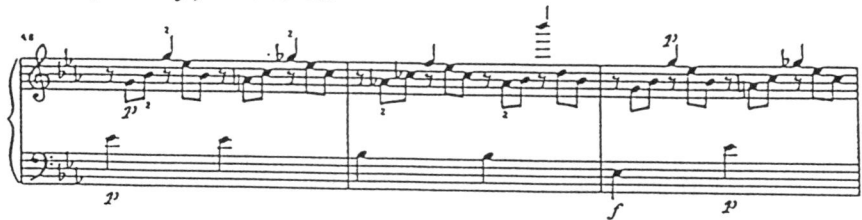

As mentioned earlier, an autograph of this final movement still exists. Curiously, the title page (probably added by Fuchs, from whose collection of Voříšek manuscripts this originally came) states that the work is a rondo, even though it is clearly a sonata, complete with repeated exposition, development, and recapitulation. The autograph score itself (a fair copy) is untitled but has the tempo marking *allegro di bravura*, a common marking for the composer. That the score is indeed an autograph is stated by Fuchs on his added title page by the words "Manuscript des Verfassers." Fuchs also gives the date as July 1822, possibly the date of his acquiring the manuscript, since it is dated 19 September 1817 at the end.

The autograph differs considerably from the first printed edition—the basis for all subsequent editions. The primary difference between the autograph and the printed version is the inclusion of a "second theme" in the printed version that is not present in the autograph. Following the four-page autograph score, however, there is an extra page (also in Voříšek's handwriting) that contains the new theme that is added to the published version. (See Example 8) This theme is given twice, once in E-flat major and again (slightly altered) in C minor—the keys in which the theme appears in the printed version. Apparently, the contrasting idea was an afterthought and was inserted later as part of the revisions made prior to publication. Moreover, the development section of the printed version differs from that given in the autograph, being six measures longer in the printed version and substantially re-written. It is probable that the autograph was originally conceived as an independent piece which was substantially revised at the time of publication and preceded by a newly composed opening section to form the two-movement work as it now stands. The inclusion of the new "second theme" represents a substantial improvement from a melodic point of view and provides relief from the relentless,

Example 8. *Fantasy in C major*, **autograph, extra page.**

driving triplets. The development section too is strengthened by greater intensity in the modulatory passages and by a treatment of the newly included "second theme" which provides an added measure of overall thematic integration.

Despite the unifying features that are clearly present-sonata form and thematic transformation-the total impression that Voříšek's Fantasy makes is not entirely satisfactory to modern ears. It is not only the bewildering kaleidoscope of styles presented—that is expected in a fantasy; it is more that the quality of the ideas themselves is rarely striking: for the most part they are commonplace and derivative rather than truly inventive. Furthermore, the very clarity of the formal structure is at variance with the wide variety of ideas presented and creates a conflict between the implications of the ideas and the externally imposed sonata structure. While a certain stylistic and formal looseness is expected in a fantasy contest, the sheer number and extent of the Baroque elements strike an odd note in a work that is essentially classic or post-classic in its fundamental stylistic stance. In the long run the Fantasy lacks intrinsic musical strength and ultimately sounds too much like a pastiche. Musically, the second section is the stronger of the two (largely through its stylistic consistency) and is similar in quality to the finale of Beethoven's Piano Sonata in F minor, Op. 2, No. 1, a work which may also have been in the back of Hummel's mind as well. A taste for this style of music has yet to become part of the current Romantic revival, a factor which will likely inhibit its acceptance into the standard repertoire.

As suggested at the outset, the Fantasy style, while explicit in the work just discussed, is also implicit in other works by the composer. One instance can be seen in the independent piano piece which Voříšek entitled *Le Désir*, Op. 3, which was published about 1820. A fantasy-style character piece, intended to portray in musical terms the emotional state of romantic longing, it is an early instance of the type of extra-musically inspired piano miniature brought to perfection in the works of Schumann. Once again it may have had its inspiration in a pre-existing work, this time possibly Hummel's *La Contemplazione*, which he subtitled "una piccola Fantasia. (Examples 9 and 10) Voříšek's *Le Désir* contains many of the features previously cited that were associated with the fantasy style: the presentation of several intense, fragmentary ideas; abrupt changes in mood and figuration; the juxtaposition of strict and free styles; sudden changes in dynamics; and the regular, if casual, organization of rhythm and phrase structure. The affect of "yearning" is expressed immediately by the sweetness of the opening chromatic parallel sixths and by the harmonic inflection toward the subdominant (mm.

Example 9. J. N. Hummel: *Fantasia "La Contemplazione"*

Example 10. *Le Désir*, Op. 3, 1–18.

1–2). The mood is heightened by the rise and fall of the melody, which reaches its apex in measure three with a carefully placed, if rather conventional, appoggiatura. The first four measures form a large "sigh" and set the emotional tone for the entire composition. Even in these opening measures, however, the fantasy element is present. The full sonority of the opening is abandoned in the second measure in favor of a single melodic line supported only by occasional chords. The thematic connection between the measures is made by the retention of the chromatic line, and the difficulty of developing the implications of the opening measure is circumvented by an abrupt shift to a lighter texture which is easier to handle. The technique of picking up an idea and freely expanding it is followed throughout the entire passage: in measures four through seven, the upbeat rhythmic figure derived from the preceding sixteenth notes is combined with a diatonic inversion of the opening figure to make a free repetition of the first phrase. This motive is then treated in a quasi-contrapuntal style, with the cadence coming in measure seven instead of measure eight. The three-measure answer to a four-measure phrase is an indication of Voříšek's disinclination to sustain the contrapuntal texture in an improvisatory context; the result is an early cadence and, as before, a shift to a lighter texture. Nevertheless, the serious, expressive note has been struck, and for the purposes of a fantasy the point has been made. In the following measures (mm. 10–13), the sixteenth-note figure is given greater rhythmic definition and is used to make a rising sequence in a homophonic style. The sequence is quite simple, suggesting that it could be invented on the spot, and the flow of "inspiration" leads to a fortissimo outburst in measure fourteen. This climax is quickly broken off by two soft cadence chords that are connected to the previous events only by the retention of the appoggiatura from measure fourteen.

The fantasy element can be observed in the way in which the ideas are adopted, lightly developed, and then abruptly dropped. The breaking off of a climax is also a feature of the fantasy style and is used to suggest great tension and deep, inner emotion. This rhetorical gesture, a stock-in-trade of the early nineteenth-century fantasist, is employed here to convey a feeling of passion and to make the climax of the first paragraph of music. The entire passage is sixteen measures long, but it is not conceived as a conventional double period: apart from the opening four measures, it forms one unbroken, freely constructed section of music-its sixteen-measure length the result of Voříšek's deeply imbedded sense of regularity, not the outcome of intrinsically symmetrical phrase structure. The passage gives the effect of spontaneity, yet it also preserves the large-scale measure-grouping of a composed style: the free flight of fantasy submits ultimately to a formalistic conception of musical structure.

Whereas *Le Désir* is an example of a free fantasy which employs the fantasy style to enhance the mood creating aspects of a proto-romantic character piece, Voříšek's one piano sonata shows his treatment of the fantasy style in a sonata context. The Piano Sonata in B-flat minor, Op. 20, is one of Voříšek's final works and may never have been completed to the composer's satisfaction. It was composed in 1824, a year before the composer's death. The autograph, located at the Gesellschaft der Musikfreunde, is not a fair copy but contains many crossings out and false starts, suggesting that it is a working draft. The autograph contains the designation "Sonata quasi una Fantasia," a designation that for unknown reasons was not included in the version printed shortly after the composer's death in 1825. That Voříšek was concerned to provide a type of overall unity to the sonata similar to that found in the Fantasy in C minor is apparent from the revisions he made to the finale, revisions the intent of which are clear but which were abandoned or never completed. The finale, a *moto perpetuo* movement like the final section of the Fantasy in C major, was composed before the other movements and was printed as an independent piece in 1820 in Starck's *Weiner Pianoforte Schule*. In the 1824 autograph, this rondo finale is reworked: several sections are elaborated, and there is even a new large passage added. All these changes were, however, crossed out, and the first edition of the original 1820 version was printed unchanged at the time of publication. One of these planned changes was the insertion of an extended section in B minor toward the end of the movement, a section that contains a striking shift to the Neapolitan key and one which parallels a similar Neapolitan passage which opens the development section of the first movement. In fact, Neapolitan harmonic coloring is a notable element in the sonata as a whole. Clearly matters of harmonic and thematic interconnection were important structural issues to Voříšek and an essential feature of his approach to the fantasy style.

The fantasy elements in the sonata are not as prominent as in the Fantasy in C major, but the device of thematic transformation—present in Voříšek's other fantasy-related works—can be observed in several ways: the two principal themes of the first movement employ the same basic phrase structure and rhythmic pattern (Example No. 11, mm. 1–5 and 26–30); and the themes of the first two movements both begin with striking octave leaps. Furthermore, all the important thematic ideas, including those for the rondo finale, are comprised of five-measure phrases. This slight rhythmic irregularity, maintained in a consistent fashion throughout the sonata, binds the different melodic ideas together through the presence of a unifying rhythmic sub-structure. Instead of being fragmented and manipulated, the themes are generally developed through ornamentation, harmonic coloration, and textural variety-techniques characteristic of the fantasy style.

The Sonata begins with a thirteen-measure period in which the initial five-measure phrase is answered with a repeated four-measure consequent. (Example No. 11) Comprised of a mosaic of short, unrelated motives, this opening unit immediately establishes the movement's fantasia character and its pervasive mood of minor-key brooking. The octave opening is quietly repeated over a rapid Alberti bass and is extended through overlapping three-measure phrases, repeated three times, to reach the dominant of the the relative major (D-flat) in measure twenty-two. Although a double statement of the opening theme is an expected feature of Classic- and Romantic-period sonata movements, the abrupt change of atmosphere and texture in measure thirteen is unexpected. The sudden change, providing contrast and yet unified by the presence of the head motive of the main theme, also contributes to the sense of fantasia-style variation. (Example 11)

The intensity of the opening is relaxed in measure twenty-six by the appearance of the second theme in the relative major. As mentioned before, this theme is rhythmically related to the opening idea and shows

Example 11. Piano Sonata in B-flat minor, Op. 20, Movement I, mm. 1–27.

the same two-plus-three phrase structure. Olga Zuckerová describes this theme as a musical *Doppelgänger* and cites it as an example of Voříšek's subjective and romantic tendencies:

> The symbol of the split personality plays a significant role in Schubert's "Der Doppelgänger" and is an important symbol for romanticism, as is evident by the fictional personalities of Florestan and Eusebius. If we compare the two themes of Voříšek's piano sonata, we find that they remind us more of the later thematic dualism ... than of other pieces by Voříšek's contemporaries.[22]

While it is possible to view the relationship between the two themes in this way, as an inherent poetic and psychological romantic phenomenon, it is also possible that it is an expression the movement's fantasia character.

The fantasy style is present in much of Voříšek's work, ranging from such overt instances as the Fantasy in C major discussed here, to the sets of variations for piano and orchestra, the piano sonata, and even to the piano miniatures. It is worth mentioning in this regard that even Voříšek's best-known and most polished works for keyboard, the Impromptus, Op. 7, carry a title which conveys a sense of improvisation—in this instance the title provided by the publisher to whom, presumably,

---

[22]Olga Zuckerová, "J. V. Voříšek" unpublished monograph, p. 86.

they suggested such a character.[23] Even in the earlier piano rhapsodies the improvisatory element is both implied in the title and conveyed in the pieces themselves. While Voříšek did not live long enough to develop his musical style to full maturity, a sense of the direction in which his music might have evolved can be found in two of his later and finest works, the *Sonata for Violin and Piano*, Op. 5, and the *Symphony in D major*. In both of these compositions the fantasy element is present but is now integrated more completely into the musical structures, leaving behind both the relics of the Baroque style and the tendency to adopt a somewhat artificial musical pose—features that occasionally mar his earlier, more student-like, works. As with Beethoven, the fantasy style was an important component in Voříšek's growth towards compositional maturity, one which provided a continuing source of musical inspiration. With Voříšek, an early death prevented the fulfillment of a remarkable potential. But in his one completed fantasy, short piano pieces, and piano sonata, one can sense the force of a strong musical imagination—an imagination cultivated through hours of private fantasizing while a young man, an imagination powerful enough that during his mature years it enabled him to be compared with Hummel and Moscheles as one of the best exponents of the keyboard fantasy.

---

[23]DeLong, "Voříšek," p. 141.

Part 4:

Editorial Approaches to Janáček

Perhaps the greatest difficulty for scholars working in Eastern Europe over the last forty years has been the isolation. While isolation can sometimes be a positive thing, encouraging self-reliance and individuality (Ivan Klima recently gave a talk entitled "On the Unexpected Benefits of Oppression") it can also keep scholars from coming to grips with new techniques and normal scholarly practices. This is nowhere more obvious than in the area of editorial activity.

One of the more exciting, but also disturbing events of the Janáček and Czech Music Conference was the confrontation between different worlds of editorial practice. This confrontation was rendered particularly poignant for many of us because one of the prime movers behind the Complete Edition of Janáček's Works is Jarmil Burghauser, a highly respected and greatly beloved figure. Yet Paul Wingfield, who has made extensive and detailed studies of Janáček's manuscripts, argues that these editorial principles must be redefined, almost from the ground up.

The most notorious aspect of the Janáček Edition has been the enharmonic respelling of some of Janáček's music. This had been particularly difficult for such figures as Rudolf Firkušný and Charles Mackerras, who have come to learn Janáček's music in one form and do not see the need to transform it. Wingfield's objections, however, go far beyond this.

There is no point in trying to blame anyone for this impasse. To my mind the problem has always been a political one: the editorial board was set up by Czechs and for Czechs, and consisted only of Czechs. Despite the fact that there were many scholars and musicians who ought to have been consulted in the process of designing an edition, political conditions made this at best inconvenient, and at worst, impossible.

Thus it is my belief that a truly representative and high quality Janáček Edition will only be possible when the editorial board consists of the most highly qualified scholars and musicians, whatever their country of origin.

The Principles of the Janáček Critical Edition

Jarmil Burghauser

Jarmil Burghauser is one of the great figures of Czech musical life. He is a serious composer, a fine conductor, and a richly imaginative musicologist, author of books on Dvořák and the editor of The Complete Dvořák Edition. *In his short essay presented here he responds to some of the criticisms levelled against the* Complete Edition of Janáček's Works, *and tries to distinguish between the ideas of Urtext and his notion of Canonic text.*

I fear my contribution to the discussion will sound more like a kind of plaint, *seufzer, Klagelied, threni, eikhah,* if you wish, coming out of the depth of my sore heart.

Alfred Dürr began his contribution to the International Musicological Congress in Berlin in 1979 by complaining of the humble status of a scholar working in an editorial institute. Not only does such an activity not bring any particular advantage but no personal prestige either: "The initial satisfaction with a feeling of seeing one's own output printed soon gives way to the sobering experience that those are generally ignored by the professional public." I would allow myself to add a third point, by changing the introductory passage to the main part of his speech a little. He says: "Musicology as a young discipline still has much to catch up with regarding editorial technique as compared with classical philology..." I would put it rather this way: Musicology—and the average professional musician—still have much to catch up with in regard to the existence of textual criticism in music as an already constituted discipline.

Indeed, the notion of this discipline, having its own philosophy, methodology and technique, is still very hazy for the average professional musician and musicologist, even for those who happened to work on editions of one or two works. Some forty years ago when I began to prepare revisions of musical texts (Fibich and Janáček) I entered this field with only the standard education in musicology at the Prague Charles University—historical training, including the classical *recensio, examinatio, emendatio,* etc., of sources as exemplified in early music. My theoretical and analytical training was due to my principle profession (composition and conducting) at the Prague Conservatory of Music. Only during the years when I worked on the Dvořák Complete Edition, as collaborator with such excellent editors as Otakar Šourek or František Bartoš, did I gain experience and search also for the theoretical background of this evolving discipline, parallel with the progress in the field in Germany, England and the USA after the Second World War.

I always felt that in the past the main stress of editorial praxis was placed on the examination and evaluation of sources, whereas much less attention was paid to the other end of the "editorial chain," the notational image of the canonical text to be published. And, moreover, some important principal points were almost entirely ignored, such as the fact that the musical work must not be confused with its graphic description, the notational image, which is a phenomenon of quite a different category. A musical work, being a non-material structure, exists objectively only in the moment when it is realized acoustically, whereas its graphic conveyance is only a device enabling that acoustical realization. The volume *Musikalishe Edition im Wandel des historischen Bewußtseins*, edited by Professor Georgiades, gives excellent examples of the many possible ways (not all of them optimal, of course) to express the same musical content. And, stemming from this dichotomy—the work as such on one hand, and its graphic conveyance on the other—the task standing before the editor is not only to establish the true substance of the work, on the strength of the external and internal critique of the sources, but also to find the optimal notational image, combining scholarly exactitude with practical viability. While much has been established here for the music of historically more remote periods—the principle of correspondence of the notation to the style of the period having now won—very little attention has been paid to the notation of the works of the 19th century, under the tacit—and false—assumptions that there are no problems and that we have a fixed definite system which has not changed since about Beethoven's time. It is true that the last principal and conspicuous change in European notation, generally accepted, was the introduction of the bar line; but our "usual" notation, in fact, keeps evolving constantly, even if imperceptibly. I do not refer, of course, to all of the innumerable proposals of revolutionary changes in notation, emerging mostly at the beginning of this century, with no chance of coming into general use, or to the innovations connected with the rising of the "New Music." One principle of the main stream remains unchanged, and that is that our musical notation is a *code*, generally established and understandable to everyone in Western music, irrespective of nationality. When a composer needs a new graphic element in order to express a new musical proceeding, as it is in the New Music, he is obliged to include an explication of it at the beginning of his score. Janáček never had in mind such an intentional deviation from the established code (with only one potential exception which I will mention later); he explicitly dissented with Riemann's view that enharmonic spelling could have any real bearing on musical performance. (I must admit I dissent from Janáček in this, as the orthographic spelling facilitates understanding of the work, and makes it easier to perform, especially on string instruments.)

Since our introduction of a strict musical orthography in accidentals in our Critical Edition cannot be seriously objected to, much less obvious and more daring, but perfectly logical, was our analogous step dealing with metrical questions. Our only precedent here was rather unfortunate: some disciples of Riemann introduced additional metric signatures to the original time-signatures in their editions of standard works, like Beethoven sonatas. They also used the interruption of barlines between the staves to show their concept of the real metric structure—although this may seem similar to our practice, it is almost totally different. I cannot enter into a detailed analysis about what was wrong in their approach, but would like to point out only one simple (but maybe surprising) circumstance, it is to be said that the usual time-signature fraction is not able to serve this purpose. The metric signature which we use in the Critical Edition is based on the only potential exception of the standard notational code which Janáček proposed himself in one of his theoretical studies (but did not use in his praxis): the signature in which the denominator in the fraction, expressing the actual metric pulse unit, is given as a note value (crotchet, quaver, etc.), rather than a numeral. I will pass over other notational details in our Critical Edition which are based on similar considerations of principle, and move directly to another common misunderstanding: the non-discerning of an edition of source (or sources) and the edition of canonical text.

Maybe the term "Urtext" has contributed to the ambiguity, by its seeming definiteness. Resulting from a reaction to various practical (like Bülow's) or theoretical (like Riemann's) revisions of classical pieces of music and taken up as a battle-cry (and surviving up to now as a commercial denomination), the term "Urtext" conveys in fact nothing definite. Does it mean that the edition gives an exact reading of the autograph? Or the last authorized copy? Or the first authorized print? In an excellent article in *Musica*, which is even comprehensible for the average musician, Paul Badura-Skoda shows that there exists more than one "Urtext"(for many classical works). In fact—in the best instances—the term means that the text is devoid of any errors or deformations, no matter who is their originator, not excluding the composer. The poetic saying that we must have our composer "warts and all" is wrong exactly in its principal point—where the warts are. If they are in the work itself, then well, nobody is entitled to remove them. But if they are only in the notation, distorting the means by which the work is conveyed to the interpreter, then the duty of the editor is to remove all such static. Janáček would be the first to protest against the practice of drawing any interpretative conclusions from his sometimes irregular notational style, just as he had protested against similar views voiced by Riemann.

We prefer to designate such a musical text, based on a thorough examination and comparison of sources and cleared of all interfering static, with the term *canonical text* (as in literary criticism)—even if we know that a work of music is a living and evolving organism, which never becomes tomblike and rigid. It is conceived in and born of the composer's mind, takes its first and subsequent graphic image from the composer, the copyists, and engravers, always acquiring some changes in graphic and compositional detail— and on and on is recreated in an interpreter's realization. In order to illuminate this process, we do not need to resort to examples like the beginnings of Gregorian chant or Beethoven's changes in copies since Janáček was almost never satisfied with any of his work—remodelling it again and again not only in the various manuscript stages, not only during the process of publication in print, but with nearly every new important performance (see the substantially different instructions given to the Czech Quartet and to the Moravian Quartet in connection with his first string quartet.)

We were glad that a figure like Professor Carl Dahlhaus understood the principal new traits of our Critical Edition at once, and even if he did not always agree with the concrete decisions touching on some details, greeted our approach as something that "sensibly contributes to progress of the methodology of editorial technique." And the core of my complaint, which now ends and for which I apologize, is that people who have only a limited notion of the philosophy, the principles, and the regulations of the discipline, dare to deliver categorical judgments, not refraining from demagogy when arguments fail.

Editorial Guidelines for The *Complete Edition* of Janáček's Works

Publishers: Barenreiter and Supraphon

We present here an English translation of the Editorial Guidelines for the Complete Edition of Janáček's Works which was distributed to all the participants at the time of the session.

In our presentation of the complete works of Leos Janáček we begin with the essential and fundamental differences between the musical work and its notated form. While the work itself is a non-material structure which grew out of the mind of its creator, only taking form in acoustical reality, the notation of the work is an aid, a guide for its implementation, which is not identical to the work itself, and should not be confused with it.

The interpretation of graphological musical notation depends on its historical development. In different eras of music history the notation shows varying degrees of precision. Various analyses have convincingly shown that there exists *no* notational system which is able to perfectly represent all acoustical parameters. This is due to the fact that the musical artwork always involves a certain degree of uncertainty, and even haziness, which makes creative interpretation possible.

Accordingly, it is among the main tasks of an editor to derive the intentions and conceptions of the composer from the notation, which may be hidden and distorted, especially if there are errors and slips of the pen (also perhaps on the part of the composer).

Furthermore, one must take into account changes made by the composer for premieres and first editions. In Janáček's case it is particularly significant that the genesis of a work is a multi-level process. Often when he returns to a work it leads to changes, not only in the notation, but also in the substance of the work itself.

The *Complete Edition* of Janáček's works has as its special goal the presentation of Janáček's notation in terms of a newly developed, systematic and unified format. This summary of the editorial guidelines offers an introduction to the ideas involved. For more details see *Ediční zásady a směrnice* (Editorial Principles and Guidelines) henceforth abbreviated as EZS, which is also published by the same editors. (Also see EZS for an amplified treatment of the different chapters in this essay).

Our principles are based on a systematic analysis of the historical development of musical textual criticism, which is roughly outlined in the first chapter of the book, and analogous to the criteria of modern textual criticism involving literary works. In this procedure the determination of the final text involves the demand for an updated orthographic norm.

1.1 The Sources

Janáček's autographs consist mostly of connected, worked-out sketches on single sheets of inexpensive paper which were lined by the composer himself, or printed by a rubber stamp. Sometimes he used paper which contained discarded compositional material on the reverse side.

These "original texts" were given by Janáček to one of his regular copyists who put it on conventional musical paper. Janáček continued to make corrections on these copies. Already, in this phase of his work, there are a number of misspellings which remained undetected by the composer, and thus occur in the final version. At the same time, this process has deprived us of certain of the peculiar modernisms of Janáček's notation, which were transformed in the hands of the copyists and the first editors.

Janáček continued his work on the first copy of his compositions with erasures, additions, and often long interpolations (partly on note paper fastened on with glue). Often he ordered a new copy of the manuscript made because it was so difficult to read. Sometimes he even worked simultaneously on two different copies of the same work and made different changes in each, on the basis of whether it was for two different performances or a premiere plus a forthcoming first edition. As a result of this kind of compositional process there are inconsistencies in the sources which cannot be clearly resolved. Also, during the publication (and during rehearsals or performance) Janáček continued to correct, and these corrections were absent from the former sources.

As the main source for the edition of Janáček's complete works we most often use the last authorized print, which is compared with the fair copy to eliminate possible slips on the part of the first copyists. In addition, documented instructions which the composer gave to the performers of the premieres are taken into consideration. The editor must also examine every section which does not sound well, and this on the basis of inner musical criteria, because Janáček was not a trustworthy corrector in either a visual or an auditory sense. If the editor comes to the conclusion that in spite of the concurrence of sources there nevertheless could still be an error, he adds an "ossia ES" (ossia from Editio Supraphon) in small print, to offer another version for the interpreting artist.

Variants which were added by the composer in earlier sources are only listed up to the last handwritten source. In other sources they are only listed when they illuminate the development of a compositional idea. An example of this is the critical edition of *Taras Bulba*, a work for which there exists a relative proliferation of sources.

In addition, older and less important sources are also taken into consideration if the main source is unclear, unsatisfying, or controversial. In special cases, the orchestral parts can be important as sources, as in the small cantata *Na Solaní Čarták*, where the main source for the second final version is lost. For the evaluation of the sources, the above rule concerning the importance of a source in terms of the composer's "final intention" cannot be mechanically invoked. The so-called "final intention" of the composer—if it can be traced at all—could have come about accidentally; this is especially true in certain cases where interpreters claim a kind of authority through contact with Janáček which is now considered dubious.

1.2 Critical Apparatus

At the beginning of the critical commentary the description of the sources can be found—first the handwritten sources, then the printed ones; first in Czech and then in German. Then follows the section entitled "Editorial Principles" which has the same basic form for all the volumes of the *Complete Edition*. This section gives the respective main sources, and also gives information about methods of source comparison and changes in Janáček's notation. The editorial guidelines are also outlined here. A special section explains symbols and abbreviations which are to be used in the following Table of Variants. The Table of Variants uses common siglas as much as possible. Only in the case of difficulties, which cannot be explained by these abbreviations, will additional explanations be given in Czech and German.

The siglas are to be used as follows: the first Arabic number = measure; additional subscript Arabic numbers = the note or chord in the measure (rests are not counted). This is followed by instrumental specifications (siglas as in the score) and source siglas. After a colon the corresponding variant follows; after a semicolon the explanation of the editors authorized reading if there is no further variant listed in another source. Because of this, different readings of sources can be offered.

Example: $118_{2,3}$ Vn 1, 2 C^1 : *hes*; C^2: [?] ; ES = HM

Solution: The first and second violins have a B-flat in the second and third notes of measure 118 in the first copy. In the second copy this part is illegible. The *Complete Edition* (ES = Editio Supraphon) uses the version of the print taken from the publisher, Hudební Matice.

In the formation of source siglas the following system is used: handwritten sources are identified with single letters (e.g. *S* = sketch; *A* = autograph; *C* = copy), printed sources are identified with two letters (e.g. *HM* = print from Hudební Matice, Prague; *UE* = Universal Edition, Vienna; *ES* = Supraphon Editions, Prague), and handwritten entries are signified by three letters (e.g. *Jan* = Janáček; *Bak* = Bakala; *Inc* = entry of unknown hand).

Further siglas are: *Vers.* I, II = the older successive version in the same source; *ex. anal.* = an emendation of the editors in concordance with an analogous place; [!] = for mistakes of writing and printing; and [?] = for unclear and illegible sources.

For additions or corrections of unimportant symbols the *Complete Edition* follows the rule that no brackets or any other typographical differentiations are used, but in clear cases (missing accidentals, rests, etc.) tacit emendations are made. If there are, however, reasons to suppose that a variant reading of the source is possible, then the most probable variant is chosen for the main text, and the circumstances are described in the Table of Variants. By this process the edition has done away with the uncomfortable position of the editor as "correcting teacher", thus closing the gap between a critical and a practical edition.

Larger connected passages or single parts of a composition which were handed down in earlier divergent versions (for example discarded sections) are presented as supplements following the main text, and if necessary have a special critical commentary and table of variants.

1. 3 Introductory Text and Preface

The Preface, Table of Contents, and Introductory Text are in five languages: Czech, German, English, French, and Russian. The text contains facts about the origin of the work and its place within Janáček's oeuvre. Information about the premiere is also included (and if necessary, facts about the preparation of the work, whether or not the composer was taking part in the production, and whether any changes were made); and finally a short overview of the authorized prints is offered.

The introductory text closes with a short characterization of the work, which is meant to be neither a scientific analysis nor a musical aesthetic study. Directly preceding the first page are symbols representing the duration of the work. These timings are derived from different recordings where the extreme limits (longest and shortest) are taken into consideration. For example:

Durata

8:30 (A) - 9.10 (T)

which means that the duration of the shortest recording, with Ančerl, lasts eight and a half minutes, while the longest version, with Talich, lasts nine minutes and ten seconds. The meaning of the symbols is explained at the conclusion of the critical commentary. On the same page which contains the duration of performances, the orchestration in Italian is found under the heading *Esecutori e strumenti* with the same abbreviations for the instruments found in the score. Also given is the minimum number of players which may be used for the percussion ensemble.

2. Notational Graphics

In the above-mentioned book, EZS, editorial guidelines and purely graphical guidelines for the printer are presented. Here is a summary: For the arrangement of notation the most important principles are simplicity, clarity, and comprehensiveness. The musical text must be so clear that one does not need any additional explanations. Furthermore, the notation should be equal to the content of the musical material and style, and should be strictly logical in itself. Thus the inner logic and substance of the music must be communicated by the notation itself. This is especially true in Janáček's work, since he sometimes composed in small snippets, and was so careless that he occasionally combined sections of a work which reflect different notational styles. Because of this it is important to remove illogical notation which is sometimes contradictory in an orthographic sense. Complaints concerning these difficulties, especially in relation to rehearsing orchestral works, have been more than justified. However, all the idiosyncrasies of Janáček's writing in the autographs which are of true importance to the interpreter (articulation, beaming, etc.), and which were wrongly changed by copyists have been retained.

2.1 Arrangements of Systems, Main System

On any page of the score—even on the very first page of the work or a movement—only the lines which contain actively playing voices are presented. This is true of Janáček's notation as well as standard modern usage. Before each system the active voices are noted with their symbols, which are presented in front of the first page of the score in an easily legible format. Exceptions to this manner of presentation are vocal and chamber works, where the participating instruments are only given at the beginning of a work. To the left of the main staff line there is a thick bracket which delimits instrumental groups or choral voices. Solo voices and instruments which form no special groups, such as the harp, are not included in the bracketing. The lines which contain closely related or identical instruments receive additional thin brackets which are closed (as an example of this we have the flutes and piccolo and the two violin groups, but *not* the violoncelli and contrabassi). The ornamental quarter-circles which appeared conventionally at the ends of the main staff have been eliminated. A bow-bracket is used for instruments which require more than one line. Within a staff line we also use incomplete lines (such as those which stop or start in the middle of a page) in the following instances: when a soloist steps out of a vocal or instrumental work; in case of an "ossia ES"; or if for a shorter period, during "divisi," a violin part must be notated separately (Examples 1-3).

Example 1.

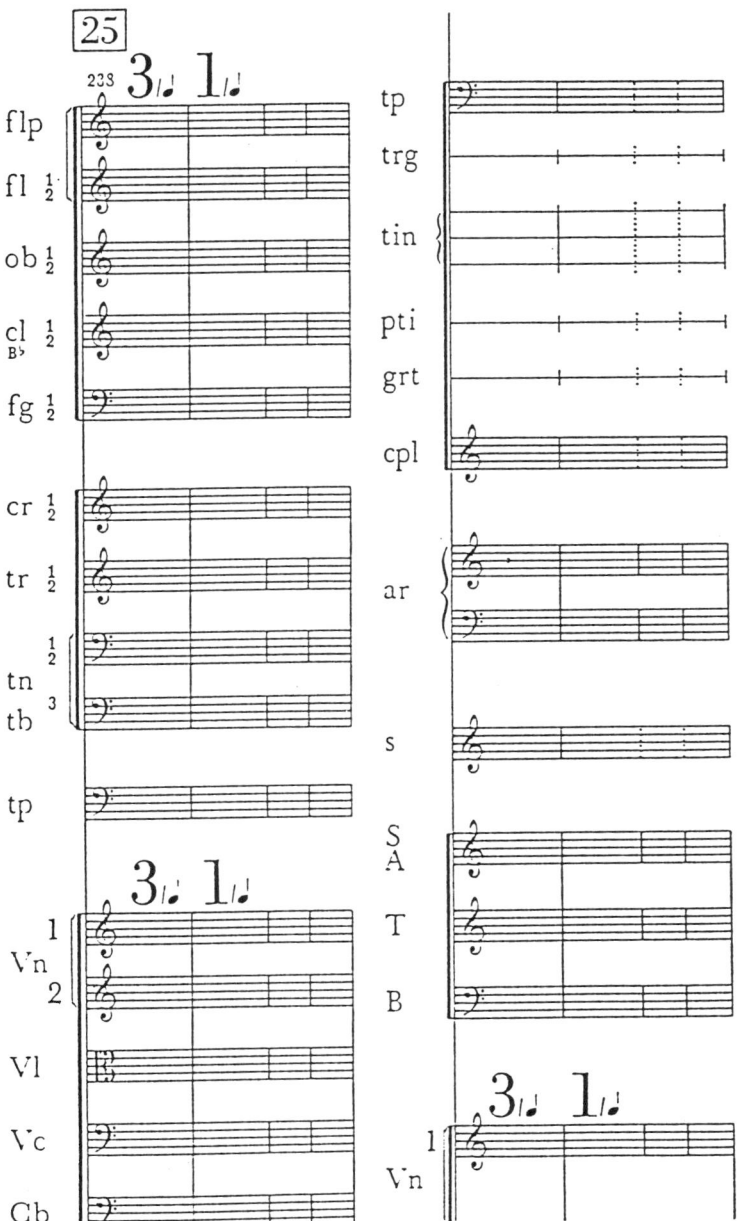

Example 2.

Example 3.

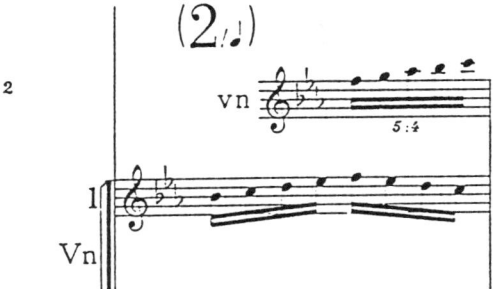

2.2 Clefs and Bar Lines

The types of clefs employed in the Janáček *Edition* are: treble, bass, and viola. Sections for bassoon and cello in the tenor clef are changes into treble or bass clef and trombones are always notated in the bass clef. The original clef is given in the critical commentary.

When the clef changes within a voice, the new clef is printed in the same format as the first clef; small print for clefs is only used within single voices for cues if there are different clefs needed.

The bar lines are handled as in example 1 which also shows how the bar lines in one-beat measures are broken. Double bars are used only for the main formal units of a composition, but not mechanically for each key signature, time signature, or tempo change. Double bars which are not found in the sources are only added if they are missing at signs such as "Fine" or "D.C. al Fine." A closing line is only placed at the ending of a composition, or at the conclusion of an entire movement. The sections designated as "attaca" by the composer, and others which obviously succeed each other immediately (variations etc.), are marked with a double bar composed of two thin lines.

2.3 Musical Pitch and Accidentals

One of the main reasons for the difficulties in deciphering Janáček's scores involves both his idiosyncratic marking of accidentals and his sometimes unusual rhythmic subdivisions. Mistakenly, those idiosyncrasies have been interpreted as something important and relevant for his compositional style. In reality, the peculiarities in this area of notation are only an expression of carelessness concerning that problem. These questions are dealt with in detail in an article by Jarmil Burghauser in the Brno music journal *Opus musicum* (1978, Nr. 5/6, pp. 147–52). Because of his quick and hasty notational style, Janáček preferred to use flats, which are easier to write than sharps. Often we find cases in which he starts writing flats, but then without obvious harmonic reason switches to sharps, probably because the new way of writing seemed simpler to him. Although Janáček preferred certain keys (such as C-sharp minor or B-flat minor) and earlier editors were asked to retain these keys, one must contradict the opinion that Janáček wanted to stress certain parts through the use of wrong or unusual accidentals. Janáček was unaware that he was violating the rules of notation, and if he had to give special instructions for interpretation, he used verbal means. If someone had told him that his notation of musical pitch suggested something *more* than musical pitch, he would have rejected the idea out of hand. The inconsistency with which he uses accidentals and key signatures in musically analogous places shows clearly that he pursued no special intention with his unusual manner of notation. The *Complete Edition* of Janáček's works seeks to proceed in such a way that the use of accidentals reflects the inner logic of the music, something which is easier to grasp when the proper orthographical notation is employed.

2.3.1 Key Signatures

In his early works Janáček employes the usual system of key signatures although these may not represent the actual key of a given passage. Later he discards key signatures, which is certainly justifiable in modulatory or tonally free passages. This results in longer tonal (or modal) passages with more numerous accidentals, making his scores appear somewhat chaotic and difficult to read. The *Complete Edition* uses general key signatures which approximate the basic key or mode of the passage concerned, and uses the possibilities of enharmonic respelling to the fullest extent. Single notes are tacitly respelled, while the sources of longer passages are explained in the critical commentary. The condition of the sources concerning the general key signature of a work may be found in the section of the volume entitled "Editorial Guidelines." When a key signature is changed, our edition does not give a cancelling signature, except in the course of a keyless body of sound within a movement.[1]

2.3.2 Local Accidentals

Janáček preferred to use superfluous accidentals which are tacitly eliminated in this edition. Because of different interpretations which concern the importance of certain accidentals (especially wrong accidentals), our guidelines show strict and logical rules which are shown and commented upon with examples in EZS. We offer the main guidelines here:

   1. A constitutive accidental covers all notes of the same absolute pitch within the context of a single measure. The note with the accidental should be thought of as an absolute entity, which cannot be influenced by a preceding note with different accidentals, nor can it be raised or lowered by the original key signature. Therefore this edition uses *no* key signature cancellation if after a D flat a D# follows, or after an F double sharp a single F flat sounds (not F[natural] flat). If, in the space of a measure, the same note occurs without being raised or lowered, it received a natural sign. If this happens in one octave it is a

---

[1]This rule was only established after the first volume of the Complete Edition (F/1, Compositions for Piano) and is therefore not applied within.

constitutive accidental, and if it is in a different octave it is a warning accidental.

2. Warning accidentals, which are used for a quicker orientation, are always placed where a note with a different key signature occurs in the following measure (without concern for the tessitura). Such warning accidentals are not used in our edition in cases where the musical content is clear at first sight and where an analogous alteration of the note concerned would be senseless.

2.4 Notation of Voices

If two voices are notated on one line, the *Complete Edition* follows conventional procedure:

If two voices are rhythmically identical they are noted with one stem. If their rhythms are different, each voice gets its own stem and its own markings (e.g. p or forte). The *Complete Edition* does not use the common notation "á 2" "á 3" for unison passages, but rather employs the designation *unis*. This is not specifically noted at the beginning of a system in each case, but it remains in effect until several full-measure rests appear in the text.

A doubling of the note heads while using one stem is not allowed in the *Complete Edition*, although it is frequent in Janáček's autographs and common in earlier prints.

The instruments used in a line are given only by the direction of the stems and by the rests, but *not* by ordinal numbers (1st, 2nd). In addition, the instrumental symbol in front of the line specifies the needed instrument. If, for example, the first clarinet plays in the first line, there is a Cl1 in front of the staff line, and no additional rests will be given for the second clarinet. For further information about such details see EZS.

2.5 Rhythm

The *Complete Edition* uses the modern form of flagging for shorter note values ♩ ♪ ᵥ (Example 4), because it guarantees a better overview, and furthermore clarifies the connection between flags and beams. The beaming follows Janáček's autographs because his idiosyncrasies do make sense in this case.

Example 4.

Vocal parts are treated the same way as instrumental parts in terms of beaming. (See Examples 19 and 20, pages 173 and 174.)

2.5.1 Heterogeneous Separation of Rhythmic Stress

This term refers to rhythmic segments which imply a metrical arrangement outside of the fundamental metrical order, such as an uneven segment in an even metrical order (triplets, quintuplets) or vice verse (duolets, quadruplets). Janáček himself suggested a rule with an uncommon solution to this problem in his theoretical works, which he follows only partially in practice. Furthermore, the fact that Janáček often has a higher rhythmic level in mind in his notation of heterogeneous segments tends to complicate his notation. So, for example, he thinks of a quadruplet in terms of a duolet and writes ; sometimes he mixes us different rhythmic stresses, as shown by the example from *Kátya Kabanová*.

Example 5.

In order to avoid ambiguity concerning the marking of such sections, the *Complete Edition* adds figures which give the number of stresses in a normal rhythmic figure in the form of a *proportion*, as is often the case in newer notation. So, for example, 2:3 signifies that two notes are played for three notes of normal division. Janáček's markings—which derive from his notion of higher rhythmic levels—are kept only if the heterogeneous divisions appear in part.

Example 6.

Following the guidelines of the Complete Edition, Example 5 from *Kát'a Kabanová* would appear as in Example 7.

Example 7.

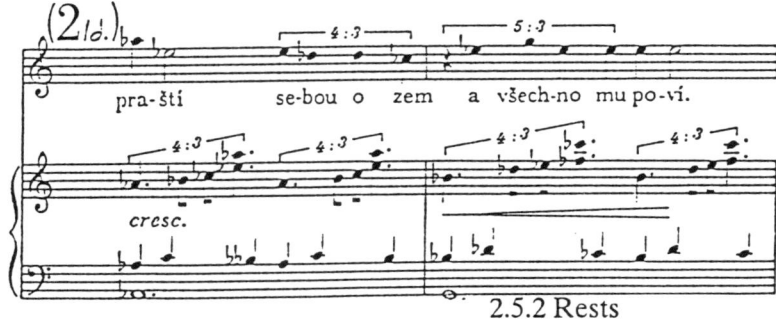

2.5.2 Rests

Considering the variety of notations available for rests, the Complete Edition has decided the following rules:

> a) A full measure rest has no specific rhythmic value, and cannot be used for the completion of a measure when the time signature exceeds 4/4. In such cases the rest must be shown with exact rhythmic values.

Example 8.

> The full measure rest is not used in the spurious one-beat measure; only rests which reflect the actual rhythmic value are used (e.g. in the 4/4 measure, a quarter-note rest is used).

b) A multi-measure rest is represented by a long, thick horizontal bar which has short vertical lines on both sides. The duration of the rest in measures is shown by a figure above the horizontal line. This rest appears almost solely in single voices.

c) Several succeeding rests within one bar are always connected if the basic metrical structure of the bar is not disturbed. It must be simplified in the following way, without taking the notation of the sources into account.

Example 9.

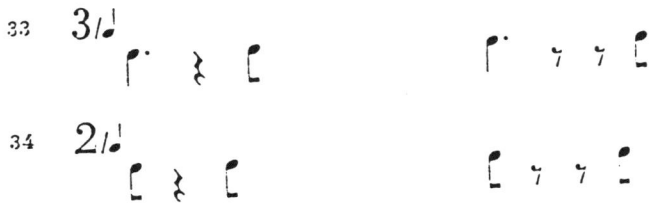

In measures in some type of triple meter, one must distinguish between those with three beats and those with a triple subdivision.

Example 10.

2.6 Meter

The designation of meter in the *Complete Edition* follows Janáček's own description in his theoretical studies[2] (he himself did not

---

[2] A detailed analysis of the manner in which Janáček's theoretical works deal with these questions can be found in a study by Jarmil Burghauser included the *Festschrift zum 60. Geburtstag von Prof. Dr. Jiri Vyslouzil*, Brno, 1984.

employ this system in his notation): instead of the common fraction 4/4 or 3/8 the "denominator" is replaced by the note value so that we see the signs given in Example 11.

Example 11.

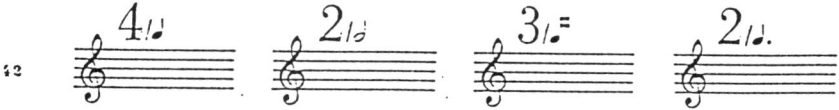

The *Complete Edition* also departs from usual practice in relation to signalling metrical changes at the end of a system. We feel that a warning of the new meter is superfluous, because the more important changes of tempo are not forewarned. The siglas C and ₡, which derive from mensural notation, are not used in the *Complete Edition*.

Janáček's own signs are sometimes confusing. In this sense they are rather similar to certain conventions in the notation of music in the Classical period, whereby in a quadruple-meter Allegro-Finale the composer writes ₡ to advise the conductor to conduct in "two" rather than in four. This does not mean that the Allegro (126-152) should be played at twice the speed; but sometimes ₡ does mean that the half-note is the real beat, which results in an undesirable ambiguity. For example, in Janáček's *Po zarostlém chodníčku I* (Along the Overgrown Path), the piece "Štěbětaly jak laštovičky" (They chattered like swallows) is notated in 4/8, but tempo and metronome markings clearly reveal that it is in 2/4 time. In such cases the editor must choose the appropriate metrical notation for the main text, and explain the sources in the editorial guidelines.

Traditional theories of meter pay scant attention to uneven meters, although such meters are common in the east and appear occasionally in Janáček's works. In older forms of notation they are very difficult to represent graphically. Our new mode of notation is able to express such metrical constructs through the use of the " + " sign in round brackets, instead of a single number.

Example 12.

If the meter changes in the course of a work, or the editor cannot develop a clear perspective concerning the metrical structure, the composer's original sign is given in round brackets after the large number, which gives the number of beats according to the form of the *Complete Edition*.

Example 13.

$$2_{(5/\sconcat)}$$
$$3_{(7/\sconcat)}$$

The *Complete Edition* retains Janáček's notation of single-beat measures for different reasons, although we believe it to be a *contradictio in adiecto*, along with Janáček's own view that at least two beats are needed for one measure. Janáček writes such measures in two cases:

1. In larger sections where such a measure forms only one beat, and two or several measures form the metrical structure.

2. With single measures which are placed between longer measures, and are equally long, or sometimes shorter, than a beat of the neighboring measures, and are thus in reality only metrical additions to the antecedent or consequent measures.

The *Complete Edition* leaves the measures in concordance with the sources in order to give an idea of the original; however, the measures in this case are not lined all the way through, thus preserving the true metrical structure (see also Example 1, page 159).

2.7 Tempo

Basic tempo signs (e.g. Allegro, Andante) and signs for tempo changes (rit., accel., a tempo) are always put above the line at the same place as metric signs. From the detailed instruction in EZS we mention here only that the *Complete Edition* does not allow the connection of an "a tempo" marking with a basic sign, because the validity of a changing sign is cancelled by the basic sign or a "tempo I" sign. This principle is also in effect if such a double marking is found in the sources. If the composer shows the relation between two "neighboring" tempi with two notes and an equal sign (=), we place this sign exactly above the bar in which the change occurs.

Example 14.

2.7.1 Metronome Markings

The metronome markings (in round brackets) are given in the *Complete Edition* only if they have been handed down by trustworthy sources. If the sources give only the metronome markings, but *not* the tempo indications, the brackets are not used.

2.8 Dynamics

The *Complete Edition* gives dynamic indications for each instrument (voice) of the score in concordance with the sources. If there is another instruction given in later sources (with "general dynamics" deriving from the original) it is simplified in the above-mentioned way. Indications such as "*accel. e cresc.*" or similar ones, are not allowed above the line. All instructions concerning dynamics are printed in italics under the line; however those for vocal parts are *above* the line.

2.8.1 Additional Instructions for Dynamics

Dynamic instructions are supplemented if it can be shown by comparison of analogous passages that the absence of such instructions is due to an error by the composer, or if an instrument appears with only a relative instruction (such as *cresc.*, *sf*). In clear cases the editorial changes are done tacitly, in less clear cases the added indication is mentioned in the Table of Variants (in the text of the sigla—e.g. 184 fg *mf* = ES).

2.8.2 Elimination of Dynamic Instructions

A dynamic indication is in force as long as it is not replaced by another. In the case of a crescendo marking which is accompanied by the abbreviation *cresc.*, the editor must decide whether the double marking is redundant (then he leaves the crescendo marking in shorter passages and leaves the abbreviation *cresc.* in longer ones), or whether the *cresc.* was not really meant for a longer passage and the crescendo marking is more of a local indicator which will usually be replaced by a decrescendo marking. Superfluous dynamic instructions are tacitly eliminated.

2.8.3 Accents

On principle, accents are set up according to the notation of the composer. One must only recognize that the several variants of sfz, ffz, etc. have been standardized into sff or sfff. Obvious redundancies have been eliminated (> or ⌃ *and* sf).

2.9 Articulation

Here the *Complete Edition* follows the critically examined notation of the sources. The exact position of ties and slurs, which are not nowadays set up in a standardized manner, is explained in detail in EZS. For example, if, in the sources, during a longer tremolo one slur (or several) is used, or the editor discovers that several successive notes should be connected with a tremolo, but without strong metric accents, we use a line slur, and mention at the end in the Editorial Guidelines that this is an editorial addition. The Complete Edition uses neither group ties (cornered brackets marking the various partitions) nor does it use vocal ligatures. (On several notes, therefore, only one syllable is to be sung).

2.9.1 Supplementation of Articulation

Articulation is supplemented only in necessary cases. If the composer noted the articulation for the first group in repeating configurations, the editor can show the common articulation for all groups by using the word "simile." The editor cannot mechanically provide additions for instruments playing simultaneously; thus analogous passages do not necessarily have the same articulation. For example, marks which give the bowing of the strings are usually shorter than the slurs and phrase marks of the winds. Concerning the overlapping of various articulation signs, or articulation signs with other indications (tempo, dynamics, technical markings) we have presented detailed guidelines which are explained in EZS.

JANÁČEK EDITION: EDITORIAL GUIDELINES

2.9.2 Phrasing

Phrasing in the *Complete Edition* of Janáček's works—following the sources—is expressed through phrase marks, and through two additional signs: a. breath marks and b. cut marks (caesura).
Example 15.

2.10 Instructions Concerning Expression and Performance Technique

All these instructions remain unchanged by the *Complete Edition*, and as a rule such instructions are not supplemented. An addition will only be considered in those cases where the composer forgot to indicate a return to the normal mode of playing after a marking such as "con sord.," "sul pont.," etc. Supplementations of this sort are listed in the Table of Variants in sigla (i.e. 201 archi s. sord =ES). Instructions concerning expression are always put under the line in italics (with the exception of the vocal parts.) If they were originally formulated in Czech, the editor adds the Italian equivalent in angular brackets (the only time angular brackets are used in the Complete Edition). Instructions for performance technique are always put above the line and are printed in normal lettering. Only the sign P for pedal (and the lying cross for cancellation of the pedal), and instructions like *una corda* (tre corde) are put beneath the line.

2.11 Ornamentation

We briefly quote the following rules from the detailed material in EZS concerning the usage of ornamentation:

    a. The sign for a trill is printed in normal lettering. If it is a double (repeated) trill we simply add wavy lines. If the trill sign also gets an accidental we put the accidental between the sign and the wavy line.

b. Janáček's notation of the trill with the lower neighbor is difficult to understand. In this case we use a notation from the time of Franois Couperin (the so-called pince continu or long mordent) (Example 16 - Janáček's notation, Example 17 - notation of the Complete Edition). In orchestral scores the editor can also use tremolo notation[3].

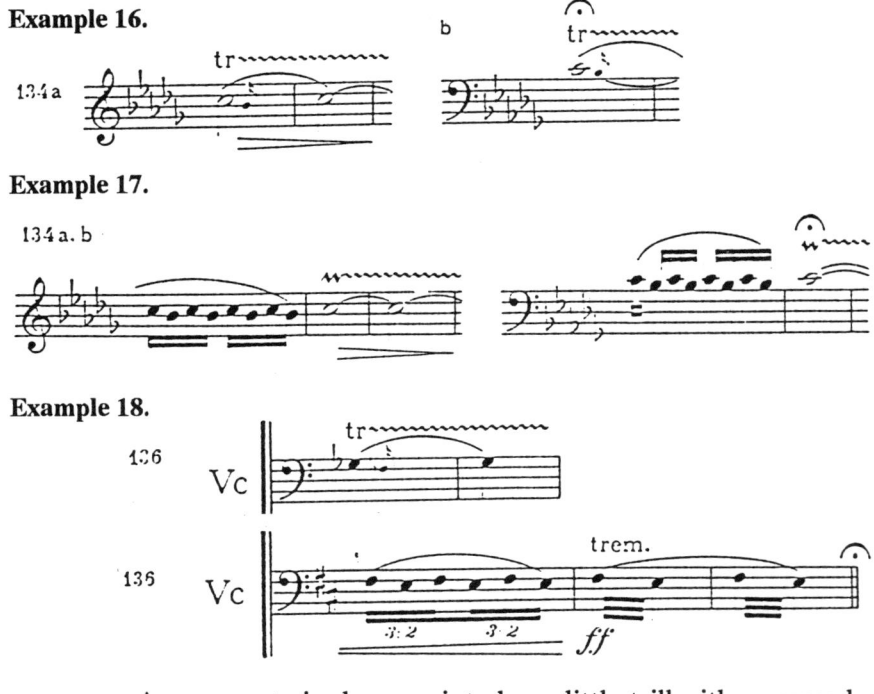

c. A grace note is always printed as a little trill with a crossed flag and no tie. The slides are printed without ties when they are not in the autograph. Ties are only used with grace-notes.

2.12 Shortened Notation

The guidelines of the *Complete Edition* always recommend a shortened form of notation when it leads to a clearer overview (especially with tremolos, octave shifts, and repetitions). For additional details see EZS.

---

[3]In the examples which show the notation of the *Complete Edition* we always place one bar of the original before the example to allow the reader to compare it with the solution offered by the *Complete Edition*.

JANÁČEK EDITION: EDITORIAL GUIDELINES

2.13 Notation of Transposing Instruments

a. Instruments which differ from the notated pitch by an octave are still notated as they are in the sources (this is true for the English Horn and Clarinets as well).

b. The bass clarinet is continuously transcribed into the so-called "French Notation," which fits the fingering of the instrument (notated in G clef a major ninth above its real pitch). The mode of notation in the sources is given in the critical report.

c. Only F-notation is used for the French Horn; differing notation in the sources is noted in the critical report. When the bass clef is used, the instrument is notated lower than it sounds. Signatures are not noted.

d. The trumpets are always notated in C (the choice of instrument is up to the player. Janáček often demands trumpets in F, which were outdated long before his time). The signatures for the trumpets are set up in accordance with the rest of the orchestra.

2.14 Special Procedures for Individual Instruments and Voices

The relationship between notes and syllables in the vocal parts is determined by exact textual underlay, not by slurs between the notes.

Example 19.

When several voices are noted on one line they do not all have their own separate dynamic and technical markings, or their own text. If such indications are in force for all voices, it will be shown by a half-bracket with a partially dotted line.

The Performer as Co-editor: Proposals for a New Complete Edition of Janáček's Works

Paul Wingfield

Paul Wingfield received his Ph.D. at Cambridge University and has written several articles on Janáček's music, focusing particularly on editorial problems. He has recently completed a book on the Glagolitic Mass. In this study he outlines his objections to some of the practices of the Complete Edition and makes a series of suggestions for its improvement. In the process, he also argues for a new view of Janáček's final decades which is refreshing and provocative.

The Collected Edition of Janáček's works has provoked surprise and even consternation on account of its notational alterations.[1] However, the notation is only one of the edition's problematic features. Equally contentious are the musicological methods on which the edition is based and the underestimation on the part of the compilers of the modern performer's editorial awareness. I would like to consider these two less publicised issues today.

The first section of this paper begins with a general survey of the commentaries in the *Complete Edition*. It then outlines modern musicological techniques relevant to Janáček source studies that might have been employed during the preparation of this edition. The second part of the paper examines the layout of the Collected Edition, and it proposes a different method of organization, which allow performers to make their own informed editorial decisions.

It is now widely accepted that in order to produce a reliable edition of a piece of music we must establish the precise contents and the internal chronologies of, as well as the relationships between, all its surviving primary sources. Very often, an editorial problem can be solved only with reference to an early draft or sketch, because many composers, including Janáček, made mistakes when recopying material. Moreover, most collected editions now include lists of manuscripts either presumed

---

[1] J. Vysloužil and others, eds.: *L. Janáček: souborné kritické vydání* [L. Janáček: Collected Critical Edition] (Prague, 1978–)

or known to be lost. The *New Bach Edition*, for example, incorporates such lists, because the rediscovery at a future date of a currently missing source would certainly place several present readings in a new light.[2] Unfortunately, most of the source catalogues in the Janáček Edition are incomplete and few of them acknowledge the possibility that some material might have been mislaid or concealed deliberately. For instance, the volume of the Edition containing the *Lachian Dances* fails to describe one of the surviving authorized copies of *Starodávný* II.[3] Also, the same volume does not make clear that the autograph of the final version of *Starodávný* II is missing.

Sets of individual parts are usually listed in the Collected Edition, but their variant readings are seldom catalogued in detail. Recent Mahler research by Paul Banks and others has shown that parts often contain authorized last-minute changes that are not in any other source. Janáček editors could therefore benefit from this potential gold-mine of information. Indeed, the extant 1927 parts for the *Glagolitic Mass* contain so many problematic late alterations that they are as important to the editor as the two authorized copies of this work.

If the Janáček Edition's catalogues of the the sources are inadequate, its assessments of the relationships between these manuscripts are misleading. We are informed in the solo piano music volume that the surviving first- and fourth-movement autographs of *In the Mists* belong to different stages of the piece's development, when these autographs were actually written as a single revision layer.[4] We are also led to believe that there are two complete authorized copies of *In the Mists*, although there are in fact three. The first two copies of this piano cycle are now fragmentary, because several pages of the first copy were incorporated intact into the second.

A further problem with the source chronologies in the Collected Edition is the inconsistent nomenclature that they employ. First drafts, for instance, are accorded six different appellations. This random labell-

---

[2] Johann-Sebastian Bach Institut, Göttingen, and Bach-Archiv, Leipzig, eds.: *Neue Bach-Ausgabe* (Kassel and Basle, 1954–)

[3] R. Eliška and J. Burghauser, eds.: *L. Janáček: souborné kritické vydání; řada D/svazek 4; Lašske tance* [L. Janáček: Collected Critical Edition; Series F/Volume 4; *Lachian Dances*] (Prague, 1982)

[4] L. Kundera and J. Burghauser, eds.: *L. Janáček: souborné kritické vydání; řada F/svazek 1; klavírní skladby* [L. Janáček: Complete Critical Edition; Series F/Volume 1; Piano Works] (Prague, 1978)

ing of manuscripts compares unfavorably with the precise nomenclature devised by the compilers of the Collected Edition of Wagner's works.[5]

The accounts in the Janáček Edition of the contents and internal chronologies of individual sources are the least informative of all. There are even some astonishing basic errors of fact: the fragmentary autograph of movement I of *In the Mists* is stated to consist of five leaves, when it really has only four. Furthermore, these accounts omit many vital details. Particularly unfortunate is the absence of an attempt to discover the relationships between the valid rectos and discarded versos of Janáček's hybrid autographs, the final layers of which are written on rectos only. In fact, we can usually discover the exact order in which each layer of every page of a multi-layered autograph was written. This may seem to be an esoteric exercise, but it is actually an essential part of the editorial process. A reconstruction of the genesis of movement I of the First String Quartet alone sheds light on about 20 textual problems in the finished work, ranging from missing dynamics to problematic tempo markings.[6]

That concludes our brief examination of the commentaries in the *Complete Edition*. We can now turn our attention to the methods we need to employ in order to establish the genesis of a Janáček manuscript. These methods are similar to those developed by Bach and Beethoven scholars. In his introduction to the admirable volume *The Beethoven Sketchbooks*, Douglas Johnson remarks:[7]

> The means for ... clarifying the actual state of the [Beethoven's] sources are not very sophisticated, at least technically, but they are perhaps not obvious.

Since these methods are not immediately apparent, it is worth outlining them and then considering their significance here. I will therefore consider the following 13 subjects: paper-types, watermarks, gathering structures, paper profiles, rastrology, ink blots, handwriting, ink types, pen strokes, trimming, erasures, numeration sequences and, finally, draft continuity.

---

[5] C. Dahlhaus and others, eds.: *R. Wagner: Sämtlich Werke* (Mainz, 1970–)
[6] For a detailed evaluation of the various stages in the genesis of Janáček's First String Quartet see P. Wingfield: *Source Problems in Janáček's Music: Their Significance and Interpretation* (Ph.D. Diss., Univ. of Cambridge, 1987), 32–71.
[7] D. Johnson, A. Tyson and R. Winter: *The Beethoven Sketchbooks* (Oxford, 1983), 11.

First of all, the *Complete Edition* of Janáček's music offers insufficient information about changes of paper-type within manuscripts. The study of paper-types is an important part of Janáček research, nevertheless. For example, examination of the three types of paper used in 1917, 1918 and 1919 respectively for *The Diary of One Who Disappeared* helps us to date specific musical revisions. Thus the Janáček Edition should contain complete lists of paper-types, as does the *New Berlioz Edition*.[8]

Watermarks are also very significant. In the age of machine-made paper the earlier elaborate watermarks were replaced largely by simpler marks produced by means of a dandy roll, but the less ornate devices in Janáček's manuscripts are equally useful for scholarly purposes. The various types of both watermarked and unwatermarked plain paper that the composer used for most of his non-operatic works were bought as loose bifolia. Each bifolia of the watermarked paper-types constituted half a sheet and therefore contained half a watermark. Before he began composing, Janáček generally divided each of his bifolia into two leaves, hence further subdividing the watermark. Of course, in drawing conclusions from our reconstructions of whole watermarks we must exercise caution: the composer may not have used his leaves in the order which they came out of the packet. Nevertheless, we can draw some tentative hypotheses: for example, leaves whose partial watermarks match exactly are likely to have belonged originally to the same layer of drafting, whatever their positions in the final multi-layered autograph.

The gathering structures of authorized copies of Janáček's music are invariably illuminating, in fact, they actually help us to establish the number of copies of *In the Mists*, a problem that I referred to earlier. The fragmentary binding arrangement of the volume in the Janáček Archive containing all the extant copied material for *In the Mists* indicates clearly that parts of the first complete copy were torn out and placed directly into the second.

Closely related to the question of gathering structures is that of paper profiles. If the editors of *In the Mists* for the Collected Edition had matched the profiles of the two surviving autographs they might not have made their incorrect assumption that these autographs belong to different stages of the compositional process. For the two autographs Janáček divided his bifolia of plain paper into four. The first cut was made with a paper-knife and the second with a pair of scissors. If we

---

[8]H. Macdonald and others, eds.: *New Berlioz Edition* (Kassel, 1967–)

match up all the sheets in the two manuscripts according to their profiles, we discover that some bifolia provided half-leaves for both autographs. This suggests that the autographs were written consecutively, as does all the other available physical evidence.[9]

The rastrology in Janáček's manuscripts is particularly interesting. For non-operatic pieces the composer generally ruled each line of every stave separately on plain paper, although in later life he sometimes used a rastrum. He employed both methods of staff-ruling in the drafts and autograph of the third movement of the First Quartet. If we group the relevant pages according to rastrological type, we can clarify several matters of internal chronology.

Janáček's manuscripts are almost as liberally bespattered with ink blots as Beethoven's sketchbooks. Some of Janáček's blots seem to have been caused by his placing leaves face down on top of one another before the music on their rectos had dried. Naturally, the composer's practice of writing revisions on the blank versos of rejected folios meant that the leaves of a manuscript frequently swapped positions during its development. Pages that were contiguous in earlier drafts can therefore often be pinpointed through the matching of ink blots.

The Janáček Edition accords especially scant consideration to handwriting. No attempt is made to chart the development of the handwriting of either Janáček or his copyists. Moreover, little effort is made to identify the authors of some unsigned copies. The three copies of *In the Mists,* which are all unsigned, are claimed to have been written by an unknown copyist, although they are obviously the work of V. Ševčík, who wrote other signed copies for Janáček.

The importance of close study of the handwriting copies of Janáček's music cannot be overestimated. There is always the chance that unauthorized revisions have been made by the copyists themselves or by editors and engravers, particularly in copies of works published posthumously. Also, a secure knowledge on the modern editor's part of various copyists' main handwriting characteristics and habitual orthographic errors is vital, especially in relation to works whose autographs are now missing. If we know that a certain copyist frequently omitted accidentals, for example, we will be more confident about adding necessary editorial accidentals in a piece for which the only surviving source is a score written by that copyist.

---

[9] A complete examination of the sources of *In the Mists* can be found in P. Wingfield: *Source Problems in Janáček's Music*, 12–31.

A subject only recently investigated in any depth by Beethoven and Bach scholars is that of ink types. In an article published in 1987 Barry Cooper argues that our knowledge of the chronology of the sketches in the Kafka Miscellany can be increased through detailed examination of the ink.[10] Moreover, the German scholar Rainer Kaiser has developed a near-infrared spectrograph for determining the ink types in Bach manuscripts and his research has helped to identify many spurious editorial ornaments and phrase markings in these sources. Similarly, the three distinct ink types in the sketches for Janáček's *Diary* provide much important information about the chronology of the work.

The thickness of pen strokes is another factor not taken into account in the Collected Edition. Pen strokes can be of considerable significance. The clear change of pen in the *Sinfonietta* manuscripts would appear to be the result of an interruption in the piece's genesis cause by Janáček's May 1926 trip to England. The pen strokes here thus aid us to determine how much of the *Sinfonietta* was finished prior to May 1926. In turn, once we discover that Janáček had not drafted some parts of the work before he went to London, even though the *Sinfonietta* received its premiere in June 1926, we realise how quickly the full score and parts had to be copied and hence why the authorized copy contains so many mistakes. These errors include the misplacement by one bar of the cymbal crash at the return of the fanfare in movement V, a mistake that has yet to be corrected in any published edition of the piece.

Although seemingly insignificant, evidence of trimming in authorized copies can be revealing. The fact that a copy has been trimmed may help us to find out whether insertions made at the outer extremes of pages by persons other than the composer were written out before or after the copy was bound and thus whether alterations made in the same hand in the musical text were made prior or subsequent to the composer's death. (The authorized copies of Janáček's works were not bound until many years after he had died.)

Erasures and paste-overs are common in autographs and copies of Janáček's music. The original versions of emended passages must be deciphered if we are to establish the precise relationships between sources. We must also bear in mind the possibility of accidental erasure. Many dynamics and phrase marks that are obviously missing from printed editions of Janáček's works appear to have been lost owing to

---

[10]B. Cooper: "The Ink in Beethoven's 'Kafka Sketch Miscellany,' " *Music and Letters*, lxviii (1987), 315–32.

the composer having mistakenly erased more material than he intended during the revision of authorized copies.

Pagination and foliation sequences in autographs invariably clarify the nature and extent of revisions, so it is surprising that they are never listed in full in the Janáček Edition. In addition, examination of the pagination in authorized copies can be fruitful. For instance, the last movement of the *Sinfonietta* copy is paginated separately, although the other four movements have a continuous sequence. If we study other features of this score, we soon see that the fifth movement was actually the first to be copied, a finding that lead us to many more important discoveries about the work's genesis.

Searching for musical continuity between the layers of the valid and discarded sides of an autograph is perhaps the most obvious way of evaluating that manuscript's genesis, but draft continuity is ignored in the Collected Edition. Of course, Janáček might not always have worked on the sections of a piece in their correct sequence, and indeed one revision of movement III of the First Quartet appears to have been carried out in reverse order. But musical continuity sequences must always be evaluated.

It should now be clear that the techniques of Bach and Beethoven studies can be applied to the editing of Janáček's manuscripts. The benefits of employing these methods also extend beyond the bounds of editorial work In the 1950s a close examination of Bach's Cantata manuscripts inspired a radical re-evaluation of that composer's stylistic development. Similarly, my own study of Janáček's sources is beginning to alter the current view of his final decade. This period is generally presented in the literature as a sudden creative flowering, which followed a fallow period between the Brno and Prague premieres of *Jenůfa*. However, manuscript evidence indicates that several of Janáček's major works of the 1920s originated before the First World War. The initial version of the First String Quartet was largely a rearrangement of the Piano Trio of 1908–09.[11] More startlingly, the earliest draft of the *Glagolitic Mass* was modelled closely on the incomplete didactic Mass of 1907–08. Thus, Janáček's final decade can in some ways be seen as a tidying-up of the composer's workshop in which several shelved projects were finally completed. We might need to modify our hitherto one dimensional view of the composer's final years.

---

[11] For a fuller consideration of this matter see P. Wingfield: "Janáček's 'Lost' Kreutzer Sonata," *Journal of the Royal Musical Association*, cxii/2 (1987), 229–56.

As I stated in the introduction to this paper, the second major problem with the Collected Janáček Edition is its layout. The actual musical texts contain virtually no editorial apparatus. Instead, an allegedly complete list of alterations is supplied in every commentary. The compilers assert that editorial markings in the text would clutter it up unnecessarily. Scholars, they claim, will be able to determine the musical content of the original sources from the commentaries.

This approach is unsatisfactory. It suggests, quite unjustifiably, that a definitive text can be established for each of Janáček's works. In fact, the primary sources of the composer's music are so ambiguous that hundreds of difficult editorial decisions have to be made for every piece, and often two or more readings for particular passages are equally feasible. If performers are to have the opportunity of producing convincing interpretations of Janáček's pieces, the edition that they are working from must be honest about the ephemeral nature of many of its readings. Editorial information should as far as is practicable be included in the musical text. Moreover, editorial apparatus need not clutter up the musical score. The *Complete Debussy Edition* identifies editorial emendations by means of small print rather than square brackets.[12] It also denotes editorial phrasing and *crescendo* and *diminuendo* markings by a vertical dash through the relevant symbols. In places where two or more readings appear equally likely extra staves are used. This layout neatly avoids the problem of some bars containing too many markings, while at the same time showing editorial modifications quite unambiguously.

Not only are the texts of the Janáček Edition unrealistically inflexible, but the editors' claim that their commentaries reveal the contents of the original manuscript is difficult to substantiate. Each set of editorial notes is actually a mixture of genuine variant readings and versions unequivocally discarded by Janáček. This type of layout can only confuse anyone who does not have detailed knowledge of the relevant sources. Other modern editors limit their commentaries to variants that affect readings in the final version only. Earlier, rejected versions are shown in facsimile or transcribed separately in appendices.

A further problem with the commentaries in the Janáček Edition is the number of mistakes they incorporate. Let us take the commentary for *In the Mists* as a test case. Of the 148 entries here as many as 57, some 38%, contain factual and/or notational errors. A further ten

---

[12]F. Lesure and others, eds.: *Oeuvres complètes de Claude Debussy* (Paris, 1985–)

entries reach debatable conclusions without fully examining the issues involved. Also, in my opinion, 71 significant problems concerning *In the Mists* are not mentioned. All the commentaries so far published are similarly inaccurate.

Clearly, it is difficult, if not impossible, for performers and scholars to make their own editorial decisions from the Collected Edition's commentaries. But even if these commentaries were completely accurate, the Edition's layout would still be unconvincing, because it assumes a distinction between the needs of performers and those of musicologists that is fast disappearing. As early as 1957 the Bach scholar Walter Emery wrote:[13]

> It is . . . important that musicians in general should have some idea of what editing means: some idea of the process that . . . music has gone through . . . before it reaches their hands. . . .

With the rise of the performance-practice movement, so much progress has been made in this area that editors have begun to expect performers to play a vital role in determining the musical texts for their interpretations. As Roy Howat comments in his explanation of the structure of the *Complete Debussy Edition*:[14]

> The main priority is that variants and associated source evidence be available, allowing performers to judge.

The Janáček editors' assumption that performers need to be spoon-fed is therefore contrary to contemporary editorial trends. A complete edition that will not be finished until next century must look to the future. Recent developments in the computer printing of music mean that it is feasible to issue editions complete with alternative readings on disc. Performers and conductors could decide which variants they wish to include in their interpretations and then print out their chosen texts. Janáček editors should be working towards such a flexible format, which accommodates the genuine cases of doubt concerning the composer's intentions.

In the course of this short paper we have established that the Collected Edition of Janáček's works is in many ways outdated and is limited in the musicological techniques that it employs. A change of approach to the Edition is therefore necessary. Such a course of action may seem impracticable, but the alternative is for Janáček source studies to con-

---

[13] W. Emery: *Editions and Musicians* (London, 1957), 5.
[14] R. Howat: "The New Debussy Edition: Approaches and Techniques," *Studies in Music* (Univ of W. Australia), xix (1985), 94–113 (p. 97).

tinue to be viewed as primitive and marginal by both experts and the musical public at large. Only when Janáček scholars show that they can learn from techniques developed in more advanced areas of musicology will their work be taken seriously and Janáček's music achieve the enlightened critical acclaim it deserves.

Part 5:

Janáček and the Contemporary World

All too often Janáček has been viewed as a quirky and isolated phenomenon, too much an individual to be associated with any broader trends, movement, or contemporaries. This perspective, far from the truth, has merely revealed the sometimes limited quality of our imaginations: first, because no figure is immune to the virus of contemporary culture, and second, because Janáček drew from the streams of culture in a way which was uncommonly rich.

The papers presented here reflect only a tiny fraction of the influences and issues which were a part of Janáček's world and shaped his thought. From the novels of Dostoevsky, to the theoretical texts of Hermann von Helmholtz, and from the operas of Charpentier to the sound of the waves, Janáček was immoderately involved in his world. It is only his uniquely framed surface which sometimes resists comparison; but the meaning behind the surface, the techniques, content, and substance of his work, tie him in countless ways to his contemporaries.

Dvořák and Janáček: New Insights into an Old Friendship

Alan Houtchens

Alan Houtchens has been a significant part of the movement to build a field of Czech and Slovak music research in the United States. He is a specialist in the work of Dvořák and has recently completed an edition of Dvořák's Vanda. *He has contributed to numerous periodicals in this country and in Czechoslovakia.*

The friendship between artists is of interest to us for numerous reasons. The first involves scholarly concerns, documentation, and even such questions as influence, mutual or otherwise. Yet there are metaphysical aspects as well which attract our attention: there is something magical about the social interaction of our "heroes," for like it or not, that is the way almost all of us, since the 19th century, have treated the figures which we study. The Dvořák-Janáček relationship is one of the great composer friendships, and in this study Houtchens reviews the nature of the interaction and tries to come to an assessment of it.

Do you know what it is like when someone takes the words out of your mouth as you are about to speak them? For me it was always like that in Dvořák's company. I can interchange his personality with his work: he also took his melodies from my heart. Nothing in the world can destroy such ties.[1]

These oft-quoted words of Janáček, written several years after Dvořák's death, reveal a friendship that was especially close. The two composers met for the first time in the fall of 1874, just after Janáček had moved to Prague to attend the Organ School, and their appreciation for each other never flagged during the next thirty years.

One can imagine that their outward personalities were not so much alike as complimentary. Dvořák was quiet, reserved, taciturn. He was a

---

[1] Leoš Janáček, "Za Antonínem Dvořákem," *Hudební revue* 4, no. 8/9 (October, 1911): 432.
  Znáte to, když někdo Vám z úst slovo bere, dřív než jste je vyslovil? Tak mi bylo vždy ve společnosti Dvořákově. Mohu osobu jeho zaměnit s jeho dílem. Tak ze srdce mi bral svoje melodie. Takový svazek nic na světě neroztrhá.

deliberate, careful person who took a long time to make decisions, especially with regard to matters of business. Janáček, on the other hand, was impulsive, restless, impetuous, perhaps even violently so. Still, he had all the characteristics of a born teacher: he was patient, persistent, outgoing and outspoken, talkative, instantly likeable.

Although they may have had fundamentally different temperaments, Janáček and Dvořák shared so many common experiences, interests, values, and aspirations that it is easy to see why they became steadfast friends. Both faced professional adversities and personal tragedies. Dvořák lost three children in infancy; Janáček similarly witnessed the untimely deaths of his two children. Both had to overcome the petty prejudices held by important members of the artistic communities in Prague and Brno. The story of Janáček's twelve-year struggle to get *Jenůfa* performed at the National Theater in Prague is well-known. Few people are aware, however, that early in his career, Dvořák weathered a blistering attack in the press. Someone writing in the Prague music journal *Dalibor*—most likely the chief editor, V. J. Novotný—strongly admonished Dvořák for allowing Simrock to publish two of his song cycles with German texts only. The vehemence with which the writer pursued this subject is indicative of the volatile nature of the times, and his remarks reflect the general tenor not only of this particular journal but also of the wave of nationalism that had spread among the Czech intelligentsia. In the process of commenting upon an announcement that had appeared in the *Signale für die musikalische Welt* of the new edition of Dvořák's *Zigeunermelodien* (*Cigánské melodie*, Gypsy songs), the journalist quipped:

> Nowhere is it mentioned that the poems are translated from the Czech (the text is only in German), as though our Czech composer Antonín Dvořák not once so far as even cared whether the Czech text enjoyed a place alongside the German in his hitherto published works. It would be advisable after all in this regard for Dvořák to adopt Smetana's manner.[2]

The last gibe seems to imply that Dvořák was thought to be in a class quite apart from Smetana and that some kind of rivalry was seen

---

[2] "Drobné zprávy," *Dalibor* 2, no. 28 (1 October 1880): 222.
Ze jsou básně ty překladem z češtiny, o tom nikde není zmínky, text jest pouze německý, jako vůbec náš český skladatel Antonín Dvořák nikdy se o to dosud nestaral, aby vedle německého i českému textu místo bylo popřáno v dosavádě uveřejněných jeho skladbách. Bylo by záhodno, aby Dvořák i v tomto ohledu konečně Smetanův ráz si osvojil.

to exist between the two composers. On the same page, but in a separate entry, Dvořák is chided again, this time with regard to the *Klänge aus Mähren* (*Moravské dvojzpěvy*, Moravian duets):

> The composer sold this work to the Berlin publisher Simrock, who printed it only with German text. No one here has the [publication] rights for a new Czech edition, so our public is obliged to buy the German translation. A composer like Dvořák, after whose works German publishers are clamoring, could command the publication of each of his vocal works in five languages, not to mention German and Czech, and it could be so merely at his whim. However, we must observe with regret that so far Dvořák has not shown enough consideration for our musical heritage and our public to provide for the printing of Czech texts and titles in addition to the German. We are convinced—and it won't be long in coming—that the covetous Germans will be writing about our highly gifted Dvořák: "unser Dworzak"! If it matters to Dvořák to remain one of us—and we think it does matter—he should forestall any further unpleasant consequences while there still is time by vigorously standing up against the German publishers.[3]

One of the "consequences" may have been that during the next three months nothing at all concerning Dvořák appeared in the pages of *Dalibor*. Since 1873 at least, and especially after Novotný took over the duties of chief editor from Jan Ludevít Procházka in 1875, Dvořák's compositional activities and the performances and publications of his new works had heretofore been noted on a regular basis in the "Zprávy" (reports) section of the journal, and occasionally full-length reviews or analyses of his compositions had been featured. Dvořák had been viewed as the darling of the Czech musical establishment, next in im-

---

[3]Ibid.
   Skladatel prodal toto dílo berlínskému nakladateli Simrockovi, který je vytiskl pouze s německým textem. K novému českému vydání právo u nás nikdo nemá, a tak jest obecenstvo naše nuceno kupovati německý překlad. Skladatel jako Dvořák, o jehož práce se němečtí nakladatelé derou, mohl by si poručiti vydání každého svého vokálního díla třeba v pěti jazycích, neřku-li v německém a českém, a stalo by se vždy po jeho vůli; s politováním však musíme poznamenati, že Dvořák dosud neměl tolik šetronosti k naší literatuře hudební a k našemu obecenstvu, aby se postaral o tisk českých textů a titulů vedle německých. Jsme přesvědčeni, a nebude to dlouho trvat, že hrabiví Němci psáti budou o genialním našem Dvořákovi: "unser Dworzak"! Záleží-li Dvořákovi na tom, aby zůstal našincem—a myslíme, že záleží—tož at' rázným vystoupením vůči německým nakladatelům předejde pozdějším neblahým konsekvecím ještě v čas!

portance to Smetana, and he had his works had been discussed only in glowing terms. Perhaps the hiatus in attention given to him now was a deliberate and calculated way of showing disappointment in the way he seemed to be courting a German audience.

This silent treatment lasted until January 1881. Finally a slightly conciliatory notice appeared wherein the situation was reviewed and certain assurances were given:

> I have regretted very much that from his oeuvre of songs Dvořák published his most perfect and respectable work [*Cigánské melodie*] at Simrock's in Berlin with German text only, and I told him openly and directly in these pages, as is well-known, that the Czech public deserved greater attention on his part, that a Czech composer must write above all for a Czech audience. What good would Dvořák be to us if his works were not accessible? And they would not be accessible to our public published only with German text. I found out, however, that Dvořák did not act in this way intentionally; for I have just been told that Simrock will publish for our public a new edition of these excellent songs in Czech, and that in the future each vocal work by Dvořák will always be issued with the Czech text in addition to a German translation. For this we are grateful to our composer, as generally there would be a danger in letting his compositions be stolen from our musical literature.[4]

If he had not been naturally inclined to embrace either the specifically Czech or the pan-Slavic nationalistic ideals espoused by his compatriots in Prague, and if Janáček's fervent sentiments had had no impact on him, Dvořák in any case could hardly have been expected to ignore the criticism he received in the pages of *Dalibor*. He henceforth took care not only to inform Simrock and other foreign publishers that his works should include the original Czech texts and titles, but also to

---

[4]"Dvořák co skladatel písní," *Dalibor* 3, no. 1 (1 January 1881): 7.

Že Dvořák toto z oboru písně nejdokonalejší a nejčestější dílo vydal u Simrocka v Berlíně pouze s německým textem, toho mi právě bylo nejvíce líto, i řekl jsem mu na tomto místě, jak známo, otevřeně a zpříma, že české obecenstvo zasluhovalo si větší pozornosti s jeho strany, že český skladatel především komponovati musí pro české obecenstvo. Co by nám byl Dvořák platen, kdyby nám díla jeho nebyla přístupna? A pouze s německým textem vydána stala by se obecenstvu našemu nepřístupnými. Přesvědčil jsem se však, že Dvořák neučinil tak zúmyslně; neboť dovídám se právě, že Simrock vydá pro naše obecenstvo nové vydání těchže znamenitých písní s českým textem, a příště, že každá vokální práce Dvořákova vydána bude vždy s českým textem vedle německého překladu. Jsme za to povděčni našemu skladateli, neboť tím odpadne nebezpečí, že by skladby jeho mohly býti odcizeny naší hudební literatuře.

make his intentions clear to his compatriots.[5] The announcement of the sale of the score of *Vanda* to August Cranz that appeared in the 25 May 1881 issue of *Divadelní listy*, for example, included this telling statement: "At Dvořák's insistence the piano arrangement also will be printed with Czech text."[6]

At the international conference entitled "Dvořák, Janáček and Their Time" held in Brno four years ago, Dr. Jiří Vysloužil presented a very interesting and informative paper comparing some of the stylistic features of Dvořák's and Janáček's music, and Dr. Theodora Straková summarized the available documentary evidence of the personal interaction between the two men.[7] Dr. David Beveridge has addressed several matters of style in his contribution to the present volume.[8] Other insights can be gleaned from the principal biographies of each composer.[9] Still, with regard to the influences each composer may have had on the other, there are still several topics that deserve closer scrutiny. One concerns the interest both composers showed very early in their lives in the folk poetry and music of Slavic peoples other than the Czechs, Moravians, and Slovaks. There is no indication that Dvořák and

---

[5]Even after Dvořák and Simrock had reconciled the various differences that had created a gulf between them, the composer still felt compelled to advise his publisher that all titles should be printed in Czech as well as German. See his letter dated 3 October, 1895, quoted in Šourek, *Antonín Dvořák in Briefen und Erinnerungem,* 100, or, in English translation, in *Antonín Dvořák: Letters and Reminiscences,* trans. Roberta Finlayson Samsour (Prague: Státní nakladatelství, 1954), 185.

[6]"Zprávy," *Divadelní listy* 2, no. 15 (25 May, 1881): 136. "Klavírní prava bude k naléhání Dvořákovu vytištěna též s českým textem."

[7]Jiří Vysloužil, "Dvořák and Janáček: Their Time and Work," in *Colloquium "Dvořák, Janáček and Their Time" (Brno 1984)* (Brno: Česká hudební společnost, 1985), 9–16; Theodora Staková, "Leoš Janáček a Antonín Dvořák (ve světle korespondence a dokumentů)," in *Colloquium,* 177–181.

[8]See Dr. Beveridge's paper, "Romantic and Twentieth Century Styles in the 1870's: Music for String Orchestra by Dvořák and Janáček," in this volume.

[9]Important biographical studies of Janáček include Jan Racek, "Janáček a Praha," *Musikologie* 3 (1955): 11–50; Jaroslav Šeda, *Leoš Janáček* (Prague: Státní hudební vydavatelství, 1961); Hans Hollander, *Leoš Janáček: HIs Life and Work,* trans. Paul Hamburger (London: John Calder, 1963); Jaroslav Vogel, *Leoš Janáček: Život a dílo* (Prague: Státní hudební vydavatelství, 1963), rev. English ed. prepared by Karel Janovický, trans. Geraldine Thonsen-Muchová (London: Orbis Publishing, 1981); Bohumír Štědroň, *Leoš Janáček: K jeho lidskému a uměleckému profilu* (Prague: Panton, 1976).

Relevent sources concerning Dvořák include Otakar Šourek, *Život a dílo Antonína Dvořáka,* rev. ed., 4 vols. (Prague: Státní nakladatelství, 1954–1957); Jarmil Burghauser, *Antonín Dvořák,* trans. Jean Layton-Eislerová (Prague: Státní hudební vydavatelství, 1967); Jiří Berkovec, *Antonín Dvořák* (Prague: Supraphon, 1969); John Clapham, *Dvořák (New York:W. W. Norton, 1979).*

Janáček knew each other before 1874, but it seems very curious, even considering the general interest shown by everyone at the time in the critical situation in the Balkans, that both composers turned first of all and perhaps simultaneously to Serbian texts, Janáček for his *Ženich vnucený* (The imposed bridegroom, 1873) and Dvořák for his *Čtyři písně na slova srbské lidové poesie* (Four songs to the words of Serbian folk texts, 1872).

In addition, it is not outside the realm of possibility that Janáček influenced Dvořák in some way during 1874 and 1875 in his selection of a libretto for a new, large-scale opera. Dvořák eventually settled on Václav Beneš-Šumavský and František Zákrejs's *Vanda*, which relates the legend of the Polish queen Vanda, who sacrificed her own life so that her people would prevail over an aggressive German tribe.[10] If Janáček did not have any direct say in Dvořák's subsequent choice of Marie Červinková-Riegrová's libretto *Dimitrij* for his next serious opera, which was first performed in 1882, we can be certain that he would have heartily approved.

By the same token, Dvořák may have steered Janáček towards Julius Zeyer's *Šárka* as material for an opera. During the years 1878–1880 Dvořák himself had sketched the music for a scene or two but put the project aside. Jaroslav Vogel may be more correct, however, in assuming that Zeyer's *Šárka*, which had been published in installments in three issues of *Česká thalie* during January and February 1887, was brought to Janáček's attention by Karel Sázavský.[11] In either case, it is significant that both composers were attracted to this particular Czech legend.[12]

Janáček's pan-Slavic orientation led him to seek out the multifarious riches of Eastern Slavic, especially Russian, cultures. It seems all the more likely, therefore, that he had become acquainted with the liturgy and music of the Russian Orthodox and Slavonic Churches long before 1896, when he actually visited Russia. In his biography of the composer, Vogel writes that the *Hospodine pomiluj ny*, which Janáček composed early in 1896, is "so impregnated with the spirit of the music of the Russian Orthodox Church, that it is difficult to believe that he

---

[10] Concerning other factors that may have influenced Dvořák in this regard, see my dissertation "A Critical Study of Antonín Dvořák's *Vanda*" (University of California, Santa Barbara, 1987), 1–45.

[11] Jaroslav Vogel, *Leos Janáček*, rev. English ed. (London: Orbis, 1981), 86.

[12] In 1897, Zdeněk Fibich composed his own opera *Šárka*, based on the same material.

wrote it before his journey [to Russia]."[13] Indeed, aside from his early experiences at the Queen's Monastery school in Brno under the tutelage of Pavel Křížkovský, an ardent supporter of the Cyrilo-Methodius movement, Janáček very well may have become acquainted with Orthodox chant during the 1870s as a result of his friendship with Dvořák. Jarmil Burghauser has pointed out to me that Dvořák's wife, Anna Čermáková-Dvořáková, sang in the church choir of Svatý Mikuláš (St. Nicholas) in Prague I (Old Town) at least from the year 1880 and presumably earlier. Karel Bendl, a fine composer and Dvořák's good friend, was choirmaster there during the years 1877–1878 and from 1886 to 1890, and Zdeněk Fibich served in the same capacity from 1878 to 1881. Janáček must have been friendly with these composers, especially Bendl, as well; and it seems likely that he would have had occasion to attend services at Svatý Mikuláš.

It is worth noting parenthetically that Bendl's fame as a choral conductor and interpreter of Russian chant spread from France across the Atlantic Ocean to America. From 1878 to 1881 he served as choirmaster in the splendid musical establishment of Baron Paul von Dervies, a fabulously wealthy Russian nobleman who, besides owning several estates in Russia, maintained a summer castle near the lake of Lugano and a winter villa at Nice. Bendl was in charge of a mixed chorus consisting of about 48 singers, all Bohemians. Aside from singing Russian liturgical chant in Dervies's private chapels, these vocalists made up the chorus for performances of opera that were scheduled regularly during the winter. Charles Martin Loeffler, a virtuoso violinist, previously a student of Joachim, later the second concert master of the Boston Symphony Orchestra for over twenty years, and a composer in his own right, played in Dervies's orchestra, which was conducted by Karl Muller-Berghaus. Loeffler apparently learned much from Bendl and was especially impressed by the Slavic music that the choirmaster conducted.[14] Dvořák must have dedicated his *Slavonic Rhapsodies* (1878) to Dervies on Bendl's recommendation.

To return to the subject at hand, one last similarity between Janáček and Dvořák should be noted. Both drew strength and inspiration from nature, and both were especially fascinated by birds. There is a wonderful photograph of a white-bearded Dvořák entertaining, so it seems, a group if pigeons—and being entertained by them—while sit-

---

[13]Jaroslav Vogel, *Leoš Janáček*, rev. English ed. (London: Orbis, 1981), 124.
[14]Carl Engel, "Charles Martin Loeffler," *The Musical Quarterly* 11, no. 3 (July 1925), 316–317.

ting on a bench at his summer cottage near Příbram. He bred pigeons as a hobby. Janáček made pets of hens. Vilem Tausky relates how he had trained two of them to jump up on a table every night so that he could caress them and wish them goodnight.[15] Janáček was in the habit of putting down on paper bird calls or any other sounds in nature that seemed special to him. He would notate the pitches and phonetic sounds made by a bird and describe in detail the specific interactions between the bird and other living things, or between it and the forces of nature.

Still further inquiry into the personal, professional, and artistic ties that bound Janáček and Dvořák together—ties that, for Janáček, "nothing in the world could destroy"—would surely reveal even more about the close friendship of these two composers and about the very nature of their creative personalities.

---

[15]Vilem and Margaret Tausky, eds. and trans., *Janáček: Leaves from His Life* (New York: Taplinger Publishing Co., 1982), 86.

Romantic and Twentieth-Century Styles in the 1870s: Music for String Orchestra by Dvořák and Janáček

David Beveridge

Alan Houtchens' paper deals with the personal relationship between Janáček and Dvořák, while David Beveridge looks at musical relationships. Beveridge, who was the guiding spirit behind the Dvořák Festival in New Orleans, and author of numerous articles in American and Czech journals, has been exploring formal questions related to Dvořák's work for almost a decade. In this study he finds some kinship between the two figures, but even more significantly, some rather pronounced differences.

In discussing Janáček's *Idyll* for string orchestra, commentators have often remarked that the work owes a great deal to the style of Dvořák. In particular, it has been observed, this piece by Janáček calls to mind the earlier composer's *Serenade* for strings. The comparison is indeed apt in a number of ways. The two works are similar in scoring (a normal string orchestra in both cases), length (roughly twenty-five minutes), number of movements (more than four: Dvořák has five, Janáček seven), and general character (music that is fairly light in tone—not as serious or profound as a symphony would be). External factors, too, indicate a close connection: Janáček wrote his *Idyll* in 1878, just three years after Dvořák composed his *Serenade*, and at a time when the two composers had recently established quite a close friendship. It is not surprising, therefore, that Janáček's work should draw on the style of Dvořák, and for most listeners upon first hearing there is in fact a remarkable resemblance between the two pieces.

My purpose in this study, however, is to discuss not the similarities between these two works, but rather the differences. These differences, upon close examination, become more and more apparent, and are ultimately of greater interest than the similarities. Some of them, of course, have to do with Janáček's relative lack of experience as a composer at the time his work was written (he was about twenty-four years old when he composed the *Idyll*, as compared with Dvořák who wrote the *Serenade* in this *thirty*-fourth year); not surprisingly, Janáček's work sounds less polished in places than Dvořák's.

More importantly, though, Janáček shows many signs in this work of something that he may not have realized himself at the time, but which we today recognize very clearly—that he would ultimately achieve fame in a style very different, in fact in some ways *fundamentally* different, from that of Dvořák. And here we find a very valuable opportunity. For if we compare Janáček's *mature* style with Dvořák, the contrasts are so great that it is sometimes difficult even to make comparisons. But in the *Idyll*, which is superficially similar to Dvořák, the differences stand out in a way which is much easier to comprehend. And these differences, as we shall see, represent not just a contrast between the styles of two individual composers, but a contrast between the approaches of two musical eras. In several ways Janáček, already in 1878, was writing in a style more characteristic of the twentieth century than of the Romantic period, as can be seen in his rhythmic, melodic, and harmonic structures, and perhaps most importantly in the way these various parameters combine to produce an overall aesthetic.

Janáček's approach to rhythm is evident in the structure of many of the themes in the *Idyll*, which contrast markedly with those found in Dvořák's *Serenade*. As is well known, the asymmetrical rhythms of Janáček's mature style stem in large part from his concern with imitating the rhythms of speech in the Czech language, and it would appear that this was already a factor (subconsciously?) in the composition of his *Idyll*. The Czech language has a rhythmic peculiarity (peculiar to Western ears, that is) which is well-illustrated by Janáček's own name, in which the first syllable is the most accented but not the longest. (The čarka, which appears to Westerners as an accent mark, actually locates the syllable of greatest length and does not indicate stress.) This same characteristic may be found in five of the principal themes of the *Idyll* (See Example 1, opposite), in each of which the first note, appearing on the downbeat, is relatively short, and leads directly or very shortly to a longer note at a less stressed point in the measure. The theme from the sixth movement (1c) is an especially clear example, where the rhythmic structure is essentially identical to that of Janáček's name; one should note that, while this example appears to lack the character of a theme, it is actually the principal melodic material of the trio section of this movement. The theme quoted from the seventh movement (1e) also requires special comment, for here Janáček has placed an accent mark over the longer notes in the theme, which would seem to disqualify

Example 1. Janáček *Idyll*

it as an example of the phenomenon in question. The context of this theme, however, makes it clear that the marked accent is secondary to that felt on the downbeat of the measure.

The contrast with Dvořák in this matter is quite strong, as there is not a single theme in the *Serenade* with the characteristics just described. It would be foolish to claim that Dvořák never wrote such themes in any of his works, but his tendencies in this direction are clearly less strong than Janáček's. His thematic rhythms, while by no means dull or commonplace, do lie somewhat closer to the nineteenth-century main-stream tradition.

The accentual pattern of Janáček's themes tends to weaken the sense of regular metric structure somewhat, but certainly does not destroy it. In other ways, Janáček tampers with metric regularity more seriously. One example is the use of quintuple meter, an asymmetrical pattern which of course is quite common in the twentieth century, but very rare in the nineteenth century outside of Russian music (and practically non-existent in Dvořák). Quintuple meter may be seen in the theme quoted from the third movement in Example 1a, and also in the opening section of the fifth movement (not quoted).

Of even greater rhythmic interest is the passage from the seventh movement quoted in Example 2. This is the original (and ironically more complex) version of the theme quoted in Example 1e; that is, it appears earlier in the movement than 1e. Whereas in example 1e the regular metric structure is weak, in Example 2 it is effectively nonexistent. Despite the time signature and evenly-spaced bar lines, to the listener the number of beats

Example 2. Janáček *Idyll*

in a metric group is variable, as one might expect in a twentieth-century composer like Stravinsky. Some readers may disagree with my scanning of the beat groupings (as indicated by the numbers above the staff), as there are ambiguities in some places, but it is quite clear that the perceived metric structure is not that of the time signature. Nor is there any substitute time signature that could account for the groupings consistently throughout the excerpt.

Proceeding from rhythmic matters to questions of melodic structure, we find again a difference between the procedures of Dvořák and Janáček, in at least one respect. This is the use of motivic repetition. Dvořák's normal practice in keeping with the practice of Romantic composers generally, is to extend and develop melodies in an evolutionary process, or to to on to completely new melodic material. Apart from some of his later works, particularly the "American" works, extensive reiterations of small motives occur only occasionally and for special purposes. In the *Serenade*, one such instance may be seen in the fourth movement, mm. 28–33 (Example 3a), in which the energy of the opening section of the movement is "wound down" through a brief passage of stasis. Note, however, that the end of this passage is actually *not* static; the speeding-up of the reiteration contributes to the reestablishment of momentum leading to the next section at m. 34. Another case may be found in the opening movement, mm. 50–59 (Example 3b), where a repeating motive "winds down" the central "B" section of the movement, and is then maintained not as the primary melodic material but as an accompanimental pattern which established a link between the "B" and the returning "A" sections. The only place in the *Serenade* where a substantial section of primary melodic material consists of numerous repetitions is the second theme of the Finale (Example 3c). This passage is quite exceptional for Dvořák, and the reiterations are clearly intended to produce a humorous effect. Moreover the melodic stasis is completely contradicted by the gradual thickening of texture, and the swell in dynamics from pianissimo at m. 287 to fortissimo at m. 311. (This contradiction contributes to the humor.)

Example 3. Dvořák *Serenade*

For Janáček the use of motivic repetition is more normal, especially in his mature style but even to some degree in the *Idyll*. The opening of the second movement, for example, is based on a theme whose material consists essentially of a three-fold statement of a one-measure motive, followed by one measure of new material (Example 4). After

Example 4. Janáček *Idyll*

the first four bars, the theme is repeated in an ornamented version which is structurally different from the original only in the last measure. Then the key changes and we hear another reiterative theme of two four-bar periods, where the periods are almost literally identical. Such use of juxtaposed planes, with the small-scale reiterations denying any sense of direction toward a goal, is reminiscent not only of the later Janáček, but of Debussy, Stravinsky, and many other twentieth-century composers.

In examining harmonic progressions, one finds a similar contrast between Dvořák and Janáček: Dvořák does truly "progress," while Janáček is more inclined to remain static for substantial periods. One of the most stable passages of harmony in Dvořák's *Serenade* occurs at the very beginning, where of course his purpose is partly to establish the key. But even here the harmony of E Major is maintained for only four measures, and acts as a springboard for the very purposeful progression to the dominant which follows (Example 5).

Quite foreign to Dvořák is the type of construction Janáček uses in the opening of his third movement, where the first fourteen measures form a closed period with virtually every measure centering on the tonic harmony. The motivic structure of this passage is also quite static in some ways. Dynamics, it must be admitted, are not static at all, and may be compared with those of the second theme in Dvořák's Finale (discussed above); in both cases the crescendo contradicts the static pattern of melody and harmony. In Dvořák's case, however, the crescendo leads on into the next section of music, whereas in Janáček it collapses on itself with an abrupt return to "piano," so that the section seems to end exactly where it began.

Example 5. Dvořák *Serenade*

In passages where Janáček does fashion harmonies into progressions, there is still a difference between his procedure and that of Dvořák. The contrast is especially clear if one compares the beginning of Janáček's first movement with that of the Dvořák movement which most resembles it in general character, namely the second. In Dvořák the harmonic arrival points at mm. 5, 10, 15, 20, 37, and 46 are very clear and direct, so that one senses the cadential arrival at a definite point in time. On the other hand, in Janáček the arrivals are blunted in one way or another. At m. 11 the tonic (B minor) arrival on the downbeat is in first inversion, with the root position following on the second beat. The subsequent D major arrival occurs prematurely on the second half of the first beat in m. 17, with a brief root position chord clouded by sixteenth-note appoggiaturas; the arrival at the end of the phrase, on the downbeat of m. 18, is in first inversion. Likewise the cadences at mm. 28, 34–35 and 68–69 are all more or less oblique, so that any sense of a goal-directed harmonic progression is weakened.

In conclusion, I should like to cite some fairly extended passages from these two works in which various of the tendencies discussed above can be seen operating together to create an overall aesthetic which distinguishes Janáček from Dvořák quite sharply. For Dvořák one passage will suffice: mm. 174–286 in the Finale. The passage corresponds to the "first theme" and the "bridge" segments, such as they are, within the recapitulation section of this quasi-sonata-form movement. As in many Romantic sonata forms, the "first theme" section is not really stable, but rather leans toward the "second theme." In this case the "first theme" and "bridge" combine to form a sort of second development section, or perhaps the primary development section, since the development preceding the recapitulation is highly unconventional. Whatever the interpretation, the passage in question is one in which melody, harmony, texture and rhythm combine to drive the music continually forward in what seems to be some kind of quest—a quest whose goal is reached precisely at m. 287 (the beginning of the "second theme"). To "take the needle off" at any point before this arrival produces a strong feeling of frustration, while on the other hand, to *hear* that arrival is immensely satisfying. All of this is consistent with the Romantic fondness for extended patterns of tension and release, with all the emotional connotations involve.

In Janáček's *Idyll* the passage which most closely resembles that just described in Dvořák occurs in the fourth movement, mm. 39–66. This is the only place in the work where Janáček seems to be attempting something like a development section, and the result is rather less than impressive.

To find Janáček at his best we must look elsewhere, to a pair of passages where progression toward a goal is the farthest thing from his mind, where instead the listener experiences a gentle rocking motion which actually does move to a new tonal area, but where that motion seems charmingly incidental. I refer to the opening and closing sections of the fifth movement, Here Janáček's penchants for rhythmic asymmetry, motivic repetition and harmonic stasis combine to produce a total effect which is completely at odds with Dvořák's norm. In the opening section the principal tonality of B minor is established by assertion, sounding on every downbeat for the first seven measures. In mm. 3–4, however, the instruments come to rest on a D major chord for the second half of the measure in such a way that it seems about equal to B minor in stability. In the ninth measure D major appears on the downbeat, and by the second half of m. 11 it seems to have been established as the key.

At the close of the movement the opening section returns in a modified version, with mm. 3–4 repeated literally at mm. 76–77. Our original impression that D major could as well be the key here as B minor is now confirmed, as Janáček takes the D major chord from the second half of m. 77 as tonic, and brings the movement to a close with eight gentle measures of tonic and dominant (mostly the former) in D. We have thus an instance of what in Mahler would be called progressive tonality, where the movement ends in a different key from that in which it began. However the Romantic concept of "progression" is not at all in evidence here; rather the two keys appear to be juxtaposed, or even to coexist. It seems almost not to matter which key has the last word.

Ironically, in the final measures of this movement there is a strong resemblance to Dvořák, as the quiet pentatonic melody in the cello calls to mind the end of the second movement from the "New World" Symphony. But this similarity only illustrates once more my overall point: when the styles resemble each other superficially, then one more easily understands the essential differences. In Janáček's *Idyll* we can see the path from Dvořák's Romanticism to a fundamentally twentieth-century style.

The Program of the *Balada blanická*

Hugh Macdonald

Hugh Macdonald is General editor of the Complete Edition of the Works of Hector Berlioz *and one of the most versatile scholars in the profession. Although a noted expert in French music, he has found it hard to keep away from Czech topics. Macdonald is also a performing pianist. In this essay he looks at the connection between Janáček's* Balada blanická *and the poem which, somehow, inspired it.*

Janáček's *Balada blanická*, composed in 1919,[1] follows treatments of the same subject by Fibich and Smetana with which Janáček must have been very familiar. Fibich's opera *Blaník* was written in the mid-1870s and performed in 1881. It had been revived in Prague in 1894. Smetana's symphonic poem *Blaník*, composed in 1879, was the last of the *Má Vlast* cycle and was already a Czech classic in Janáček's time.

Smetana's *Blaník* uses the Hussite chorale to depict the warriors who sleep in the heart of the Blaník mountain (a hill in the south of Bohemia) waiting for the day when they will ride out to save the Czech nation in its hour of need. A pastoral episode paints a picture of rustic life outside over a long held F major chord in the strings, a symbol of the army sleeping within. The glorious march that closes the work not only strikes the rousing chord of Czech nationalism, it also acts as coda to the cycle of six symphonic poems, recalling the *Vyšehrad* theme from the opening piece.

Fibich's opera *Blaník*, dedicated to Smetana, had a fictional libretto by Krasnohorská, set in 1623, shortly after the Battle of the White Mountain. The legend of the Blaník knights acts merely as background to a tale of love and heroism. Another work on the Blaník theme, Suk's *Pod Blaníkem*, a rousing patriotic march with words by Suk himself, belongs to 1932. There must surely have been other Blaník works by Czech composers.

Janáček's purpose in composing *his* Blaník may be seen in the light of the assured spirit of Czech national identity following the establishment of an independent state of Czechoslovakia only a year earlier, also as a sequel to the two earlier symphonic poems *Šumařovo dítě* ("The Fiddler's Child") and *Taras Bulba*. It is explicitly based on the version of the Blaník legend

---

[1] The date of the composition of *Balada blanická* is always given as 1920. It was first performed in Brno on 21 March 1920, and since he began work on *Kát'a Kabanová* in January 1920 it must have been substantially written in 1919.

told by Vrchlický in his Selské ballady of 1885. The poem is not printed in the 1958 Artia score, nor has it been translated into English. (I append an English version at the end of this article.) The poem is a clear narrative recounting how the mountain of Blaník opens up every year on Good Friday. If anyone is unfortunate enough to set foot in the mountain he must wait a full year before he can escape. One Good Friday, while everyone else is in church, a peasant, Jíra, wanders to the foot of the mountain and enters where the rock wall is open. At the end of a long passage he comes to a stone hall where the Hussite warriors, fully armed, stand beside their horses beneath St. Václav's banner, plunged in sleep.

Suddenly the rock door closes with a clang behind him; Jíra falls asleep. When he awakes the scene is transformed. The men and horses still stand in a circle beneath St. Václav's banner. But instead of weapons of war they now carry the emblems of peace: plows, spades, sickles, scythes. The mountain is open, Jíra flees. Back in the old world Jíra glances at his reflection in a stream: he is transformed into an old, old man, and the villagers do not recognize him. He has been gone for a hundred years, perhaps more. Larks sing overhead.

Vrchlický's poem had clear utopian significance for those who longed for a world in which destructive weapons might give place to productive tools, swords to plowshares. There was no nationalist emphasis. The knights do not ride out to save their country, they are always asleep. But time effects a wonderful change on their power for good.

In the post-war world of 1919, and in a newly founded republic, such a tale had an unmistakable message of peace and production, which Janáček unquestionably wished to reinforce. Pacific intent might be hard to express in music, but the narrative is full of sound and incident, highly suitable for musical treatment within the widely understood conventions of the symphonic poem: there is the Passion Hymn sung on Good Friday, the murmuring of the forest as Jíra wanders out, the atmosphere of the dark mountain passage, the sudden revelation of the warriors and their horses in the heart of the mountain, their resplendent armor, the banner of St. Václav, the clang of the rock door closing, Jíra falling asleep, the passing of time, the transformed vision of the warriors and their horses when he awakes, his breathless flight, the discovery of his aging, the song of the skylarks in the final line.

There is a certain symmetry in the story, beginning and ending in the village, with scope for transformation techniques of various kinds since both Jíra and the warriors undergo physical transformation. There are realistic noises such as the Passion Hymn, the clang of the door, and the song of the birds.

Yet although every commentary and program note emphasized the dependence of Janáček's music on Vrchlický's poem, there is very little connection between them. If we did not know it was based on Vrchlický, it would be impossible to guess. Nor is there anything in the music to suggest the mountain of Blaník and its legend.

For a symphonic poem from the era of Strauss and Suk it is extremely short, at eight minutes one of the shortest of all symphonic poems. With a certain amount of pressing and squeezing some of the music can be interpreted to fit the poem, as Vogel has demonstrated,[2] although his interpretation can easily be challenged at many points.

In formal terms the works has an exposition divided into first and second sections (mm. 1–75 and 76–157), development (mm. 158–260), and recapitulation (m. 261 to the end). The first part of the exposition can be related to the poem with some degree of success. Ex. 1 (m. 1) perhaps represents placid village life, while Jíra himself has the more forthright theme (Ex. 2, m. 10). In m. 28 the distorted chorale, Ex. 3, may be the village passion hymn from which Jíra has escaped, the violent music at m. 46 representing his flight. The next hymn, Ex. 4, in m. 54, is presumably a representation of the knights of St. Václav.

Example 1.

Example 2.

Example 3.

[2]Jaroslav Vogel, *Leoš Janáček* London 1981, pp. 250–3.

Example 4.

Example 5a.

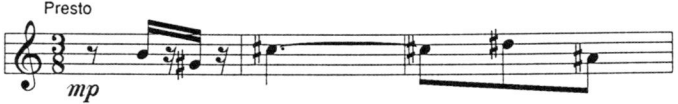

Example 5b.

Example 6.

Example 7.

Example 8.

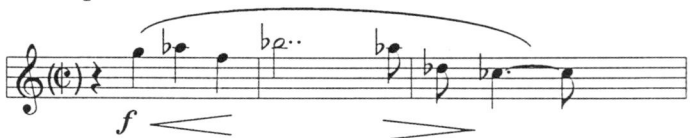

Thus far the meaning of the music, as a rapid telescoped representation of the first part of the poem, is more or less straightforward. But hereafter there are considerable difficulties. There is no crash of the rock door, although Vogel says: "Most probably it occurs at the end of the harp episode [m. 75] where the septuplets of the strings tumble downward without, however, reaching any emphatic conclusion." But tumbling strings do not convey a crashing rock, and the fact is that Janáček, for his own good reasons, did not represent this effect at all.

There follows a long lyrical passage, mm. 76–157, whose meaning is baffling. It is relaxed and melodious, in light 3/8 rhythm, Ex. 5. It ought to represent Jíra falling asleep and the passing of many years, but it does neither of those things in a conventional way despite the marking "un poco meno mosso" twice and "dim. e rit." once. We have to see it as Jíra falling asleep, though Vogel interpreted it quite differently as Jíra's call for help and his running back and forth searching for a way out of the mountain. It is a congenial episode, free of stress and unrelated musically to anything heard so far, comparable to a symphonic second group.

The next section, from m. 158 to the climax at m. 248 is involved and developmental. It introduces a distorted version of Jíra's theme, Ex. 2, a new theme, Ex. 6, not used elsewhere, a new version of the knights" music, Ex. 4 (shown as Ex. 7), an echo of the passion hymn, Ex. 3 a recapitulation of Ex. 5 from the previous relaxed episode, a dramatic transformation of the opening pages, a triumphant diatonic version of Jíra's theme, Ex. 2, and a *sforzando* climax.

In symphonic terms this is evidently development. In narrative terms it suggests Jíra's dramatic quandary, a new picture of the knights, the sound of the village outside, more time passing, and an increase of tension toward the climax. This is far from anything in Vrchlický's poem. In only one respect does it fit, in the transformation of the knights' music (m. 178). But as warriors the knights were presented with far greater nobility, as in Ex. 4. As harbingers of peace in Ex. 7, they are dignified certainly, but no more glorious or more optimistic than they were before. If the twist in Vrchlický's poem is the pacifist interpretation of the Blaník legend, Janáček makes no special point of that at all. The echo of the Passion hymn at M. 187 could fit the line of the poem "The dying sound of the Passion hymn is lost in the mountain," but why does the relaxed 3/8 music, Ex. 5b, recur immediately after (m. 205)? If it was a representation of sleep or of time passing it has no place. Only if it were Jíra's search for escape would it belong here. Why does Jíra's theme then (m. 233) become diatonic and triumphant, suggesting heroism and youth? (Vogel sees this as Jíra's flight, followed by his horrified glimpse of his reflection in the stream at the climax at m. 248) Where is the picture of Jíra in extreme old age? Could it be the new theme, Ex. 8, at m. 251? If that is so. why is it a new theme, not a transformation of the first one?

Recapitulation occurs at m. 261, with a calm return to the opening, Ex. 1, followed by the "knights" music, Ex. 4, in its first warlike form, full of nostalgic longing with a big Mahlerian cadence in D-flat major, as if that was the true image of the Blaník warriors.

If it is relatively simple to interpret the first 75 measures in parallel with the poem, the remainder (over 200 measures) has the most tenuous relationship with it, ignores the opportunities for musical illustration it contains and makes no attempt to underline the poem's message. Janáček has, in sum, merely taken the poem as his starting point and then gone on to write a symphonic movement rich in ideas and marvelously varied in texture but having nothing whatever to do with Vrchlický or Blaník.

Svatopluk Cech's poem *Šumařovo dítě* is the literary source of the first symphonic poem, and although Janáček himself gave some clues to its programmatic interpretation the narrative is by no means clear. *Taras Bulba* is based on Gogol's tale, which is full of action and detail. Yet to marry the story to the music is not at all easy. *Balada blanická* takes this process even further in a symphonic poem which shares with many illustrative pieces of the time a literary source and, apparently, a narrative content. Yet the narrative is abandoned mid-way. If Janáček is telling a different story, he did not tell us what it is.

What is most perplexing about this is that Janáček's symphonic poems appear to fall into the category of narrative, like Liszt's *Mazeppa*, Dvořák's Erben pieces, Balakirev's *Tamara*, or Tchaikovsky's *Voyevode*. In contrast to Suk he did not choose abstract or philosophical subjects. In his operas, furthermore, action and speech are vividly captured in music. Such a technique equipped Janáček to write symphonic poems of considerable force and realism. Yet in all three symphonic poems realism is largely renounced. He is perhaps not a realist at all. These are abstract poems. Perhaps there is a clue here to his failure to complete the *Dunaj* symphony, which carried so much "programmatic baggage"[3] that a coherent outcome could not be devised. In *Balada blanická* we find realism spurned and narrative con-

---

[3]M. Beckerman in "Janáček's Unfinished Symphony," *Stagebill*, May 1988.

fused; he was composing with his head and heart in the sky, and with Vrchlický's little volume of poetry firmly closed.

The Ballad of Blaník

by Jaroslav Vrchlický

Every year on Good Friday,
As the Passion is sung, Blaník opens up.
Woe, woe to him who sets foot there,
He must wait, wait for a full year to pass.
In truth he is fortunate
If he can endure the year's misery
Until again on Good Friday,
As the Passion is sung, Blaník opens up.
Much worse is it for him on whose eyelids
Sleep heavily presses,
He must sleep there for a hundred years.
Oh, what woe dogs his errant steps
One Good Friday was an unhappy day
Good friend Jíra came out of his gate
and instead of going to church, where they were singing the Passion,
He turned toward the woods. The day was dark and gloomy,
How desolate were the trees, how sad their murmuring!
Jíra was, by common consent, a thinking man.
Gloomy woods held more for him than God's house.
Further and further on he goes, to the foot of Blaník.
Old stories swarmed in his brain,
He smiled. —Ah, this rock wall
Beneath the pine roots is enticingly open
Jíra enters, lowering his head.
The distant Passion hymn echoes through the woods.

Before him is a long passage; at the end is a glimmer
Like a bright star, or a shining cloud.
Toward that light Jíra steps closer and closer
Till he comes suddenly upon a hall of stone.
Neatly around the wall stood rows of horses;
Some wore bells on their stirrups and harness;
Some shook their heads, some pawed the ground
Raising echoes in the dark hollow passage.
Beside the horses, as told by legend,
Stood a band of dark-visaged knights
Clothed in stillness, arrayed in a circle,
As if plunged in deepest reverie.

At their feet shone mounds of weapons,
On their heads flashed helmets like the stars,
Huge shields, their surfaces sparkling like silver,
Covered their whole body and the horses too,
Great swords, mightily sheathed,
Catapults and slings with volleys loaded,
Ball-and-chains, pikes and daggers,
Maces and spears. Marshaled in lines
God's troops stood clothed in stillness,
Ready to fight but plunged in sleep.

From the midst of that horde a banner arose
On which St .Václav's eagles spread their wings.

Jíra looked close, anxious to understand.
Boulder doors closed with a terrible clang.
Through the desolate wood the Passion lament
Reverberated weakly here in the rock,
As when a bird with wounded wings rears up
And flutters in empyrean, dying.

BALADA BLANICKÁ

Suddenly Jíra felt a heaviness in his limbs.
He sinks down, thinking to take a rest.
He sinks and dozes in that living grave.

God knows how long he slept. When he awoke
It was a time when Blaník was open.
Unaware, he looked around.
He rubbed his astonished eyes, and again took fright.
Neatly around the wall stood rows of horses;
Some wore bells on their stirrups and harness,
Some shook their heads, some pawed the ground,
Raising echoes in the dark hollow passage.
Beside the horses again stood a row of men,
Swaying like shadows that flicker in the trees,
Clothed in stillness, arrayed in a circle,
Still plunged in deepest reverie.

But at their feet the weapons were gone.
In place of huge shields like the moon
Shone plows, farrows in place of slings,
Instead of swords could be seen
Scythes, spades, flails, harrows,
Hoes and sickles newly forged.
From the midst of that horde a banner arose
On which St. Václav's eagles spread their wings,
Fluttering with joy...

The dying sound
Of the Passion hymn is lost in the mountain.
Hola, Jíra, bestir yourself, go seek the woods,
Take the road home!

But look back!—The horses neighed,
Jíra breathlessly fled Blaník's rock.

God orders the passing of the years
Jíra happened to lean over a stream
And trembled to see his flickering image,
His whole head now a color of gray
His pallid temples lined with wrinkles,
Like the man who has read many books of wisdom
Which God seldom gives to us to read
And for whose deep understanding
There is only indifference—the rest are blind.

A bewildered Jíra came to his village,
They did not know him, and he too knew no one.
In the fields all were at work, the only sight to see,
And above the smiling country the joyful skylarks sang.

A Reappraisal of Janáček as Realist

Marilyn S. Clark

As we already stated, one of our tasks, in dealing with any artist, is to balance the effects of individuality and community. This is particularly true when one tries to see where a creative figure fits in terms of the larger movements of the day, the so-called "isms." In the case of Janáček, arguments could be made for his nationalism, his pantheism and atomism, his symbolism, his expressionism, and even perhaps impressionism and surrealism. Yet it is perhaps Janáček's relationship to realism that is both most compelling and most elusive. In her study on Janáček's realism, Marilyn Clark, a noted librarian and scholar, draws on the writings of Dahlhaus and others, and explores realist tendencies in Janáček's operas.

While Janáček is increasingly considered to be a complex and difficult composer, Janáček scholars and devotees have for many years commonly agreed on certain characteristics of the composer's musical and literary legacy. This brief essay examines the widely held opinion that Janáček was a realist composer. The essay argues that although there are numerous elements of realism in Janáček's most well-known work *Jenůfa*, he should not be construed as a realist composer throughout his creative life. To maintain such a stereotype constricts our understanding of Janáček and blinds us to various evolving stylistic trends in his work.

There is no doubt that realism was a prominent trend during Janáček's formative period. However, by the turn of the century the style, if it should be called so, was largely played out—in a period of decline.[1] In literature and the arts during the first decades of the twentieth century several new trends followed each other in quick succession and overlapped. These include impressionism, expressionism, surrealism, neoclassicism, vitalism, and so forth. Janáček, always intellectually stimulated by the new and experimental, sampled, tasted, savored a number of these styles.

---

[1] I agree with Professor Jaroslav Volek and other commentors that to say a particular piece is "realist" or "romantic" is incorrect, because music is largely abstract and such labelling is misleading. However, I do feel that one can add to the understanding of a piece of music by saying that it has certain elements or characteristics of a style. I would even agree that a preponderance of certain elements can lead to a realist or romantic trend. But I do not agree with Professor Dahlhaus that a piece of music can simply be termed "realist."

For many years, when *Jenůfa* was by far the best known opera of Janáček, it is evident that those who know only this work concluded that he was exclusively a realist composer. This stereotype overlooks both the complexity and stylistic evolution of his later creative work. In examining the works of Janáček I have largely been concerned with the dramatic aspect of his operas. While we cannot say that a holistic judgment of Janáček's works can be derived only from the dramatic side, we certainly should agree that drama is one important aspect of them.

I think Carl Dahlhaus provides good arguments that *Jenůfa* (*Její pastorkyňa*) has many elements that he characterizes as realism in music.[2] Janáček's use of speech melodies throughout the fabric of the score, not only in the vocal parts, his use of the regional Moravian-Slovácko dialect and local color are realist elements in the opera. Janáček's reaction to the subjectivism and sentimentality of the romantic era is evident. Supernatural mysteries and nationalistic mythology are superseded by narratives of the lives of common people. The composer becomes an objective observer penetrating the psychological depths of individual characters. Janáček has not substantially altered the basic concept of Gabriela Preissová's village dramas, which are generally considered to be prominent examples of realism in Czech literature.

That is not the case in many other texts that Janáček adapted during his creative life. I hope to demonstrate here that his choice and application of dramatic themes in his operas show an evolution through a variety of stylistic characteristics—from romanticism, to realism, to psychological melodrama, through vitalism, and expressionism.

For example, the early operas *The Beginning of a Romance* (*Počatka románu*) and *Šárka* are works primarily from a formative period. Both have many of the characteristics of romanticism. *The Beginning of a Romance* is a primitive folk opera and we can see some influences of a lyrical romanticist such as Josef Kajetán Tyl, while *Šárka* reflects the characteristics of the opera's librettist Julius Zeyer, including his interest in the distant past, in mysticism, and in legendary heroes.

The opera *Fate* (*Osud*), which followed *Jenůfa* turns from the local village to a middle-class setting at the spa of Luhačovice. The story is of a mother's self-consuming hatred of her daughter's lover and husband, Míla's supposed unfaithfulness to Živný, the mother's insane act of pull-

---

[2]Particularly the chapter "Realistic Melody and Dramaturgical Construction," in his *Realism in Nineteenth-Century Music*, trans. Mary Whittall (Cambridge: Cambridge University Press, 1985), 95–106.

ing Míla to her death along with herself, Živný's futile attempt to write an autobiographical opera and the strange lack of a conclusion to the opera. While the spa and the middle class setting of the opera are banal and common, typical of the early decades of the twentieth century, the main characters have little control over their fate; one tragedy follows another, the bizarre is accented. I would characterize this as psychological melodrama—and the beginning of a tendency by Janáček to use fewer realist elements in his operatic writing.

At the time of writing this opera, Janáček was engrossed in works by psychologist Wilhelm Wundt and Ernst Meumann. Was there some influence there? While we can derive very little from Wundt and Meumann that directly points to such melodramatic material, we are more certain that the field of psychology was at the time young and controversial, and we can surmise that any artist who wanted to be abreast of the times read and reflected this psychological work. We should also consider the climate of this opera as typical of the decade before the first World War—a time of fruitless struggle and rising tensions, despair over tragic events that can only have been caused by uncontrollable external powers. The effect of the opera is of heightened intensity of emotion.

In *The Excursions of Mr. Brouček* (*Výlety pana Broučka*), Janáček used stories of Svatopluk Čech written in 1888 and 1889. That Janáček had difficulty in adapting Čech's work and giving the work the atmosphere he desired is evident from the unusual number of contributions to the libretto by several writers, including Viktor Dyk, František Procházka, František Gellner, Karel Mašek, and Max Brod. The themes are of Matěj Brouček's trip to the moon where he is satirized as a bourgeois "beetle," and then returning to the glorious Hussite period of Czech history.

The opera is a humorous fantasy, which on the one hand satirizes youthful flights of fancy and the older generation's stodgy habits. On the other hand, the strong nationalism of the war-time years is reflected in the portrayal of the Hussite period—a theme which was very popular during that period just before the war. This kind of interest is also reflected at that time in the great popularity enjoyed by the historical novels of Alois Jirásek. Janáček's opera, however, has moved away from the purely historical romanticism of Jirásek. The elements of humor and satire predominate the nationalism in this work.

The opera *Kátya Kabanová*, adapted from Červinka's translation of the play *The Storm* by Aleksandr Ostrovsky, was composed in 1921—

more than sixty years after the play was written in 1859. The play criticizes the stolid society and the moral decadence of the late Russian empire and the vast Volga and the storm are symbolically important. Some critics consider that the play follows the trend of naturalism prominent in the latter nineteenth century; others cite it as an example of critical or psychological realism.[3] In 1859 this approach was new and fresh—a rebellion against long-standing romanticism; in 1920 the style was long overused and in decline. In his adaption of the play, Janáček gives greater emphasis to the psychological tension, and foreshortens some of the realistic aspects of the original play, de-emphasizing the social commentary, turning the external violent storm of Ostrovsky into inner turmoil.

I would have to agree with producer David Pountney's interpretation in John Tyrrell's book that these aspects give the opera an expressionistic character that emphasizes individual characters much more than does the play by Ostrovsky.[4] And yet some aspects of realism remain. The piece is set in a definite milieu—the ever present and dominating Volga River gives an important atmospheric affect. We sense throughout the opera the crushing moral atmosphere of the traditional Russian village. However, the twentieth-century opera, it seems to me, is an opera that has a quite different affect than the nineteenth-century play. Even though Janáček was not intimately involved with the individuals in the *Literární skupina* (Literary Group), the expressionistic atmosphere of this and later operas was probably influenced by this Brno literary group, led by theoretician František Götz, which at this time developed a trend of expressionism in Czech literature.

I would have to hasten to explain here that I do not necessarily mean the expressionism of Schoenberg. The atonality of Schoenberg was only one of several ways expressionism developed in music. By expressionism I am referring to elements of music and drama which were used to portray an intense expressiveness.[5]

---

[3]M. Hoover, *Alexander Ostrovsky* (Boston: Twayne, 1981), 56–59.
[4]David Pountney, "Producing 'Kátya Kabanová'," in *Leoš Janáček: Kátya Kabanová*, comp. John Tyrrell (Cambridge: Cambridge University Press, 1982), 185.
[5]Here I defer to two articles by Miloš Štědroń which relate Janáček to expressionism from a musicological viewpoint: "Janáček und der Expressionismus" *Sborník prací Filosofické Fakulty Brněnské University*, Rada hudebnívěda 19/5 (1970), 105–27, and "K podstatě tzv. sociálího a slovanského expressionismu u Leoše Janáčka," *Česká hudba světu svět České hudbě : Sborník původních statí československých a sovětských hudebních vědcůk roku české hudby* (Praha: Panton, 1974), 119–50.

Janáček's animal opera *Adventures of the Vixen Sharp Ears* (*Příhody lišky Bystroušky*), based on Rudolf Těsnohlídek's novel, is quite a substantial change of climate after the intense emotionalism of *Kátya*. In reading Janáček's numerous essays and "fejetony" we become quite conscious of his love of nature, his efforts to hear and record the sounds of birds, insects, and other wildlife into musical terms. With *Bystrouška*, Janáček gives us the operatic side of these fejetony. As in the fejetony, the music of this and other operas has many impressionistic aphorisms— short sketchy outlines of statements. I feel that this opera comes closest to the impressionism that Czech literary critic Arne Novák found in Janáček's work.[6]

The animals of this world have taken on the attributes of humans— they tease their tormentors, they incite rebellions, they love, and they yearn for a home with domestic tranquility. It seems to me that Janáček was to some extent influenced by the Czech literary trend called vitalism in this opera. The vitalists, including Stanislav Neumann and František Šrámek, turned their backs on the despair and the alienation of the war years and celebrated youth, primitive nature, and life itself. In the opera, gone are the crushing local mores, nationalism has been supplanted by primitive animal rights, and the existence of life itself is celebrated.

In *The Makropoulos Case* (*Věc Makropulos*) Janáček has transformed Čapek's humorously conceived play into a deeply emotional opera. The local color of Janáček's earlier work has disappeared; the opera has no particular local setting; the background of the current action is vaguely urban and cosmopolitan. Emilia Marty in her various epoches has lived in Greece, Spain, and Scotland. This plot gives a new twist to the common expressionist theme of disillusionment and distrust of modern industrial progress. In the *Makropoulos Case,* the long-sought-after wonder drug has prolonged life, and the result is not a celebration of life and youth, but Marty's extreme disillusionment, utter despair, and alienated boredom. The long tenure of Marty's life is unrealistic, and the prolongation of life becomes a tragedy in itself. How different is this material from Preissová's local village tragedies. The uncertainty, despair, and alienation of Čapek's relativism are expressed in

---

[6]A. Novák, "Leoš Janáček: Der Schriftsteller," in *Feuilletons aus den "Lidové noviny"*, ausgewählt, erweitert, mit Beitragen und Anmerken versehen von Jan Racek. Im Auftrage der Deutsches Akademie der Kunste, herausgegeben von Leos Spies (Leipzig: Breitkopf & Härtel, 1959), 186.

Janáček's opera, and give it a twentieth century outlook—far from the realism of the latter nineteenth century.

The last opera to be considered here, *From the House of the Dead* (*Z mrtvého domu*), is adapted from Dostoevsky's novel of 1862. As such, the novel derives from the central era of realism in Russian literature. However, for some authors, Dostoevsky's contribution to expressionism was considerable. To quote R. S. Furness's book on expressionism,

> He shares with Nietzsche and Strindberg an emphasis on extreme, often pathological psychological states, on the rejection of "normal" canons of thinking and feeling, on the need for a daring transvaluation of values. Both Nietzsche and Dostoevsky stress the need for a spiritual revival, a New Man born of suffering and passion.[7] It is exactly these aspects of Dostoevsky's novel that Janáček emphasizes in the 1920s.

In his final two operas, *The Makropoulos Case* and *From the House of the Dead*, I feel that Janáček makes increasing use of expressionistic elements. We have seen that Janáček's creative work began in the romantic period with the operas *The Beginning of a Romance* and *Šárka*. His next, and most well-known work for many years, *Jenůfa*, reflects the realism of the late nineteenth century, and we can see many traces of realism in his subsequent operas. After Janáček's experiment with satire and fantasy in the Brouček operas, and his use of aspects of impressionism and vitalism in the Vixen, I believe that the dominating direction of Janáček's remaining late works is expressionism. This does not mean that Janáček should be considered a pure advocate of any of these styles. He was always an experimenter, an individualist, and an eclectic.

Czechoslovak Presence at Schoenberg's *Verein*

John H. Yoell

Just as important as the study of things Czech is the study of the musical interaction between the Czech Lands and elsewhere. Dr. John Yoell is a physician and scholar who has made many valuable contributions to our field in terms of discography and bibliography. He has also sought links between events in the Czech Lands and outside in his studies of Mahler's Czech roots. In this study he demonstrates potent connections between Vienna and Prague in the realm of new music performance.

Introduction:

Considering the close historical ties between the Austrian and Czech musical communities, even antedating Mozart's day, the paucity of demonstrable communication between Arnold Schoenberg and key Czech contemporaries like Leoš Janáček might seem disconcerting.[1] Their careers rarely crossed.[2] But distance between these two prominent men of music, long living and working in geographic proximity at both ends of the same trolly line, need not imply that Schoenberg's circle and counterparts in the Czech lands were natural enemies, even recalling that German-Slav animosity frequently rose to a high pitch during the sunset years of the Habsburg empire. Several of Janáček's compatriots looked upon the progress of Schoenberg's controversy-ridden climb to fame with keen interest; many personal and professional connections can be demonstrated.[3] To unravel these relationships it is useful to focus on Schoenberg's short-lived but highly visible music society which he founded immediately after the guns of World War I had ceased firing.

---

[1]Václav Holzknecht, *Tschechoslowakisch-Österreichische Musik Spaziergänge* (Prague: Orbis, 1971).

[2]Jaroslav Vogel, *Leoš Janáček*, revised edition prepared by Karel Janovicky (New York: W. W. Norton & Co., 1981), pp. 12, 42, 309, 332, 349, and 350. Miloš Štědroň, "Janáček a Schönberg," *Časopsis Moravséo musea: vědy společenske* 49 (1964).

[3]Schoenberg's leading advocate in Prague was his onetime teacher and brother-in-law Alexander von Zemlinsky, conductor at the German Theater from 1911 to 1927. The network of associated professional relationships is explored by Jitka Ludvová, "Pupils of Schoenberg in the Czech Lands," translated by Max Bloch (MS). Also see Frank Schneider, "Schönberg und die tschechische Musik," *Beiträge zur Musikwissenschaft* 23, No. 1 (1981), pp. 26–30.

The Vienna *Verein*

By organizing and directing the *Verein Für musikalische Privataüffuhrung* (Society for Private Musical Performances), Arnold Schoenberg showed himself among the first to directly address the special problems related to 20th-century music in performance.[4] Headquartered initially at Türkenstrasse 17—not far from the residence of Dr. Sigmund Freud—the Society attacked a grueling schedule which emphasized the meticulous preparation of its concerts. Rules governing attendance were stringent: admission by subscriber pass only, no applause or expression of disfavor and no music critics.

The founding date of the *Verein* (23 November, 1918) hardly looked promising. Four years of ruinous war had left the Austro-Hungarian Empire torn apart by its ethnic minorities. Starvation stalked the streets of Vienna; fuel supplies dwindled almost to nonexistence. In the words of Schoenberg's biographer H. H. Stuckenschmidt, defeated Germany and Austria "had become a witch's cauldron of vanishing values."[5] But to Schoenberg, economic and military calamity shrank to mere annoyances as he geared his iron will to establish a proper forum for contemporary music. "Our Society," he proclaimed, "will have educated a public which will have knowledge of modern music as no other public in the entire world."[6]

Assisted by a small corps of pupils and disciples, Schoenberg threw time and full energies into the *Verein* with burning zeal. His will was law, down to the last detail. At the heart of the project was a repertoire drawn from Mahler onwards; "whatever," Schoenberg decreed, "had a real face or name." Works selected for performance showed praiseworthy concern for what the past quarter century had produced in various parts

---

[4]General information about the *Verein* may be found in: Hans Moldenhauer and Rosaleen Moldenhauer, *Anton Webern: A Chronicle of his Life and Works* (N.Y.: Alfred A. Knopf, 1979), pp. 223–241. Malcolm McDonald, *Schoenberg* (London: Dent, 1976), pp. 31–34. Joan Allen Smith, *Schoenberg and his Circle* (N.Y.: Schirmer, 1986), pp. 81–102, 245–268. Bryan R. Simms, "The Society for Private Musical Performances: Resources and Documents in Schoenberg's Legacy," *Journal of the Arnold Schoenberg Institute*, 5 (Oct. 1979), pp. 127–149. Leonard Stein, "The Privataufführungen Revisited," in *Paul A. Pisk: Essays in his Honor*, ed. John Glowacki (Austin: University of Texas, 1966), pp. 203–207. Judith Meibach, "Schoenberg's Society for Private Musical performances, Vienna 1918–1922: A Documentary Study" (dissertation, University of Pittsburgh, 1980). Judith Meibach, "The Society for Private Musical Performances: Antecedents and Foundation," *Journal of the Arnold Schoenberg Institute*, 7 (Nov., 1984), pp. 159–176.

[5]A comprehensive account of the politics, pressures and privations in wartime Austria-Hungary is Arthur J. May, *The Passing of the Hapsburg Monarchy*, 2 vols. (Philadelphia: University of Philadelphia Press, 1966).

[6]Simms, "The Society for Private Musical Performances, p. 127.

of Europe. The *Verein* did not exist for the exclusive promotion of Schoenberg's own music or the products of his inner circle.[7]

By its third season the Society had rehearsed and presented over 200 works, many in repeat performance and special arrangements. The subscriber base—remarkable considering the social and economic considitions at the time—rose to about 300 persons.[8]

So far, a growing literature on the *Verein* has barely touched on the intimate relationship beween its activities and supporters of Czechoslovak background. Their participation took various forms: as performers, staff members, rehearsal coaches and composers represented on the Society's programs. In fact, Schoenberg himself had strong ancestral ties both to the Czech and Slovak areas of the newly-formed republic which conditioned his official nationality.[9] Although conceived and born in Vienna, his *Verein* died and was buried in the capital of Czechoslovakia, Prague. So the story of Schoenberg's music society truly becomes a tale of two cities.

Prominent among Schoenberg's pupils present at the *Verein's* first general meeting (6 December, 1918) were Josef Travníček (a.k.a. Traunek, born 1893 at Olomouc) and the ill-fated Viktor Ullmann (born 1898 in Austrian Silesia). Travníček was appointed a recording secretary and member of the all-important music committee. Later on, both he and Ullmann became active conducting in and around Prague, as did other *Verein* charter members like Karl Rankl and Anton Webern.[10] Paul A. Pisk, the Society's first general secretary, was born in Vienna, but parental origins lay in Moravia (his father, an attorney, drew up the bylaws). Ullmann's first wife, Martha Koref, studied with Schoenberg and hailed from Prague. Although not a founding member of the *Verein*, Heinrich Jalowetz (born 1892 at Brno) served as a coaching assistant (Vortragsmeister); he considered his teacher Schoenberg as "one's artistic and human conscience."[11]

---

[7]McDonald, *Schoenberg*, pp. 31–32. For a translation of the prospectus, see Meibach, "Antecedents and Foundation," pp. 164–169. For detailed programs of the Society's concerts with participating artists see Walter Szmolyan, "Die Konzerte des Wiener Schönberg-Verein," and Ivan Vojtech, "Die Konzerte des Prager Verein," in Heinz-Klaus Metzger and Rainer Riehn, eds., *Schönbergs Verein fur musikalische Privataufführungen*, Musik-Konzepte, 36 (Munich: edition text + kritik GmbH, 1984), pp. 101–118.

[8]Moldenhauer, *Webern*, p. 240.

[9]Upon dissolution of the Austro-Hungarian Empire, Schoenberg's official nationality became Czechoslovak due to parental ancestry. Pertinent original documents are in the archive of the Arnold Schoenberg Institute, Los Angeles. Also see McDonald *Schoenberg*, p. 30 (footnote).

[10]Ludvová, "Pupils of Schoenberg's." Also Max Bloch, "Viktor Ullmann: A Brief Biography and Appreciation," *Journal of the Arnold Schoenberg Institute*, 3 (Oct., 1979), pp. 151–157.

Even a cursory glance at the roster of the *Verein's* performing musicians brings up many Czech-sounding names: viola player Ernst Moravec (Morawetz), cellist Josef Haša, flutist E. Kliopera, clarinet player Viktor Polatschek, violist Jaroslav Czerny, double bass player Karl Fiala—not surprising since thousands of Czech dwell in Vienna. One of the *Verein's* leading pianists, the young Rudolf Serkin, came from the Sudentenland. Another, who doubled at the harmonium, Olga Novakovic might show Czech ancestry, but Croatian seems more likely.[12] In any event, closer scrutiny of the Society's records and the sorting out of often obscure biographical details would probably add more Czech names to this list.

As for composers born or resident in Czechoslovakia whose works received performance at the *Verein*, the attention paid looks reasonably generous. The experimentally-minded Alois Hába (a known admirer of Schoenberg) was there, along with Dvořák heirs Josef Suk and Vítěslav Novák. Honored too were Otakar Ostrčil, Bohuslav Vomačka and Josef Gustav Mraczek. What was heard from the German wing of native sons brings in Fidelio Finke, Gustav Mahler, Erich Wolfgang Korngold, Franz Schmidt, Egon Kornauth, Viktor Ullmann and Erwin Schulhoff. Since Alexander von Zemlinsky composed some of his best works while a resident of Prague, he might be included. So might Ernst Krenek, born in Vienna but with both parents Czech. Collectively, this group of Czechoslovak or Czecho-German composers made a formidable addition to the repertoire of the *Verein*.

There are, however, exclusions to explain. By 1918 Schoenberg could hardly have been unaware of the growing significance of Leoš Janáček. In fact, in an important issue of the Society's prospectus (September 1919), Alban Berg made a passing reference to "Leo Janáček."[13] Possibly something from this Brno-based composer got as far as rehearsal, but in terms of actual performance, Janáček drew a blank at the *Verein*. While several of his more characteristic and rewarding concert pieces—two string quartets, *Mladi* and the *Concertino*, for example—came into view only after the *Verein* ceased to function, his omission nevertheless semms glaring in retrospect.

---

[11]Smith, *Schoenberg*, p. 129.

[12]Karl Steiner, formerly a pupil, has written "to the best of my recollection" the ancestry of his teacher Olga Novakovic "was Yugoslav rather than Czech." (Personal letter 23 May, 1988).

[13]The original printed prospectus is in the archive of the Arnold Schoenberg Institute. Janáček's pivotal opera *Jenůfa*, with Maria Jeritza in the title role, saw performance at Vienna's Imperial Court Theater in February, 1918. Despite a flurry of political controversy, this well-prepared performance went ahead by royal command. The music made a deep impression.

Left out of the picture too was Josef Bohuslav Foerster. This prolific composer, journalist, husband of a noted opera singer, and good friend of Gustav Mahler, was then about to end a fifteen year residence in Vienna. He duly took notice of Schoenberg and his circle, but the reverse does not seem true.[14] Possibly Schoenberg found him irritating as a critic, or thought his compositions lacked a "face."

The Prague *Verein*

In March, 1920, the *Verein* took to the road for a series of four closely-spaced concerts at the Mozarteum in Prague under the sponsorship of Dr. Vilém Zenánek. The ensemble's dedicated level of performance created a splendid impression, particularly on Georg Alter, astronomer and amateur violinist. Soon Alter was going about badgering various local musicians to set up a similar organization in the capital of the new Czechoslovakia. The *Verein* players came again in 1921, this time offering a Schoenberg-coached *Pierrot lunaire* (by no means the Prague premiere). The return visit catalyzed action. At a charter meeting, in the Spring of 1922, the Prague branch of Schoenberg's stimulating *Verein* became a reality. Original officers included Zemlinsky as President with Alter as Secretary; Schoenberg subsequently accepted title as Honorary President. Otherwise, the Prague *Verein* essentially adopted the practices and procedures of its Viennese parent.[15] The players, initially coached by Erwin Stein and Anton Webern, made the trip up from Vienna. But in time, the Society drew more and more on local personnel. All told, the *Verein* in Prague mounted a total of twenty concerts between 25 May, 1922, and a final amtinee on 31 May, 1924.

Meanwhile, the Vienna counterpart had dissolved in December, 1921, after concert number 113, leaving Prague to carry on. Support in more prosperous Czechoslovakia reached to about 400 subscribers, among them some of the capital's more prominent musical personalities. And its cause enjoyed a good outlet in a progressive music journal, *Der Auftakt* (The Upbeat).

The full story of the Prague *Verein* remains to be told. Clearly it represented an important, if temporary, adjunct to German musical

---

[14]Josef Bohuslav Foerster, *Poutnik v Cizine* (Prague: Orbis, 1947), pp. 301–312. Under the title *Marja*, Foerster's realist opera (Now titled *Eva*) was produced at the Vienna *Volksoper* on 21 December, 1915. The composer-journalist resided in Vienna from 1903 until 1919.

[15]Alexander Ringer, "Schoenbergiana in Jerusalem," *The Musical Quarterly*, 59 (Jan. 1973), pp. 1–14. Also Ivan Vojtech, "Der Verein fur musikalische Privataufführung in Prag," in *Schönberg Gedenkaustellung*, pp. 312–315.

presence in Bohemia, yet the wide-ranging programs reasonably paid heed to the state of recent Czech composition; music students were admitted free and the prospectus came out in both Czech and German.

What about audience reactions? These ranged from enthusiasm to overt hostility. Repeat performances of Schoenberg's *Pierrot lunaire* proved particularly abrasive. Unlike Mozart, Schoenberg did not experience the immediate understanding and loving embrace of Prague's music lovers. The short-lived *Verein*, however, did fill a niche for the city's more sophisticated audiences and helped pave the way for later contemporary music forums in the Czech capital such as the left-wing *Přítomnost* (The Present) and the *Mánes* group. In fact, during the early 1920s, no city had greater exposure to the challenging messages of Arnold Schoenberg than Prague.[16] Biased reactions sometimes reached dismaying lengths, as when Rudolf Serkin invited Josef Suk to lend his presence at the debut of the visiting *Verein* enxemble. "I shall say not!" Suk exploded. "Why in the world would I want to come?" This flat refusal cut especially deep because surely Suk realized that Schoenberg himself would be making introductory remarks at the concert, while Serkin was to play a major piano cycle, *Life and Dreams* by Josef Suk.[17]

Inflation and difficulties raising funds usually are advanced as main reasons why the *Verein* eventually folded. Probably just as important was the shift in Schoenberg's attention to other matters. Zeal has limits. Having done their duty boosting the cause of modern music, personnel in the Society doubtless felt a measure of relief that demanding rehearsals and weekly concerts became things of the past. Yet all concerned could pack up their instruments and disband with pride at a job beautifully done. If the *Verein* truly uttered Vienna's last gasp as a cosmopolitan music center, it accompanied a noble exit.

Persons of Czechoslovak background took part at all levels of Schoenberg's Society for Private Musical Performances—players, officers, composers, subscribers. Without this participation, the Society might not have achieved the high degree of artistic success shown by its history. A later era sees the *Verein* as a model showcase for the promotion of 20th -century musical culture. To what extent this vital organization affected the development of new music within post-1918 Czechoslovakia, however, remains a topic ripe for further investigation.

---

[16]Ivan Vojtech (personal communication).

[17]Meibach, "Schoenberg's Society" (dissertation), p. 172.

Henry Cowell, Leoš Janáček, and Who Were the Others?

Eva Drlíková

Eva Drlíková has, as editor of the Brno journal Opus musicium, *played a large role in shaping Czech musicological discourse. Her contribution to this volume comes as a welcome tonic. All too often, especially in light of events in the last forty years, we regard Czechoslovakia as isolated from mainstream events, particularly from events in the United States. Though Dvořák's journeys to the United States are amply documented, it is easy to think of Janáček as a more local phenomenon, as distant from the United States of Woodrow Wilson and Herbert Hoover as was Mozart from George Washington and Thomas Jefferson. By placing the composer Henry Cowell in Moravia, and trying to fully establish the nature of his relationship to Janáček and others, Drlíková adds further dimensions to our vision of Brno in the 1920's and Czech-American cultural relations between the wars.*

Janáček's relations with the United states are documented in only one instance—when he met with the American composer Henry Cowell. This incident has only been described in Czech literature.[1] English-language scholars of Janáček and of Cowell may know about it in a rather vague sort of way, but they probably do not know all of it.[2]

In 1923 Henry Cowell made his first tour of Europe to play his works and demonstrate his new way of playing the piano. In the spring of 1926 he also performed in Warsaw and from there came to Brno, both to lecture on his new way of playing the piano and to give a concert to demonstrate his abilities as a composer and pianist. It was organized by the Association of Moravian Composers (Klub moravských skladatelu) headed then by Leoš

---

[1] *Pazdírkův hudební slovník naučý* (Brno: O. Pazdírka, 1933–37), 2: *Část osobní,* 151; *Hudební rozhledy,* 3 (1969), 72. See the study by Miloš Štědroň about Janáček and his connection with contemporary composers.

[2] For example, *The New Grove Dictionary of American Music* (1986), s.v. "Cowell, Henry," by Bruce Saylor; William Lichtenwanger, *The Music of Henry Cowell: A Descriptive Catalog,* I.S.A.M. Monographs, 23 (Brooklyn: Institute for Studies in American Music, 1986); and "Leos Janáček," by John Tyrrell, in *The New Grove Turn-of-the-Century Masters* (New York: Norton, 1985).

Janáček. Cowell's lecture was held on 8 April, 1926, and his concert, sponsored by the Moravian Urania Society, was held the next day. The Czech general public in Brno knew Henry Cowell from hearsay as an ultramodernist, which was the description used by Hans Heinz Stuckenschmidt in a German-language Prague journal, *Auftakt*.[3] Cowell's lecture and his concert received deserved acclaim, particularly his piano playing and his composition oriented to support it. As a composer, however, Cowell appealed to the Brno public for his technical inventiveness rather than for his supreme artistic qualities. Dr. Ludvík Kundera, an excellent pianist of contemporary music and writer on Janáček's work, described Cowell's concert in the journal *Hudební rozhledy* (1926, p. 127):

> ... his works incorporate a lot of new techniques and their quality determines the success or otherwise of the work in question. Cowell, therefore, stresses primarily the quality of his compositions and only secondarily points to the new techniques, and to implement them he uses his musical ideas and explains them. And at this point I should like to state that Cowell as a composer was a complete disappointment. ... His innermost expression is, however, very simple, usually one-part melody, accompanied and apparently thickened by noises of some kind, either clusters of all diatonic or chromatic tones on the piano, or analogous clusters on his "string piano," or finally the accompaniment of the primitive native instrument, a "thunderstick" used by the Red Indians. The source of all of Cowell's inventions is his interest in the color of the sound ... he is extremely daring in his harmonies, documenting it with his clusters of minor or major seconds. ... To be able to play these clusters he made a gradual and a very natural shirt to a new method of playing the piano, which requires a systematic use of his hands and forearms ... fists, palms. ... The second new aspect also concerns the color of the sound: to play the piano, he uses the string directly. ... Cowell is no charlatan; he is a serious musician, who is important primarily for his attempts to enhance our existing possibilities in expressing the color of the sound.

The next year, Leoš Janáček received a letter from Cowell requesting him to accept honorary membership in the New Music Society of California (together with Bartók, Bliss, Malipiero, Hába, Křenek, and others), and at the same time informing him about Cowell's publishing

---

[3]*Auftakt* 3 (1926): 81; see the study "Die neue Klaviervirtuose," Chapter 4.

activities in the field of contemporary music in the United States (see the copy of Cowell's letter).

In June, 1929, almost exactly three years after his first visit, Cowell made another appearance in Brno. This time his visit was advertised in the newspaper *Lidové noviny*, which published a Czech translation of Cowell's essay entitled "Folk Songs as a Basis of New Music."[4] In his study, Cowell describes his method of collecting Irish folk songs and in the process refers to Janáček's method of recording Slovak songs, because in his view, the character of the songs is so distinctive that no other method is viable:

> ... this music is not based on scales but on elementary units [phrases, strains]. Each of the strains, tied to the meaning of the words, comprises such a unit that would be difficult to dissect or break down into smaller units, no less tones. It is interesting to compare Janáček's discovery concerning elements of Slovak songs and the language in general, which show similarities so close that they are practically identical.

The second concert was certainly more significant for both Cowell and his audience than the first one in 1926.[5] This time, Cowell's music was played next to the works of leading Moravian composers (Janáček, Václav Kaprál, Vilém Petrželka), all by the Moravian Quartet, and the concert became a major event.[6] It took place in the music room of the Brno Faculty of Arts under the auspices of the progressive Ethical Movement of Czech Students. The students were highly interested in Cowell's music (*Movement for Strings*, 1928), as well as his way of playing the piano. As recorded by a correspondent of the journal of the Ethical Movement of Students,[7] a long discussion ensued, with the composers giving both an oral explanation and practical examples.

In 1929, Cowell—as pianist and composer—came to Brno for the last time. Cowell is also mentioned in Czech musical literature as a author of a series of articles, "Composing Music for Americans," written for the magazine *Rhythm*.[8]

---

[4]"Lidová píseň jako základ nové hudby," *Lidové noviny*, 6 June, 1929.

[5]In 1926, after Cowell's Brno concert, the pianist and composer gave the same program for the Modern Music Association (Spolek pro moderní hudbu) in Prague at the Mozarteum, April 16. The second concert of Cowell's music was held only in Brno, and Cowell took his presence as a "persona grata." As far as I know, after this occasion he visited Bratislava, the capital of Slovakia, and from there, perhaps, went on his way to the U.S.S.R.

[6]Among other things, it was broadcast by the Brno radio station at a very advantageous time.

[7]"E," *Journal of Ethical Movement of Czech Students* 3 (1929): 11.

[8]Cowell, "Hudební tvorba pro americký národ," *Rytmus* (1937–38): 74, 97.

The above are all facts. Now the questions begin: How did a young American composer happen to come to Brno? Who introduced him to Janáček? Who was instrumental in introducing Cowell to the Brno audience? Two hypotheses can be put forward, but unfortunately neither can be entirely substantiated:

1. In the early 1920s, the Ethnographic Department of the Moravian Museum was headed by Dr. František Pospíšil (1890–1951), well-known throughout Europe, England, and the Middle and Near East (later also in the U.S.) as a specialist in so-called "sword and war dances" (including those from Scotland and Ireland).[9] The private archives of Pospíšil were destroyed after his death in 1951, and no written documentation exists to prove that these two "collectors," Pospíšil and Cowell, ever met.

However, oral evidence of Dr. Ludvík Kunz, a younger collaborator of Pospíšil, seems reliable. He claims that Pospíšil mentioned several times that he had "met" Cowell over Irish folk dances. It was Pospíšil and his beautiful Slovak wife who were said to have introduced this inquiring American to Slovak folk songs and dances.[10]

2. The Association of Moravian Composers was approached by Dr. Vladimír Úlehla, a biologist, physiologist, and later also ethnologist, to organize the first concert by Cowell in Brno. Úlehla was staying at the Desert Laboratory in Arizona and California during the second half of 1925, having received a grant from the Rockefeller Foundation's International Education Board. When searching through Úlehla's diaries and itineraries, I was unable to find any other mention of Cowell except this: "July the 4th, a trip with Cowell" (1).[11] Other friendly meetings cannot be ruled out.[12]

No printed program for either of Cowell's concerts in Brno has been found. We know only that in 1926 Cowell played mostly his own pieces (*Suite*, *Episode*, *Advertisement*) with violinist Leo Lindner, and

---

[9]After his American trip in 1930, Pospíšil wrote a very respectable book about the southwestern Indians: *Etnologické materiály z Jihozápadu USA* (Contribution to the Ethnology of the Southwest USA) (Brno: Nákladem vlastním, 1933).

[10]In a short news item in the newspaper *Lidové noviny*, 6 June 1929, p. 7, Cowell is described as a collector who was also interested in Slovak folk songs.

[11]Brno University Archives, B 57/21–22.

[12]Working on this subject, I received a very interesting letter from Vladimír Úlehla, Jr., the son of Vladimír Úlehla. He writes about a big private party in his parents' house in Brno with many important persons, and Cowell as a star of this event. This happened in the second half of the 1920s.

that in 1929 the Moravian Quartet played his *Movement for String Quartet*, and that for an encore Cowell played his *Irish Legends* on the piano.

According to information from Czech ethnographer Dušan Holy, there are two lectures or studies by Cowell[13] (for American and Russian journals) on the technique of folk string players from Velká (a village in Moravian Slovakia), which Cowell visited for the first time with Vladimír Úlehla in 1927.

Besides Cowell's letter to Janáček, the only direct document about the two meeting is found in Úlehla's memoirs. In his book *Zivá píseň* (*Living Song*), Úlehla writes: "Of all our composers, Janáček was practically the only one Cowell regarded favorably. They met several times and had very long discussions."[14] Úlehla describes Cowell as a friend he met during his American stay.[15]

What may also have happened is that Janáček, who was at that time writing his *Capriccio* for piano left hand, found some inspiration for the unusual model of the piano in Cowell's music, which was revolutionary at that time.

The question of Cowell and Janáček and the others is one of many incidents forming a mosaic of connections and relationships between Moravia and the United States that strengthened Masaryk's Czechoslovakia and that formed a rich source for the whole of Czech modern art. In this connection, I should also mention the second American trip of Tomáš Baťa, Vladimír Karfík's studies in Frank Lloyd Wright's Studios, the conductor Břetislav Bakala's performances as an organist, regular information on American musical life written by Vladimír Políkva, and a large number of other items which need to be placed in their proper context. Henry Cowell's contribution to Czechoslovakian musical culture lies in the fact that he was the first American to enrich significantly the Czech and Slovak musical scene with his non-European musical thinking.

---

[13] Vladimír Úlehla, *Studiem lidového života na Moravské Slovensku k ideové základně státu* (The study of Folk Life in Moravian Slovakia and the Ideal Basic of Czechoslovakia)(Bratislava, 1947), p. 6.

[14] Úlehla, *Zivá píseň* (Prague: F. Borový, 1949), p. 62.

[15] Ibid., pp. 202 and 339.

Leoš Janáček and His Influence on Slovak Music

Milan Adamčiak

Two of the Janáček myths which have survived intact to this very day are: a. that Janáček somehow embodied a "Moravian" attitude, both musically and ideologically, and b. that he was too much of an individual to have influenced subsequent generations. Both of these are neatly punctured by Milan Adamčiak, a member of the Slovak Academy of Sciences and a noted theorist and musicologist. In his study he gently but firmly suggests how important Slovakia was in the development of Janáček's thinking, and also shows the way Janáček's influence, both directly and indirectly added to the tremendous vitality of Slovak musical development.

When I was informed about the possibility of appearing in front of you with a report on Leoš Janáček and Slovak music I asked myself how to formulate this problem. How could I contribute at least in a small measure to the rich and fruitful contact between Janáček and Slovakia? I had in my mind many constructions and associations, e.g. Janáček and Slovakia, Janáček and the Slovaks, Slovakia in Janáček's works, Janáček the Folklorist and Slovak Folk Creations. Since I devote myself more to the music of Slovak composers than I do to our folk song or Janáček's works, I chose as the topic for my contribution the title: "Leoš Janáček and his Influence on Slovak Music." I would like to introduce a few composers, in whose music we can detect Janáček's echo.

First of all, let me mention some well-known facts about Janáček's personal relationship to Slovakia. He often expressed his sincere respect and admiration for the land and its people. It is known that he was concerned with the fate of our nation and culture in the context of the Austro-Hungarian monarchy, and later was interested in the common life of Bohemians, Moravians, and Slovaks in the Czechoslovak Republic. For Janáček, there were no frontiers between Moravia and Slovakia; they were amalgamated in his mentality, his humanism, and his national and social feelings. He visited Slovakia a few times for different reasons — traveling and searching for folk songs in northwestern Slovakia, going to the High Tatras for relaxation, and journeying to Bratislava several times for premieres of his works. Along with some harmonizations and adaptations of Slovak folk songs and some of his choral compositions, he made many notes of speech melodies and the sonic environment, including waterfalls and bird sounds from the High Tatras. In Bratislava he was inspired to compose the symphonic work the "Danube." But his most intensive interest in Slovakia and its national identity was awakened when it became useful in the support of his own theoretical and compositional attitudes.

At a time when Slovakia was largely unknown and thus had almost no contact with European musicians, Janáček found confirmation of his theories of folklore. He considered Slovak singing as the model manifestation of Slavic musical thinking. The very rich and individual strains of Slovak folklore supplied a broad background which could be developed, and confronted him with the equally rich musical traditions of other Slavic groups. The backward, poor and miserable Slovakia of the early 20th century was the home of a certain measure of archaism or primitivism of musical thinking, which was emphasized by Janáček. It is natural that Janáček, as an admirer of folk expression and the creator of a new and deep relationship to a type of musical folklore stripped of romantic rusticity and idealization, supported this state with his critical realist attitude. We thus find the roots of what we may consider echoes of Janáček in many works by Slovak composers.

The efforts of Janáček as a folklorist deeply influenced the need of Slovak ethnographers, musicologists, and composers to cope with the traditional music of their homeland in the early 20th century. In spite of the efforts of Czech musicians and collectors, it was only after World War II that Slovak musicology penetrated more deeply into the structure of Slovak folk songs; especially important here are the works of Jozef Kresánek. Janáček's influence upon the work of Slovak composers took place a bit earlier and involved the relationship between Art music and national song and dance.

In speaking about Janáček's relation to Slovak composers we cannot avoid his contact with the Nestor of our modern music, Ján Levoslav Bella (1843–1936). Janáček showed interest in his string quartet and wanted to perform it on a concert by the Brno Beseda as early as 1880. But Bella, though pleased by Janáček interest, as the two letters by Bella from Transylvania show, had disagreements with Janáček about his approach to the score. These two figures have, however, much in common. For example: at Kremnica Bella worked as a organist, conductor, pedagogue and organizer of musical events, and he devoted himself to improving the quality of musical life in middle Slovakia; these were the same kinds of activities which Janáček performed in Brno. Bella's fight for the professionalization of Slovak composers in the contemporary cultural context of the Slovak musical public did not gain much support; and for a long time his music, like Janáček's, remained unknown and unappreciated.

Janáček's organ school in Brno also influenced the relationship of Slovakia to the Moravian master. In Bratislava, between the two wars, a number of students and graduates of Janáček's school performed in concerts, and it was thus possible to get a real sense of their style and approach. Perhaps more than any other figure Fraňo Dostalík (1896–1944), who wrote about several concerts of faculty and students of the Slovak Academy of Music and Drama, oriented himself towards the works of Janáček's disciples and Czech composers of the 1920's. I believe Janáček's influence in Slovakia was promoted by a number of Czech and Moravian musicians working here, but especially by this legendary composer and pedagogue. His articles, concert reviews, notebooks and quotations by those who knew him make this clear. Dostalík did not neglect any opportunity to show his admiration for the great Moravian master. Let me say a few words about the relationship between Dostalík and Slovak composers. Even today he is looked upon as an outsider in Slovak music, standing apart from the main trends, and his Janáčekism played a large part in creating this situation. Dostalík is said to have been an eccentric, erratic enthusiast for everything new, a representative of immature modernism, an admirer of polarities for their own sake, and an obstinate supporter of everything that interested him.

In composition he was a self-taught man, incorrigible, and perhaps even incomprehensible. Between 1919 and 1921 he studied at the Brno Conservatory and attended Janáček's lectures in composition. In those years he was already very much interested in the musical avant-garde. He was attracted to Bartók, Hindemith, Milhaud, Stravinsky and Mosolov. He knew the works of the Second Viennese School, and was interested in the work of Roslavec, Alexanderov, Ježek, E.F. Burian and others. He followed the efforts of Alois Hába in microtonality, in the quarter-tone and sixth-tone system, and it is reported that in the thirties he constructed a quarter-tone harmonium. In the years 1922–27 he taught at pedagogical schools, later he led a graduate course at the Hungarian Pedagogical Institute in Bratislava. Dostalík also worked as a reviewer for some Slovak newspapers, writing primarily about performances of choral and contemporary music. In 1929 he reviewed a lecture and concert by Henry Cowell in Bratislava. He devoted himself to musical analysis (Bartók, Hindemith and Janáček), and was occupied by theoretical points concerning harmony and modality.

He wrote five violin sonatas, some piano compositions, congs, choruses, a melodramatic cantata and an opera, *Radúz and Mahuliena*. According to the musicologist Štefan Čurilla, Dostalík sent the opera to a competition held by the Association of American Slovaks. Only a few of his compositions were performed for an audience. His music reveals the striking influences of Janáček's texture, terseness of melodic-rhythmic fragments, and richly structured metrorhythmical elements. His music is considered bold in harmony, but unbalanced in form. It is a pity that a great portion of his work is missing, and that his archives are now considered lost. Some of his books and collections of music, many of them richly annotated, have been dispersed in various private archives. It is quite important for Slovak musicology to settle its debt to this noteworthy personality of our twentieth century musical culture. In the context of the development of Slovak music in the twenties and thirties, Fraňo Dostalík—as one of the few people who did not follow in the footsteps of Vítězslav Novák's conception of modern Slovak national music—introduced himself as a enthusiastic proponent of Janáček's music and tried to penetrate into the heart of Slovak musical folklore.

It is a paradox that Josef Grešák (1907–?), a disciple of Fraňo Dostalík in composition, had a similar fate in terms of his position in Slovak music in general, and in his relation to Janáček in particular, for in the work of Grešák the balladic tone and seal of individual primitivism that tied Janáček to the Slovak folk song was projected into reality. Josef Grešák was born in north-eastern Slovakia and became involved in Slovak music in an individual way. He began his career by writing music full of vitality and stayed with it throughout his life. He became Dostalík's most loved student and it is evident that he always had a great admiration for Janáček's music and for his uncompromising attitude. On the basis of good reviews in the twenties (Grešák was esteemed by Josef Suk and Václav Talich), he gained a place for himself in Slovak music only decades later; first in the fifties, as a composer with a lasting relationship to national folk music, and later as a composer of rich invention and individual expression. Grešák's distinctive style, which grows out of his individual musical poetics, about which he expressed himself with enthusiasm, is very similar to that of Janáček. Grešák did not speak much about Dostalík—perhaps he was too much marked by the stamp of his personality—and to be quite honest, he was considered his epigone. Of course this perceived status did not contribute to a proper evaluation of Grešák's work. In terms of his compositional approach, he accentuated the rhythmical-motoric aspect of his works, which was basically related to the East Slovakian dance called Karičy, and which he specified by irregular metric notation. He used this as the basis for his theory of pulsation, which is immediately attractive by virtue of its graceful terminology and the way it discusses the independence of common rhythm and meter. In the sphere of melos and interval construction, Grešák employs serialism and selective modalities, and this gives his works a particularly individual, compact homogeneity, in spite of their structural variability. In his accent on detail, the variability of the fragmentary "cells," and in his use of carefully framed diction in vocal parts of his compositions, Grešák may be considered one of the composers who creatively seized direct inspiration from Janáček's music.

When we speak of Grešák's relation to Janáček, it is necessary to mention one more dimension, a dimension, I am convinced, that plays a most remarkable role. It is his humanism, his deeply human, socio-critical feeling, which is reflected in many of his works, especially in those places where he accentuates his respect for the hard fate of human beings. He was inspired by the strong social motivation in Slovak literature evident in figures such as Vincent Šikula (*Rozárka*), Martin Kukučín (*Neprebudený*, (Unawaken)), Pavel Országh Hviezdoslav (*Zuzanka Hraškovie*). Grešák not only felt both passionate interest in and compassion for human relations, but he also revealed an awareness of its cruel fate, and appealed to contemporary ethical standards. His character types have much in common with Janáček's figures in *Zápisník zmizelého* (The Diary of One Who Vanished), *Jenůfa*, and *Kátya Kabanová*. The balladic mood, which is characteristic of Slovak music in the first half of our century, is quite clear in Grešák's work with naively sincere outlines. His *Panychida* is, for example, a work outside any time. There the *Ballade of an Unborn Child* by the modern Czech poet Jiří Wolker is juxtaposed with the Old Slavic text of funeral cere- monies, reminiscent of Janáček's *Glagolitic Mass*. Grešák's position in Slovak musical culture has not yet been fairly appraised until the present day, and we can see an analogy between his fate and that of Janáček—there is a similar controversy concerning the hegemony of Vítězslav Novák's conception, activities on the periphery of musical events, a similar refining of his own characteristic style independent of topical trends, as well as a similar impulsive mentality and vitality continuing into the extraordinary late creative periods of both Grešák and Janáček.

Despite the fact that in the last few decades we meet Janáček's name only sporadically in connection with Slovak music, we must say that his echo is heard from many works of composers from several generations. The rustic sense, the rhapsodic quality, and the role of the dance movement found in Janáček's works are reflected in some works of Andrej Očenáš, for example in his orchestral suite *Ruralia Slovaca*, and in his symphonic poems, which display a relationship to the instrumentation of Janáček's *Lašské tance* and *Taras Bulba*. Expressivity of detail is found in some of Očenáš's chamber music, e.g. in the First String Quartet, and in the piano phantasy *Pl'úšt'* (The Flurry).

Among the composers who entered Slovak music in the fifties and sixties, it is Juraj Pospíšil who most inclines towards Janáček's approach. Born in Northern Moravia, he was a student at the Janáček Academy of Music Arts in Brno, studying with Vilém Petrželka. Pospíšil has maintained an admiring affinity for Janáček and for Bohuslav Martinů, who especially influenced his early works. He is particularly interested in instrumental music, and is clearly influenced by Janáček's texture (e.g. in the suite of lyrical pictures for strings *In Dreaming*, in the First Symphony, and in the symphonic poem *Mountains and Men*). Signs of Janáček-like fragmentary composition, an accent on details and a rich variability of expression, are first found in Pospíšil's work in connection with rhapsodic and program music. Later there is the very strong influence of Webern's miniatures, and a serial organization of intervalic material. These two impulses, Janáček and Webern, appear in Pospíšil in a particular symbiosis, in which proper dramatic lyricism, economy of material and force of musical idea combine harmoniously.

Expressive lyricism is evidently one of the fundamental characteristics of Moravian musicality. This view is supported by the work of another Moravian-born composer, Hanuš Domanský, who graduated from the Brno Conservatory and from the Academy of Musical Arts in Bratislava where he studied with Dezider Kardoš. Domanský is one of those who were seriously interested in the work of Janáček and Martinů; yet his work reflects a great deal of individuality. He is a composer with an expressively linear kind of musical thinking, known for formal austerity, metrorhythmic ideas, and a sense of dramatic contrast. His music is effective in the way various ideas are joined together (e.g. Dianoia for Violin Solo, the First String Quartet, or a Fragment of a Sonata for Piano). The basis of his composition became a three to five tone motive which was treated as if it were observed from several angles, corresponding to the particular text and in dialogue with contrasting parts. Domanský's music achieves effective tension, dynamic of musical process through the nuances of the basic form, and through the effect of dynamic variability and accent on the evolutionary aspect, in which the contour line of melody and harmony is arbitrary. For those who know Domanský personally (a well-balanced man, smiling and quiet), the rapacity of his music comes as a burst of hidden energy.

Last but not least, I would like to mention a young composer, Vít'azoslav Kubička, a representative of the generation entering Slovak music at the beginning of the eighties. Kubička is a disciple of Dezider Kardoš, and has devoted himself mainly to instrumental and electronic music. He is the chief of the Electroacoustical Studio of Czechoslovak Radio in Bratislava. In forming his personal compositional style, an outstanding role was played by his knowledge of the music of Brahms, Mussorgsky, Stravinsky, Janáček and Ilja Zeljenka, at present the leading personality of Slovak music. Kubička appropriated various impulses from these composers, but in such a concentrated manner that we feel that his compositions come from a single focus. Yet his admiration for Janáček's motivic work and his attention to detail is clear. The compositions of Kubička, with their variability of stimuli and dominating linearity, become effective through their homogeneity and their compactness, where stress is on the ripeness of the idea. He builds upon the vaulted arches of expressivity with a great deal of introspection and self-reflection. His expression possesses something Satyr-like, erotic, vital, and ravenous. Simply said, the spirit of Janáček's scores is preserved and developed in an individual way.

Finally, I would like to apologize to all those who have expected to hear more about Janáček, or about those composers for whose musical expression Janáček's work was a clear and important stimulus. His contributions to the formation of Slovak operatic diction by Ján Ciker or Eugen Suchoń has been dealt with several times, and some of that material has been published. I thought it was perhaps more important to call your attention to the importance of Janáček's ideas and music in those places where our history is silent, and offer a summary of what is still to be elucidated by historical and analytic research of specific authors and works.

Part 6:

"The Danube" Symphony

One of the highlights of the festival which accompanied "Janáček and Czech Music" was the American premiere of Janáček's "Unfinished Symphony," titled "The Danube" performed by the St. Louis Symphony Orchestra under the baton of Leonard Slatkin. Even though he made no written contribution to this volume, we are indebted to Maestro Slatkin for his efforts, both in performing the work and generously sharing his time with us during the discussion section and making some pointed remarks about performing the work, and particularly about the impracticality of certain sections.

It is rare that a conference such as ours has a work like "The Danube" to discuss. The story of the work is told in several different ways on the pages that follow, a bit like a musicological Rashomon. Though we are all in agreement that Janáček would undoubtedly have made changes before allowing a performance, we nonetheless felt that such a work poses a whole range of musicological, musical, and even philosophical questions well worth asking.

Was Janáček Satisfied with his Symphony "The Danube"?

Alena Němcová

Alena Němcová has been an influential figure in the creation of Czech musical studies as an international field. As a scholar she has written numerous articles on Janáček and Czech contemporary composers, and has contributed to the New Grove. In her role as head of the Music Information Center in Brno, housed in Janáček's old organ school, she has aided dozens of scholars, musicians, and journalists in the pursuit of their work. In this study she has assembled and commented on the documents central to the study of the context of the "The Danube" Symphony, and poses telling questions about Janáček's intentions.

The first news of Janáček's intention to compose a symphony appeared in print in 1924. At the end of his autobiographical sketch, published by Adolf Veselý[1], we read an interesting reflection by Janáček on "The Danube." In the text, dating from 2 October, 1924, Janáček spoke of a symphony evoked by a view of the river "some time ago, a year earlier," and which he "hoped to complete with a clear head perhaps during 1925." During this period filled with activity, a year was a very long time for the composer. Janáček's biographer Jaroslav Vogel inserted the date 1923, originally printed in the margin, directly into the text of this passage and thereby pushed the inspiration of the work even further into the past.[2]

On 2 June, 1925, Veselý, printed an article in *Lidové noviny* entitled "At Leoš Janáček's" in which he mentioned that the composer "for over a year now has had in mind a new work, a symphony about the Danube." Further evidence of the symphony comes from the pen of Ludvík Kundera in his article "Janáček's Compositional Nachlass," printed three months after the composer's death.[3] In it Kundera

---

[1] Adolf Veselý, *Leoš Janáček. Pohled do života a díla* (Prague, 1924), pp. 96–99.
[2] Jaroslav Vogel, *Leoš Janáček. Život a dílo* (Prague, 1963); English version (Orbis, 1981), pp. 286–290.
[3] Ludvík Kundera, "Skladebná pozůstalost Janáčkova," *Hudební rozhledy*, iv, (November, 1928). In the same issue appears a reminiscence by Adolf Veselý—"Poslední roshovor s Leošem Janáčkem" ("The Last Talk with Leoš Janáček")—in which he repeated some of Janáček's thoughts from 1925 on "The Danube."

described a manuscript, which he classified as a sketch but which "gives the impression of a definitively completed work." He added, however, that this sketch "in the course of further work would certainly have undergone basic changes," a conclusion based on Janáček's compositional practice as deduced from the examples of other autographs, .

After the premiere of the opera *From the House of the Dead*, which Janáček's pupils Břetislav Bakala and Osvald Chlubna prepared in 1930, Chlubna turned his attention to the sketch of "The Danube." He assumed that it would be possible, as in the case of Janáček's final opera, to make a performing version, and the conductor Zdeněk Chalabala planned to give the premiere during the concert season of 1932/33. In his article "The Last Work of Janáček — The Danube"[4] Chlubna reflected on the ideas behind Janáček's composition and discussed some problems in deciphering the manuscript. The nut was too hard to crack, it seems. While the opera was a fully complete autograph reflecting the composer's ideas and lacking only the final corrections of the fair copy, it was uncertain at that time whether the rough sketch of the symphony corresponded to the composer's intentions which, in themselves, seemed a bit unclear.

News of the symphony is encountered again on 8 May, 1948, in a brief item by Chlubna in *Lidové noviny*.[5] Shortly before it was published, "The Danube" was performed in Brno on 2 May by the Czech Radio Orchestra under Břetislav Bakala. In an article entitled "My Part in Janáček's Symphony" Chlubna gave an account of the work he devoted to the symphony between October 10, 1947 and January 6, 1948.

In his 1958 monograph Jaroslav Vogel summarized all the information known about the symphony at that time. According to Vogel, Janáček was impressed by the mighty flow of the Danube during a visit to Bratislava in March 1923, and it was this impression that marked the beginning of Janáček's idea of composing the symphony. In his account of Janáček's sources of inspiration (the poem "Lola" by Alexander Insarov and Pavla Kříčková's "The Drowned Girl"[6]), Vogel derived his information from Chlubna's first article (1932), while at the same time adopting a critical stance towards Chlubna's later reconstructions. As a hypothesis he suggested a certain parallel with Smetana's symphonic poem *Vltava* and also

---

[4] Osvald Chlubna, "Neznámé poslední Janáčkovo dílo Dunaj," *Divadelní list Brno*, vii, (March, 1932), pp. 306–308.
[5] Osvald Chlubna, "Má účast na Janáčkově symfonii Dunaj," *Lidové noviny*, 8 May, 1948.
[6] The poems were published in *Lidové noviny*. Alexander Insarov was a nom de plume of the female writer Soňa Špálová.

mentioned also an unfinished project of Richard Strauss. In his article "Janáček's Danube Symphony in the Conception of Osvald Chlubna,"[7] Miloš Štědroň analyzed Janáček's autograph and Chlubna's reconstruction. He pointed out characteristic traits of Chlubna's arrangement in the first movement, demonstrating convincingly how far the arranger had departed from Janáček's compositional principles, shifting the work into quite a different stylistic sphere. Štědroň stressed the need for a new critical transcription for the collected edition, one that would show the stage of completeness in which Janáček had left the work. According to Štědroň, any performing version should adhere to the composer's original as far as possible. A further Štědroň paper given at the 1978 Brno conference[8] is concerned with the same set of problems. On the occasion of the first performance of the new reconstruction, an article, "A New View of Janáček's Symphony,"[9] was published by both its editors Leoš Faltus and Miloš Štědroň. The article can be taken as a brief critical report, providing basic details about the manuscript and a description and justification of essential editorial decisions. Finally, an article by Jakob Knaus[10] is, in essence, an interpretation of the points made by Czech scholars, above all Vogel and Štědroň.

Janáček made a public announcement concerning his intention to compose a piece about the Danube at the end of 1924, which he confirmed in an interview for the *Lidové noviny* in June of the following year. The very fact that the composer talked publicly about an unfinished composition was unusual. Janáček did not generally announce his compositions in advance—it was even difficult for his pupils to penetrate into his creative workshop. These public utterances were accompanied by the even greater concern with the work which we find in his personal correspondence. For Janáček, letters functioned as a kind of work-diary in which he expressed his satisfaction with a work or the difficulties that he had encountered, and thereby relaxed from the pressures of his creative energy. They are thus an invaluable source for researchers in which they can learn about the progress of a given work, its hidden designs, as well as what prompted or inspired it. Many of Janáček's own letters are missing, but in the Janáček Archives in Brno

---

[7]Miloš Štědroň, "Janáčkova symfonie Dunaj v pojetí Osvalda Chlubny, *Hudební věda*, XV, No. 4 (1978), pp. 326–332.
[8]Miloš Štědroň, "Chlubnova verze Janáčkova Dunaje," in *Colloquium Leoš Janáček ac tempora nostra Brno 1978* (Brno, 1983), pp. 169–175.
[9]Leoš Faltus and Miloš Štědroň, "Znovu Janáčkova symfonie Dunaj, *Opus musicum*, No. 7 (1985), pp. 193–196.
[10]Jakob Knaus, "Leoš Janáčeks 'Donau' Symphonie," *Oesterreichische Musikzeitschrift*, 4 (1987), pp. 173–178; and in *Leoš Janáček-Gesellschaft, Mitteilungsblatt*, No. 51 (1987).

some of the replies to these missing letters can be found; they illuminate many diverse aspects of his creative development. Let us, therefore, consider the sources that have survived and attempt to trace Janáček's work on the symphony.

It seems that the river Danube struck Janáček's fancy long before the idea of setting it to music occurred to him. As early as the summer of 1911 he considered taking a trip to Bratislava and from there traveling down the Danube by boat.[11] The idea surfaced again in 1923 during his stay in Bratislava where he attended a performance of his opera *Kátya Kabanová* on 24 March. He wrote about it to Kamila Stösslová:[12]

> The beautiful old town, the fast-flowing Danube. I've a mind in the holidays to take a trip down the Danube right up to where it flows into the sea — or at least to Belgrade.

At that time Janáček had probably already begun sketching the new work, for he finished the second movement on 18 June. Dr. Alois Kolísek, professor of theology at Bratislava, whom Janáček had contacted about folkloristic matters during this period, was consulted about the plan for his trip. On 6 June Kolísek sent Janáček detailed information about the departures of boats to Belgrade from Bratislava, including the fare, adding:[13]

> Can I draw your attention or rather invite you to come to Bratislava the day before your departure to Belgrade. You can stay with me. At the moment the steamer goes every day from Bratislava to Děvín — in the afternoon, it's a pleasant and instructive outing. It would make a prelude to sailing to Yugoslavia.

The date of the journey was set precisely, as we learn from another letter Janáček wrote to Kamila:[14]

> On 1 July I want to make a trip along the Danube by ship. If I manage to find a companion, I would travel to Pest — Belgrade and beyond Belgrade to the Danube rapids, which are very beautiful. That would take 5 days. Then I would return again to the Tatra mountains.

Perhaps Janáček did not find a companion—after the middle of June he clearly had no long journey in mind, for in further post cards Kolisek

---

[11] Janáček's postcard to Zdenka Janáčková, 24 August, 1911, JA 5802, B 977.
[12] Janáček to Kamila Stösslová, 3 April, 1923, JA E 1399.
[13] Dr. Alois Kolísek to Janáček, 6 June, 1923, JA 2062, B 478.
[14] Janáček to Kamila Stösslová, 9 June, 1923, JA 8405, E 211.

only looks forward to seeing Janáček again in Bratislava and towards a possible trip to Děvín. Meanwhile there was no word about the composition.

The next bit of information about the symphony is in effect, a poetic nature painting in which the river grows into the musical conception out of which the symphony is born. At the end of the passage about "The Danube," Janáček wrote:

> And some time perhaps in the year 1925, with a clear head, the work will ripen as if in the sun.

What is interesting is the following note, which dates these lines and which also provides information about Janáček's intention to incorporate the Lola episode into the symphony:

> Yesterday, the 1st of October, it occurred to me that Insarov's Lola will certainly drown in it (i.e. in the Danube).

In the last days of 1924 Janáček worked on the symphony in Hukvaldy, and on December 31 he wrote to his wife:[15]

> I've got nice weather, a dry frost, snow only five-fingers deep. It's warm inside. I work on The Danube and walk assiduously.

According to Chlubna, Janáček had completed the sketch of the four-movement symphony in May 1925, but wanted to postpone its completion until after a trip down the river, which he planned again in the summer of 1925. Chlubna's testimony agrees with Janáček's words in the *Lidové noviny* interview:

> Mr. Vavrečka promised me that he would draw up a plan for sailing down the Danube. I want to see the Danube along its whole length. And so sometime in the summer I will sail right up to where it meets the sea, and then I will get to work on my symphony.

This is a clear announcement that the composer did not consider the existing sketch to be definitive, and that only after a trip would he return to the work and put it into its final shape. In two long letters to Janáček, Hugo Vavrečka, representative of the Czechoslovak Embassy in Budapest, did indeed describe to him in detail the course of a cruise along the Danube, sending him timetables of steamship companies. Vavrečka drew up a plan for the trip and recommended the best time of the year to go, either in June, September or October. It was already too late

---

[15]Janáček to Zdenka Janáčková, Hukvaldy, 31 December, 1924, JA 7815, A 4994.

for a June departure, but in July Janáček was still thinking of going when he wrote to Kamila:[16]

> I flee from place to place since I can't be where I would like to be. Luhačovice, Hukvaldy. Venice, down the Danube: but everywhere it's just misery for me.

On 27 July, writing from Hukvaldy,[17] he told his wife that he had finished revising Act II of *Věc Makropulos* and that he had completed one movement (by now the last) of the symphony, which he confirmed a week later in a letter to Kamila:[18]

> But I have also looked over the symphony, The Danube. There will be the interesting Lola episode in it. At first — and then she shivers with cold and hunger before jumping into the Danube.

In the autumn of 1925 Janáček traveled to Venice most unwillingly, and the trip down the Danube dropped out of his calendar again. In May of the following year he was in England, where he probably talked about the new symphony with Rosa Newmarch, who, after his return home, sent him some advice from London: "Take a little rest now and finish the symphony."[19] (We cannot be quite sure whether the symphony mentioned by Rosa Newmarch was "The Danube" symphony or the *Sinfonietta*, which Janáček had finished just before leaving for England, and which he was in the process of revising.)

On 19 August, 1926, a letter reached him in Luhačovice reminding him once again of the unfinished piece. Otakar Ostrčil, chief conductor of the National Theatre in Prague, asked him if he would entrust him with the score of the new symphony for a premiere at a concert of the Czech Philharmonic on 30 January, 1927. This was a very concrete proposal which came in relatively good time to allow Janáček to make final corrections and prepare the work for performance. And Janáček's response? We know his reaction in great detail from a letter to Zdenka, whose directness and sincerity has all the hallmarks of authenticity:[20]

> The post has just come. Ilona writes that Hoffmann called on her and asked her to play the Concertino with the Czech Quartet in Vienna. So

---

[16]Janáček to Kamila Stösslová, 7–8 July, 1925, JA E 315.
[17]Janáček to Zdenka Janáčková, 27 July, 1925, JA 7833, A 320.
[18]Janáček to Kamila Stösslová, 5 August, 1925, JA 8513, E 324.
[19]Rosa Newmarch to Janáček, Leamington Spa, 23 May, 1926, JA 5466, B 909.
[20]Janáček to Zdenka Janáčková, Luhačovice, 19 August, 1926, JA JA 7850, B 1389.

that will now be the third performance in Vienna. She sends you her greetings. And there is an express letter from — Ostričil from Soběslav. I'll read that after lunch! [He put off reading the letter as if he suspected something unpleasant.]Roast chicken for lunch. Yesterday I had nothing for supper — I couldn't stand the veal. So what is Mr. Ostrčil writing to me about? Does he want Věc Makropulos? Let's read it now. What a mistake! He wants my symphony The Danube, which is far from ready. He'll have to go on waiting for it. Sometimes one makes mistakes.

Punctum satis. The very same day he replied briefly to Ostrčil:[21]

> Dear Friend. "Our" Danube is not so tempting that I'm in a hurry to finish my own Danube!

For the moment Janáček put a full stop after the letter and the symphony. It was not meant to be definitive, but unfortunately turned out to be. There remained to him two years of life in which he began and finished a number of compositions, but never returned to the symphony. Why? The answer can only be hypothetical, based on an analysis of the sort of composer he was, and on his views of the psychology of composition.

If we survey Janáček's works, we see that with the exception of early pieces, which were mostly lost, Janáček wrote nothing in the spirit of purely absolute music. His sonatas have extra-musical content (in the piano sonata it is clearly defined, in the violin sonata in a more general manner, or rather one that was created in the course of composition, which itself lasted seven years!). The same is true of the quartets, the *Sinfonietta*, the wind sextet *Mladi*, the *Capriccio* (originally to have been called "Defiance") and the piano *Concertino*. For the individual movements of the *Concertino*, Janáček employed, curiously, several explanations:

1. The Suite "Spring," with the following movements: Beetle, Deer, Cricket, Torrent;

2. The Spring—featuring a cricket, midges, a roebuck, a healthy, fast-flowing stream—and, yes, and man, too;

3. the whole work grew out of the youthful mood of my sextet Mladi;

4. officially for Pult and Taktstock:

---

[21]Janáček to Otakar Ostričil, Luhačovice, 19 August, 1926, JA 11.334, A 6060.

I —an angry hedgehog is upset by being forcibly awoken from his winter sleep

II —the squirrel jumping in a cage

III —the owl and other night animals looking critically into the strings of the piano,

IV —as if everything, as in the fairytale, was talking about a "new penny"

No matter — today we need no explanation when we listen to the work, and Janáček provided his program after the piece was written, and furthermore, gave a different one every time. He was not concerned with literary descriptiveness, but with extramusical motivation which, as a committed realist, he needed for his work. It is possible that in the period leading up to his seventieth birthday, i.e. in the year 1923, when he was at the peak of his creative powers and had found a clarity in his compositional principles, he longed to create a large scale orchestral work in the classic symphonic genre. (Up to this time he had written only orchestral dances, dance suites, the Idyll and three symphonic poems.) Also, we must not belittle a certain ambition to be on equal footing with composers of the past and with many of his contemporaries. But to write a symphony without a concrete stimulus went against all of Janáček's previous principles and experience. Therefore, he sought for his symphony a large-scale subject which seemed to be provided by the big river whose gushing floods in the spring in Bratislava made such an impression on him. As Vogel has pointed out, and after him Knaus, water attracted and inspired Janáček. For him the river was a symbol of purifying change and of time flowing to an eternal rhythm. His imagination created associations—Slavonic nations living on the banks of the Danube, pictures of nature (which he wanted to see with his own eyes), the fates of people linked with the river, poems which he himself set by the Danube. In a lecture on "Naturalism in Art,"[22] which he worked on at the beginning of 1924 at the very time he was engaged with the composition of "The Danube," Janáček wrote of the workings of external stimuli on the composer's creative process. Among other concrete examples, he cites the view of the Vltava from the Prague embankment:

O/ = visible sensation/: the silhouette of Hradčany—the flowing of the Vltava: in the rhythm which has lain there for centuries; the movement of an eye—time

---

[22]Leoš Janáček, "Naturalismus v umění," sketches for a lecture, dated 25 February, 10 March and 24 March, 1924, JA S 72, S 73.

U/ = audible sensation/: when the ice floes get lifted up—the noise, the creaking; how long—similarly thickly—like a noisy wall! The screech of seagulls—black and white spots—the line of their flight

Extended these fields—to man

With his appearance /O/ "the golden section" / with his laughter—his crying—his speech /U/ and to oneself /T = bodily sensation/

A thousand rhythms!

And their emotional undertow!

This emotional undertow is a sort of bridge, along which the stimulus goes to its connection with sound—to composition.

I stood on the bank of the Vltava. A hole cut in the ice. In it a fisherman with a rod in his hand is reflected in the white snow. Dusk towards four o'clock. Biting cold, ice blown over with snow: *expectation*.

All this flashes past in one's head—so that I don't know what sparks off the real sound!

Janáček went on to analyze the effect of external circumstances on what he called the internal circumstance of the creative artist. He included in this concept

> "the sequences of all things perceived" or, "superficially all consciousness. All that falls into it—even if unnoticed—dissolves, sums up, mixes with, suppresses, flows out of or disappears—but never gets lost completely ... were it to be forgotten forever the serious, emotional part would also fall away. Untruth."

After this detour into Janáček's theory, let us return to the symphony. Janáček must have still sensed some gaps in its conception, which was on a large scale, and may not have been supported by adequate emotional engagement. The short stretch of the Danube which he saw from the Bratislava embankment, was not enough to inspire a large symphonic composition. Thus he wrote to Ostričil that " 'Our' Danube is not so tempting", and thus he wanted to "experience" the river fully with his own senses. But in the last years of his life Janáček was assailed by subjects which he experienced deeply, and which were immediately transformed into rhythms and notes. In order to write everything that he still had to write, there was no time for the Danube excursion, and Janáček never found the time to return to the composition which had become blocked. The symphony, completed only as a preliminary sketch, was never authorized by the composer and remained at the most only interesting evidence of Janáček's unending creative struggle to fill out a large-scale symphonic form.

Janáček's "Danube": Some Notes on the Montage of the Symphony by the Composer and on its Reconstruction from an Autograph Draft

Miloš Štědroň

Miloš Štědroň is a leading figure in the Czech music world. A composer of some distinction, he is also an expert on 17th century music, especially the works of Monteverdi. His contributions to Janáček research are numerous and involve analysis, archival work, and humanistic interpretation. In this essay he discusses the reconstruction of "The Danube" Symphony.

1. Janáček's Montage

Before I touch on the problematic questions of the reconstruction of "The Danube" Symphony I should like to explain in condensed form how I understand Janáček's montage. When I came up with the "montage conception" of Janáček's creative method 20 years ago, the term was not attractive to the older generation of theoreticians and musicologists. Far from it. Very often I was told that Janáček was not a "monteur." Now, however, I reproach myself for not having stuck firmly enough to my conception of Janáček's montage. In the meantime many articles and books have appeared, whose authors I find myself in sympathy with, for they have arrive at views similar to mine, although perhaps not always in connection with Janáček's music.

Janáček composed in layers that were related to his conception of time and density. This method taken by itself is very closed to that of the montage, in the sense introduced into the arts by the technology of the cinema and theatre. Eisenstein's montage could already be found in music as early as the turn of the 20th century in the form of a technique for the gradual linking and combining of layers. The openness of Janáček's method was due to the character of his work with the material.

---

[1] Editor's note: Here Štědroň is referring to Janáček's concept of *sčasování*. Although Janáček used the word in sometimes contradictory ways, its basic sense is "the way events unfold in time." The derivative "sčasovka" denotes a concrete rhythmic utterance, created by making selections from different rhythmic layers.

The montage was an open-ended process which could be taken up again and again. The composer implanted layers into the "finished" scores already being copied by the copyist, and the process was not finished even during the performance itself and after. The idea of different timing layers can be conceived of as an idea of different kinds of density.[1] Janáček is very concise in his message. His layers tend more towards simple heterophony than towards filling in the sound space. These days the importance of heterophony is growing due to the compository techniques of the seventies and eighties, whereas in the middle and late periods of Janáček's work this problem looked quite different in many situations. Contrastive and sonically antithetical layers very often have a polyrhythmical or even polymetrical effect. Janáček usually made use of this simple stratification as a contrast in the closing parts of the motifs, while the motif was disintegrating (as, for example, *From the House of the Dead*). The repetition of the timing-tunes contributes to their harmonic importance. I consider them colors or rhythmic ostinatos. This is Janáček's point of contact with the Impressionists. Genetically, his path of development had been quite different, to be sure: compared with Debussy's isolated chords, his timing tunes developed in a different way, from folk music and its persistent ostinato.

These isolated static chords, which often tend towards quartal, second-quartal or quintal structuration, became, above all, a new sonic quality. This aspect is emphasized by the montage character of Janáček's tectonics, too. In saying this, I do not want to argue that the significance of the center, key and tonality becomes weaker in Janáček. Nevertheless, the tectonics and form take on another dimension, and it is possible to observe a freer re-grouping of nuclei taking place, which gives the impression that Janáček frees himself from the traditional relations of harmony. All in all, it is no more than a masterly exploitation of rhythm, shift, heterophony and manipulation of density. Besides his strong and impressive harmony, Janáček exploits the system of chords (quartal- and quintal-chords), which either constitutes a special sphere, and then is impressive mainly owing to its novelty, primarily in the sonic aspect, or is integrated in a contrastive way into the traditional harmony, from which it is effectively set off in both extreme cases.

I have tried to expound briefly and concisely which aspects, in our opinion, represent the main phenomena of Janáček's montage. After this rather generally conceived introduction, I am now going to concentrate on several problems relating to the reconstruction of "The Danube" Symphony.

A: The number of movements of the Symphony and their sequence

The autograph draft at our disposal has four movements. They are numbered by Roman numerals; it is obvious, however, that the numerals have been re-written. The designations of time and expressions are not helpful because they are mostly absent. According to the general principles of editing, the composer's last version is decisive, so the score should be without problems in this respect. The numerals I, II and III are written in Janáček's own hand; the first page of the fourth movement (the reconstruction of which we shall comment on presently) is missing.

Example 1. (first page of the" Danube" Symphony)

Nevertheless, immediately after Janáček's death, when the score left on the composer's desk during the registration of Janáček's posthumous papers, Ludvik Kundera referred to the opening of another unknown part which we did not have at our disposal. The final movement has its catharsis, no doubt, but its fast closing part with rather modest instrumentation gives evidence for the supposition that the Author would have applied a sort of intensification, which he really did in many other cases. Otakar Trhlk (the conductor who asked for the reconstruction and who was its first performer) went to the extent of transposing the sequence of movements and used Janáček's third movement as the final one. This movement is in the nature of a scherzo, but in spite of this the conductor considered the movement more suitable for closing the musical whole. I mention these circumstances in order to stress that the sequence of movements does not create the impression of unchangeability and necessity, especially in the case or the last ones. Describing Janáček's posthumous papers, Kundera also registered a motif which, in his opinion, is a part of the first movement. This is missing now, so the first movement is a fragment. Even if Kundera associated the unknown part X with the first movement by error, we are deprived of it. It may possibly have been lost together with the first page of the fourth movement.

B: The missing introductory page of the fourth movement and its reconstruction

At first it seemed that the loss of one page might be very awkward, because the opening of the movement is unknown to us. Later, however, we realized that we could overcome this loss with the aid of Kundera's description of the opening in the article on Janáček's compository legacy.

Example 2. Kundera's Testimony

Způsob práce ve všech pozůstalých skladbách je týž jako v posledních orkestrálních dílech mistrových: několik motivů nemnoho obměňovaných a neustále opakovaných.

Ludvík Kundera.

The opening was sufficient and, together with the bar of the first bar of page two (which is preserved), it gave us a good basis for determining the movement's instrumentation and repetition.

Example 3.

C:

Differentiating between two systems when one appears above the other in the score, is not always an easy task, especially if the designation of instruments and key are missing at some places. I should like to demonstrate this kind of situation by an example on page 2–3 where the bar lines in the two systems, one above the other, correspond.

Example 4.

It is no exception that in his autograph drafts Janáček designated in this rather enigmatic way the circumstance that the new page was the result of a contraction of the two preceding ones, i.e., the result of a process of elimination; such extensive elimination are very frequent, sf. pp. 13–18. In the first system four flutes, oboes, a cor anglais, four French horns and a tuba are playing; in the second system, strings "pp con sordino." Therefore the suspicion arose that two score pages with incidentally identical bars are at issue.

D:

It is evident that the closing part of the first movement is unfinished. In Janáček it is not common to finish with a single and even harmonic layer.

Example 5.

E:

The timpani in the second movement have been drafted by Janáček in chordal sequences which could only have been performed in the twenties with the utmost difficulties and with many instruments and players taking part. The performers wanted to preserve the only and typical harmony, and for this reason we intensified the chordal contour of the sequences with the help of trombones.

F:

Example 6a.

Example 6b.

The viola d'amore as a sonic phenomenon in Janáček has been investigated separately by John Tyrrell.[2] We should only like to say that the short solo in the second movement does not present any problems for performance. The same applies to the high-pitched imitation passages in the third movement, where Janáček himself cast doubts on their interpretation with his own note "a cello would be better."

[2] John Tyrrell, *Leoš Janáček: Kat'a Kabanová* (Cambridge: Cambridge Univ. Press, 1982), pp. 154–161 ("Janáček and the Viola d'Amore").

Example 7a.

The real problem is the solo viola d'amore part in the fourth movement. The instrument has been placed in contrast to the strings with octave runs of extreme difficulty, which very probably cannot be played on a single instrument. (Example 7b)

Example 7b.

G:

"Song Solo Oboe" is Janáček designation of the melodic part, sung to the accompaniment of "echo" imitations on the viola d'amore or either cello or flute. We have fully respected the connection of the oboe and the human voice singing the vowel "A" (Janáček added the letter to the score in pencil). The "Song" is one of the most outstanding timbres of the composition and makes it a vocal symphony *sui generis*.

Example 8.

H:

In any possible later versions of the closing part of the fourth movement the development would undoubtedly have resulted in more extensive exploitation of the factura [sic?] tutti. After the dialogue between the viola d'amore, conceived as a solo, and the strings, the beginning of the orchestral block would be problematic as well as surprising, so far we have not made use of it.

Example 9.

Is "The Danube" Symphony an incomplete autograph draft and are we entitled to reconstruct it? So far there have been two answers to this: O. Chlubna's endeavour is the first and our reconstruction the second.

"The Danube" was nearly completed. It is possible that as early as 1928, after finishing the opera *From the House of the Dead*, Janáček would have continued work on the piece. Perhaps it would have taken the form of the sonic reinforcement of the score, which usually occurred during the process of copying; perhaps some more substantial interventions into the musical logic of the work would have taken place. We are aware of the incomplete nature of some places which would have been finished and perfected by Janáček's original method of montage.

In spite of these problems we consider "The Danube" a remarkable manifestation of Janáček's musical thought in the twenties, some of the unique methods and procedures of which should not be forgotten, especially since we do not know any counterparts to them in his masterpieces.

Leoš Janáček's "Danube" Symphony—Original and Chlubna Versions

Jakob Knaus

Jakob Knaus has been a pioneer in Janáček studies outside of Czechoslovakia. In addition to his role as President of the Janáček Society in Switzerland, he has published several important collections of letters and essays. Here, he turns his attention to two main elements: the numerous differences between the Chlubna and Štědroň versions of the symphony, and the relationship between Janáček, the Danube River, and the women, poetic and otherwise, who he associated with it.

The *Sinfonietta* by Leoš Janáček, written in 1926, is well-known, and we are sure that it was intended in this extraordinary way:

Sinfonietta, Beginning 0'30"

Frantisek Jílek/ Brno Philharmonic Orchestra (1986)

♩ = 63 (1st movement 2'11")

Thirty years ago, however, it was still performed like this:

Sinfonietta, Beginning 0'45"

Jascha Horenstein / Pro Musica Symphony Orchestra Vienna (1955)

♩ = 40 (1st movement 3'27")

Such differences of approach would be impossible now in the case of the *Sinfonietta*. But the same problem (just a little bit more complicated) arises with Janáček's "Danube" Symphony the original title of which is "Dunaj." Janáček first conceived this symphony shortly before the *Sinfonietta* in 1925 and almost finished it, leaving it nearly ready for performance. The third movement of this four-movement symphony may sound in two different ways, both based on autograph sketches:

"Danube," 3rd movement, beginning (Štědroň version) 1'20"

Libor Pešek / Slovak Philharmonic HK Marco Polo 8.220362
with Soprano solo (see Music 12)

"Danube," 3rd movement, beginning (Chlubna version) 1'10"

Jiří Waldhans / Brno Philharmonic Orchestra Prague Radio
with violin solo and castanets!

Both times the first example belonged to the reconstructed version by Miloš Štědroň and Leoš Faltus, the two Czechoslovakian musicologists from Brno—the second example was taken from the version by Osvald Chlubna, who, in 1948, made a performing edition for a broadcast in Brno. But here there are such immense differences to the original score that this is rather an adaptation or an arrangement. The differences are greater than those between Moussorgsky's original "Boris" and the version by Rimsky-Korsakov. Chlubna claimed that Janáček wrote a letter to Otakar Ostrčil, the opera intendant in Prague, in August 1926: "Neni ten "naš" Dunaj lákavý, abych chvátal svuj dunaj zakončit!" (Our Danube is not so tempting that I should be in a hurry to finish the Danube!) Still, three movements may be considered finished, the fourth part remained unfinished—and no reconstruction can change this fact.

I will now try to explain why Janáček might have put away the score as unfinished. The beginning of the first movement is typical of Janáček as we know him from his works of his last ten years: a rising fourth and a rising second—you remember the music of his opera *The Cunning Little Vixen*.

Example 1. "Danube," 1st movement, beginning (Štědroň version) 0'45"

The music of the first movement is less compact than the beginning of the *Sinfonietta*, for example. The treatment of the motivic material is less consistent. Janáček, in the *Sinfonietta*, gets a lot of variants from two motives by splitting them up and altering them and then by regrouping them establishing new relationships between them. Here, in "The Danube" Symphony, he quickly introduces a new motive which then functions as a ostinato formula or as a short insert. Still, this first movement is the most consistent. For instance, here he combines two bars changing their order:

Example 2.

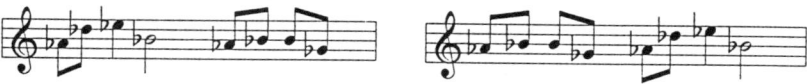

Nevertheless, he soon inserts a contrasting bar group which connects two versions of the same motive but sounds somewhat isolated and unfunctional. In the *Sinfonietta* Janáček would have gained an ostinato figure from this, or he would have chosen only one motive and split an ostinato figure from it, as a mono-thematic tendency shows in a lot of his works.

The second movement contains a great solo for kettle drums—something Janáček always liked to do. He provides for four pairs of kettle drums playing chords, whose extended rolls produce a menacing mood. (We may remember here the third movement of the Berlioz *Symphonie Fantastique* or his *Requiem*—and Janáček himself used the kettle drums as solo instruments in *Taras Bulba*, in his opera *Katya Kabanová* and in his *Glagolitic Mass*.)

In the "Danube" Symphony—in bars 106 to 147 of the third movement—he works with a staccato sequence behind which may be a speech melody taken from a line of poetry:

Example 3.

At this point it is necessary to mention the two poems which inspired Janáček in some way: "Útonula" (The Drowned Girl) by Pavla Kříčková and "Lola" by Alexander Insarov. Janáček had found these two poems—like many of his other inspirations—in his favorite newspaper *Lidové noviny* (*People's Newspaper*).

The first poem describes a bathing girl. Hidden in the bushes a boy, a stranger, discovers her. Ashamed of her naked body she jumps into the pond. The poem "Lola" by Insarov is about a young prostitute. First she wishes for a palace—this is fulfilled in the first stanza. In the second stanza she looks for it in vain and in the third she is no longer desired by anybody. She feels cold and only wishes a warm stove.

To this poem Janáček added a curious but typical hand-written appendix: ". . . jumps into the Danube . . ."—the open ending in the Insarov poem is completed in an abrupt way. Already twenty years before he had composed "Maryčka Magdonov," a ballad for male choir on a text by Petr Bezruč, containing a great deal of social criticism. There the title figure escapes the law (or better: she saves her soul) with a jump into a river—into the Ostravice. Katya Kabanová also jumps into a river—into the Volga.

In this "Danube" symphony Janáček does not intend any nature painting—for him and for all the Slavonic peoples of the southern region, that is for the Moravians, the Slovaks, but also for the Russians in the Ukraine, the river Danube has a mystical aura. And in many popular texts the river Danube brings death. And moreover: the word "Dunaj" (Danube) is in the Slavonic languages of masculine gender, whereas it is feminine in German.

And another point: at the same time Janáček was occupied with his opera *The Makropulos Case*—the common feature: compassion for the title figure—Elina Makropulos, the 300-year-old singer who cannot die. And as the subtitle of his first String Quartet (1923) and his letters tell us it was again compassion for the tormented woman in Tolstoy's "Kreutzer Sonata" that triggered his work. So we are not astonished to find pity for a woman as the subject of the "Danube" Symphony. This even finds expression in a speech melody, as for example in the second movement:

Example 4.

Ach je to sot-va ho-di-nu, co vi-del ta-dy div - ci - nu

And now, the girl in Pavla Křičková's poem "Útonula" is dead. The speech melody of the Czech phrase "Ach je to sotva hodinu co viděl tady divčinu" shapes the four-bar motive. It is not the descending second that shapes the motive, but the rhythmical contrast between the aggressively hammering falling motive and the repeated eighth notes that characterize this passage. The four-bar speech melody is to be considered therefore as a variant of the descending motive:

Example 5. "Danube," 2nd movement, bar 109ff

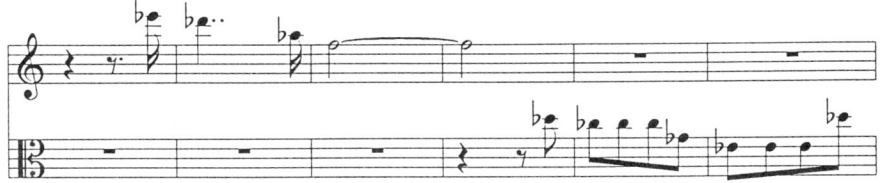

If we compare this with the third movement of the *Sinfonietta*, where we find similar motives in competition, we realize that Janáček works here far less consistently.

In the third movement, from which you have already heard an example, a high soprano sings a vocalize ringing up to top E:

Example 6. "Danube," 3rd movement, bar 77ff

Lola, the prostitute, is in the center—her first triumphant gesture at the first entry of the soprano gives way to naked fright, and—in a trill, to despair. Two beats of the full orchestra express her tragic end. "Yesterday, on the first of October 1924, I had the idea, that Insarov's Lola will drown in the Danube. And one day, perhaps in 1925, this work will ripen in my relieved heart like a fruit in the sun."

But he never finished the work. The final bars are sketched. Osvald Chlubna turned the movement into some sort of pomp and circumstance. His alterations are so far-reaching that we cannot speak of a reconstruction—it is an arrangement.

Example 7. Final bars in the Chlubna version, 25 bars

In the original score the ending sounds rather casual. And this might be a reason why Janáček put away the unfinished work and turned to others, like the *Sinfonietta* and the opera *The Makropulos Case*. So we may say, Janáček ended this work, but he did not really finish it.

Example 8. Final bars in original score (Štědroň version) 12 bars

The Vocalise in Janáček's "Danube" Symphony

Peter Susskind

We were indeed fortunate to have two conductors speak at our session on the "Danube Symphony." The first, of course, was Leonard Slatkin, but more detailed remarks were also made by Peter Susskind, formerly Assistant Conductor of the Saint Louis Symphony Orchestra, and now music director and conductor of the South Bay Youth Orchestra. In this study, Susskind tries to make sense of the enchanting yet enigmatic vocalise which occurs in the third movement of the work, by putting it into a larger historical, programmatic and musical context.

The vocalise traces its history to the training of the voice. There are innumerable examples in the works of early Italian and French composers for the voice. Some of these are purely technical exercises, indeed some are fearsomely difficult, some have a more expressive function.

But if one thinks carefully about the nature of vocal and choral lines, the vocalise, if not in name, was also used by the great composers for the voice as a means of extra expression. A long melisma on a single syllable of a word is in its nature on one vowel. This is very similar to what we think of as a vocalise. One just has to consider the solo and choral melodies of Bach and Handel to be able to bring to mind instantly wonderful melodic spans which are entirely wordless. Nominally they are of course means of heightening the expressive message of the given text, but in fact they are wordless melodic lines. Think for instance of the very first recitative from the *St. Matthew Passion* on the word *crucified* or, to express a completely different emotion, the ferocity of the *Messiah* aria "Why Do the Nations So Furiously Rage Together?" and the seemingly endless triplets on the vowel 'a' from the word *rage*. On a slightly frivolous note, I can't help reminding you of the wonderful quintet from Act I of *The Magic Flute* where Papageno's complete opening statement is perforce wordless. There are of course numerous more serious examples throughout the operatic literature, including the Queen of the Night's celebrated aria also from *The Magic Flute*.

Bearing in mind then, these two types of wordless vocal lines, we must now consider the vocalise proper—namely a complete work for performance which is neither a vocal training exercise nor a momentary excerpt from an aria or chorus. The famous vocalise by Rachmaninov would be the obvious example from the solo repertoire but there are notable examples from the symphonic repertoire as well. The wordless choruses in Ravel's *Daphnis and Chloë*, in Debussy's *Nocturnes*, in Vaughan Williams' *Sinfonia Antartica* and in Holst's *Planets* come to mind. One has to think long and hard, however, to find an example of a totally wordless section for solo voice and orchestra. Vaughan Williams' *Third Symphony*, Nielsen's *Third Symphony* and the *Concerto for Coloratura Soprano* by Glière are among the most important works in this category. And it is this exceptionally rare and unusual sound that makes this movement such a breathtaking surprise when it comes in Janáček's "The Danube." Even for listeners familiar with Janáček's operas, choral and vocal works, the sound of a high soprano adding a completely unexpected color and certainly a very puzzling new mood to this symphonic work comes as something of a shock. And yet, when one thinks of other purely orchestral works by Janáček, the conception of a vocal line becomes less strange. After all, the three wonderful symphonic poems are all based on literary works—*The Fiddler's Child* subtitled *Ballad for Orchestra*, *Taras Bulba* from Gogol's novel and *The Ballad of Blaník*. So the notion of telling a story by purely instrumental means was quite natural to Janáček. It is one small step then to use the voice as an extra orchestral color. It would be tidy to feel that this comfortable notion ties up all of our thoughts about the mysterious vocal line in the third movement of this altogether rather enigmatic "The Danube." But one cannot help feeling that there must be something more than simply the use of an additional tone color to the choice of a female voice, particularly in such close conjunction with the *viola d'amore*. Usually when a vocal part is unexpectedly added to an instrumental work the text gives us the clue as to its meaning—Mahler's Fourth Symphony and Schoenberg's Second String Quartet come immediately to my mind in this context. But with "The Danube" Symphony we are left on our own to puzzle out the significance.

Much has been written about the possible themes and ideas absorbing Janáček as he wrote this work. The ones that seem relevant to this discussion are the notions of Nature as depicted by the female voice, the content of the two poems found with the manuscript (one about Lola, a prostitute and the other called *The Drowned Girl*) and lastly, some more general expression of his passion for Kamila Stösslová. Are any or all of these to be found in the substance of the music?

This third movement certainly starts joyfully enough with a feeling of serenity and peace with the world and nature, but even before the voice enters there is a slightly menacing motif from the violins. This orchestral introduction does seem to suggest some sort of expression of Janáček's love of Nature. When the voice enters it is immediately answered by Janáček's beloved *viola d'amore*. We know that this instrument had a very special significance for him and I find it hard to believe that he would associate this intensely personal instrument with Lola the prostitute. We might theorize then that he is leading us to thoughts about Kamila or possibly about the unfortunate protagonist of *The Drowned Girl*. At this point there is a dialogue between voice and *viola d'amore*. The serene mood is temporarily recaptured but with the sudden *meno mosso*, a more plaintive quality is introduced. The sound of the oboe, in particular, which until now has doubled the voice throughout, is revealed at this point in a much more transparent texture. Janáček is able with a subtle change of instrumentation to suggest considerably more agitation in the succeeding *più mosso*. The bassoons with contra and the cello and bass pizzicato lend a feeling of greater urgency which in turn seems to develop into near desperation as the voice is forced up to the high E in the next *più mosso*. Still the *viola d'amore* follows the singer until just before the final *meno mosso* where the instrument temporarily takes the lead—in a way, guiding the listener to this most melancholy passage in the movement. However dissatisfied Janáček may have been with the work—and we have the famous remark, "This Danube of ours is not sufficiently attractive to make me want to hurry up and finish it"—this wonderful passage with this flute and harp figuration is clearly the work of the master. Curiously, this is also the moment where Janáček chooses to have the *viola d'amore* actually double the vocal line pretty well consistently to the end of the movement. So what does it all mean?

It is tempting to construct one's own scenario. One could suggest a fanciful plot line where the composer leads us from his personal love of Nature to the relationship with Kamila, with its undertones of regret and nostalgia (the age difference and the fact that she was already married, as indeed he was, must play some part here!); the emotion becoming ever more strained and agitated with the dialogue between composer and beloved eventually leading to a unison statement and ending in some kind of forceful denouement. Another possibility is Vogel's somewhat vague hypothesis[1] that this movement "represents Vienna."

[1] Jaroslav Vogel, *Leoš Janáček: His Life and Works*, trans. Geraldine Thomsen-Muchová (London: Paul Hamlyn, 1962).

Yet another possibility is *The Drowned Girl* poem where the innocent girl, preparing to bathe naked in the river, is startled by the surreptitious onlooker, with her desperate running and leaping into the river represented by the *accelerando* to the end of this movement.

As ever, when we start to fantasize in this way we tend to put the music into the background. This may not be the greatest movement Janáček ever wrote, and indeed the whole work lacks the inevitability of his greatest pieces but there can be no doubt that this music is by Janáček—the fingerprints are all there, and as with all his mature works the style is unmistakable. I hope that by raising some of these questions we may listen even more carefully to the music itself. Ultimately, it is of course entirely irrelevant what Janáček had in mind when he used the wordless vocal line with its *viola d'amore* accompaniment, if indeed he had anything other than purely musical thoughts. With Janáček there so often seems to be some extra-musical content and it has been argued with some justification, I think, that in this case there may actually be too much programmatic "baggage" attached to the work. It may even be true that this excess "baggage," so to speak, was one of the reasons why he had problems finishing the piece. As a performing musician, however, I think of two quotations by great composers whenever literary programmes are forcibly attached to music, the first from Mozart's letters:

> My very dearest Papa! — I cannot write poetically, for I am no poet. I cannot artfully arrange my phrases so as to give light and shade. Neither am I a painter; nor can I even express my thoughts by gesture and pantomime, for I am no dancer. But I can do so in sounds. I am a musician.

The other is Mendelssohn's unforgettable aphorism, "The meaning of music is too precise for words." Needless to say, these *bon mots* do not preclude the possibility of extra-musical content being perfectly relevant to certain works, and "The Danube" Symphony is surely a prime contender here. They do, however, put into perspective, I feel, the obsession which occasionally attacks some of us to overlay perfectly wonderful, self-sufficient music with literary or philosophical themes.

What is important here, I feel, is that a fascinating work by one of this century's most original geniuses, which has not been heard frequently until now, is being discussed and listened to with new and serious concentration.

Part 7:

Janáček: Past, Present and Future

The last series of essays comprises material from three different conference sessions and tried to present several types of studies dealing with the way Janáček has been, and is, perceived. Thus we have a largely bibliographic study by Jaroslav Mráček followed by three essays of a general, searching nature, which attempt to come to grips with the phenomenon of Janáček on the broadest possible plane.

The Reception of Leoš Janáček as seen through a Study of the Bibliography: A Preliminary Report

Jaroslav Mráček

Jaroslav Mráček has been most influential in the creation of the new field of Czech and Slovak music studies in the United States. His "Smetana Centennial Conference" of 1984, which as already been noted several times in this volume, has become a model for subsequent conferences on Janáček, Dvořák, and Martinů, and his Friends of Czechoslovak Music has played an important role in promoting musical and intellectual activities. In addition to his work on Rorate chant, Jan Löwenbach, Smetana, and Canadian music, he is also a Janáček bibliographer, and in this essay he outlines the main contributions to Janáček studies.

This paper may be considered a brief introduction to a larger project, namely a research manual and bibliography about Leoš Janáček.[1] An attempt will be made to demonstrate the impact which his music has had on the world outside his native Czechoslovakia since his death sixty years ago. It is beyond the scope of this paper to present a complete presentation of all the research which has taken place. The citations will of necessity be very selective.

Prior to the premiere of *Jenůfa* in 1904, Janáček first became known as a musician from Moravia with an enthusiasm for the classics, for the new music of his day, and for the folk music of his native Moravia. In the first bibliographic citations, he appears along with his mentor and colleague František Bartos, with whom he began in 1888 the systematic collection of Moravian folksongs and dances. Their first collaboration was the *Národní písně moravské v nově nasbirané* (Moravian folksongs newly collected), first published in 1899. Earlier in 1884, Janáček had founded and edited a music periodical, *Hudební listy* (Musical Letters), which published reviews and notes on musical events in Brno. Leoš Firkušný, in 1935, published Janáček's reviews which appeared in

---

[1]The author is preparing *Leoš Janáček: A Guide to Research* for Garland Publishing Inc., New York.

Hudební listy between 1884 and 1888. Throughout his life, Janáček continued to contribute articles to many newspapers.[2] The two theoretical texts, *O skladbě souzvukův a jejich spojův* (The composition of chords and their connections),[3] and *Návod pro vyučování zpěvu* (A manual for teaching singing), were published in Prague in 1897 and Brno in 1899 respectively. One of Janáček's articles, "Pavla Křižkovského význam v lidové hudbě moravské a v české hudbě vubec" (Křizkovsky's role in Moravian folk music and Czech music generally), honoring his teacher, appeared in *Český lid* in 1902. By 1912, he had published his *Úplna nauka o harmonii* (A Complete harmony manual).[4] Other collections of his writings have been edited by Bohumír Štědroň, Jan Racek, Theodora Straková, Jiří Vysloužil, and others.

By 1904, the year of the premiere in Brno of *Její pastorkyňa* (Her foster daughter; Jenůfa), he had written two operas, a folk ballet, numerous choruses for men's women's and mixed voices, and many arrangements of folksongs. In spite of Dvořák's support until his death, Janáček remained a regional composer.

The struggle for acceptance continued after the Brno premiere. National and international recognition was not forthcoming until the performances of *Jenůfa* in Prague in 1916 and Vienna in 1918. As Charles Susskind observed in his recently published *Janáček and Brod*,[5] credit for establishing Janáček's fame abroad rests with Max Brod, the Prague-born German writer and friend of Franz Kafka and Franz Werfel. The composer Josef Suk had urged Brod to attend the Prague performances of *Jenůfa*. Brod's review for the Berlin theatrical weekly, *Schaubühne*, appeared on 15 November 1916 and was reprinted immediately in Czech in Prague and Brno. The means were at hand for Janáček's acceptance on the international scene. Max Brod became the chief collaborator who provided translations for *Jenůfa* and all the succeeding operas except the *Excursions of Mr. Brouček*. Susskind believes it was Jan Löwenbach, the Czech music critic and copyright attorney, who first suggested the translation of *Jenůfa* to Brod.[6] Susskind gives considerable detail about the Vienna premiere which took place on 16 February 1918. Some of the sources are preserved in the

---

[2]Jan Racek, Arn Novák, Vladimír Helfert, and Leoš Firkušný, *Fejtony z "Lidových Novin"* (Brno: Krajske nakladatelstvi, 1958).

[3]Leoš Janáček, *O skladbě souzvukův a jejich spojův* (Prague, 1897); ed. in *Hudebně teoretické dílo, 1* (1968): 183–296.

[4]2nd ed., 1920; ed. in *Hudebně teoretické dílo*, 2 (1974): 169–328.

[5]Charles Susskind, *Janáček and Brod* (New Haven: Yale University Press, 1985), pp. 40ff.

[6]Ibid., pp. 42ff.

Löwenbach Collection at San Diego State University. Brod also wrote the first biography of Janáček. The Vienna premiere was followed by other German performances in Cologne on 16 November, 1918, conducted by Otto Klemperer. Many other performances of *Jenůfa* followed. The Vienna premiere also led to a publishing agreement with Universal Edition for the score of *Jenůfa* and subsequent works, with translations by Brod. A collection of Brod's writings from this period including his reviews of *Jenůfa* were printed in 1923, *Sternenhimmel: Musik-und Theaterlebnisse*, and translated into Czech as *Pražské hvězdné nebé* (Stars in Prague's heaven) in 1989.[7] Also, he wrote the first biography of Janáček in 1924.[8]

Czech music had become popular and accepted in England during the nineteenth century largely due to Dvořák's visits. Just as Janáček's fame was spread in Germany largely through the writing of Brod, so too his cause was taken up in England by the distinguished critic and Russophil Rosa Newmarch. In 1919, the Prague National Theatre Orchestra under Karel Kovařovic and the Moravian Teachers' Choir performed in London as part of a Czechoslovak music festival. Rosa Newmarch had been instrumental in publicizing the tour of Britain. She first visited Prague and Moravia in the summer of 1919 at the invitation of Kovařovic. On her return to England, she arranged for a visit of Janáček to London in April and May of 1926. One of her earliest articles about Janáček, "Leoš Janáček and Moravian Music Drama," appeared in the *Slavonic Review* in 1922. She continued to champion Janáček's music and write reviews of his works as they were premiered in England. The friendship and collaboration between Janáček and Newmarch is preserved in the letters they exchanged and in some of the personal papers and articles of Rosa Newmarch recently published by Zdeňka E. Fischmann, the *Janáček—Newmarch Correspondence*.[9] Besides the translations of Janáček's letters, Fischmann has produced a very well-documented account of the period, roughly from 1919 to 1931.

Janáček's success continued to grow during this last period of his life. After very successful performances of *Jenůfa* in Berlin and at the Metropolitan Opera in New York in 1924, the opera continued to be performed in its German edition, much as Smetana's *The Bartered Bride*

---

[7]German ed., (Munich: Kurt Wolff Verlag, 1923); Czech trans., B. Fučik (Praha: Editio Supraphon, 1969).

[8]Czech ed., trans. by A. Fuchs: Max Brod, *Leoš Janáček: Život a dílo* (Prague: Hudební matice Unělecké Besedy, 1924); id., *Leoš Janáček: Leben und Werk* (Vienna: Wiener Philharmonisher Verlag, 1925); rev. German ed. (Vienna: Universal, 1956).

[9]Zdeňka E. Fischmann, *Janáček—Newmarch Correspondence* (Rockville MD: Kabel Publishers, 1986).

had earlier entered the international repertoire. Before his death in 1928, Janáček's opera *Kátya Kabanová*, the song cycle *The Diary of One Who Vanished*, the *Sinfonietta*, and several other of his late works attained international stature. Several writers besides Brod began writing about Janáček before his death. Osvald Chlubna, composer and pupil of Janáček, was one of the first Czechs to write about Janáček: his orchestration and theoretical teachings (1924–25),[10] the opera *From the House of the Dead* (1929–30),[11] the study "Neznáme poslední dílo Janáčka *Dunaj*" (An unknown last work, Dunaj),[12] and other articles. Jan Mikota, Janáček's secretary, wrote "Leoš Janáček v Anglii" (Leoš Janáček in England) in *Listy hudební matice*, 1926. The writer and editor Adolf Veselý wrote many articles about Janáček and collaborated with him in the compilation of the sborník, *Leoš Janáček: Pohled do života a díla* (Leoš Janáček: a survey of his life and work), published in Prague in 1924. Rosa Newmarch authored the Janáček article for the third edition of the *Grove's Dictionary* (1927), and later the fourth edition (1940).

After Janáček's death on 12 August 1928, the world reacted to the loss of this remarkable creative genius with tributes and performances of his works. The Second String Quartet was first played on 11 September 1928. His almost completed opera, *Z mrtvého domu* was premiered in Brno on 12 April 1930. Numerous articles and books appeared in tribute: obituaries by Newmarch, in *The Chesterian*, 1928, *Musical Times*, 1928, and the *Slavonic Review*, 1929. In 1929 Hans Hollander wrote, "Leoš Janáček and his Operas," for the *Musical Quarterly*. In 1930 the books *Leoš Janáček*, by Daniel Muller, and *Po stopách dra Leoše Janáčka* (In the footsteps of Dr. Leoš Janáček) by Adolf E. Vašek appeared. The International Society for Contemporary Music, meeting in Geneva in 1929, paid special tribute to his memory.

In 1934, a Janáček Society was established in Brno to promote his works. The Janáček Archive was founded in Brno and a series of publications were undertaken beginning with the letters of Janáček and various individuals. The first volume appeared in 1934 containing correspondence between Janáček and the first editor, Artuš Rektorys. The series was later taken over by Jan Racek. Bohumír Štědroň wrote "Leoš

---

[10]Osvald Chlubna, "Janáčkova orchestrace," *Hudební rozhledy*, 1 (1924–25): 45; "Teoretické učeni Leoše Janáčka" (Janáček's Theoretical Teachings), ibid., 57, 77, 114.
[11]Chlubna, "Z mrtvého domu," *Divadelní list Národního divadla v Brne* 5 (1929–1930).
[12]*Hudební rozhledy*, 7 (1931–32): 302.

Janáček na mužskem učitelském ústavě v Brně" (Janáček at the men's teachers' institute in Brno) for the magazine *Tempo*.[13] In 1934 the young musicologist Leoš Firkušný completed his dissertation on Janáček under the guidance of Vladimír Helfert.[14] The following year he wrote about Janáček as music critic of the operas in Brno.[15] Janáček's wife, Zdeňka Janáčkova, wrote a manuscript, "Můj život" (My life) in 1936. In 1937 Firkušný wrote about Janáček's last opera, *From the House of the Dead*.[16] In 1938, ten years after Janáček's death, the 1935 Ph.D. dissertation (Brno) of Hyněk Kašlík, *Retuše Karla Kovařovice v Janáčkově opeře "Její Pastorkyňa"* (Kovařovic's revisions in Janáček's *Jenůfa*) was published in Prague. In that year, Otakar Jeremiáš published a biography, and Jan Racek his *Leoš Janáček: poznámky k tvurčímu profilu* (Remarks on Janáček's creative image). In the fateful year of 1939, there were publications by Vladimír Helfert, Leoš Firkušný, and Bohumír Štědroň.[17] Contributing to his English reputation, Wilfred Mellers wrote "[Janáček:] A great Czech Composer."[18]

The outbreak of World War II interrupted plans for the performances in England of Janáček's and other Czech operas, such as Dvořák's *Rusalka*. As has been observed in the literature, Rosa Newmarch never lived to hear Janáček's operas performed in her own country. Limited performances of his chamber music did continue to take place in Czechoslovakia, as Zdeňka Pilková has demonstrated in her article and catalogue.[19] On 26 March 1940, Miloš Sádlo played the *Pohádka*; Ilja Hurník, on 4 February 1941, played selections from *Po zarostlém chodníčku*; on 23 April 1941, Ivan Vectomov repeated *Pohádka*; on 29 September 1942, the *Sonata pro housle a klavír* was played (performers not specified); Ludvík Kundera performed *V mlhách* on 5 October 1943; on 23 November 1943, František Smetana arranged and played *Lístek odvanuty*; and on 18 January 1944, the

---

[13]*Tempo*, 13 (1933–34): 315.
[14]Leoš Firkušný, "Vliv lidové hudby lašské a valašské na skladatel. rust Leoše Janáčka."
[15]Leoš Firkušný, *Leoš Janáček, kritikem Brněnské opery* (Brno: Pazdirek, 1935).
[16]Leoš Firkušný, "Poslední Janáčkova opera, Z mrtvého domu," *Divadelní list [Národního divadla] v Brně* 12 (1937).
[17]Vladimír Helfert, *Leoš Janáček*, 1 (Brno: Pazdirek, 1939); Leoš Firkušný, *Leoš Janáček a Brněnské divadlo* (Prague: Knihovna unie, 1939), et al.; Bohumír Štědroň, *Leoš Janáček a Luhačovice* (Brno, 1939), et al.
[18]*The Listener*, 21 (20 April 1939): 861.
[19]Zdeňka Pilková, "Hudební uterky Umelecké besedy v letech 1935–1951 (studie a soupis)." (Musical Tuesdays of the Umelecka Beseda in the years 1935–1951), *Příspevky k dějinám české hudby*, 1 (1971): 67–172.

Sonata was played by Milán Valter. No concerts were held between 3 October 1944 and 9 October 1945. Although this is not a large list, Janáček was in the company of Karel Boleslav Jirák, Vítězslav Novák, Ladislav Vycpálek, Rafael Kubelík, Jaroslav Křička, Jaroslav Vogel, Pavel Bořkovec, Karel Weis—to name a few—and the Czech classics Mysliveček, Dusík, Smetana, Fibich, Dvořák, Suk and many west European composers. It should be mentioned that Rudolf Firkušný, the younger brother of Leoš, had been active in playing the music of his teacher Janáček in Czechoslovakia and, after 1939, in the West.

Examples of wartime publications include Jan Racek's *Bratři Mrstikové a jejích citovy vztah k Leoši Janáčkovi a Vítězslavu Novákovi* (The Mrstik brothers and their emotional ties with Janáček and Novák), Brno, 1940; and Racek, "Leoš Janáček v tradici české hudby" (Leoš Janáček in the tradition of Czech music), in *Leoš Janáček a současní moravsští skladatele—nastín k slohovému vývoji soudobé moravské hudby* (Leoš Janáček and contemporary Moravian composers: an outline *apropos* of the stylistic development of contemporary Moravian music), Brno, 1940. Hans Hollander published "Leoš Janáček—Slav Genius," in *Music and Letters*, 1941.

After World War II, there is virtually a publishing explosion. Many publications seem to gravitate around the years ending in the numbers four and eight, corresponding to the decades of his birth and death, and frequently emanate from festivals, conferences, and congresses. The year 1948 produced an important collection of studies by Straková, Veselý, Fric, and Raab, edited by Jan Racek in *Leoš Janáček: obraz života a díla* (A picture of Janáček's life and works). Robert Smetana wrote *Výpravení o Leoši Janáčkovi* (Stories about Janáček). The second edition of the correspondence between Janáček and Rektorys appeared. Bohumír Štědroň in 1949 edited a posthumous volume of the writings of Vladimír Helfert, *O Janáčkovi: Soubor státi a článku* (*About Janáček: a collection of essays and articles*). Desmond Shawe-Taylor wrote about Janáček in 1949.[20] Other writers in the decade of the 50s include Koppenburg, Montagu, Stuart, Stuckenschmidt, Kubelík, Böhmer, Gorer, Krause, Erdmann, Bollert, Clarke, Herbst, Šeda, Trávniček, Černohorská, Fiechtner, Honolka, Müller-Röffs, and many others.

The centenary of Janáček's birth was marked by special celebrations and publications. It was the Year of Czech Music and a publication was is-

---

[20]Desmond Shawe-Taylor, "Leoš Janáček," *New Statesman*, 37 (15 January 1949): 53–54, et al.

sued edited by Mirko Očadlík, *Rok české hudby. O živote a díle skladatelů, jejichž jubilea slavíme v roce 1954.Hudební rozhledy* published a special issue, and *Musikologie* 3 published a special issue: *K stému výroči narození Leoše Janáčka (On the 100th anniversary of the birth of Janáček)*, 1955.

In 1958 an international congress was held in Brno. The *Proceedings* were published together with exhibition catalogues.[21] Many articles and books by Czech, Slovak and foreign writers emanated in this year. Ivo Stolařík published the correspondence between Jan Löwenbach and Leoš Janáček.[22] Jaroslav Vogel completed the most definitive study of Janáček's life and works, published first in German, and later in English and Czech.[23] Papers were published for a cancelled conference, *Colloquium: Leoš Janáček et Musica Europaea*, which was to have been held in Brno in 1968.[24] The *Colloquium: "Dvořák, Janáček and their Time,"* Brno 1984, was chaired by Jiří Vysloužil and the papers were edited by Rudolf Pečman. The papers of the symposium *Operní dílo Leoše Janáčka*, papers of the international symposium at Brno, in 1965, were published by the Moravian Museum in *Acta Janáčkiana*.[25] Volume 2 of *Acta Janáčkiana* appeared in 1985, edited by Jiří Vysloužil and others, and published by the Společnost Leoše Janáčka. Volume 3 of *Acta Janáčkiana* (1988) contains additional articles and reviews about Janáček. Three documents, Vincenc Janáček, *Zivotopis Jířika Janáčka*, Leoš Janáček, *Dopisy strýci*, and *Dopisy matky*, have been edited by Jiří Sehnal and Svatava Přibáňova, and published in Brno by *Opus musicum* in 1985.

In 1980, the Leoš Janáček Society (Společnost Leoše Janáčka) began publishing a *Newsletter*.[26] The English edition, *Leoš Janáček Society Newsletter*, printed for foreign distribution, and the Czech edition, *Zpravy společnosti Leoše Janáčka*, for domestic circulation. Issue No. 5 (1988) contains a retrospective reprint of articles published between 1948 and 1958 by Jan Racek, Jan Kapr, Ludvík Kundera, Antonín Sychra, and Jiří Vysloužil. A selected bibliography for those years is included.

---

[21]*Leoš Janáček a soudoba hudba: mezinárodní hudebně vědecký kongres,* Brno 1958 (Prague, 1963).

[22]Ivo Stolařík, *Jan Löwenbach a Leoš Janáček: vzajemná korespondence* (Opava, 1958).

[23]Jaroslav Vogel, *Leoš Janáček: Leben und Werk* (Kassel, 1958); Czech original, 1963; Eng. trans., 1962, 2nd rev. ed. by Karel Janovicky, London, 1980, New York, 1981.

[24](Brno, 1970). Jiří Vysloužil was to have been the chairman. The papers were edited by Rudolf Pečman.

[25]*Acta Janáčkiana*, 1 (1968), edited by Theodora Straková and others.

[26]It is published for the Leoš Janáček Society by the Czech Music Society, Prague. The address of the Secretariat of the *LJS* is: Fil. fac. Masaryk University, A. Nováka 1, 602 00 Brno.

In addition to the foregoing, writers about Janáček in the late 60s include McCredie, Wörner, Fukač, Fiala, Němcová, Sychra, Vrba, Bajer, Burghauser, Příbaňova, Tučapsky, Jiránek, Lebl, Tyrrell, Abraham, Pospíšil, Pensdorfova, Pulkert, Miloš Štědroň, and others. In the 1970s some new authors are Knaus, Geck, Kaderávek, Josephson, Renton, Schön, and Ströbel. Some of the last-named have become specialists in Janáček in a way not always possible to scholars of the 50s and earlier in that they were able to write dissertations about some aspect of Janáček because the groundwork had been prepared by the generalists of previous generations. There is some crossover in the groups, for example, Abraham, Wörner, Vysloužil, and Tyrrell represent the meeting of several generations. The list goes on. In the 80s we have recently seen writing by Beckerman, Beveridge, Erismann, Fischmann, Honolka, and Charles Susskind. Some dissertations on Czech music recently completed or in progress are by Beckerman, Deylampour, Freeman, Houtchens, Renton, Skoumal, and M. Smith.[27] Earlier studies include Geck, Kaderavek, and Tyrrell.[28] In 1978, a collection of reminiscences by Rudolf Firkušný, Rafael Kubelík, František Smetana, and Karel Boleslav Jirák was published.[29] This list makes no pretension of being complete or definitive.

To sum up—in the 1980s performances and subsequent reviews of Janáček's works, particularly his operas, are taking place all over the world—San Francisco, Houston, New York, Vancouver (Canada), Melbourne (Australia), Cardiff (Wales), Nottingham, Cologne, Stuttgart, Münster, Bonn, Frankfurt, and Paris. The new Janáček edition is well

---

[27]M. B. Beckerman, "The Theoretical Works of Leoš Janáček: An Exploration," (Ph.D. diss., Columbia University, 1982); F. Deylampour, "Motiv und motivische Arbeit in spät Instrumentalwerken von Leoš Janáček," (Ph.D. diss., Technische Universität, Berlin, in progress); D. E. Freeman, "The Opera Theater of Count Franz Anton von Sporck in Prague (1724–1735)," (Ph.D. diss., University of Illinois, 1988); H. A. Houtchens, "The Operas of Antonín Dvořák," (Ph. D. diss., University of California at Santa Barbara, in progress); B. H. Renton, " " ; Z. Skoumal, "Structure and Tonality in the Later Instrumental Music of Janáček," (Ph. D. diss., City University of New York, 1992); M. Smith, "A Study of the Unaccompanied Secular Choral Works of Leoš Janáček," (Washington University, 1988).

[28]A. Geck "Das Volksliedmaterial Leoš Janáčeks. Analysen der Strukturen unter Einbeziehung von Janáčeks Randbemerkungen und Volksliedstudien," (Ph.D. diss., Frei Universität, Berlin, 1970); M. R. Kaderavek,"Stylistic Aspects of the Late Chamber Music of Leoš Janáček: An Analytic Study," (D.M.A., University of Illinois, 1970. 2v,); J. R. Tyrrell, "Janáček's Stylistic Development as an Operatic Composer as Evidenced in his Revisions of the First Five Operas," (Ph.D. diss., Oxford University, 1969).

[29]*O Janáčkovi* (Collected reminiscences by R. Firkušný, R. Kubelík, F. Smetana, and K. B. Jirák) Commentary by F. Schwarzenberg and J. Zástěra. Intro. by František Svejkovský. (Chicago: Velehrad, 1978).

under way. Musicologists and performers are looking at notation and interpretation from several and/or different points of view.

In closing it must be said that Janáček, once considered an unknown provincial composer from Moravia, has emerged as an international figure, no longer the exclusive property of a handful of devoted admirers. Is the internationalization of Czech music inevitable? Consider what has happened in the case of Smetana and Dvořák. Are the once revered interpretations of great Czechs of the calibre of Václav Talich being challenged or equalled by a new generation of jet-setters, most of whom do not even speak Czech? There is, however, a new generation of scholars, many of whom do have a command of the Czech language, who are writing penetratingly about Janáček, and who *can* contribute to the establishment of a definitive critical edition of the master's works. It was once thought that only Germans could understand and interpret Beethoven. Can Janáček survive a similar internationalization? It appears that the answer is yes.

Leoš Janáček Today

Jiří Vyzloužil

Jiří Vyzloužil has been associated with the music of Janáček for over forty years and has contributed greatly to our understanding of the composer. His collection Leoš Janáček: O lidové písni a lidové hudbě *(Leoš Janáček: On Folk Song and Folk Music) is an invaluable introduction to Janáček's activity as an ethnographer. He has also written books on Hába and 20th-century music. In his essay presented here he offers a broad overview of Janáček's style and its implications.*

In his creative development and work Leoš Janáček (1854–1928) represents the exceptional case of a composer difficult to categorize unambiguously in terms of style. The phenomenon of his style and musical poetics is new, incomparable, and unique in relation to Czech and European music.

1.

The difference between Janáček and the Czech national school of the 19th century, including Antonín Dvořák who was nearest to Janáček, is not only chronological and biographical, but involves differences in the style and musical poetics of the works as well. As an introduction, we will briefly point out some easily discernable differences between the classical-romantic sources of inspiration in the music of Smetana, Dvořák and Fibich, and the more modern inspirations in Janáček's work (including realism as a movement of art and what we might call "imaginary realism").

Both romantic classicism, which associates Dvořák's works with those of Schubert and Brahms, and romanticism, which connects Smetana's and Fibich's compositions with the New German school of Liszt and Wagner, have only a limited importance in Janáček's artistic production. Echoes of the classical-romantic stylistic orientation of the Czech national school can be discerned only in a few of Janáček's early compositions (eg. *Suites, Idyll*). However, if we want to apply the criteria of this category to classicistic (that is neo-classical) elements in some late compositions—a possibility suggested by the names "quartet," "wind sextet" (*Mládí*), "symphony" ("The Danube"), as well as *Sinfonietta, Concertino* and *Capriccio*—we will encounter some difficulties, for these compositions depart significantly from the classical formal models indicated by their titles. Neither the selection of instruments, nor the method of orchestration is classicist or romantic, and the musical material departs significantly from the Brahmsian-Beethovenian manner.

2.

Janáček is related to the 19th century and the Czech national school (especially to Dvořák and Pavel Křížkovský, Janáček's teacher and the founder of Czech national music in Moravia) by his use of the poetics of folklore as a basis for artistic innovation. Folklorism is a fundamental and persistent component of Janáček's musical style, which, however, underwent radical transformations. In the case of Janáček we have two types of folklorism:

a) The first type, which might be called "Dvořákian," can also be denoted as "echo folklorism."[1] The basic form of musical style in this type is the echo, i.e. a composition which uses folk texts or melodies, or is based on a folk model. Janáček's orientation towards this "echo poetic" corresponded to the dynamics, needs and level of Czech cultural life in Moravia during the second half of the 19th century. Artistically, Janáček's choral and instrumental music of this type is similar to Dvořák's echo compositions, such as his world-famous *Moravian Duets* (Op. 28 and 32, 1876) and *Slavonic Dances* (Op. 46, 1878, and Op. 72, 1887). But Janáček's attempt to use "echo poetics" in the one-act opera *The Beginning of a Romance*, which must be considered a developmental set-back, demonstrates the limitations of this approach. In comparison to the more modern-oriented, that is romantic, *Šárka*, *The Beginning of a Romance* appears as an uninspired and dramaturgically static type of early song opera, namely a Singspiel.

b) The second and more decisive type of folklorism can be designated "idiomatic." At its root is Janáček's innovative and individual adoption (or absorption) of the expressive and stylistic principles of folklore. In fact, this approach can already be observed in some of the music of Dvořák, but, with the exception of compositions such as the *Biblical Songs* (Op. 99, 1984) composed to psalm texts with free rhythm, Dvořák did not in essence abandon the metric-syntactic quadrature form of the major-minor system.[2] Though Dvořák made significant steps

---

[1]The Czech word is "ohlas." It is used frequently to apply to compositions which might be referred to as stylized folk music. *Editor*

[2]The term "quadrature" refers to a norm which is based on four-measure phrases. *Editor*

in the direction of artistic folklorism, his folklorism is not "idiomatic" in a sense that involves a fundamental change in style or musical poetics.

3.

Among Czech composers, only Janáček may be considered to have adopted a folklorism which is "idiomatic" in the full sense of the word. This is due partially to Janáček's systematic study of the musical material of the archetypal East Moravian and Slavonic folk song, and partly to Janáček's remarkable ability to assimilate folklore idioms while composing original music. Janáček's style and musical poetics are of an artistic folklore type, though not always folk-like (the music of *The Makropulos Case*, for example, is quite remote from folklore). These archetypal folkloric idioms, however, have an additional property: they free Janáček and his music from connections with the classical-romantic tradition, and forge a link with modern streams of musical impressionism and expressionism, which were definitely nearer to him than neoclassicism. Janáček himself was well aware of the connections between his work and the musical modernism of the first decades of the 20th century. When Janáček voiced his thanks for being awarded an honorary doctorate by the Philosophical Faculty of Masaryk University in Brno in 1925, he confessed his affinity in feeling and thinking (especially in terms of harmony) with the "modern streams of Debussy, Schreker and Schoenberg" (he had in mind Schoenberg's pre-dodecaphonic period). In other words, he claimed that he felt and thought like a modern composer who espoused the Modern or Art Nouveau style.

Folklorism, as conceived by Janáček in a novel manner—as a kind of neofolklorism—does not clash with his claim to be modern. After all, it is generally admitted today that the modern style (Secession) not only includes exotic elements (the Japan series) or purely folkloric ones, but also urban and even trivial elements. And the last named characteristic feature applies particularly to Janáček and the whole of Czech modern creative production (primarily that of visual arts), the art of the painter and graphic artist Alfons Mucha (also a native of Moravia) being a prominent example, along with the folkloristic lyrical Seccesionist architecture of Janáček's friend Dušan Jurovič. We do not intend to overestimate the presence of modern stylistic elements in Janáček's work (it is not easy to identify them musically). The subject matter and style of his fourth opera *Destiny*, however, are clearly in the spirit of the modern style. This opera is also a work which announced a fundamental change in the orientation of Janáček's style and content, a movement away from the rustic folklore of *Jenůfa* towards modern conceptions (socially critical, civic, fantastic, and other) of music drama (in operas), vocal music (notably in the *Diary of One Who Vanished* and the *Glagolitic Mass*) and instrumental music (with such outstanding compositions as the orchestral *The Fiddler's Child*, both Quartets, *Sinfonietta*, the "Danube" Symphony, as well as the piano *Concertino* and *Capriccio*).

By "separating," "moving away" (secessio) from the stylistic and aesthetic maxims of the 19th century, Janáček reached a mature musical style—a style that was still developing in conjunction with his musical poetics, which could boldly match the musical poetics of the avant-garde of the 1920s (the confrontation did take place at the ISCM festivals in which Janáček took part between 1923 and 1927).

4.

Let us now turn our attention specifically to Janáček's musical poetics, which may be briefly summarized by the following statements:

a. The modal character of his horizontal lines:

Triadic and scalar intervals of the major-minor harmonic system are not the dominating melodic principle. Melodic organization is determined rather by tones of tetrachordal, quintachordal, and multi-dimensional modal structures, whose diatonic framework is enriched through the addition of chromatic pitches which help to define expressivity. The tetrachordal interval structure of the perfect fourth and the upper and lower major seconds, a principle which originates in folk music, represents the tonal basis of Janáček's horizontal organization. Even as they are transformed through motivic development, the modal melodies in Janáček's music do not lose that quality of spontaneous generation found in the folk music models.

b. The modal character of tonality (extended tonality):

The modal organization of the horizontal lines brings about the change of the functional major-minor system into a system of modal, i.e. extended tonal harmony. Vertical composition no longer depends on tertial structuring, and the chordal succession is not governed by functional diatonic tonic-dominant relations. In terms of harmonic development, the modal organization of horizontal lines produces a system of characteristic tonal suspensions with free harmonic connections. The tonal centers are then controlled by the outer notes of the horizontal modal plane—in the case of tetrachords the prime (tonic) and the fourth (subdominant). Atonal moments in a Schoenbergian sense are rare in Janáček (although we do have analogies in some works, as in the second theme of the first movement of the *Concertino*).

c. The tendency of Janáček's musical form towards asymmetry: Characteristic formal approaches in Janáček's music are connected with the above-mentioned modal melodic and harmonic syntax, which departs from the symmetry of major-minor relations and corresponds to the metrical rhythmic asymmetry through a kind of "aquadrature" of musical form. In its asymmetric tendencies, Janáček's musical form approaches the rhythmically "non-versified" expressive forms of prose. In compositions with prose texts this new stylistic feature is especially evident; it is marked with rich and varied rhythmic patterns within compound and changing meters, reflecting the rhythmic principle also found in non-measured, drawn-out folk tunes. In the work of a composer who, beginning with *Jenůfa,* set prose texts, the tendency towards a "prosification" of music makes sense. The principle of "prosification," however, does not result in the loss of a clear sense of self-contained musical form. The reiteration of characteristic motifs and dance rhythms, derived not only from folk music but also the waltz, may strengthen the rhythmic "organization" of musical forms through their fixed meters. This applies primarily to instrumental compositions. But within the metrically unfolding musical stream there also pulsate asymmetrical elements which make the expressive form rhythmically livelier.

The asymmetry of motivic segments (musical microstructures) produces asymmetry in the form of larger units (musical macrostructures), which, in a sense, depend on them. This asymmetric tendency in Janáček's musical thinking (aquadrature) made it difficult for him to resort to classical and preclassical models constructed on the basis of symmetry (quadrature). On the one hand, the forms of Janáček's compositions (mainly in the vocal parts) show a tendency towards "quasiathematic" looseness. On the other hand they also employ the technique of "montage," involving symmetrical rhythmic motifs and themes outside the thematism of quadrature forms.

d. The form-shaping role of the word (principle of prosification): This feature of Janáček's style is also connected with his primarily folkloric orientation. In some early choral "echoes" Janáček had already abandoned the symmetrical rhythmic principle based on the fixed measure, a musical counterpart of verse foot, and imitated the quasi-recitative (parlando) style of drawn-out, non-measured folk tunes. Through its loosened form this music approximates prose, yet the principle of prosification matures in Janáček's work only at the moment when he decided to set prose in *Jenůfa* (1894) and when, wishing to justify his new vocal principle aesthetically and theoretically, he eagerly studied speech intonation (from 1897 onward) in his celebrated "theory of speech melodies." This study influenced Janáček so strongly that he began setting some versified texts to music as if they were prose (*Amarus, Destiny*). On the other hand, it must be said that Janáček also treated some of his texts in prose as if they were versified. For example, he adapts the celebrated scenes of Kostelnička in *Jenůfa* as well as the prose of his male chorus *The Wandering Madman*, both rhythmically and metrically.

The theory of "speech melodies" had a fundamental influence on Janáček's musical thought, particularly on his "prosification" principle. In vocal compositions and operas, which occupy a key place in his work, the musical motifs spring from the "word," that is from its sound, syntax and semantics. On the basis of this prosifying principle, Janáček built up his entire poetics of vocal music, particularly in opera. The impact and importance of this prosifying principle was not only stylistic (formal) but also expressive. Insofar as we speak about "realism" in Janáček, not only with regard to the subject and orientation of some works (*Jenůfa* but also to those works of "imaginary realism" *The Cunning Little Vixen, The Makropulos Case*), this principle of prosification occupies the key position in his style and musical poetics. It also penetrates into the instrumental accompaniment from the vocal component. The prosifying tendencies dynamise the musical form of purely instrumental compositions. The small characteristic rhythmic figures in the instrumental scores can partly be explained by the influence of prosifying tendencies.

e. The role of musical expression:

The musical forms of Janáček's works are not purely musical forms; they are expressive musical forms. In their content the role of the objective background (setting), which Janáček always creatively approached with ardent personal engagement, cannot be neglected. The spectrum of the objective background in Janáček's works is fairly broad and comprises folklore subjects and language phenomena (in various types of "echoes"), his personal life (in the string quartet "Intimate Letters"), a public event (apotheosis of the death of the demonstrating Czech worker František Pavlík in the piano sonata "1. X. 1905"), everyday reality (choirs in the "Russian" operas *Kátya Kabanová* and *From the House of the Dead*), or on the contrary, rather remote reality (in the science-fiction opera *The Makropulos Case*), and others. In the topology just given are, of course, overlappings and interpenetrations of the real and the imaginary within individual works. For example, there is also much which is subjective in the rustic folklore-like *Jenů fa*. In contrast, the science-fiction story of Emilia Marty in *The Makropulos Case* is framed dramatically by the reality of the modern world. The omnipresence of personal vision and the experience of reality, or only fictitious reality, is a constant and an inexhaustible source of the expressive power of Janáček's music.

f. Special features of orchestration:

Janáček was reproached by interpreters of his works and by his pupils for a lack of knowledge of instrumentation. In reality, however, he was also extremely original in this sphere of his art. He "instrumentated," or rather used instruments and their groups in bare tone colors, without a stylistic covering. The raw natural sound of Janáček's scores and solo instrument parts suggest the sound of East Moravian folk bands. He used instruments and voices primarily as expressive factors and did not hesitate to expose them in extreme and often unperformable positions, having little respect for what was and was not instrumentally or vocally possible. This clear idea of orchestration made him reject preprinted music paper for his composing. He drew the staves for individual instruments and their groups himself in agreement with his exact sound conceptions. He did not want printed manuscript paper to induce him to fill up the score with irrelevant voices.

5.

Janáček, who entered the musical world as a member the the 19th century Czech national school, grew up during his artistic development to become a leading personality of modern music. The Brno musicological school of Vladimir Helfert (*Česká moderní hudba* 1936) placed him in the generation of Smetana, Dvořák and Fibich, though it could not ignore the avant-garde traits of his compositions from the last decade of his life. Realistic moments in Janáček's works led the West-German musicologist Carl Dahlhaus to link Janáček with 19th century musical realism (in his book of 1982). But *Jenůfa,* composed between 1884 and 1903, can be regarded as a work reflecting the stylistic turn of "the epoch of 1900." A decisive step toward a "modern style" was made with the opera *Destiny*. The dynamising modal character of Janáček's melodies, tonality and harmony, his developing and "idiomatic" use of folklore principles, the prosification and asymmetric character of rhythmical and musical forms, the technique of "montage," the "natural" instrumentation, and in general his whole human and artistic physiognomy place Janáček undoubtedly among the eminent composers of the first third of the 20th century. That Janáček belongs stylistically to the music of this century is witnessed also by the interest in his work on the part of contemporary audiences, interpreters and composers.

The Conflict between Reality and its Living in the Work of Leoš Janáček

Jaroslav Jiránek

Jaroslav Jiránek has been a truly independent musical thinker for over forty years. He is equally at home in the fields of philosophy and music, and has written monographs on Smetana's dramatic works and on musical semiotics. In his essay Jiránek tackles the extremely difficult question of the relationship between objective reality and Janáček's subjective experience of it (the "living" of the title).

The conflict between reality and its living which always haunted Janáček as a man and artist because of his strange nature appeared to be a "blessing" and "damnation" simultaneously. For Janáček, conventional European musical romanticism was just as attractive as it was unacceptable. It was unacceptable to him not only as a Moravian, taking into account the historical, cultural and political situation of Moravia in the 19th century, but it was also unacceptable to him personally. He could never stand anything that was "second hand," he wanted to have everything "from his own hand." As soon as he understood that the folk song was a unique source, serving as an aid to understanding the *life* of the people, rather than an artistic end-in-itself, he advanced a step further. He began to be interested in the incentives, inspirations and the very beginnings of the songs, as well as their environment, conditions and their "outside linguistic" situations. This was, in fact, the starting point for Janáček's studies of the "speech tunes" of people in all kinds of situations; later on he studied the tunes of nature and the surrounding world in general. These tunes were transformed into Janáček's main means of communication with reality; they became the basis not only of his individual *style of musical realism*, but, at the same time, they integrated Janáček the musician and the man of letters to form one uniform artistic personality.

Speech tunes were, by themselves, neither a discovery nor any privilege of Janáček. Long before Janáček, they had been taken into account by every composer working with musical declamation. They also appeared in various "pure" or "absolute" musical representations of the word (for example, the well-known "Liebe-wohl!" in Beethoven's piano sonata *Les Adieux*, and Erben's verse "Shed light, my little moon, shed light" in Dvořák's symphonic poem *The Watersprite*). Unique, however, is Janáček's very specific conception of all the tunes as well as the fact that he managed to transform them into a *universal system*, the basis of his own artistic style. Janáček's concept of speech tunes is quite individual. In the well-known polemic between Janáček and Otakar Hostinský about Czech musical declamation, Hostinský started from the phonological basis (*O české deklamaci hudební—On Czech Musical Declamation*, Prague, 1868), while Janáček stood on the phonetic basis (in his review of Kuba's collection, *Slovanstvo ve svých zpěvech—Slavs in their Songs,* printed in the collection *On the Folk Song and Folk Music*, pp. 129–131). Hostinský was right when he pointed out the influence of some specific phonological characteristics of the Czech language, e.g. the accent on short syllables at the beginning of words. This characteristic has inevitably had an impact on the musical declamation of the Czech language. From this standpoint, Janáček got closer to a perfect understanding of the practically limitless emotional subtext of the spoken language. Janáček was always more interested in the *parole* than the *lingua*, he was more interested in spoken dialect and not as much in literary language — if language in general interested him at all. Through his speech tunes, Janáček not only collected linguistic expressions, but he also studied them as documents reflecting or manifesting the immediate acoustic expression of the human mentality, its outside form.

Just like a fiction writer who collects basic material first— i.e. the facts, the time, social, psychological or ethnographic data which inspired and stimulated his own emotions and experiences, i.e. the whole substance which then produces the work of words, the verbal work— Janáček also collected the potential theme and foundation of his own artistic creation by systematically retrieving and recording musical tunes.[1]

It can be justly stated that among musical artists and composers he was quite unique in that he systematically exploited the *objective, outside musical reality* of everyday life; and at the same time, through these musical themes, he also recorded and classified the life fiction in himself, in his mind and soul. This very close connection with objective reality caused some critics to wonder whether his work and creative attitude should be called realism, or rather naturalism. I think that Janáček's critics including Nejedlý are wrong. It is true that the territory

---

[1] More accurately: as soon as he found this original way.

of Janáček's unique realism reaches the very border of naturalism[2] and — on the other hand—the very border of expressionism[3]. However, in none of the quoted cases did he step over the borderline. He just oscillates between the two extreme poles as determined by the already characterized and so very characteristic conflict between the *objective* reality and its *subjective* living. Sometimes the extent to which Janáček's restless spirit tried to track and catch reality in twists and outside details of the world is quite astonishing. Sometimes, he is even seduced by the temporal moment; he falls into the trap of description, of detail under the cool appearance of the outside. He is protected, however, by the hot breath of his own life experience which, in turn, could drag him to a subjective distortion of such reality.

But the very idea that Janáček copied reality naturalistically in his tunes is totally wrong. First of all, these tunes are not merely an acoustic, but rather a musical reflection of reality, representing a dialectic unity of lived reality and at the same time reality as lived by Janáček. But even his style does not constitute any mosaic of potential tunes. Their system does not represent any "atom" of his artistic expression, but only a *potential substance to be artistically formed*. Just as an author of fiction carries the theme and substance in his mind for a long time before putting it into an artistic form, Janáček offers us an interesting testimony about his process of creation as recorded by his biographer A. Veselý: "It is quite certain that each of my operas went on growing for one, two years in my mind without my stopping that growing by one single note. With every work of mine, I had only terrible worries."[4]

---

[2] Even Sychra speaks on his study "Janáčkův sloh, klíč k sémantice jeho hudby" (*Estetike* 1, 1974)—(Janáček's style, the key to the semantics of his music), about his "neck-breaking courage to land in the arms of *naturalism*—though in principle that trend was totally alien to him." (p. 122). Similarly, Arne Novák puts a question: "why was he so attracted by a genre which is only an artistic preparation for integral realism, why didn't the Maestro feel its interfering evil power which then turned to be fatal—not only because of the libretto—for both *Výlety pana Broučka* (The Excursions of Mr. Brouček) and for the pub scenes in *The Cunning Little Vixen*; why didn't he wish to leave the too human banality when he himself had enough force and strength for take-off and flight?" in *L. Janáček—Feuilletons, Lidové noviny*, Brno 1953).

[3] I have tried to characterize the features of expressionism in Janáček's work in the already quoted study as a stylistic microcosm of Czech music in the XXth century.

[4] A. Veselý, *Leoš Janáček. Příběh života a díla* (*Leoš Janáček. The Story of Life and Work*) (Praha 1923), p. 96. Vogel—in his *Leoš Janáček. Život a dílo* (*Leoš Janáček. Life and Work*) (Praha, 1963)—quotes another part of Janáček's letter to M. Brod of 31/10/1924: "It is not good to write immediately after very strong personal impressions. When all these perceptions are coated with another life layer—the richer and more rapid the idea is. It penetrates as an Artesian well."

Only in this sense (i.e. as the potential thematic material for artistic forming) can we understand the principle that the tune system forms as the initial basis of Janáček's style of musical realism. It goes without saying that Janáček's original theme resisted current musical technique —just because it was so musical par excellence. This is the objective correlate to Janáček's dislike concerning pre-existent techniques.[5] Some critics speak about Janáček's monothematism. But his has nothing to do with Beethoven's or with Smetana's monothematism, both of which are based on the musical logic of motivic work. Janáček's, on the other hand, grows out of the *uniform mood of the life moment*. His desire to grasp the moment results in repetition, a characteristic technique of Janáček's compositional style. Similarly, we could mention Janáček's tendency toward harmonic inertia,[6] when he lets the same chords sound for several metrical units, or when he modifies it on the basis of the psychologically supposed consciousness of its original form. This uniformity of mood is also important when considering his ostinatos of basic rhythms combined with permanent changes of rhythmic detail creating characteristic "sčasovky"—a word which does not even exist in the Czech language. But, on the whole, it is not difficult to find a very close relationship to the principle of folk numbering and folk variation techniques in general. The principle of Moravian folk variation technique has always been very close to Janáček's attitude. Janáček—just as the old folk musical poetry—was oriented to the psychological aspect of man in his individual life situations. In his general style, this tendency was reflected in a preference for discontinuous static variation forms and in the curious fragment and suite approaches so very typical of his style. This is why Janáček is strongest as a composer whenever and wherever he can base and found the unity of the musical work on the outside musical unity of life itself as represented by the word (vocal creation) or even better by a scene (as in his operas, where he represents rather a musical theatrical or musical dramatic type getting nearest to the Italian opera out of all Czech composers). Thanks to his life force and the vigor of his musical creation he was able to apply his static technique in major musical forms, whether symphonic or cham-

---

[5]For the first time I dealt with the original features of Janáček's technique in my study "On some issues of the relation of Leoš Janáček to Czech and world music," in *Leoš Janáček a soudobá hudby* (*Leoš Janáček and Contemporary Music*), Prague, 1963.

[6]Interesting data about Janáček's harmonic inertia are quoted by Jarmil Burghauser in his study "Janáčkova tvorba komorní a symfonická" (Janáček's Chamber and Symphonic Works), *Muzikologie*, Praha–Brno, 3, 1955.

ber; he was capable of making the popular principle of numbering and variation modifications a basic tectonic element. Even the figurations so typical in Janáček's works, usually thematic in terms of his individual concept of monothematism,[7] are never merely secondary, inferior or simply evocative elements. On the basis of a suite principle they help create a uniform expression and — for Janáček — the formal structure of composition. It is quite interesting to note that Janáček uses, in individual details, quite current means (e.g. in chords and harmony). But even the means and context of the application are very original.[8] On the whole as an organic system, Janáček's musical technique is so original that we can speak not only of a personal musical style but also of an individual attempt to work out an "East-European" musical conception with "neologisms"[9] and "dialectisms"[10] standing hand in hand — just as in his literary expressions.

The "dialectisms" resulted several times in erroneous evaluations of Leoš Janáček—as if he were a purely ethnographic, marginal phenomenon. The dialectisms were also the source of negative evaluation of Janáček by Zdeněk Nejedlý.[11] Quite surprisingly, a similar evaluation was brought forward by a young West-German researcher D. Ströbel from the Eggerbrecht Freiburg school. He claimed that Janáček was a unique phenomenon suffering, however, from a strange historical "splendid isolation" aimed rather at the past than to the future.[12]

Looking at Janáček's compositions one half of a century after the composer's death tells us something quite different. The above-mentioned splendid isolation tends rather to the future than to the past. During the post-war period, Janáček's influence on future generations

---

[7] See my study "Janáček's Klavierkompositions und ihr dramatiker Charakter" in Jaroslav Jiránek, *Zu Grundfragen der musikalischen Semiotik*, Verlag Neue Music, Berlin, 1985.

[8] This is analogical to his musical speech tunes which are not his own invention but, nevertheless, their way of application is quite revealing and original. In this connection Pavel Bisner should be quoted, writing in his study about Janáček's literary style, for it is not easy to determine what is dialecticism and what is neologism: his neologisms are "antiquariantistic rather than modernistic." See Pavel Bisner, "Janáček spisovatel" (Janáček as a writer), *Hudebni rozhledy*, 11, 1958.

[9] See note 8.

[10] For details, see *Janáček's Aesthetics*, p. 204.

[11] Very characteristic for Zdeněk Nejedlý was his detailed study of Leoš Janáček's *Jenůfa*. It was a response to the Prague premiere. (*Smetana* 6, 1916). His study was published in book form (Prague, 1916).

[12] See D. Ströbel, "Auf der Suche nach Janáček's musikgeschictlichem Ort," *Colloquium Musica Bohemica et Europea*, Brno 1970, Brno 1972, pp. 397–406.

of Czech composres can be proved paradigmatically, noetically and aesthetically in the deepest sense: through the inspired and fruitful learning from the wisdom of musical folk poetry. This influence is not to be found in the sense of pre-Janáček[13] empty folklorizing (although we have survived its short relapse in Czech music from the beginnings of the 1950's), but rather in Janáček's art of immersing himself into the life of the people and in its philosophy to gain new tectonic principles from simple but venerable forms of popular art.

However, the major argument is the incandescent but highly topical nature of Janáček's composition. Let us mention only the remarkable thematic unity of the intimately personal, national and social in his themes. How near his subjects are to our present-day thinking! At the same time, they grow out of concrete historical events and circumstances in Janáček's life! Or — let us just cite the manner in which the inner dynamism of Janáček's work, growing out of the reality and his life experience, endows Janáček's creation (not only in the strict musical sense)[14] with that strange charge of "dramaticism" so apt in the dramatic movements of the present day!

Janáček's life and work constitute a unique contribution to the dialectics of personality and work, and the previous discussion is very modest due to the restricted scope of this article. We even might say that there is something very mystical in the mutual connection and predetermination of Janáček's life and work. In this sense we could even quote the very name of Janáček. Its seems as though its etymology hides by remarkable coincidence a symbolic piece of Moravian popular philosophy. While the Czech JAN (John) from the fairy tale about "foolish Johnny," symbolizes the simple feeling and wisdom of a modest hero, and while the Slovak Jáno (John once again) Jánošík symbolizes a popular rebel of the Robin Hood type, the Moravian Janíček (little Johnny) represents both the popular rebellion and the soft Slavonic nature, just as did the great composer himself. He was full of love and resentment—as given by Moravia to Czech music and world.

---

[13] The folklorizing period of young Janáček is also conceived as the "pre-Janáček" one in the spirit of our interpretation.

[14] I dealt with the dramatic character of Janáček's work and with the purely instrumental means in my study "Dramatic features of Janáček's piano style" (*Opus musicum*, 10, 1978), just as in my book selection *Muzikologicke etudy* (Musicological studies), Prague, 1981, and in my book published in the German translation, see note 7.

Janáček and the Dance of "Categories"

Jiří Fukač

Jiří Fukač has been a vital force on the Czech musicological scene since the late 1960's, organizing conferences, compiling a dictionary of music, and writing elegant, perceptive, and often incidentally, quite difficult articles about an enviably wide range of topics. As a longtime member of the musicology division at Masaryk University in Brno, and now its Chair, Fukač has had the opportunity to consider significant questions about Janáček and test his ideas at numerous conferences and symposia. Here he eloquently addresses the central themes of our conference: Who was Janáček? What was the nature of his musical speech? How have we allowed inherited myths to shape our vision of the composer? But Fukač attempts more than a mere debunking of traditional views, he tries to penetrate into the very process of "getting to know" something.

About 220 years ago, the German thinker Georg Christoph Lichtenberg wrote the following spirited aphoristic words: "Critics teach us to keep to nature. Writers know that, but they prefer to keep to those, who have kept to nature before them."[1] Certainly a writer who practices science does not have to give the same account of natural or social reality as his colleague from the area of belles lettres. It is rather his task to engage in such activities as description, analysis, classification, interpretation, exegesis and generalization in relation to the objects of investigation. Nevertheless, being active in all the above-mentioned ways, he often deals not only with the "thing-in-itself," i.e. with the pure objects of observation, but also with residues of previously accumulated cognitive reflections or explanations. So his conduct does not essentially differ from that of Lichtenberg's fictitious writer. The more a scientist is able to utilize the conceptual apparatus, patterns of thought, or methods developed by his predecessors, the more he is in a position to solve his new tasks "ex analogia." That is why the scientist of today should take notice of this in order to revive his direct cognitive contact with observed phenomena (in other words: his contact with their real "nature"). And in addition, he may recognize the cognitive myopia of his own field in the same way.

---

[1]Georg Christoph Lichtenberg, *Aphorismen und Schriften* (Leipzig, 1931) p. 130.

Some biographers turn the accepted viewpoint upside down and demythologize established idols by accentuating negative features of their personalities. Not only Mozart, Beethoven and Wagner, but also Bach have already been subjected to such revelations, which, quite surprisingly, are quite similar to those of the hagiographical type. Joseph Kerman has meritoriously drawn our attention to another "categorical misconception," namely the nationalist and religious ideology projected into biographical explanations. He cites the words with which Forkel, the first real German musicologist, ended his Bach biography of 1802.[7] We must not forget, however, that similar (and not necessarily weaker) nationalist attitudes towards Bach's supposedly essential Germanness were already put forward by Telemann, Mattheson and Marpurg shortly after Bach's death.[8] Finally, we should emphasize the incredible changeability of style and approach in cognitive reflections on music. As soon as style characterizations cease to refer to a concrete compositional approach, it becomes possible to subsume one and the same personal style under diverse style categories, the real character of which is well expressed by the German adjective "geisteswissenschaftlich."[9] In E.T.A. Hoffmann's mind, for instance, Haydn and Mozart were the first "romantic" composers, but soon both became generally accepted, together with Beethoven, as exemplary representatives of the classical style.[10]

Our introductory "discourse on method" gives us sufficient reason to put forth the following questions: To what extent is the established view of Janáček stigmatized by narrative usages or by some autobiographical, hagiographical, ideological or other similar pattern of thought? What are the sources of these models in Janáček's case? What aspect of Janáček's portrait have been misinterpreted by musicologists and what must be done to correct it? In our search for adequate answers, we shall try to demonstrate the network of "categories" dancing around Janáček's life, work and historical environment.

* * *

On the 8th of March, 1918, Janáček inscribed the following emphatic words in a "Czech Memorial Volume from the Great Year

---

[7]Kerman, p. 33–34.
[8]Alfred Schweitzer, *J. S. Bach* (Leipzig, 1955), pp. 196–198.
[9]Carl Dahlhaus, *Musikalischer Realismus Zur Musikgeschichte des 19. Jahrhunderts* (München, 1984).
[10]Charles Rosen, *The Classical Style Haydn, Mozart, Beethoven* (New York, 1976).

1918"[11]: "Držím se kořenů života našeho lidu—proto rostu a nepodlehnu." This short text is useful for musicologists and publicists as a very suitable motto, but most quotations do not mention the original source. As editor of the well-known "Iconographia Janáčkiána" (Brno 1974), Theodora Straková used it, for instance, as an appropriate introduction to the chapter called "Captivated by Folk Music." She understood Janáček's formulation "kořeny života... lidu" in the sense of "folk life's roots," while Stephan Finn, as English translator of her book, interpreted the sense of Janáček's text as follows: "I have a hold on the roots of the life of our people—therefore I grow and do not succumb." It is true that the words "folk" and "people" function, to a large extent, synonymously, though they differ from each other in their connotations. The former refers more directly to the folklore community, i.e. to the basic stratum of the population, while the latter conveys much more strongly the concept of "a profiled nation." Finn tended instinctively to the "nationalistic" conceptual variant; Straková, however, interpreted the text as a good example of Janáček's adherence to the spirit of folklore and folklorism. Which if the two interpretations is right? And what did Janáček really mean by his proclamation?

Certainly Janáček as a composer and theorist never stopped dealing with folk-song and folk-dance. He arranged some Moravian, Silesian and Slovakian tunes during World War I. The Viennese performance of his *Jenůfa* filled him with enthusiasm because, among other reasons, folklore equipment (folk costumes, a garlanded horse, etc.) had been used to great effect. But after the premiere, which took place on February 16th, 1918, Janáček said (in his letter dated the 25th of March to the choral society Hlahol in Prague) that he was glad that he had displayed a "Czech heart" in a foreign country. In other words: he felt as if he was playing the role of representative of Czech music. After so many years, during which Janáček was neglected, it was indeed a completely new mission and situation for him. And there is another argument, socio-psychological rather than subjective in its nature, which is more significant than Janáček's individual feeling: the social climate which arose after the Manifesto of the Czech writers (in May 1917), after Wilson's declaration of his 14 points (in January 1918), and after the so-called "Epiphany" declaration of the Czech deputies, directed many Czech artists and scientists towards a revolutionary and patriotic way of thinking. On the 24th of February, 1918, Vladimír Helfert, who

---

[11]The original Czech title runs as follows: "Český památník z velkého roku 1918." The Memorial Volume was edited in Prague on 10th April 1918.

was to become Janáček's biographer, published his politically courageous and risky "futurological" essay "Our Music and the Czech State."[12] Janáček's identification with this idealistic trend was expressed in two important works: his opera *The Excursions of Mr. Brouček* (completed in 1917), which was intended to make people disgusted by the national indifference of the Czech petty bourgeois, and the Slavonic Rhapsody (called *Tarus Bulba* and completed on March 29, 1918), which was composed with the intent of demonstrating that "there is no fire nor suffering in the world which could break the strength of the Russian people." The word "Russian," however, could be replaced in good faith by "Czech" or "anti-German": on the 26th of March, Janáček confided in Gabriele Horvátová that he had finished his composition under the spell of the battle on the French front.

These were the circumstances under which Janáček, as one of 50 prominent representatives of Czech cultural life, was challenged to make a contribution to the mentioned Memorial Volume. The musicologist Zdeněk Nejedlý put down in it a short passage from Smetana's *Tábor*, Josef Suk cited his *St. Venceslas Meditation*, and Janáček added to his verbal utterance a stylized Hussite Chorale song from *The Excursions of Mr. Brouček*:

Example 1.

The rhythmic model is based on another Hussite tune (Ktož jsú boží bojovníci, You who are God's own warriors), while the text comprises the first lines of the song "Povstaň, povstaň," which may be translated as follows: "Rise up (in arms), rise up, all the empire which is true to the Czech country!" Our questions seems to be answered. It is certain that there the basic folk stratum is subordinate to the national ideal: in the case of both Mr. Brouček's excursion to the Hussite fifteenth century and in the "Czech-Russian" parable of Tarus Bulba. The instinctive collective movement "from below," however, is subordinated to a superior organism, that is to say to that of one's own nation. Janáček certainly identified himself with the latter alternative.

---

[12]Vladimír Helfert, *Naše hudba a český stát* (Praha, 1918).

Was it a result of his own creative "search for Czechness in music" (in accordance with Michael Beckerman's considerations[13])? Did Janáček sacrifice his folklorism to achieve a certain status as a Czech national composer? Eighteen days before the downfall of the Austro-Hungarian monarchy, Janáček described the folklorism in *Jenůfa* in clearly political terms (in his letter to Karel Kovařovic):

> Today I got a notice that *Jenůfa* should be performed at the Viennese court opera on the 15th and the 21st of October. I supposed that they would cut me off as a citizen of an enemy state now. But this is not the case. It seems to me that the multi-colored Moravian-Slovakian stage is like a red carnation on the ministerial frock of the Viennese bubble.

* * *

The fact that Janáček arrived at his own national concept of music by employing some values of folk, folklore and folklorism entitles us to verify many other deeply-rooted interpretations. His orientation towards this value cluster represents an indispensable means, to be sure, but not the essential base of his creative development. And for this reason we are in a position to argue about all explanations which—apart from their axiological omens or tendencies—identify Janáček's type with the character of a composing folklorist, a lowly worker in the field of folk heritage, a primitive, a natural-born or barbarian talent.[14] Neither Janáček's uncurbed temperament, nor his folkloristic activity, nor his village origin legitimates such a view. Let us therefore ask the question: What parallel can be found between his individual or creative type and his ancestral, social and regional origin?

Janáček's birthplace, Hukvaldy, was surely not a typical agricultural village. Analyzing Janáček's first memories of childhood, we find almost no evidence of his relationship to rural life and its folklore. His earliest conscious and subconscious awareness seems to have been formed by such elements as the architectonic monuments manifesting the power of Bishops or Archbishops of Olomouc, figural church music, so-called "Hausmusik," and the cultural activities related to school

---

[13]Michael Beckerman, "In Search of Czechness in Music," *19th Century Music*, X, i (Summer 1986), pp. 61–73.

[14]Zdeněk Nejedlý as a critic of Janáček's opera "The Cunning Little Vixen" says that this work represents a milieu which corresponds to Janáček's primitiveness. He says that in doing so "a primitive can create a manner, but not a style." See Zdeněk Nejedlý, *Kritiky II. Rudé právo 1923–1935* (Praha, 1956), pp. 107–111.

teaching, which had been connected with the Janáček dynasty since the late 18th century.[15] As a child, Janáček was dependent upon the world of adults; this dependence was greatly intensified later during his stay among the blue-uniformed choirboys in the so-called "Thurn-Wallesessin Foundation" in Brno. Like many other Bohemian and Moravian musicians of this period, Janáček, while at Hukvaldy, was subject to a typical behavioral pattern which can be metaphorically called (in accordance with Božena Němcová's well-known tale) the "dialectics of castle and subcastle life." In this case, the concept of the "castle" implies the notion of a clerical hierarchy.

Janáček's family tradition also suggests some specific features. His ancestors were in no way simple folks.[16] Living and working in Silesian and North Moravian towns and villages (in the same region where Sigmund Freud was born), they struggled under conditions of proletarianization for their social establishment and advancement, as well as for their higher education and success. This fight stamped a special dynamic on nearly all members of Janáček's dynasty. Some of Janáček's brothers and sisters tried to make their way abroad (in America and in Russia). In Janáček's case, we must appreciate his partly ingenious, partly awkward maneuvering between different power structures, patterns of social life, and free opportunities (for example between ecclesiastical and secular institutions, Brno and Prague, motherland and foreign countries, ideal conformism and nonconformism, school discipline and verbal looseness in teaching, paternalism in his own family or surroundings and "dandyism" in public) and, finally, his spontaneous negation of aging by emphasizing some features of youth. Although it was typical for Janáček's generation, and his own family, to overcome received social status by identifying oneself with town life, Janáček never became a pure urban type. His appropriation of this living style looks rather as if the town was "captured" by an extrinsic man, who feels quite diffident or strange in town and therefore styles himself and his behavior "backwards" in "rural" manners. Let us mention some examples of this process: the growing difference between Janáček and his "city" wife Zdeňka, his long-lasting residence away from (or "below") the city center of Brno (including the tram!), his ostentatiously rural lifestyle in his garden house behind the organ school, and his need to leave Brno often not only for the countryside, but also for "Golden Prague" (". . . to stay only in Brno, I could become only a

---

[15]Jaroslav Vogel, *Leoš Janáček* (London: 1981), pp. 37–39.
[16]S. Přibáňová, "Nové poznatky k rodokmenu Leoš Janáčka" (New Knowledge about Janáček's Pedigree), in *Časopis Moravského musea 69*, 1984, pp. 129–138.

small wheel taken out from the machine ... " [17]) as an expression of the instinctive ambition to "capture" great towns. Janáček's feuilleton "My town," which is about Brno and may correspond with one of the programmatic intentions of the *Sinfonietta*, contains no reference to modern urban or civil aspects, after all: it summarizes his reminiscences and describes some attractions of Brno:

> but how could one be in love with Brno of those days? One day suddenly I saw a miraculous change in the town. My antagonism to the gloomy town hall vanished ... Over the town the light of freedom blazed, the rebirth of October, 28, 1918 ... and the vision of the growing greatness of the town, of my Brno, gave birth to my Sinfonietta.

On the other hand, we know that the *Sinfonietta* was also intended to express his fascination with the festive sound of fanfares, with Sokol, with the Czechoslovakian Armed Forces, and with "the free man of these days, his spiritual beauty and joy, his strength, courage and determination to fight for victory." Jaroslav Vogel has interpreted the final words of this passage to mean "the defense of the young state and its hard-won independence."[18] But wasn't Janáček referring here primarily to his own hard-won independence, which has been connotatively connected with so many different programmatic intentions in the semantic field of the *Sinfonietta*? His identification with the town of Brno interacts with this situation, when he, as the established national composer, felt himself to be superior to his immediate surroundings: "those days," the times namely, when it was impossible to be in love with Brno, passed away. In spite of its progressive musical equipment and euphoric spirit, the *Sinfonietta* embodies the difficulties and ambivalence of Janáček's adaptation to complicated sociological "high structures" in a romantically emphatic and autobiographical way.

The village of Hukvaldy is situated on the easternmost periphery of the historical territory of the Czech lands. From the tops of the Carpathian foothills one can see far away in all directions, mainly towards the east of Europe. A sensitive creative spirit can feel the Eastern element brought by the waves of Wallachian colonization, he is able to imagine regions stretching far into the Balkans with the Carpathian massif, to feel the dimension of history and prehistory of the Slavs, to discover the purity of the oldest levels of folk music and to identify himself with the spontaneous vitality of

---

[17]See Janáček's letter to K. Stösslová from June 28, 1918.
[18]Vogel, p. 322

Eastern musicality. Janáček, Bartók, Szymanowski, Kodály, Enescu and many of their successors, observed—and still observe—this territory, each from a different viewpoint, and arrived at long last at similar images and creative principles. In the midst of them, Janáček has chronological priority [19] and among the great Czech musicians—apart from Alois Hába—he is the only composer who was born in this region. In the days of Janáček's youth, however, this origin by itself did not guarantee such a creative orientation. We know that Janáček's earliest impressions had no connections with these phenomena. Moreover, we can suppose that Janáček, as a schoolmaster's son, was especially isolated from the real ethnic environment at Hukvaldy. As for the so-called Lachian dialect spoken in this region and also used, even flaunted by Janáček, it is necessary to emphasize that the concept "Lachia" in the sense of ethnographic unit is a comparatively recent literary mystification, the relevance of which has been strengthened by, among others, Janáček's later "Lachian" verbal and musical utterances. The "Lachian roots of Janáček's life and work"[20] are therefore just as unrealistic as the claim that Janáček was influenced by the Eastern specificity of his native place or region from the very outset. Janáček gained this specificity much later, namely during his aforementioned retrospective and subsequent identification with "rural" or "country" patterns. His approach to all values represented by the phenomenon of Hukvaldy does not differ essentially from the way in which Vítězslav Novák, as composer of South-Bohemian origin, discovered (from 1896) the sources of Eastern Moravian and Slovak folklore.

Nevertheless, in Janáček's case, Hukvaldy played a much larger and more complex role as an oasis of quiet, as a place where Janáček could represent for his local friends a "gentleman of the town" and for the visitors from the town (for example for V. Novák in 1897) a "sapient native"; as the catalyst of his retrospectively realized inquiry into elements of his own identity, as a useful resource of deep self-reflections, as an ideal terrain for his beginning folkloristic research, etc. For that matter it was not Hukvaldy alone that Janáček required for his "Eastern" views. He also studied some more authentic folk music in other parts of the Carpathian region. His conception of Czech or Slavonic music is based on his reading of Russian literature as well. The Czech (and a part of the European) art of the time was painfully seeking new

---

[19] Jiří Fukač, "Janáček's Hukvaldy and the East," *Janáček a Hukvaldy* (Brno, 1984), pp. 47–57.

[20] See the characteristic title of J. Procházka's book *Lašské kořeny života i díla Leoš Janáček* (The Lachian Roots of Leoš Janáček's Life and Work), (Praha, 1948).

patterns for its own identity, as well as a more effective approach to spontaneous folk creativity and new links to the dynamically developing folk creativity and cultures of Eastern Europe. And in this connection, in doubt as to which path of musical advancement he should take, Janáček grasped with amazement that the entire macro-world of the routes which he sought were to be found in the micro-world of Hukvaldy, in the physiognomy of this wider territory and of course in the subconscious stratum of his own experience of Hukvaldy. The myth of Janáček's Hukvaldy therefore deserves to be corrected: as a young musician Janáček did not depend on his native milieu, but the rediscovery of the world of Hukvaldy was a creative and reflective act which became a stimulus just in the nick of time for his development.

* * *

Finally, our consideration should result in some corrections concerning the understanding of Janáček's music. This may be accomplished by means of some provocative interrogatory theses which have here only "pars pro toto" character.

1. Folklorism as Janáček's style?

Janáček, very much like Bartók, explored and simultaneously exploited the Eastern type of musical folklore. The specific motivations of the two composers' sudden turn towards this kind of music were alike, anyway, but the temporal hiatus between their decisions to devote themselves to this activity led to important typological differences. Let us recall some of Janáček's remarks from his feuilletons "The Harabiš Inn" (1924) and "My Lachia" (1928) by means of a free montage:

> The Harabiš Inn stands in a narrow valley . . . In little windows of the Inn the alluring red lights were already twinkling . . . In the room a press of maids, grooms, women with children in arms . . . Body to body, passionate dancing . . . The air was full of odor of sweat . . . There was astonishment on the face of the poet Šťastný, while I eagerly followed the boiling pot of the Lachian dances . . . That was in 1881 . . . Why should the score of the Lachian Dances go out into the world? . . . The reason is the broad basis of folk art . . . in memory of that warm summer night with the starry skies above, the murmur of the river Ondřejnice, which sounds like gentle love-chatter . . . [21]

---

[21] *Janáček, Leaves from his Life*, ed. and trans. V. and M. Tausky (New York, 1982), pp. 29–32.

After so many years, the ghost of romantic attitudes toward folklore is raised, a spirit wholly foreign to Bartók. Of course this scene had to astonish the conservative poet Father Šťastný. Janáček appeared to play a double role by presenting himself as the last romantic and the first modern representative of Czech folklorism in music.

But it is not the only difference between Janáček and Bartók in this field. As is well known, Bartók used folklore patterns and impulses in many different ways or manners, from the clever arrangements to the most complicated stylizations and wittiest semantic re-evaluations. This typological spectrum is much narrower in Janáček's music. He derives different modal elements from folklore and finds the first stimuli for his "speech melody" theory and practice in contact with folk-song intonation, but as soon as he integrates these and similar stimuli, he can renounce any direct employment of folklore tunes, rhythm, etc. That is why the frequency of folk-song quotations in Janáček's work is substantially lower than, e.g., in Bartók's or Vítězslav Novák's music. Apart from Janáček's simple folklore arrangements, we might ask to what extent we could venture to characterize Janáček's ripe style as folklorism. In *Jenůfa*, whose semantic field is country life, scenes with musical and scenic folklore elements always appear with a specific function, as if they have to prepare the approaching catastrophe—in other words, as a token of the individual's alienation within the stiff mechanism of preformed collective behavioral patterns. Folklore as a source of an "estrangement effect" can already be found in the opera *The Beginning of a Romance*. Would Janáček have undertaken such a practice, if he identified his own style with straightforward folklorism?

2. A born dramatist?

Because folklorism cannot stand the scrutiny of being considered the leading principle of Janáček's whole development, some publicists have sought to identify such a principle with his "dramatism." There are at least three elements which could support this conviction: a. Janáček's stage works and plans represent the sphere of his most relevant and complex artistic conquests, b. penetration of Janáček's music into the musical life of different cities (to begin with Prague, 1916) or countries has always started with the acknowledgement of his operas, c. Janáček's dramatic qualities found expression not only in stage works, but also in other kinds of music. According to Max Brod's explanation there is no need to speak about Janáček's dramatism, however, but—in a more general sense—about his "above-average sensibility for minima," i.e. about his ability "to look into the abyss through small chinks."[22]

Nevertheless, if the publicists, speaking about "Janáček the dramatist," really mean Janáček was *born* a dramatist, they are in danger of a gross over-simplification. Janáček's dramatic feeling could have been strengthened by qualitites like his unquiet temperament, fighting spirit, internal tension and vulnerability, characteristics which accompanied him from his youth and difficult adolescence; but we have no evidence for their early transformation into the creative need to express his own internal world in a dramatic way. In the late romantic period, it was even usual for some great composers (e.g. Brahms, Bruckner, Joseph Suk and, what is more, Gustav Mahler as an opera conductor) to ignore the stage in spite of dramatic tensions in their lives or of theatrical entities in their environment.

To the best of our knowledge, Janáček as a young artist took no interest in theatre in the cities where he studied and worked. The situation changed as soon as Czech culture in Brno created its own operatic context. From that time, Janáček felt the necessity to become involved as a critic and later as a composer. In this regard his reaction, from about 1884, does not essentially differ from that of Smetana in the sixties. Does this derive from Janáček's acknowledged tendency to "capture"all the higher structures in his surroundings? And Janáček pluralized this activity as soon as he decided to penetrate into Prague's opera life, which represented a specifically difficult and historically new task.[23] We may articulate a hypothesis that his identification with the role of the leading Moravian, and afterwards of the most progressive Czech music dramatist, was primarily evoked by sociological conditions existing in a young national music culture.[24] It was precisely these conditions which mobilized all his latent dispositions or facilities, and that were necessary for his extraordinarily original development in this field.

---

[22]Max Brod, *Leoš Janáček Život a dílo* (Praha, 1924), p. 7.

[23]The well-known difficulties which Janáček had in his efforts to have his operas staged in Prague had an interesting analogy: the English-German composer Agnes Tyrrell (1846–1883) from Brno suffered similar troubles when she offered her opera to the German theatre in Prague. See Jiří Fukač, "Zur Frage der neuromantischen Stilmerkmale in der Musikentwicklung Mährens," in *Sborník prací filosofické fakulty brněnské university*, 19 (1970) H5, pp. 63–90.

[24]Jiří Fukač, "O Janáčkovi z trochu jiného úhlu. Poutník ve světě divadla" (About Janáček from a slightly different angle. A wanderer in the theatre world), in *Program Státního divadla v Brně*, 55, No. 5 (1984), pp. 194–197.

3. Was Janáček's stylistic evolution violent or retarded?

In the 19th and 20th centuries, a composer whose personal style ripens only (and suddenly) at about the age of fifty, is something quite unique, but Janáček represents such an exception to the general rule. We must admit that our field is at a loss to explain this rare case. Was Janáček so busy and disturbed, that he was incapable of concentrating on composition, or was he so depleted by his oscillation between conformism and nonconformism that he could not find his own creative solution? Did his thorough education in theory and aesthetics paradoxically block his musical imagination? Was it necessary for him to build the conditions for his own establishment by remodeling Czech musical culture in Brno in his own image, by educating his future audience and performers, by developing and then nullifying his folklorism and other conceptions, and by undergoing many private catastrophes before he developed his own musical thought? Was Nejedlý justified in his remark that Janáček as a primitive could not create any style?[25] Did Janáček instinctively reject patterns of musical romanticism so that only later confrontations with increasing verism, impressionism, expressionism and the avant garde were able to release his latent feeling of modern personal style? Or should we accept Dietmar Ströbel's hypothesis that Janáček tried to reformulate paradigms of 19th century music, and that in doing so folk music, as a new logical instance, granted a new sense to this striving?[26] I am afraid we could reformulate all these and similar interpretations presented in the abundant literature to infinity or gradate them to the nth degree without being able to discover the real situation of Janáček's creative development.

The basic problem is given by the specific interaction of all these factors, let us say by the impacts of these factors on each other. Such events generate then a typical "algorithm" of Janáček's creative behavior. Being absorbed in many activities, public tasks and contexts of functional music, he tried to achieve the creative liberty which exists in the field of autonomous music. Under Moravian conditions, this effort required him to originate the context for his own work: like Smetana's and Dvořák's generation in Prague, Janáček saturated all needs of the arising national cultural capacity in Brno, but in contrast to the situation in Bohemia, he had to do it by himself, and years later. The given norms were both a paradigm and a hindrance to him. Wishing to solve this task in an individual and specific

---

[25]See footnote 14.
[26]Dietmar Ströbel, *Motiv und Figur in den Kompositionen der Jenůfa*, (Werkgruppe Leoš Janáčeks: München, 1975), pp. 16–25.

way, he had to create a new alternative of Czech music in general and to overcome his predecessors, which took much of his time and invention. That is why Janáček oscillated between retardation and acceleration for a long time: on the one hand, he seems to be retarded in comparison with Smetana, Dvořák and Fibich, on the other hand he appears ahead of the much younger generation which brought the first wave of modern music into Czech culture.

In fact, his "getting ahead" represents rather going in a completely new and unknown direction. On the 12th of February, 1925, as a "young" honorary doctor, Janáček wrote that it is necessary to grow "from one's own inner self," in order to have a share in the flourishing field which is destined to him. He suppressed, however, the notion that, in his case, this field sometimes fatefully retarded and sometimes provoked the processes which occurred in his own inner self. Therefore the "algorithm" is based on the tenacious "improvement" of particular musical kinds, genres and subgenres. He tried to change sequentially church and choral music style, opera and piano, chamber and orchestral music, and to solve their specific problems. So he drew the autonomy nearer and nearer. After many attempts, sketches, torsos, and unconvincing results he was finally in a position to compose in his own style, to grow from his own inner self and to deviate from given norms. Many of his works (for example the sonatas for piano and violin, or the cello composition "Fairy-tale") bear witness to this difficult process of generating, although they make an impression of perfectionism. And every new subtype requires a new approach to the mechanism of seeking and improving: *Jenůfa* as a new type of modern musical drama took him 9 years to complete, but *Fate* took only 7 months; the first part of the burlesque *Brouček* took 9 years, and the second part again only 7 months. Is it simply a fortuitous numerical game?

4. Structural and semantic innovations or a fixed system of figures?

We can declare that after 1900 Janáček really "grows from his own inner core" without any hesitation, as soon as he acquires control over the "secrets" of a particular genre. Nevertheless his specific paradigm is so firmly crystallized and so exclusive that it evokes the assumption of his primitivism, mannerism or one-sidedness, of the preformed character of his creative operations. New influences arriving from contemporary music were immediately adapted to his own style as well. Observing his newly reconstructed score (such as The "Danube" Symphony, the Violin Concerto, etc.), we can only try to guess which of the well-known "elements (and with what frequency) will appear there. Under these conditions, our style designations of his music usually stay somehow "quasi" or "fuzzy" (sometimes one feels compelled to speak about Janáček's impressionism, expressionism, etc.). This is why we so often say "Janáček and the music of the 20th century," as if there were a distance between both phenomena and as if his music had to be perpetually compared with other "normal" styles, streams, idioms and idiolects of his time.

Janáček's paradigm is comparatively narrow, to be sure. It is not the repertory of his creative operations which surprises us, but rather their distribution, sequence, context and hierarchy in actual works. And it was and is a very difficult task to describe the way Janáček dealt with these entities. Nevertheless our analytical ability increases gradually. Where Vladimír Helfert observed unstylized repetitions, unsubstantial variation and simple augmentations or diminutions of the raw motivic material,[27] we detect a complicated strategy of thematicism and dethematization as a source of Janáček's latent "dramatism."[28] Janáček's ostinato figuration seems to us to represent a sphere where the thematicism can alternatively be based on melos and sonority and where the texture acquires the character of a montage which concerns the qualities of linearity, verticality and simultaneity. Instead of speaking about naturalism or realism in general, we identify the actual vehicles of iconicity and expressivity. Janáček's self-defining theoretical utterances are not to be taken literally, which was often the source of misunderstanding in the past, but we set store by them as authentically catalogued compositional operations. From our point of view it is no longer a mystery why Janáček emphasized the importance of "speech motifs" for his compositions and at the same time neglected to use them in a direct way. We have understood that in this way Janáček acquires a "store" of typified sound gestures which—like index signs—are able to represent the sphere of human expressitivity. And we also comprehend that it was no accident that Janáček named the rhythmization as "sčasování." This neologism, introduced by Janáček himself, refers to the latent co-existence of the fundamental temporal base and of rhythmic strata acquired through progressive divisions of this base in

---

[27]Vladimír Helfert, *Česká moderní hudba* (Olomouc, 1936), pp. 44–51.

[28]Jaroslav Jiránek, "Dramatické rysy Janáčkova klavírního stylu" (Dramatic features of Janáček's piano style), in *Opus musicum*, 10, No. 5–6 (1978), pp. 139–148.

musical time space,[29] while the concrete music structure is realized by situating the sound events in select strata, in other words by their "in-time-putting" (which could be the most literal translation of the Czech word). In this case there is something in common with a specific "store" of typified icon signs, because Janáček was convinced that an event in a higher stratum represents more dynamic processes in subjective and external reality. Janáček's structure is therefore similar to a flexible network of typified units with semantic predispositions. Which specific meaning is to be realized depends on the topical configuration of the operations used, and on what the composer or the recipient will project in the course of events. Janáček's music acquires its great fascination by challenging you to take an active part in the building and rebuilding of the meaning. In this sense it is not simple by any means. It represents the direct opposite pole from romantic programmaticism, of expressionist semantic clarity and of the so-called "mood-technique" long since domesticated in musical theatre and misused in incidental and film music. It is true, that some works can sometimes conduct themselves (or be understood) as program music, pure expression or a presentation of "moods," but their semantic configuration discourages such an approach. We can venture the affirmation that Janáček's music represents a re-embodied and essentially transubstantiated form of this sempiternal semantic principle which is—mainly in German musicology—characterized as "Figurik." The figure could be defined as a preformed structural unity which offers a general or typified frame for the realization of the meanings with similar designation tendencies. Otherwise Janáček's "figuration" strategy found its immediate depiction in his specific notational image. In place of rhetorical units of meaning which were typical for composition in the renaissance and baroque eras, Janáček's music uses the broad sphere of human experience with sounding and moving gestures born in physical, communicative and autocommunicative processes. That is why his music has the ability to bring our mind to resonance, and to achieve a common validity, which occurs in spite of its stylistic exclusiveness and limitation.[30]

* * *

---

[29]Vladimír Helfert (in his book *Leoš Janáček I* [Brno, 1939], pp. 318–319) drew our attention to Janáček's deep knowledge of 16th century polyphony. His knowledge supposedly included an attitude towards mensurality, as well. The Italian Ars nova notation (14th century) was not of particular interest to Janáček, to be sure, but this very type of mensural notation corresponds somehow with Janáček's theory of "sčasování."

[30]This is why when we first encounter Janáček's compositions, we are often unable to ascertain what this music could mean. We apprehend the presence of "signs" there, but these

It has not been our aim to demythologize Janáček: we have endeavored to demystify rather the process of dealing with him in a cognitive sphere. Janáček himself appears as a composer who was the tributary of different traditional and conventional contexts to a surprisingly high degree, but who nonetheless built a new typological variant of creative behavior. Most evaluative criteria derived from our experiences with 19th-century and 20th-century music and music culture fail in his case: this is why so many misinterpretations arose around him. Our stock of terms and concepts have proven to be insufficient, but Janáček appears as a very effective touchstone for musicological conceptions and misconceptions. His music represents a useful challenge for the improvement our thought about music in general.

"signs" remain "open" for us for a long time. As soon as we recognize that the courses and correlations of musical events are similar to the dynamics of our internal and external world, or provoke our need to express ourselves, we begin to create our romantic strategies which can hardly be dispersed. Janáček often projected different meanings in a single work (see our discussion of the semantic field of the *Sinfonietta*). The network of preformed figures can convincingly serve two very different semantic conceptions: although the fanfare from the *Sinfonietta* is primarily a sign of festivity and joy, the English rock group Emerson, Lake and Palmer used this music in a classical rock adaptation to express a ghostly psychic situation (without essentially changing the structure, but by means of an added text), and Janáček's music supports this intention in a very effective way!

Index

A Complete harmony manual, (*Úplna nauka o harmonii*), 348. See also Janáček, Leoš
A manual for teaching singing, (*Návod pro vyučování zpěvu*), 348. See also Janáček, Leoš
"A New View of Janáček's Symphony," 313. See also Štědroň
A picture of Janáček's life and works, (*Leoš Janáek: obraz života a díla*), 352. See also Racek
A World Revolution, 26. See also Masaryk
About Janáček: a collection of essays and articles, (*O Janáčkovi: Soubor státi a článku*), 352. See also Helfert
Abraham, (Janáček scholar), 354
Acta Janáčkiana, 353
Adamčiak, Milan, 301–307
Adieux, Les, 365. See also Beethoven
Advertisement, 299. See also Cowell
Along the Overgrown Path, (*Po zarostlém chodníčku I*) 235. See also Janáček, Leoš
Alter, Georg, 293
Alvilda regina de'Goti, 121ff. See also Vivaldi
Amarus, 362. See also Janáček, Leoš
"An unknown last work, *Dunaj*," ("Neznáme poslední dílo Janáčka *Dunaj*"), 350. See also Chlubna
Angeli cementes, 149. See also Hasse
Angelus Domini Descendit, 149. See also Zelenka
Argippo, 121ff. See also Vivaldi
Ariosti, Attilio, 149
 O quam Suavis, 149
Armida al campo d'Egitto, 124, 125. See also Vivaldi
Armida, 34ff. See also Dvořák
Arsilda regina di Ponto, 124. See also Vivaldi
Association of Moravian Composers, 295–296, 298
atonality, 57–81

Auftakt, journal, 296
August II, Elector of Saxony, 141
Badura-Skoda, Paul, 220
Bajer, Jiří, 21–31, 354
Bakala, Břetislav, 21, 299, 312
Ballad of Blanik, The, (*Balada blanická*), 273–282, 342. See also Janáček, Leoš
ballad songs, 160
Ballade of an Unborn Child, 305. See also Wolker
Barbara dira effera, 148. See also Zelenka
Barenreiter Verlag, 221–242
Bartered Bride, The, 46, 349–350. See also Smetana
Bartók, Béla, 57, 382
Bartos, František, 218, 347
 Moravian folksongs newly collected, (*Národní písně moravské v nově nasbirané*), 347
Baťa, Tomáš, 299
Beckerman, Michael, 45–53, 354
Beethoven Sketchbooks, The, 245. See also Johnson, D.
Beginning of a Romance, The, (*Počatka románu*), 8ff, 284, 288, 358, 382. See also Janáček, Leoš
Bella, Ján Levoslav, 302–303
Benda, František, 163
Bendl, Karel, 33, 43, 261
 Česká svatba, 43
 Matka Mila, 33, 43
Beneš, Eduard, 25ff
Beneš-Šumavský,Václav, (librettist for Dvořák's *Vanda*), 260
Berg, Alban, 292
 Wozzek, 91
Beveridge, David, 263–271, 259, 354
Bezruč, Petr, 338
Biblical Songs, 358. See also Dvořák
Bisner, Pavel, 369fn
Blaník, 273. See also Fibrich; See also Smetana
Blodek, *V studni*, 43

Böhmer, 352
Boettinger, Hugo, (Dr. Desiderius), 24
Bohème, La, 35, 42. *See also* Puccini
Bohemian composers, 185ff
Bohemian music, a topography of, 165–183
Bollert, 352
Bolshevik Years of Trouble and Chaos, The, 25. *See also* Nazhvin
Bořkovec, Pavel, 352
Breshko-Breshkovskaya, Kateřina, 25
Brno Conservatory, 303
Brno Organ School, 303
Brod, Max, 21, 29, 30, 52, 285, 348–349, 382
  Stars in Prague's heaven, 349
  Sternenhimmel: Musik-und Theaterlebnisse, 349
Burghauser, Jarmil, 217–242, 261, 354
Burke, Kenneth, 172
Burney, Charles, 151, 167ff
Burrows, David, 171

Caldara, Antonio, 148
  Perfice (gressus meos), 147–148
Cambridge Opera Handbook, 3
Candace, 124. *See also* Vivaldi
Cantate, 147. *See also* Zelenka
cantorial music, 165–183
cantorial music, reference list, 177–181
Čapek, 287–288
Capriccio, 299, 317, 357, 360. *See also* Janáček, Leoš
Catholic Church music, 141–154
Cavalleria rusticana, 33ff. *See also* Mascagni
Čech, Svatopluk, 278, 285
Čelakovský, F. L., 157ff
Čermáková-Dvořáková, Anna, 261
Černohorská, Milena, 45, 352
Červinková-Riegrová, Marie, (librettist for Dvořák's *Dimitrij*), 260
Česká svatba, 43. *See also* Bendl
Česká thalie, journal, 260
Český lid, journal, 348
Chalabala, Zdeněk, 312
Charles VI, King of Bohemia, 117
Charpentier, Gustave, 36
  Louise, 36ff

Chesterian, The, (Janáček obituary), 350
Chew, Geoffrey, 173
Chisholm, Eric, 46
Chlubna, Osvald, 21, 312, 335–340, 350
  "An unknown last work, *Dunaj*," ("Neznáme poslední dílo Janáčka *Dunaj*"), 350
  "Last Work of Janáček—The 'Danube,' " 312
chromaticism, 57–81
church music, 165–183
Chvalte Boha silného, 141–154. *See also* Zelenko
Cigánské melodie, (Gypsy songs), 256. *See also* Dvořák
Clark, Marilyn S., 283–288, 352
"classical" style, 374
Collected Edition, (Janáček), 243–252
Colloquium: "Dvořák, Janáček and their Time," 353
Colloquium: Leoš Janáček et Musica Europaea, 353
Complete Debussy Edition, 250ff
Complete Edition, (Janáček), 243–252
"Composing Music for Americans," (series of articles), 297. *See also* Cowell
composition of chords and their connections, The, (*O skladbě souzvukův a jejich spojův*), 348. *See also* Janáček, Leoš
Concertino, 107–114, 292, 317, 357, 360, 361. *See also* Janáček, Leoš
Concerto for Colaratura Soprano, 342. *See also* Glière
Conrad, Joseph, 40
constanza e firtezza, La, 118. *See also* Fux
constanza trionfante, La, 121ff. *See also* Vivaldi
Cooper, Barry, 248
Cowell, Henry, 295–299, 304
  Advertisement, 299
  "Composing Music for Americans," 297
  Episode, 299
  "Folk Songs as a Basis of New Music," 297
  (Cowell, Henry cont.)

Irish Legends, 299
Movement for String Quartet, 299
Movement for Strings, 297
Suite, 299
Cranz, August, 259
Cunning Little Vixen, (*Příhody lišky Bystroušky*), 25, 45–53, 83–91, 336, 362, 367fn. *See also* Janáček, Leoš
Čurilla, Štefan, 304
"Czech Memorial Volume from the Great Year 1918," 374ff
Czech National Songs,(České narodní písně), 159
Czech nationalism, 371ff
Czech Philharmonic, 316
Czech Radio Orchestra, 312
Czerny, Jaroslav, 292

Dahlhaus, Carl, 220ff, 283fn, 284, 363
Dalibor, journal, 256–258
Danube River, 311–344
"Danube, The" Symphony, 25, 83–91, 336, 362, 367fn. *See also* Janáček, Leoš
Daphnis and Chloë, 342. *See also* Ravel
de Nativitate D., 148. *See also* Zelenka
de Temp[ore], 146, 148. *See also* Zelenka
Debussy, Claude, 66, 75, 322
Nocturnes, 342
Denzio, Antonio, 117ff
works written by, 123fn
Denzio, Elizabetta, 122ff
Der Auftakt (*The Upbeat*), (journal), 293
Dervies, Baron Paul von, 261
Desiderius, Dr., 24. *See also* Boettinger, Hugo
Destiny, 359, 362, 363. *See also* Janáček, Leoš
Deylampour, (Janáček scholar), 354
Dianoia for Violin Solo, 306. *See also* Domansky
Diary of One Who Vanished, The, (*Zápisník zmizelého*), 57–81, 246ff, 305, 350, 360. *See also* Janáček, Leoš
Die schöne Galatea, 43. *See also* Suppé

Divadelní listy, (journal), 259
Dividalní noviny, (journal), 22
Domanský, Hanuš, 306–307
Dianoia for Violin Solo, 306
First String Quartet, 306
Fragment of a Sonata for Piano, 306
Dopisy matky, 353. *See also* Janáček, Leoš
Dopisy strýci, 353. *See also* Janáček, Leoš
Doriclea, 121ff. *See also* Vivaldi
Dorilla in Tempe, 121ff. *See also* Vivaldi
Dostalík, Fraňo, 303–304
Radúz and Mahuliena, 304
Dostoevsky, Fědor, 288
From the House of the Dead, (author), 28, 30
"dramatism," 370, 382ff
Dresden, royalty in, 141ff
Drlíková, Eva, 295–299
"Drowned Girl, The" 312, 342, 337ff. *See also* Křičková
Ducreux, Marc, 170fn
"Dunaj," Symphony 278. *See also* Janáček, Leoš
Dürr, Alfred, 217
Dusík, (composer), 352
Dvořák, Antonín, 9, 33 ff, 46, 263–271, 352, 355, 357,
Armida, 34ff
Biblical Songs, 358
Cigánské melodie, (Gypsy songs), 256
Critical Edition, 217ff
Four songs to the words of Serbian folk texts, (Čtyři písně na slova srbské lidové poesie), 260
friendship with Janáček, 255–262
Horymír, 36ff
Moravian Duets, (Moravské dvojzpěvy,), 257, 358
Requiem, 74
Rusalka, 351
Serenade, 263–271
Slavonic Dances, 46, 358
Slavonik Rhapsodies, 261
string orchestra, music for, 263–271
Tvrdé palice, 43
Watersprite, The, 366
Dyk, Viktor, 285

editorial guidelines, (Janáček edition), 221-242
Eggebrecht, Hans Heinrich, 373
Emery, Walter, 251
"Engraved Words," 26. *See also* Masaryk
Episode, 299. *See also* Cowell
Erdmann, (Janáček scholar), 352
Erismann, (Janáček scholar), 354
Ethical Movement of Czech Students, 297
Eva, 34. *See also* Foerster
Ewans, Michael, 45, 48
Excursions of Mr. Brouček, 8, 348, 377fn, 376. *See also* Janáček, Leoš
expressionism in Janáček's work, 283, 286, 288

Faltus, Leoš, 313, 336
Faměra, Josef, (pianist), 36
Farnace, 121ff. *See also* Vivaldi
Fate, (Osud), 284-28, 385. *See also* Janáček, Leoš
fede tradita e vendicata, La, 124. *See also* Vivaldi
Fétis, François-Joseph, 185
Fiala, Karl, 292, 354
Fibich, Zdeněk, 33, 34, 261, 273, 352, 357
Blaník, 273
Fiddler's Child, (Šumařovo dítě), 273-274, 342, 360. *See also* Janáček, Leoš
Fiechtner, (composer), 352
Finke, Fidelio, 292
Finn, Stephan, 375
Firkušný, Leoš, 347, 351
Firkušný, Rudolf, 352, 354
First String Quartet, 93-105, 245ff. *See also* Janáček, Leoš
First String Quartet, 306. *See also* Domansky
First String Quartet, 306. *See also* Očenáš
First Symphony, 306. *See also* Pospíšil
Fischmann, Zdeňka E., 349, 354
Janáček—Newmarch Correspondence, 349

Flotzinger, (Janáček scholar), 167
Flurry, The, (Pl'úšť), 306. *See also* Očenáš
Foerster, Josef Bohuslav, 34, 293
Eva, 34
folk music, 58ff
Bohemian, 156ff
18th-century, 155-163
Moravian, 156ff, 368
"Folk Songs as a Basis of New Music," 297. *See also* Cowell
folklorism, 302, 358ff, 370, 377ff
Forkel, Johann Nicolaus, 374
Four songs to the words of Serbian folk texts, (Čtyři písně na slova srbské lidové poesie), 260. *See also* Dvořák
Fragment of a Sonata for Piano, 306. *See also* Domansky
Freeman, Daniel E., 117-140, 354
Fric, (Janáček scholar), 352
From the House of the Dead (Z mrtvého domu), 21-31, 91fn, 288, 312, 322, 333, 350, 351, 362. *See also* Janáček, Leoš
Chlubna's writings on, 350
Fukač, Jiří, 354, 371-388
Furness, R.S., 288
Fürstenau, Moritz, 146, 150
Fux, Johann Joseph, 118, 142
constanza e firtezza, La, 118

Gassman, Florian Leopold, 185
Gaude Plaude (Laetere), 148. *See also* Zelenka
Geck, (Janáček scholar), 354
Gellner, František, 25, 285
"Germanness," 374
Germinal, 36. *See also* Káan
Glagolitic Mass, 27ff, 244, 249, 305, 337, 360. *See also* Janáček, Leoš
Glareanus system, 68
Glière, Reinhold, 342
Concerto for Colaratura Soprano, 342
Gorer, 352
Gorky, Maxim, 27
Götz, František, 286
Grešák, Josef, 304-305

Grove's Dictionary, Janáček article for, 350
Grundgestalt, Schoenberg's, 94fn
"Gubernatorial Collecting," 159ff

Hába, Alois, 292, 380
Haša, Josef, 292
Haec dies, 148. *See also* Zelenka
Handel, George Frederick, 148
   Huc pastores, 149
   Messiah, 341
   Poro, 148
handwriting and copyists, 247ff
Harabiš Inn, The (Janáček article), 381
Hasse, Johann Adolf, 143
   Angeli cementes, 149
Heinichen, Johann David, 142ff
Hejda, František, 40ff
Helfert, Vladimír, 351, 352, 363, 375ff, 386
   About Janáček: a collection of essays and articles, O Janáčkovi: Soubor státi a článku), 352
Her Foster Daughter, (*Její pastorkyňa*), 34ff, 348. *See also* Janáček
Herbst, 352
Hoffman, E. T. A., 374
Hogwood, Christopher, 33
Hollander, Hans, 350, 352
   "Leoš Janáček and his Operas," 350
   "Leoš Janáček—Slav Genius," 352
Holst, Gustav, *Planets, The*, 342
Honolka, Kurt, 45, 352, 354, 373
Horn, 147ff
Horymír, 36ff. *See also* Dvořák
Hospodine pomiluj ny, Janáček, 260
Hotinsky, Otakar, 365
   On Czech Musical Declamation, 366
Houtchens, Alan, 255–262, 354
Howat, Roy, 251
Huc pastores, 149. *See also* Handel
Hudební listy (Musical Letters), periodical, 4, 348
Hudební rozhledy, (journal), 296, 353
humanism, Slovak, 305
Humanitarian Ideals, 28. *See also* Masaryk
Hungarian Pedagogical Institute, Bratislava, 303
Hurník, Ilja, 351
Hviezdoslav, Pavel Országhn (*Zuzanka Hraškovie*), 305

Idyll, 263–271, 357. *See also* Janáček, Leoš
Il confronto dell'amor coniugale, 125. *See also* Vivaldi
Imperial Court Theater, Vienna, 292fn
Imposed Bridegroom, The, (*Ženich vnucený*), 260. *See also* Janáček, Leoš
impressionism in Janáček's work, 283, 287–288
In Dreaming, 306. *See also* Pospíšil
In the footsteps of Dr. Leoš Janáček, (*Po stopách dra Leoše Janáčka*), 350. *See also* Vasek
In the Mists, 244ff. *See also* Janáček, Leoš
inflection, 58ff
inganno triofante in amore, L', 121, 124. *See also* Vivaldi
innocenza giustificata, L', 124. *See also* Vivaldi
Insarov, Alexander, ('11[pálová, Soňa), 312
   "Drowned Girl, The," ("Últonula"), 312, 337ff, 342
   "Lola," 312, 337ff, 342ff
"Intermezzo erotico," 80
International Society for Contemporary Music, 350
"Intimate Letters," 362. *See also* Janáček, Leoš
Inventarium, 141ff. *See also* Zelenka
Irish Legends, 299. *See also* Cowell

Jalowetz, Heinrich, 292
Janáček, Leoš
   as dramatist, 382ff
   Collected Edition, 243–252
   "Complete Edition," 243–252
      editorial guidelines, 221–242
   Critical Edition, 217–242
   evaluated today, 357–364
   Moravian folksongs, Janáček's collection of, 347
   place in musicology, 371–388
              (*Janáček, Leoš, cont.*)

Compositions

Along the Overgrown Path, (*Po zarostlém chodníčku I*), 235
Amarus, 362. See also Janáček, Leoš
Ballad of Blanik, The, (*Balada blanická*), program of, 273–282, 342
Beginning of a Romance, 8ff, 284, 288, 358, 382
Capriccio, 299, 317, 357, 360
Concertino, 107–114, 292, 317, 357, 360, 361;
  sonata form in, 107–114
  structure of, 107–114
Cunning Little Vixen, (*Příhody lišky Bystroušky*), 25, 45–53, 83–91, 336, 362, 367fn
  organization, musical, 83–91
"*Danube" Symphony, The* ("*Dunaj*"), 278, 302, 311–344, 357, 360, 385
Destiny, 359, 362, 363
Diary of One Who Vanished, The, (*Zápisník zmizelého*), 57–81, 246ff, 305, 350, 360
Excursions of Mr. Brouček, (*Výlety pana Broučka*), 8, 285, 348, 377fn, 385, 376
Fate, (*Osud*), 284, 385
Fiddler's Child, (*Šumařovo dítě*), 273–274, 342, 360
First String Quartet, 93–105, 245ff
  motives and structure, 93–105
From the House of the Dead (*Z mrtvého domu*), 21–31, 91fn, 288, 312, 322, 333, 350, 351, 362
  Chlubna's writings on, 350
Her Foster Daughter, (*Její pastorkyňa*), 34ff, 348
Idyll, 263–271, 357
Imposed Bridegroom, The, (*Ženich vnucený*), 260
In the Mists, 244ff
"Intimate Letters," 362
Jenůfa, 3ff, 71 ff, 256, 283, 284, 288, 292fn, 305, 348, 359, 361, 362, 377, 375, 382, 385
Káťa Kabanová, 24, 29, 232, 285–287, 305, 314, 350, 337, 362
Lachian Dances, 244
Lašské tance, 306
Lístek odvanuty, 351
Makropoulis Case, The, (*Věc Makropulos*), 30, 83, 91fn, 287–287–288, 316, 338, 339, 359, 3672, 363
"Maryčka Magdonov," 338
Mladi, 292, 317, 357
Na Solaní Carták, 223
"Nursery Rhymes," 57–81
"1. X. 1905" (string quartet), 362
Piano Trio, 249
Po zarostlém chodníčku, 351
Pohádka, 351
Puppets, 25
Šárka, 8ff, 34, 284, 288, 358
Second String Quartet, 350
Sinfonietta, 248ff, 316ff, 335ff, 339, 350, 357, 360, 379, 387fn
Sonata pro housle a klavír, 351–352
Song of the Unknown, 25
string orchestra, music for, 263–271
String Quartet, 338, 360
Suites, 357
Taras Bulba, 18ff, 223, 273, 278, 306, 337, 342, 376
V mlhách, 351
Wandering Madman, The, 362
Youth, 83

Writings

editors of, 348
A Complete harmony manual, (*Úplna nauka o harmonii*), 348
A manual for teaching singing, (*Návod pro vyučování zpěvu*), 348
composition of chords and their connections, The, (*O skladbě souzvukův a jejich spojův*), 348
Dopisy matky, 353
Dopisy strýci, 353
"Křizkovsky's role in Moravian folk music and Czech music generally," ("Pavla Křižakovského vyznam v lidové hudbě moravské a v české hudbě vubec"), 348
"My Lachia," 380, 381
Our Music and the Czech State, 376
Janáček, Vincenc, 353
Zivotopis Jiřika Janáčka, 353
"Janáček: A great Czech Composer," 351. See also Mellers
Janáček Academy of Music Arts, Brno, 306
Janáček and Brod, 348. See also Susskind

INDEX

Janáček Archives, Brno, 313 ff, 350
"Janáček at the men's teachers' institute in Brno," ("Leoš Janáček na mužském učitelském ústavě v Brně "), 350–351. *See also* Štědroň, Bohumír
Janáček—Newmarch Correspondence, 349. *See also* Fischmann
Janáček Society, 350
Janáčková, Zdeňka, 316, 351
  My Life, (Můj život), 351
"Janáček's Compositional Nachlass," 311. *See also* Kundera
"Janáček's Danube Symphony in the Conception of Osvald Chlubna," 313ff. *See also* Štědroň
Jeník, Jan, 158–159
Jenůfa, 3 ff, 71ff, 256, 283, 284, 288, 292fn, 305, 348, 359, 361, 362, 377, 375, 382, 385. *See also* Janáček, Leoš
Jeremiáš, Otakar, 351
Jeritza, Maria, 292fn
Jirák, Karel Boleslav, 352, 354
Jiránek, Jaroslav, 354, 365–370
Jirásek, Alois, 285
Jírovec, Vojtěch, 185–190
Johnson, Douglas, 245
  Beethoven Sketchbooks, The, 245
Josephson, Nors S., 83–91, 354
Jurovič, Dušan , 359

Káan, Jindřich, 36
  Germinal, 36
Kadeřávek, (cantor), 175, 354
Kafka, Franz, 348
Kafka Miscellany, 248
Kahan, Arcadius, 170
Kaiser, Rainer, 248
Kapr, Jan, 353
Kardoš, Dezider, 306, 307
Karfík, Vladimír, 299
Kašlík, Hyněk, 351
  Kovařovic's revisions in Janáček's *Jenůfa*,"("Retuše Karla eKarla Kovařovice v Janáčkové opeře *Jeji Pastorkyňa*,") 351

Kátya Kabanová, 24, 29, 232, 285–287, 305, 314, 350, 337, 362. *See also* Janáček, Leoš
Kerman, Joseph, 374
kettle drums, use of, 337
Klementinum, Prague, 38
Klemperer, Otto, 349
Kliopera, E., 292
Knaus, Jacob, 313, 318, 335–340, 354
Koch, Heinrich, 186
Kokoschka, Oscar, 167
Kolísek, Alois, 314ff
Kolovraty Manuscript, 159
Komedianti, 42. *See also* Leoncavallo
Koppenburg, 352
Koref, Marta, 291
Kornauth, Egon, 292
Korngold, Erich Wolfgang, 292
Kovařovic, Karel, 349, 377
"Kovařovic's revisions in Janáček's *Jenůfa)*," ("Retuše Karla Kovařovice v Janáčkové opeře *Jeji Pastorkyňa*"), 35. *See also* Kašlík
Koželuh, Leopold, 185
Krakonoš, 39. *See also* Rozkosny
Kralická Bible, 141, 152
Kramár, František, 185
Krasnohorská, (librettist for Fibrich's *Blanik*), 273
Krause, (Janáček scholar), 352
Krenek, Ernst, 292
Kresánek, Jozef, 302
"Kreutzer Sonata," 338. *See also* Tolstoy
Křička, Jaroslav, 352
Křičková, Pavla, 312, 337ff
  "Drowned Girl, The," ("Últonula"), 312, 337ff, 342. *See also* Insarov
Křížkovský, Pavel, 261, 358ff
"Křížkovsky's role in Moravian folk music and Czech music generally," ("Pavla Křížkovského význam v lidové hudbě moravské a v české hudbě vubec"), 348. *See also* Janáček, Leoš
Kubelík, Rafael, 352, 354
Kubička, Víťazoslav, 307
Kučera, Otakar, (librettist), 40, 170fn

Kukučín, Martin, 305
  Unawaken, (*Neprebudený*), 305
Kundera, Dr. Ludvík, 296. 311, 323ff, 351, 353
  "Janáček's Compositional Nachlass," 311
Kunz, Dr. Ludvík, 298

Lachian Dances, 244. See also Janáček, Leoš
Lašské tance, 306. See also Janáček, Leoš
"Last Work of Janáček—The Danube, The" 312. See also Chlubna
Lebl, (Janáček scholar), 354
Leoš Janáček, 350. See also Muller
Leoš Janáček: a survey of his life and work, (*Leoš Janáček: Pohled do života a díla*), 350. See also Veselý
Leoš Janáček and contemporary Moravian composers: an outline apropos of the stylistic development of contemporary Moravian music, (*Leoš Janáček a současní moravsští skladatele—nastín k slohovému vývoji soudobé moravské hudby*), 352. See also Racek
"Leoš Janáček and his Operas," 350. See also Hollander
"Leoš Janáček and Moravian Music Drama," 349. See also Newmarch
"Leoš Janáček in England," ("Leoš Janáček v Anglii"), 350. See also Mikota
"Leoš Janáček in the tradition of Czech music," ("Leoš Janáček v tradici české hudby"), 352. See also Racek
Leoš Janáček Society (Společnost Leoše Janáčka), 353
Leoš Janáček Society Newsletter, 55, 353
"Leoš Janáček—Slav Genius," 352. See also Hollander
Leoncavallo, Ruggero, 33
  Pagliacci, 33, 42
Lichtenberg, Georg Christoph, 371ff

Lidový noviny, (*People's Newspaper*), 24, 297, 311ff, 337
Life and Dream, 294. See also Suk
Lindner, Leo, 299
Lístek odvanuty, 351. See also Janáček, Leoš
Listy hudební matice, (journal), 350
Literární skupina (Literary Group), 286
Living Song, (*Živá píseň*), 299. See also Úleha
Loeffler, Charles Martin, 261
"Lola," 312, 337ff, 342ff. See also Insarov
Louise, 36ff. See also Charpentier
Löwenbach, Jan, 348, 353

Má Vlast, 273. See also Smetana
Macdonald, Hugh, 273–282
Madama Butterfly, 36. See also Puccini
Magic Flute, The, 341. See also Mozart
Mahler, Gustav, 292
  Fourth Symphony, 342
Makropoulis Case, The, 30, 83, 91fn, 316, 338, 339, 359, 3672, 363. See also Janáček, Leoš
Mancini, *Resonate vos lyrae sonorae*, 149
Mánes, music forum, 294
Manon Lescaut, 42. See also Puccini
Martinius, Dresden Lutheran leader, 152
Martinů, Bohuslav, 306
"Maryčka Magdonov," 338. See also Janáček, Leoš
Masaryk, Tomaáš G., 21ff
  A World Revolution, 26
  "Engraved Words," 26
  Humanitarian Ideals, 28
Masaryk University, Brno, 359
Mascagni, Pietro, 33
  Cavalleria rusticana, 33ff
Mašek, Karel, 285
Matka Míla, 33, 43. See also Bendl
Maus, Fred Everett, 107–114
McCredie, (Janáček scholar), 354
Mellers, Wilfred, 351
Melton, James, 168
Mendelssohn, Felix, 344
Merezhkovsky, Dmitri Sergejevich, *My Notebook*, 25

INDEX

Messiah, 341. See also Handel
Metropolitan Opera, 349
Meumann, Ernst, 285
Mikota, Jan, 350
  "Leoš Janáček in England," ("Leoš Janáček v Anglii"), 350
Mikuláš, 38. See also Rozkosny
Mladi, 292, 317, 357. See also Janáček, Leoš
Muller-Berghaus, Karl, 261
modality, 360, 57–81
Modern Music Association, Prague, 297fn
monothematism, 368
montage process, 321ff
Montagu, 352
Moravec, Ernst, 292
Moravian Duets, (*Klänge aus Mähren*), 257, 358. See also Dvořák
Moravian folksongs, Janáček's collection of, 347
Moravian folksongs newly collected, (*Národní písně moravské v nově nasbirané*), 347. See also Bartos
Moravian Quartet, 297, 299
Moravian Urania Society, 296
Motetti, 145ff. See also Zelenka
Mottetto a 4, 149. See also Zelenka
Mountains and Men, 306. See also Pospíšil
Movement for String Quartet, 299. See also Cowell
Movement for Strings, 297. See also Cowell
Mozart, Wolfgang Amadeus, 344
  Magic Flute, The, 341
Mrstik brothers and their emotional ties with Janáček and Novák, The, (*Bratři Mrstikové a jejích citovy vztah k Leoši Janáčkovi a Vítězslavu Novákovi*), 352. See also Racek
Mráček, Jaroslav, 347–355
Mraczek, Josef Gustav, 292
Mucha, Alfons, 359
Mueller, Wenzel, 176
  Zauberzitter, Der, 176
Muller, Daniel, 350

Leoš Janáček, 350
Müller-Röffs, 352
Music and Letters, 352
Musica, 219ff
Musical Quarterly, 350
Musical Times, Janáček obituary, 350
musicology, as a discipline, 217ff
Musikalishe Edition im Wandel des historischen Bewußtseins, 218
Musikologie 3, 353
My Lachia, 380, 381. See also Janáček, Leoš
My Life, (*Můj život*), 351. See also Janáčková
"My Part in Janáček's Symphony," 312. See also Chlubna
My Notebook 1919–1920, 25. See also Mereshkovsky
Mysliveček, Josef, 352

Na Solaní Čarták, 223. See also Janáček, Leoš
National Czech Theater, 39
National Museum, Prague, 146
National Theater, Prague, 21ff, 33ff, 42, 256, 316
nationalist composers, 380
Nazhivin, Ivan Fiororovitsch, 25
  Bolshevik Years of Trouble and Chaos, The, 25
Nejedlý, Zdeněk, 366ff, 376, 377fn
Němcová, Alena, 311–320, 354
Němcová, Božena, 378
Neumann, Stanislav, 287
New Bach Edition, 244
New Berlioz Edition, 246
New Grove, 3, 146
New Music Society of California, 296
Newmarch, Rosa, 316, 349–351
  "Leoš Janáček and Moravian Music Drama," 349
Nocturnes, 342. See also Debussy
Novák, Arne, 287
Novák, Vítězslav, 292, 305, 352, 380, 382
Novakovic, Olga, 292
Novotný, V. J., (chief editor *Dalibor*), 33, 42, 256–257
  Sedlák kavalír, 42

397

Nowak, Leopold, 176
"Nursery Rhymes," 57–81. *See also* Janáček, Leoš

O magnum mysterium, 147ff. *See also* Zelenka
O quam Suavis, 149. *See also* Ariosti
Očadlík, Mirko, 352
    Rok české hudby. O živote a díle skladatelů, jejichž jubilea slavíme v roce 1954, 352–353
Očenáš, Andrej, 306
    First String Quartet, 306
    Flurry, The, (Pl'úšt'), 306
    Ruralia Slovaca, 306
On Czech Musical Declamation, 366. *See also* Hotinsky
On the 100th anniversary of the birth of Janáček, (K stému výroči narození Leoše Janáčka), in *Musicologie*, 353
"1. X. 1905," 362. *See also* Janáček, Leoš
opera, Italian, 34, 117ff
    composers of, 119ff
opera, Russian, 21
Operní dílo Leoše Janáčka, International symposium at Brno, 1965, 353
Opus musicum, 353
Organ School, Prague, 18, 255
organization, musical, 83–91. *See also* Janáček, Leoš
Ostrčil, Otakar, 292, 316, 336
Ostrovsky, Aleksander, 285–286
    Storm, 29, 285–286
"Our Music and the Czech State" 376. *See also* Janáček, Leoš

Pagliacci, 33, 42. *See also* Leoncavallo
Pala, František, 22, 34
Pange lingua, 148. *See also* Zelenka
Panychida, Gresak 305
paradigma, 58
pastoral, musical, 46ff
pastorella, 18th-century, 172ff
Pečman, Rudolf, 353
Pensdorfova, (Janáček scholar), 354

Perfice (gressus meos), 148. *See also* Caldara
Peruzzi, Antonio Maria, 118ff
Petrželka, Vilém, 306
Piano Trio, 249. *See also* Janáček, Leoš
Pierrot lunaire, 293–294. *See also* Schoenberg
Pilková, Zdeňka, 155–163, 351
Pisendel, Johann Georg, 148fn
Pisk, Paul A., 291
Pivoda, František, 3, 17
Planets, The, 342. *See also* Holst
Po zarostlém chodníčku, 351. *See also* Janáček, Leoš
Pod Blaníkem, 273. *See also* Suk
Pohádka, 351. *See also* Janáček, Leoš
Políkva, Vladimír, 299
Polatschek, Viktor, 292
Popelka, 39. *See also* Rozkošný
Poro, 148. *See also* Handel
Pospíšil, Dr. František, 298
Pospíšil, Juraj, 306, 354
    In Dreaming, 306
    Mountains and Men, 306
Pountney, David, 286
Prague National Theatre Orchestra, 349
Preissová, Gabriela, 42, 284, 287
Present, The, (Přítomnost), (music forum), 294
Přibáňova, Svatava, 353
Příhody lišky Bystroušky, 287. *See also* Janáček, *Cunning Little Vixen*
Proceedings of International Congress, 1958, 353
Procházka, František, 285
Procházka, Jan Ludevít, 257
Proh quos criminis, 147ff. *See also* Zelenka
Provisional Theater, 39
Psalm 150, musical setting of, 141–154
Puccini, Giacomo, 35
    Bohème, La, 35, 42
    Madama Butterfly, 36
    Manon Lescaut, 42
Pulkert, (Janáček scholar), 354
Puppets, 25. *See also* Janáček, Leoš

Queen's Monastery School, Brno, 261

INDEX

Raab, (Janáček scholar), 352
Racek, Jan, 348, 350ff, 353
   A picture of Janáček's life and works, (*Leoš Janáček: obraz života a díla*), 352
   Leoš Janáček and contemporary Moravian composers: an outline apropos of the stylistic development of contemporary Moravian music, (*Leoš Janáček a současní moravšstí skladatele—nastín k slohovému vývoji soudobé moravské hudby*), 352
   Leoš Janáček in the tradition of Czech music, (*Leoš Janáček v tradici české hudby*), 352
   Mrstik brothers and their emotional ties with Janáček and Novák, The, (*Bratři Mrstikové a jejích citový vztah k Leoši Janáčkovi a Vitězslavu Novákovi*), 352
   "Remarks on Janáček's creative image," ("Leoš Janáček: poznámky k tvurčímu profilu"), 351
Rachmaninov, Sergei, 342
Radúz and Mahuliena, 304. *See also* Dostalik
Rankl, Karl, 291
rastrology, 247ff
Ravel, Maurice, 342
   Daphnis and Chloë, 342
realism, 357ff, 365–370
   in Janáček's operas, 283–288
   in Janáček's symphonic poems, 278–279
recitative,
   "free tempo," 8
   Janáček's concept of, 319
   "motivis," 10, 11, 12
   "obbligato," 18
   "secco," 18
   study of, 165ff
   "tempo," 18
Reich, Wolfgang, 143, 147
Rektorys, Artuš, 350, 352
"Remarks on Janáček's creative image," ("Leoš Janáček: poznámky k tvurčímu profilu"), 351. *See also* Racek
Renton, Barbara, 354

Requiem, 74. *See also* Dvořák
Rhythm, (magazine), 297
Riemann, Hugo, 219ff
Ristori, Giovanni, 148
Rittersberg, J., 159
Rok české hudby. O živote a díle skladatelů, jejichž jubilea slavíme v roce 1954, 352–353. *See also* Očadlík
Robertson, Alec, 34
Rosen, Charles, 190
Rosilena ed Oronta, 123, 124. *See also* Vivaldi
Rozkošný, Richard, 33ff
   Krakonoš, 39
   "Mikuláš, 38
   Popelka, 39
   Svatojanské proudy, 39
   Záviš z Falkenštejna, 39
Ruralia Slovaca, 306. *See also* Očenáš
Rusalka, 351. *See also* Dvořák
"Russophilism," 23, 27

Sádlo, Miloš, 351
Šárka, 260. *See also* Zeyer
Šárka, opera 358. *See also* Janáček, Leoš
Sázavský, Karel, 260
sčasování, 321fn
Schaubühne, (journal), 348
Schenker, Heinrich, 93–105
Schmidt, Franz, 292
Schoenbaum, Camillo, 146
Schoenberg, Arnold, 93–105, 286, 289–294
   Pierrot lunaire, 293–294
   Second String Quartet, 342
Schön, (Janáček scholar), 354
Schulhoff, Erwin, 292
Second String Quartet, 350. *See also* Janáček, Leoš
Šeda, (Janáček scholar), 352
Sedlák kavalír, 42. *See also* Novotny
Sehnal, Jiří, 353
Serenade, 263–271. *See also* Dvořák
Serkin, Rudolf, 292, 294
Ševčík, V., 247
Shawe-Taylor, Desmond, 352
Šikula, Vincent (*Rozárka*), 305

Simrock, (Berlin publisher), 256–258, 259 fn
Sinfonia Antartica, 342. See also Vaughan Williams
Sinfonietta, 248ff, 316ff, 335ff, 339, 350, 357, 360, 379, 387fn. See also Janáček, Leoš
singspiel, 358
Siroe re di Persia, 124. See also Vivaldi
Skoumal, Zdenek, 93–105, 354
Slavonic Dances, 46, 358. See also Dvořák
Slavonic Institute, Paris, 26
Slavonic Review, Janáček obituary, 349, 350
Slavonik Rhapsodies, 261. See also Dvořák
Slovak music, Janáček's influence on, 301–307
Slovakia, Janáček's interest in, 301–302
Smaczny, Jan, 33–43
Smetana, František, 256, 273, 312, 352, 355, 357, 351, 354, 383
  Bartered Bride, The, 46, 349– 350
  Blaník, (symphonic poem), 273
  Má Vlast, 273
Smetana, Robert 352
  Stories about Janáček (Vypravení o Leoši Janáčkovi), 352
Smith, M. 354
Smolka, Jarmil, 152
Sokol, (Czech nationalist), 379
sonata form, 95
Sonata pro housle a klavír, 351. See also Janáček, Leoš
Sonata, 351–352. See also Janáček, Leoš
Song of the Unknown, 25. See also Janáček, Leoš
Šourek, Otakar, 218
Špálová, Soňa, 312fn
"speech melody," 19
speech tones, 365ff
"Společnost Leoše Janáčka," 353
Sporck, Count Franz Anton von, 117ff
Sporck Theater, Prague, 117–140
  performers at, 120ff
  Vivaldi operas at, 129–131
Šrámek, František, 287
St. Inatius Loyola, 149
St. Matthew Passion, (Bach), 341
St. Venceslas Meditation, 376. See also Suk
Stárek, Rudolf, (librettist), 36
Stamic, J. V., 163
Stanford, Charles Villiers, 34
Stars in Prague's heaven, (*Pražské hvězvdné nebé*), (translated writings of Brod), 349
Štašny, Father, 382
Statthaalterei, documents in, 119, 123fn
Štědroň, Bohumír, 350ff
  "Janáček at the men's teachers' institute in Brno," ("Leoš Janáček na mužském učitelském ústavě v Brně"), 350–351
Štědroň, Miloš, 313ff, 321–334, 336, 348
  "A New View of Janáček's Symphony," 313
  "Janáček's Danube Symphony in the Conception of Osvald Chlubna," 313ff
Stein, Erwin, 293
Steiner, Karl, 292fn
Sternenhimmel: Musik-und Theaterlebnisse, (collection of Brod's writings), 349
Stockigt, Janice, 141–154
Stoja, (Rozkosny), 33ff
Stolařík, Ivo, 353
Storm, 29, 285–286. See also Ostrovsky
Stösslová, Kamila, 30, 314ff, 342ff
Straková, Theodora, 259, 348, 375
  Leoš Janáček: obraz života a díla, 352
Strauss, Richard, 312
string orchestra, music for, 263–271. See also Dvořák
string orchestra, music for, 263–271. See also Janáček, Leoš
String Quartet, 338, 360. See also Janáček, Leoš
Ströbel, Dietmar, 384, 354, 369
Strohbach, Herman, 158
Stross, Josef, 9
Stuart, (Janáček scholar), 352
Stuckenschmidt, Hans Heinz, 290, 296, 352
style, Romantic, 263–271

INDEX

Sub olea pacis, (*Melodrama de Sancto Venceslao*), 149. *See also* Zelenka
Suites, 357. *See also* Janáček, Leoš
Suk, Josef, 273, 278, 292, 294, 348, 352, 376
   Life and Dream, 294
   Pod Blaníkem, 273
   St. Venceslas Meditation, 376
"Šumařovo dítě" ("The Fiddler's Child"), 273–274. *See also* Janáček, Leoš
"Šumařovo dítě," (poem), 278. *See also* Čech
Suppé, Franz von, *Die schöne Galatea*, 43
Supraphon, (publisher), 221–242
Susskind, Charles, 348, 354
   Janáček and Brod, 348
Susskind, Peter, 341–344
Svatojanské proudy, 39. *See also* Rozkošný
Svatováclavská (Wenceslaus) Bible, 154
Sychra, Antonín, 353, 354
syntagma, 58

Talich, Václav, 355
Taras Bulba, 18ff, 223, 273, 278, 306, 337, 342, 376. *See also* Janáček, Leoš
Tausku, Vilem, 262
Těsnohlídek, Rudolf, 25, 52, 287
Tempo, magazine 351
Third Symphony, (Nielson), 342
Third Symphony, 342. *See also* Vaughan Williams
tirannia castigata, La, 121ff. *See also* Vivaldi
Thurn-Wallesessin Foundation, Brno, 378
Tíbor, (Smetana), 376
Tolstoy, Leo, 338
   "Kreutzer Sonata," 338
tonality, 57–81
Travníček, Josef (a.k.a. Traunek), 291, 352
Treitler, Leo, 372
Trhlk, Otakar, 323

Tučapsky, 354
Tvrdé palice, 43. *See also* Dvořák
Tyl, Josef Kajetán, 284
Tyrrell, Agnes, 383fn
Tyrrell, John, 3–19, 45, 286, 329ff, 354

Úlehla, Dr. Vladimír, 298–299
   Living Song, (*Živá píseň*), 299
Ullmann, Viktor, 291, 292
"Últonula," *See* "Drowned Girl, The")
Unawaken, (*Neprebuden*ý), 305. *See also* Kukučín
"urban folklore," 159ff
Urbanek, 37ff

V mlhách, 351. *See also* Janáček, Leoš
Vavrečka, Hugo, 315
Vašek, Adolf E., 350
   In the footsteps of Dr. Leoš Janáček, (*Po stopách dra Leoše Janáčka*), 350
Valter, Milán, 351–352
Vanda, 259. *See also* Dvořák
Vanhal, Johann Baptist, 185
Vaughan Williams, Ralph, 342
   Sinfonia Antartica, 342
   Third Symphony, 342
Věc Makropulos (*The Makropoulos Case*), 287–287–288. *See also* Janáček, Leoš
Vectomov, Ivan, 351
Venkov, (daily newspaper), 29
Verein Für musikalische Privataüffuhrung (Society for Private Musical Performances), Prague, 290–294
Verein, Vienna, 290–293
verismo, (realism), 33–43
Veselý, Adolf, 311, 350, 367
   Leoš Janáček: a survey of his life and work, (*Leoš Janáček: Pohled do života a díla*), 350
Veselý, study in *Leoš Janáček: obraz života a díla*, 352
"Viennese Classical School," 186ff
Viennese string quartet, 185–190
Violin Concerto, 385. *See also* Janáček, Leoš

vitalism in Janáček's work, 283, 287–288
Vivaldi, Antonio, 117–140
  Argippo, 121ff
  Armida al campo d'Egitto, 124, 125
  Arsilda regina di Ponto, 124
  Candace, 124
  constanza trionfante, La, 121ff
  Doriclea, 121ff
  Dorilla in Tempe, 121ff
  Farnace, 121ff
  fede tradita e vendicata, La, 124
  Il confronto dell'amor coniugale, 125
  inganno triofante in amore, L', 121, 124
  innocenza giustificata, L', 124
  motets of, 148
  operas of, 129–131
  Rosilena ed Oronta, 123, 124
  (*Siroe re di Persia*, 124
  tirannia castigata, La, 121ff
Vltava, 312. *See also* Smetana
vocalise, 341–344
Vogel, Jaroslav, 21, 27, 45, 94, 107, 260, 275, 277, 278, 283fn, 311fn, 318, 343, 352, 353, 379
Volga River, importance in *Kátya Kabanová*, 286
Vomačka, Bohuslav, 292
Vota, Father Moritz, 154
Vraniky, Antonín, 185
Vraniky, Pavel, 185
Vrba, 354
Vrchlický, 274–275, 277, 279
  Selské ballady, 274
Vrtby, Count Johann Joseph von, 128
Výpravení o Leoši Janáčkovi (Stories about Janáček), 352. *See also* Smetana, Robert
Vycpálek, Ladislav, 352
Vysloužil, Jiří, 55, 259, 348, 353, 354, 357–365

Wandering Madman, The, 362. *See also* Janáček, Leoš
Weber, B. D., 159
Webern, Anton, 291, 293

Weis, Karel, 352
Werfel, Franz, 348
Winter, Peter, 176
Wolker, Jiří, 305
  Ballade of an Unborn Child, 305
Wörner, (Janáček scholar), 354
Wozzek, 91. *See also* Berg
Wundt, Wilhelm, 285

Year of Czech Music, 231
Yoell, John H., 289–294
Youth, 83. *See also* Janáček, Leoš

Zákrejs, František, (librettist for *Vanda*), 260
Zauberzitter, Der, 176. *See also* Mueller
Záviš z Falkenštejna, 39. *See also* Rozkošný
Zelenka, Jan Dismas, 141–154
  Angelus Domini Descendit, 149
  Barbara dira effera, 148
  Cantate, 147
  Chvalte Boha silného, 141–154
  de Nativitate D., 148
  de Temp[ore], 146, 148
  Gaude Plaude (*Laetere*), 148
  Inventarium, 141ff
  Motetti, 145ff
  Mottetto a 4, 149
  O magnum mysterium, 147ff
  Pange lingua, 148
  Proh quos criminis, 147ff
  Sub olea pacis, (*Melodrama de Sancto Venceslao*), 149
Zemlinsky, Alexander von, 289fn, 292–293
Zenánek, Dr. Vilém, 293
Zeyer, Julius, (librettist for *Šárka*), 260, 284
Zigeunermelodien, (*Gypsy Songs*), 256. *See also* Dvořák
Zindendorf, Count, 153
Životopis Jiřika Janáčka, 353. *See also* Janáček, Vinc.
Zpravy společnosti Leoše Janáčka, (newsletter), 353